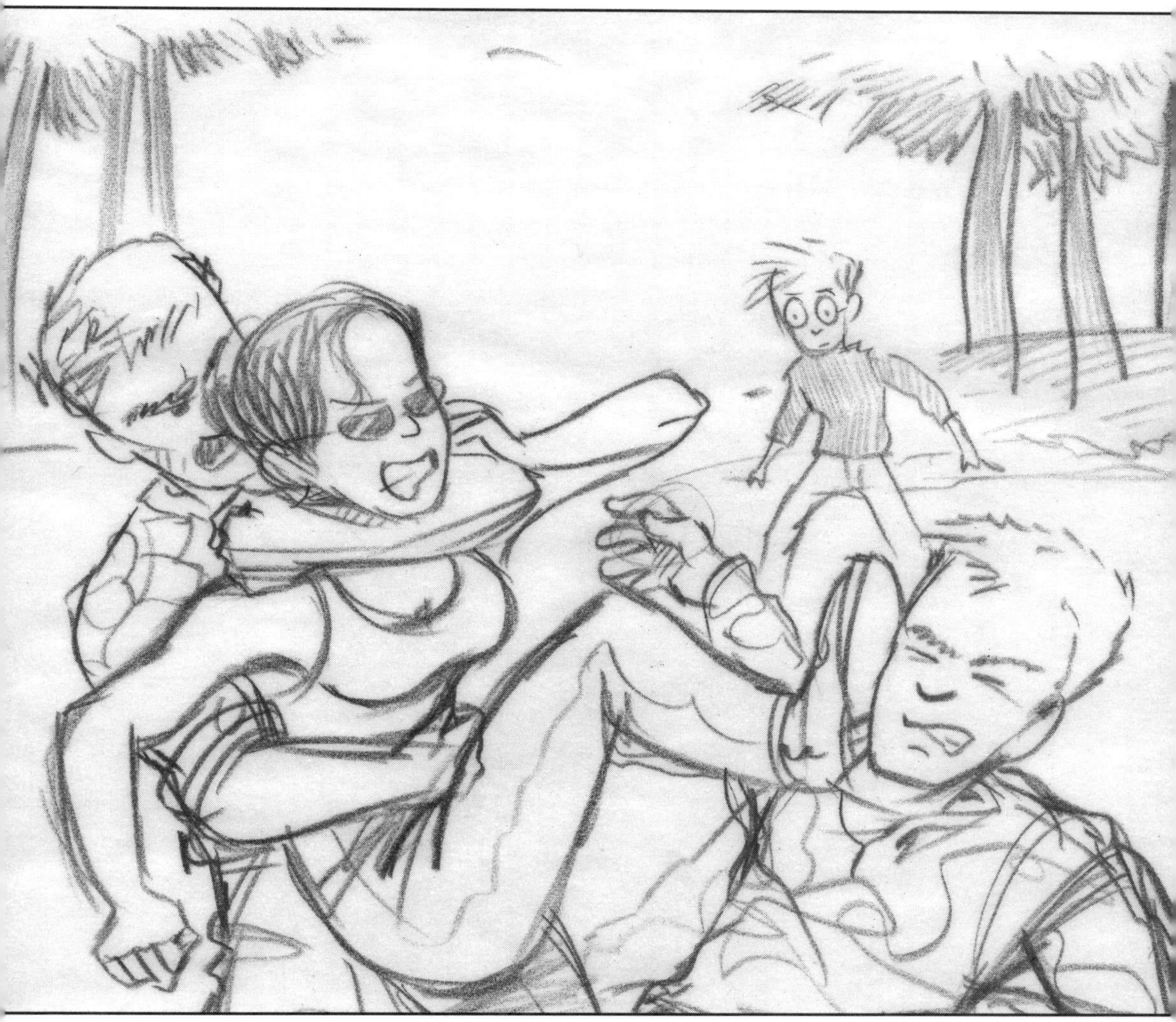

For Adrienne.

Other Jane's World trade paperbacks:

Jane's World Vol. 1
ISBN 0-9742450-0-3

Jane's World Vol. 2
ISBN 0-9742450-1-1

Jane's World, Vol. 3
ISBN 0-9742450-7-0

Jane's World
P.O. Box 88
Sebastopol, CA 95473

janetoon@mindspring.com

www.JanesWorldComics.com

Brian Miller
Hi-Fi colour design
www.hifidesign.com

PRINTED IN CANADA

jane's world

VOLUME 3

Paige Braddock
Story and art

Brian Miller
Colorist

Who's who in Jane's World...

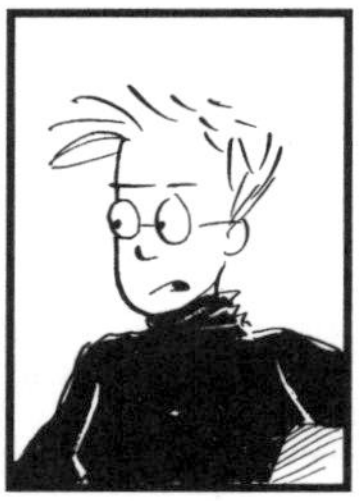

Jane
It's her comic!

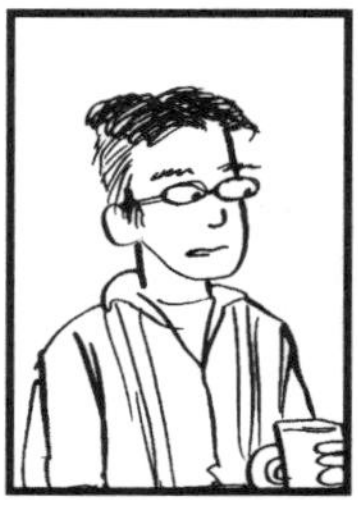

Archie
Jane's coworker

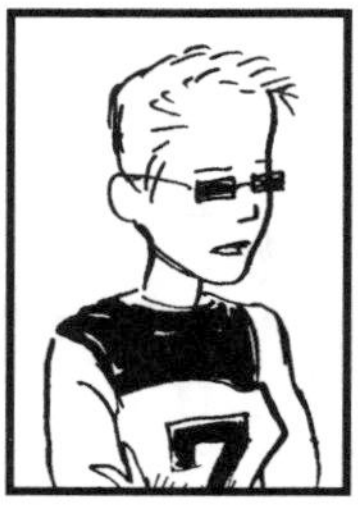

Jill
Part of Chelle's past

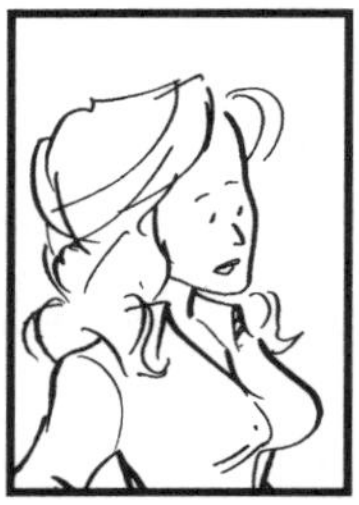

Dixie
Ethan's current girlfriend

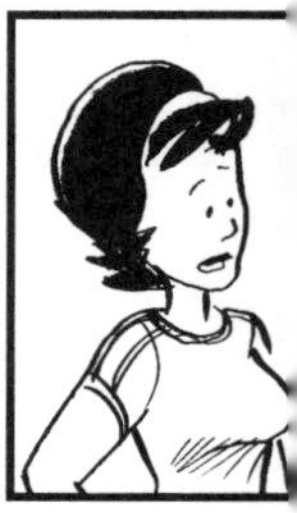

Talia
Jane's Ex GF

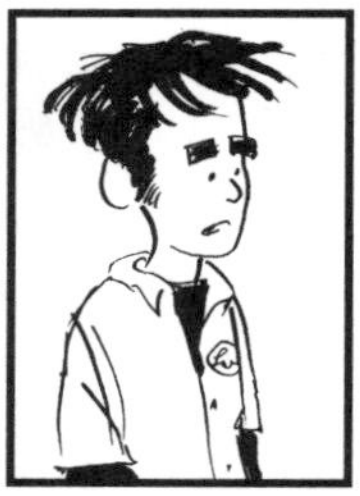

Bud
Jane's cousin

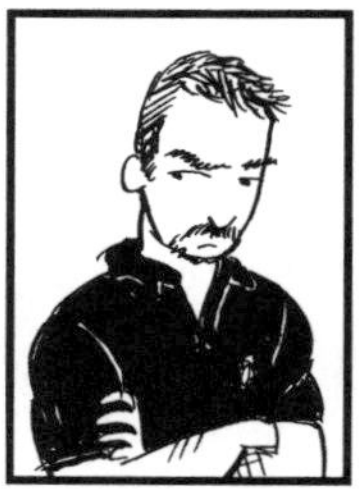

Ethan
Jane's roommate

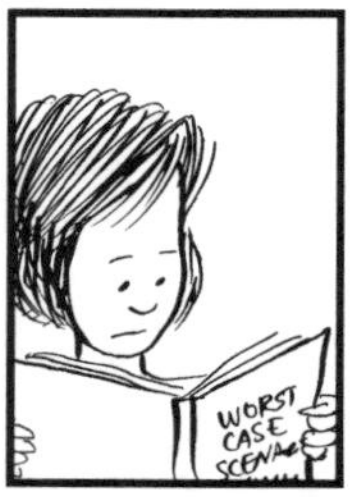
WORST CASE

Dorothy
Jane's best friend

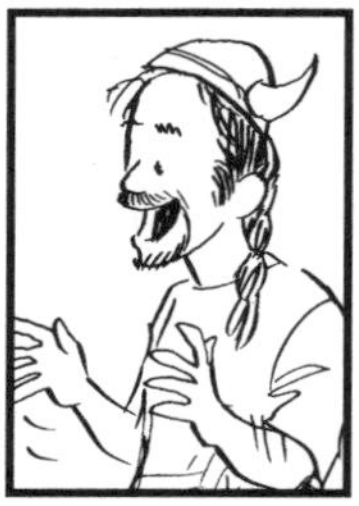

Abbott
Viking cyclist

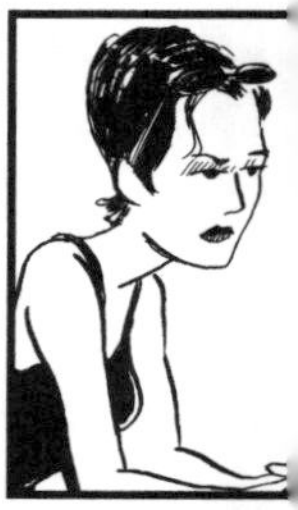

Chelle
Needs no introduction

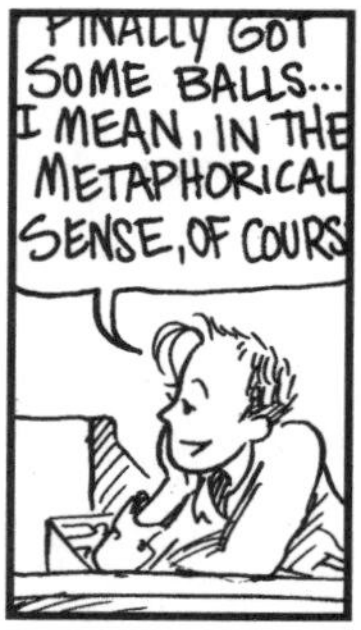
SOME BALLS... I MEAN, IN THE METAPHORICAL

Natalie
Lethal trainee

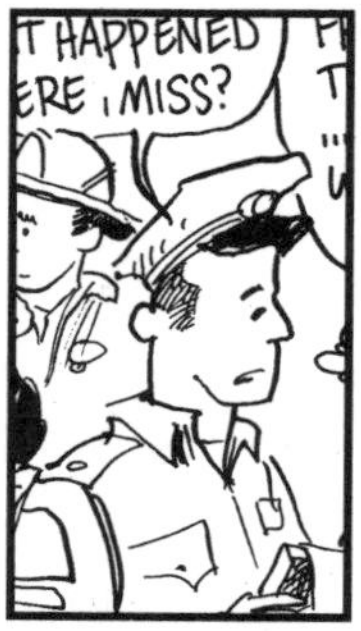

Rick
Local gay cop

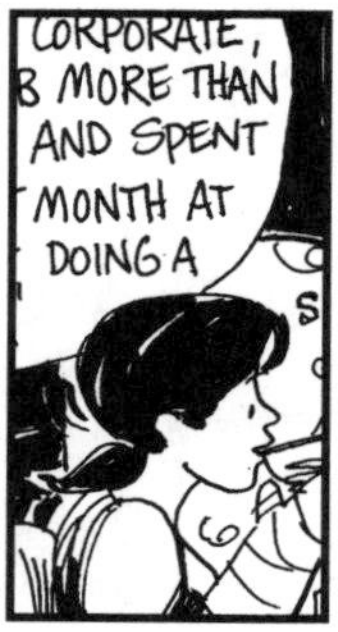
MORE THAN AND SPENT MONTH AT DOING A

Maggie
Jane had a crush on her in college

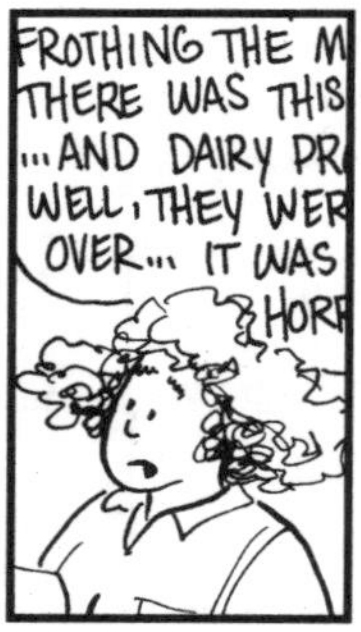
THERE WAS THIS ...AND DAIRY OVER... IT WAS

Doris
Wannabe cop

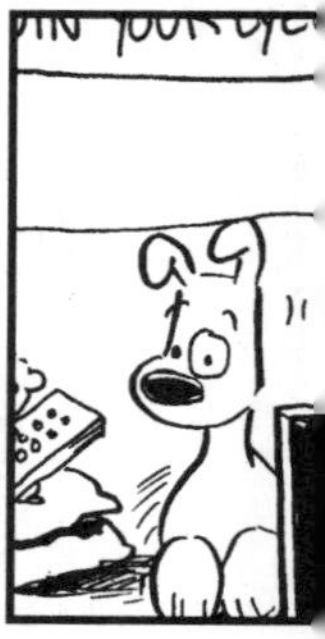

Rusty
Jane's dog

Recap of Vol. 2

Vol. 2 begins with an ill-fated ski trip.

Upon Jane's return home she gets a call for help from her niece, Alexa. It seems that Alexa's mom, Becca, has gotten dumped for a younger woman with "perky breasts" and has decided to sequester herself in a cabin in the woods. As far as Alexa is concerned this is too far off the the grid and she puts a plea out to Jane to take her back to civilization. Alexa ends up staying with Jane for a little while so Becca can regroup. While Alexa is visiting Jane learns sadly that all life's answers are found in Algebra. This explains a lot, considering Jane carried a solid "D" average in math throughout high school.

Jane trusts her cousin Bud to baby sit Alexa while she works the night shift at the Quicki-Mart and she returns home to find her niece has blue hair. Needless to say, Jane's sister Becca, is not pleased.

Jane and Chelle's more "off" than "on" romance comes to an end. No one really thought the relationship ever got off the ground, except in Jane's imagination, so no one was surprised to see it end.

Confused about the entire affair and not quite sure how to feel about it, Jane is even more surprised when Chelle asks her to go see a couples counselor. Puzzled over this sequence of events that seem out of her control, Jane decides to take some time to reflect on her life. She stops at a mountain overlook and just soaks up some wilderness. When darkness falls she discovers that her car won't start. Luckily, Cindy is near at hand and offers her a ride home. On the way back to town they run off the road trying to avoid a stray dog. Jane never wanted a dog, but Rusty turns out to be one of the best things to happen in her lonesome life.

Jane's car is on it's last leg, so Bud encourages her to sell it and buy something new. She talks Ethan into helping her buy a used Jeep on Ebay. They travel to Texas to pick up the car and during one of their roadside stops, Jane provokes God and gets struck by lightning. This little mishap leads to some killer static cling. Jane begins to pick up small furry animals without even trying.

During a mental lapse, Jane asks Dorothy (a cat person) to baby sit her dog, Rusty, while she's away. Big mistake! Dorothy manages to lose her dog. Rusty is missing for a couple of weeks. He returns without fan fair, with a tattoo!

In the final chapter of Vol. 2, an old crush from Jane's college days, Maggie, moves to town and buys the cafe. While Jane is trying to do a little friendly spying on Maggie, Doris mistakes her for a stalker and almost has her arrested. In gratitude for not having the whistle blown on her "near" stalking, Jane befriends Doris. Against her better judgment, Jane get's talked into going to the woods to help Doris find a live Christmas tree. This little outing ends with Jane looking for snacks in an old camp trailer and Doris accidentally sending it rolling down an embankment into the river!

Here is where our story begins...

Chapter 1

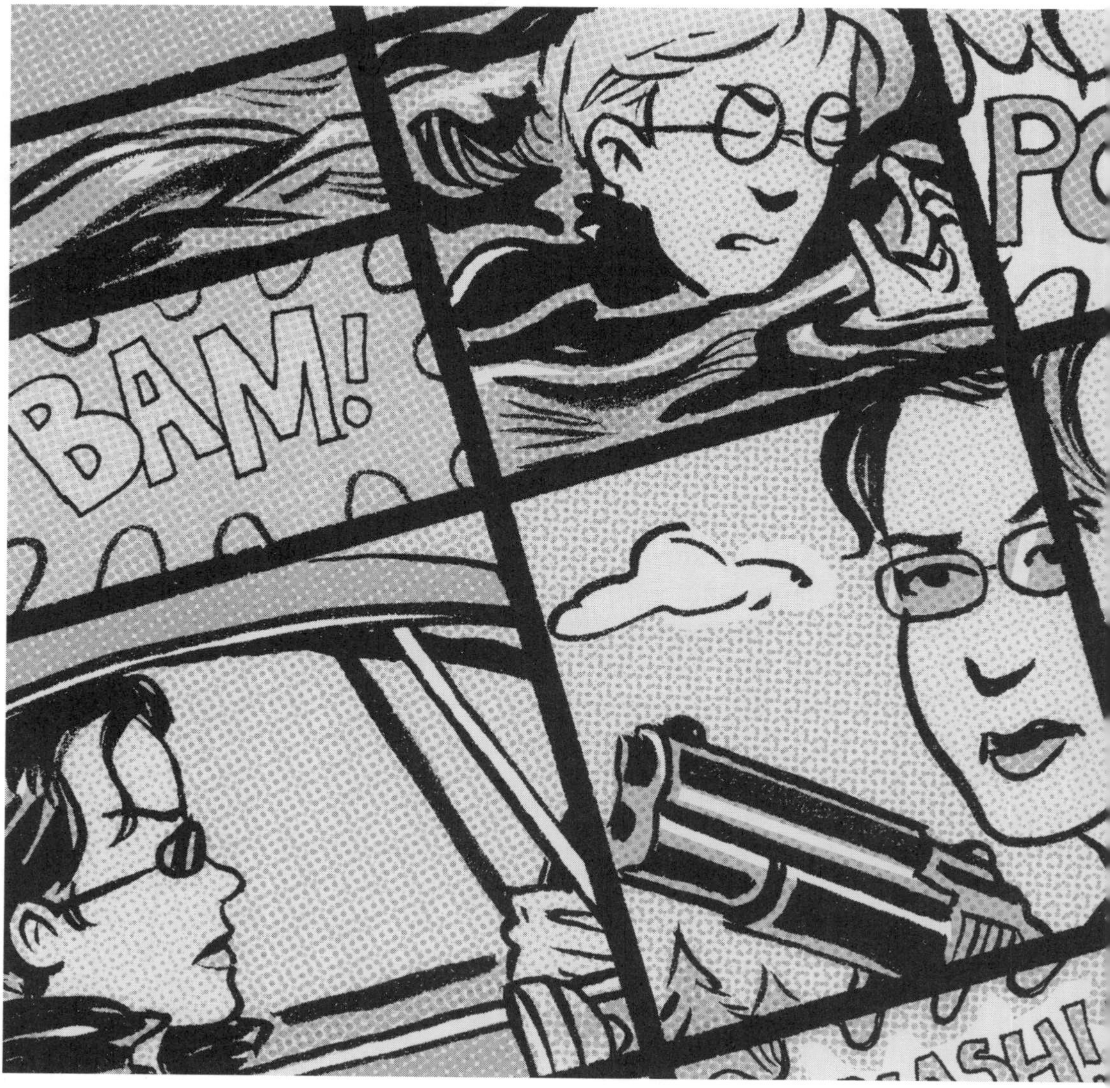
BAM!

12·18·2002
OH, NO!
JANE!!
!!!
PAIGE

OH, NO! IT'S ALL MY FAULT!!
PAIGE
JANE! LOOK OUT FOR THAT TREE!
ROCK! THERE'S A ROCK!!
12·19·2002

NOT THE RIVER!.. PLEASE, LORD, NOT IN THE RIVER!... I'LL BE GOOD... I'LL GIVE UP MY POLICE SCANNER... IF I DIDN'T HAVE LOWER-BACK PAIN, I'D PUT THE TREE BACK RIGHT THIS MINUTE!!
SPOOSH!

YES, FOLKS! JANE HAD A WILD DOWNHILL JAUNT RIGHT INTO THE RIVER!...

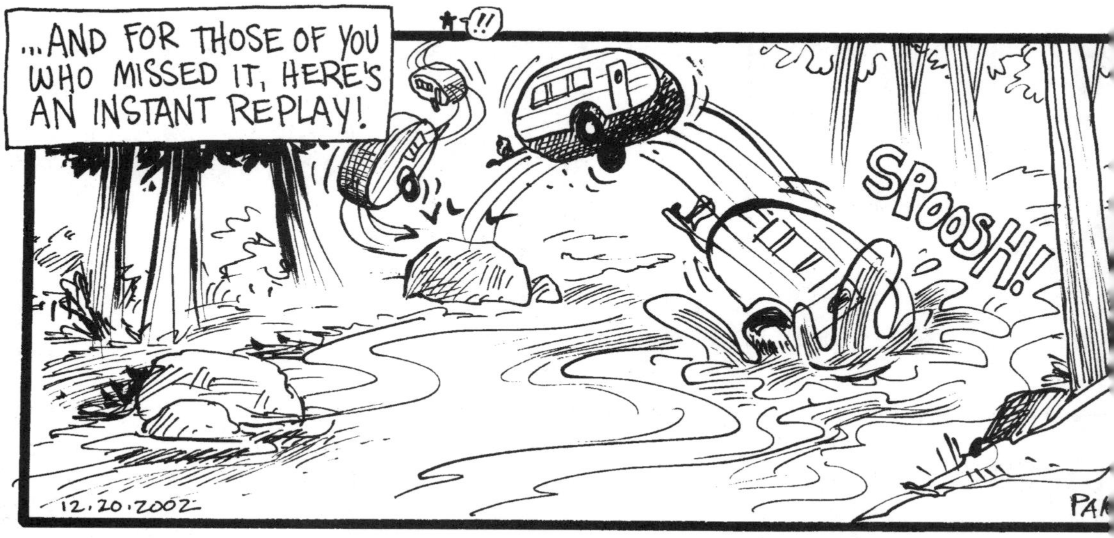
...AND FOR THOSE OF YOU WHO MISSED IT, HERE'S AN INSTANT REPLAY!
!!
SPOOSH!
12.20.2002

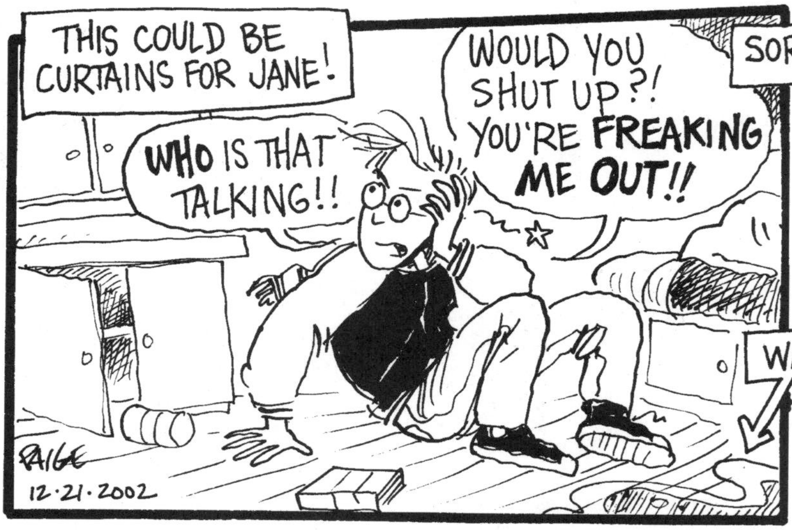
THIS COULD BE CURTAINS FOR JANE!
WHO IS THAT TALKING!!
WOULD YOU SHUT UP?! YOU'RE FREAKING ME OUT!!
SORRY...
WATER!
PAIGE
12.21.2002

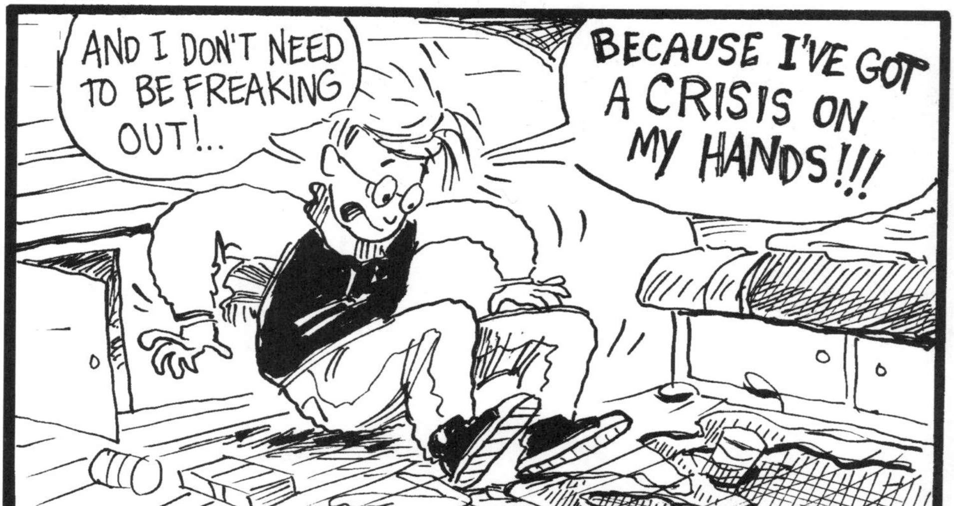
AND I DON'T NEED TO BE FREAKING OUT!...
BECAUSE I'VE GOT A CRISIS ON MY HANDS!!!

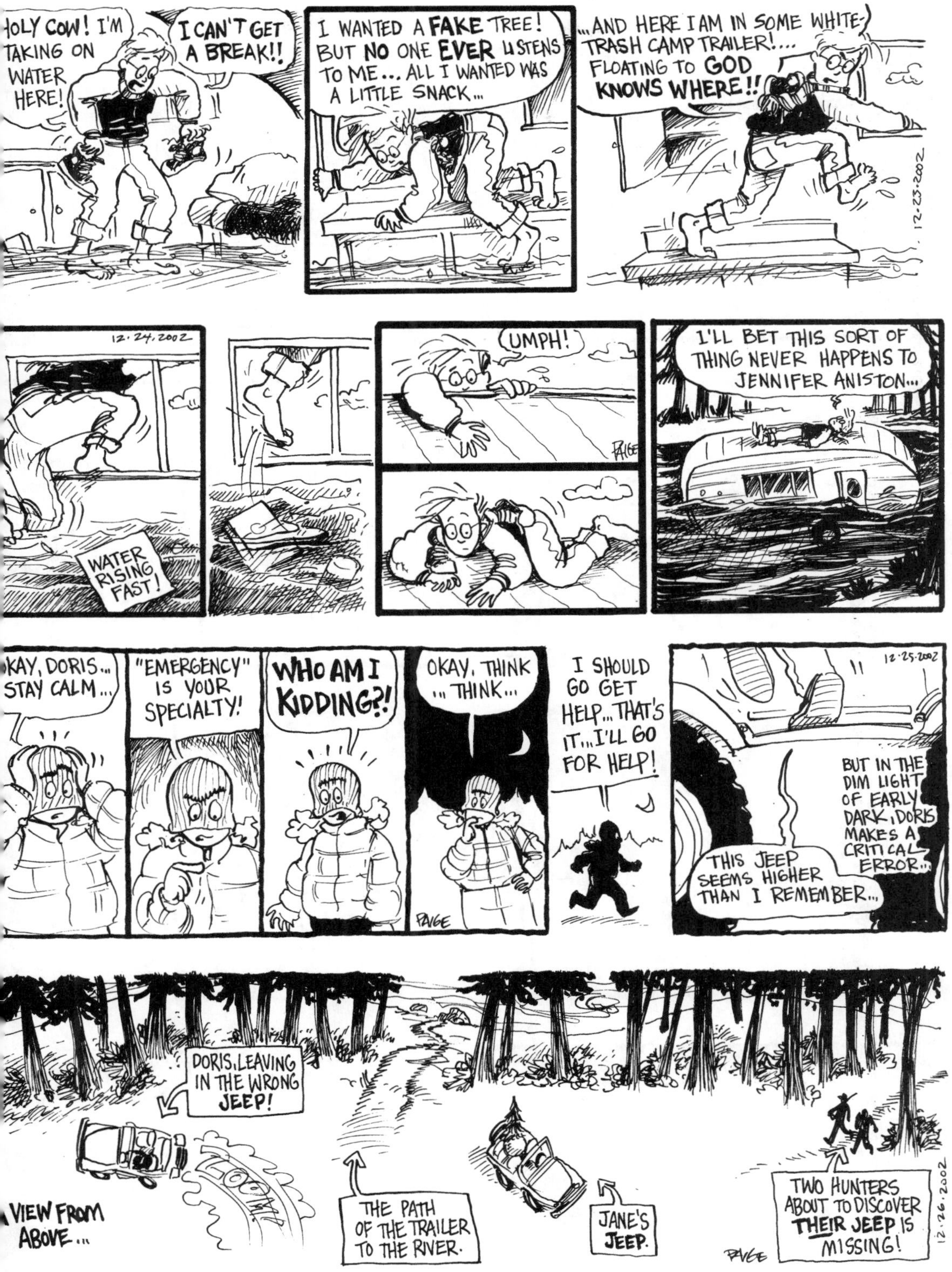
HOLY COW! I'M TAKING ON WATER HERE!
I CAN'T GET A BREAK!!
I WANTED A FAKE TREE! BUT NO ONE EVER LISTENS TO ME... ALL I WANTED WAS A LITTLE SNACK...
...AND HERE I AM IN SOME WHITE-TRASH CAMP TRAILER!... FLOATING TO GOD KNOWS WHERE!!
12·23·2002
12·24·2002
WATER RISING FAST!
UMPH!
PAIGE
I'LL BET THIS SORT OF THING NEVER HAPPENS TO JENNIFER ANISTON...
OKAY, DORIS... STAY CALM...
"EMERGENCY" IS YOUR SPECIALTY!
WHO AM I KIDDING?!
OKAY, THINK ... THINK...
PAIGE
I SHOULD GO GET HELP... THAT'S IT... I'LL GO FOR HELP!
12·25·2002
BUT IN THE DIM LIGHT OF EARLY DARK, DORIS MAKES A CRITICAL ERROR...
THIS JEEP SEEMS HIGHER THAN I REMEMBER...
DORIS, LEAVING IN THE WRONG JEEP!
VIEW FROM ABOVE...
THE PATH OF THE TRAILER TO THE RIVER.
JANE'S JEEP.
TWO HUNTERS ABOUT TO DISCOVER THEIR JEEP IS MISSING!
PAIGE
12·26·2002

Time passes slowly, as Jane floats down stream...

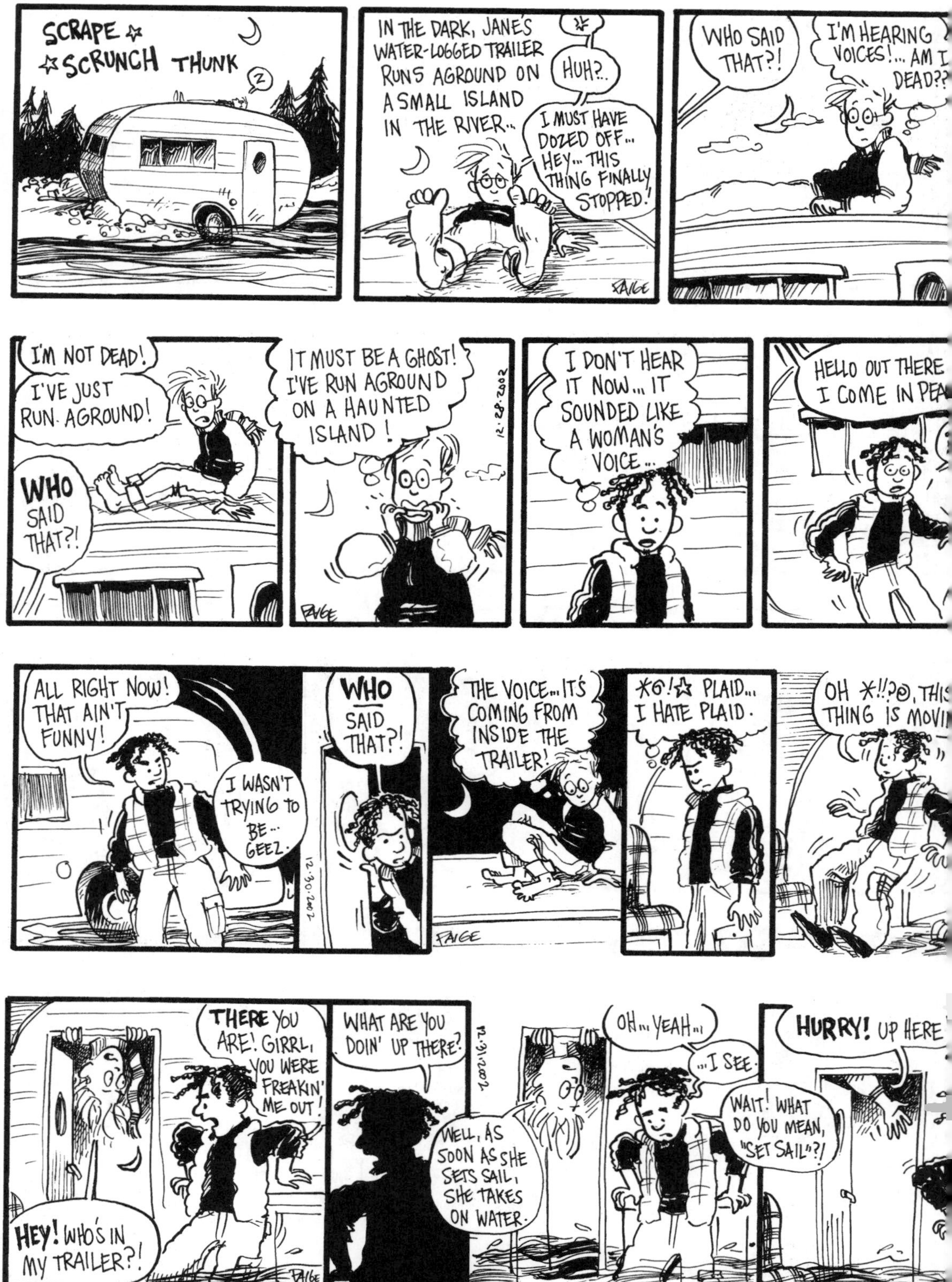
SCRAPE
SCRUNCH THUNK
Z
IN THE DARK, JANE'S WATER-LOGGED TRAILER RUNS AGROUND ON A SMALL ISLAND IN THE RIVER...
HUH?..
I MUST HAVE DOZED OFF... HEY... THIS THING FINALLY STOPPED!
PAIGE
WHO SAID THAT?!
I'M HEARING VOICES!... AM I DEAD??
I'M NOT DEAD!
I'VE JUST RUN AGROUND!
WHO SAID THAT?!
IT MUST BE A GHOST! I'VE RUN AGROUND ON A HAUNTED ISLAND!
12·28·2002
PAIGE
I DON'T HEAR IT NOW... IT SOUNDED LIKE A WOMAN'S VOICE...
HELLO OUT THERE
I COME IN
ALL RIGHT NOW! THAT AIN'T FUNNY!
I WASN'T TRYING TO BE... GEEZ.
WHO SAID THAT?!
12·30·2002
THE VOICE... IT'S COMING FROM INSIDE THE TRAILER!
PAIGE
PLAID... I HATE PLAID.
OH
THING IS
THERE YOU ARE! GIRRL, YOU WERE FREAKIN' ME OUT!
HEY! WHO'S IN MY TRAILER?!
PAIGE
WHAT ARE YOU DOIN' UP THERE?
WELL, AS SOON AS SHE SETS SAIL, SHE TAKES ON WATER.
12·31·2002
OH... YEAH...
...I SEE.
WAIT! WHAT DO YOU MEAN, "SET SAIL"?!
HURRY! UP HERE

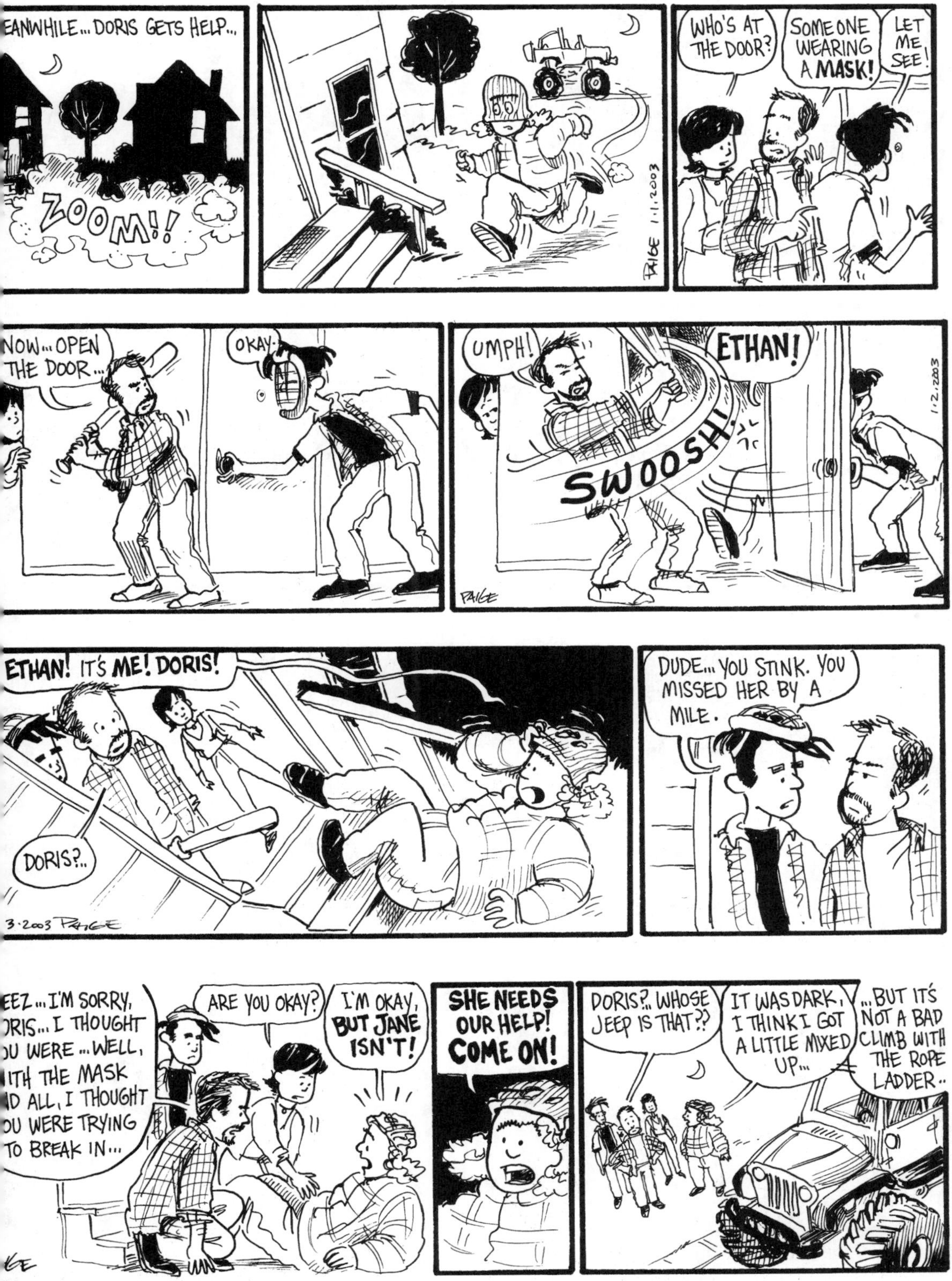
EANWHILE... DORIS GETS HELP...
ZOOM!!
PAIGE 1·1·2003
WHO'S AT THE DOOR?
SOME ONE WEARING A MASK!
LET ME SEE!
NOW... OPEN THE DOOR...
OKAY.
UMPH!
ETHAN!
SWOOSH!
1·2·2003
PAIGE
ETHAN! IT'S ME! DORIS!
DORIS?..
3·2003 PAIGE
DUDE... YOU STINK. YOU MISSED HER BY A MILE.
EEZ... I'M SORRY, ORIS... I THOUGHT U WERE... WELL, ITH THE MASK D ALL, I THOUGHT U WERE TRYING TO BREAK IN...
ARE YOU OKAY?
I'M OKAY, BUT JANE ISN'T!
SHE NEEDS OUR HELP! COME ON!
DORIS?.. WHOSE JEEP IS THAT??
IT WAS DARK, I THINK I GOT A LITTLE MIXED UP...
...BUT IT'S NOT A BAD CLIMB WITH THE ROPE LADDER..

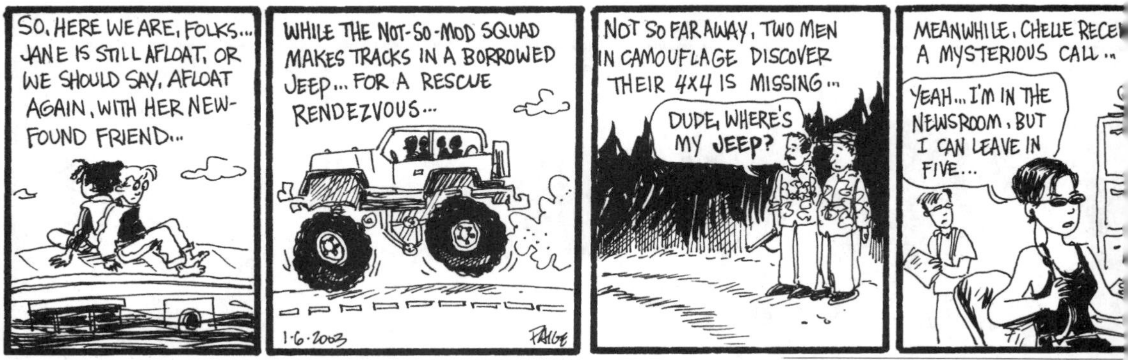
SO, HERE WE ARE, FOLKS... JANE IS STILL AFLOAT, OR WE SHOULD SAY, AFLOAT AGAIN, WITH HER NEW-FOUND FRIEND...
WHILE THE NOT-SO-MOD SQUAD MAKES TRACKS IN A BORROWED JEEP... FOR A RESCUE RENDEZVOUS...
1-6-2003
PAIGE
NOT SO FAR AWAY, TWO MEN IN CAMOUFLAGE DISCOVER THEIR 4X4 IS MISSING...
DUDE, WHERE'S MY JEEP?
MEANWHILE, CHELLE RECE
A MYSTERIOUS CALL...
YEAH... I'M IN THE NEWSROOM, BUT I CAN LEAVE IN FIVE...

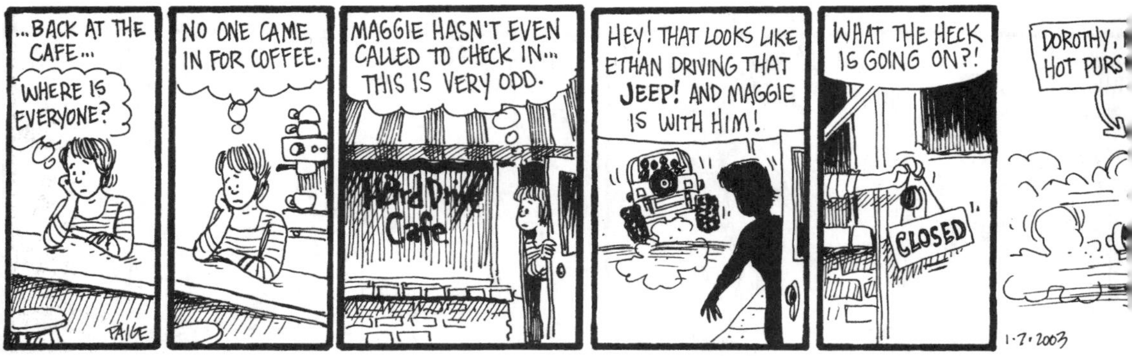
...BACK AT THE CAFE...
WHERE IS EVERYONE?
PAIGE
NO ONE CAME IN FOR COFFEE.
MAGGIE HASN'T EVEN CALLED TO CHECK IN... THIS IS VERY ODD.
Hard Drive Cafe
HEY! THAT LOOKS LIKE ETHAN DRIVING THAT JEEP! AND MAGGIE IS WITH HIM!
WHAT THE HECK IS GOING ON?!
CLOSED
1-7-2003
DOROTHY,
HOT PURS

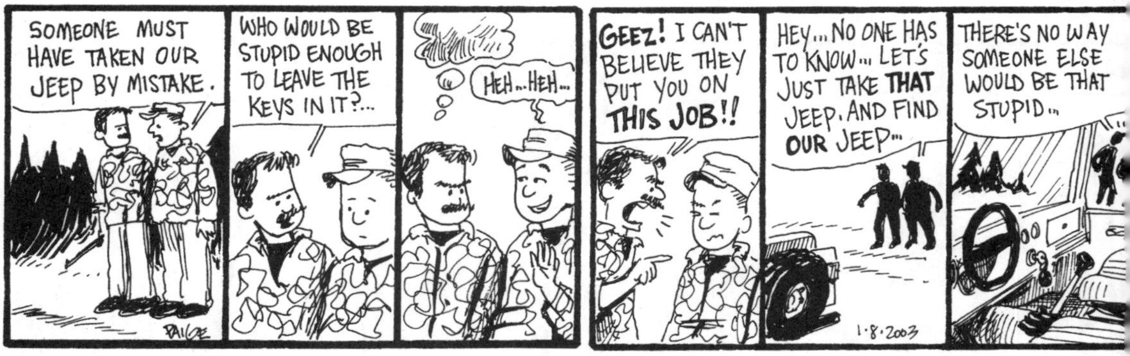
SOMEONE MUST HAVE TAKEN OUR JEEP BY MISTAKE.
PAIGE
WHO WOULD BE STUPID ENOUGH TO LEAVE THE KEYS IN IT?...
HEH...HEH...
GEEZ! I CAN'T BELIEVE THEY PUT YOU ON THIS JOB!!
HEY... NO ONE HAS TO KNOW... LET'S JUST TAKE THAT JEEP, AND FIND OUR JEEP...
1-8-2003
THERE'S NO WAY SOMEONE ELSE WOULD BE THAT STUPID...

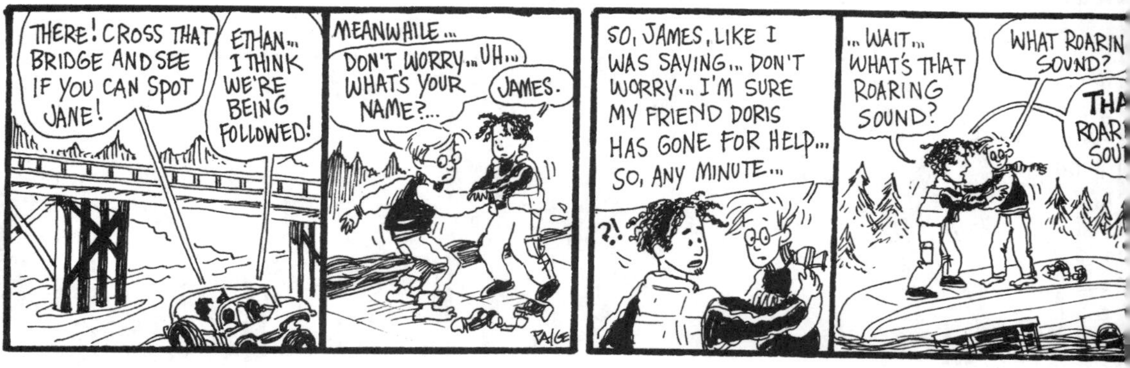
THERE! CROSS THAT BRIDGE AND SEE IF YOU CAN SPOT JANE!
ETHAN... I THINK WE'RE BEING FOLLOWED!
MEANWHILE...
DON'T WORRY... UH... WHAT'S YOUR NAME?...
JAMES.
PAIGE
SO, JAMES, LIKE I WAS SAYING... DON'T WORRY... I'M SURE MY FRIEND DORIS HAS GONE FOR HELP... SO, ANY MINUTE...
?!
...WAIT... WHAT'S THAT ROARING SOUND?
WHAT ROARIN SOUND?

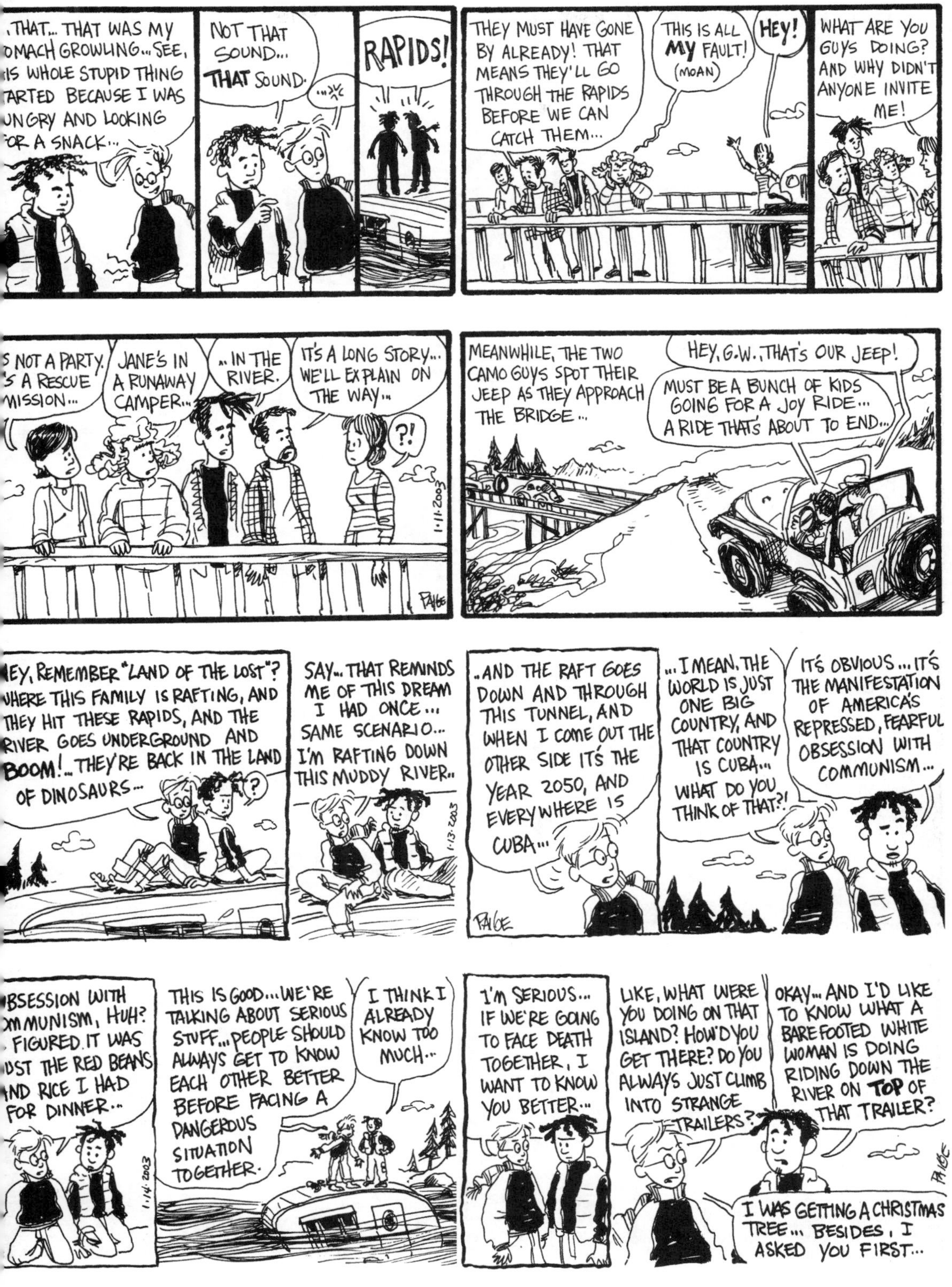

, THAT... THAT WAS MY
OMACH GROWLING... SEE,
IS WHOLE STUPID THING
TARTED BECAUSE I WAS
UNGRY AND LOOKING
FOR A SNACK...
NOT THAT SOUND... THAT SOUND.
RAPIDS!
THEY MUST HAVE GONE BY ALREADY! THAT MEANS THEY'LL GO THROUGH THE RAPIDS BEFORE WE CAN CATCH THEM...
THIS IS ALL MY FAULT! (MOAN)
HEY!
WHAT ARE YOU GUYS DOING? AND WHY DIDN'T ANYONE INVITE ME!
S NOT A PARTY. 'S A RESCUE MISSION...
JANE'S IN A RUNAWAY CAMPER...
... IN THE RIVER.
IT'S A LONG STORY... WE'LL EXPLAIN ON THE WAY...
?!
1-11-2003
PAIGE
MEANWHILE, THE TWO CAMO GUYS SPOT THEIR JEEP AS THEY APPROACH THE BRIDGE...
HEY, G.W., THAT'S OUR JEEP!
MUST BE A BUNCH OF KIDS GOING FOR A JOY RIDE... A RIDE THAT'S ABOUT TO END...
EY, REMEMBER "LAND OF THE LOST"? WHERE THIS FAMILY IS RAFTING, AND THEY HIT THESE RAPIDS, AND THE RIVER GOES UNDERGROUND AND BOOM!... THEY'RE BACK IN THE LAND OF DINOSAURS...
?
SAY... THAT REMINDS ME OF THIS DREAM I HAD ONCE... SAME SCENARIO... I'M RAFTING DOWN THIS MUDDY RIVER...
1-13-2003
...AND THE RAFT GOES DOWN AND THROUGH THIS TUNNEL, AND WHEN I COME OUT THE OTHER SIDE IT'S THE YEAR 2050, AND EVERYWHERE IS CUBA...
...I MEAN, THE WORLD IS JUST ONE BIG COUNTRY, AND THAT COUNTRY IS CUBA... WHAT DO YOU THINK OF THAT?!
IT'S OBVIOUS... IT'S THE MANIFESTATION OF AMERICA'S REPRESSED, FEARFUL OBSESSION WITH COMMUNISM...
PAIGE
BSESSION WITH OMMUNISM, HUH? FIGURED IT WAS UST THE RED BEANS ND RICE I HAD FOR DINNER...
1-14-2003
THIS IS GOOD... WE'RE TALKING ABOUT SERIOUS STUFF... PEOPLE SHOULD ALWAYS GET TO KNOW EACH OTHER BETTER BEFORE FACING A DANGEROUS SITUATION TOGETHER.
I THINK I ALREADY KNOW TOO MUCH...
I'M SERIOUS... IF WE'RE GOING TO FACE DEATH TOGETHER, I WANT TO KNOW YOU BETTER...
LIKE, WHAT WERE YOU DOING ON THAT ISLAND? HOW'D YOU GET THERE? DO YOU ALWAYS JUST CLIMB INTO STRANGE TRAILERS?
OKAY... AND I'D LIKE TO KNOW WHAT A BAREFOOTED WHITE WOMAN IS DOING RIDING DOWN THE RIVER ON TOP OF THAT TRAILER?
I WAS GETTING A CHRISTMAS TREE... BESIDES, I ASKED YOU FIRST...
PAIGE

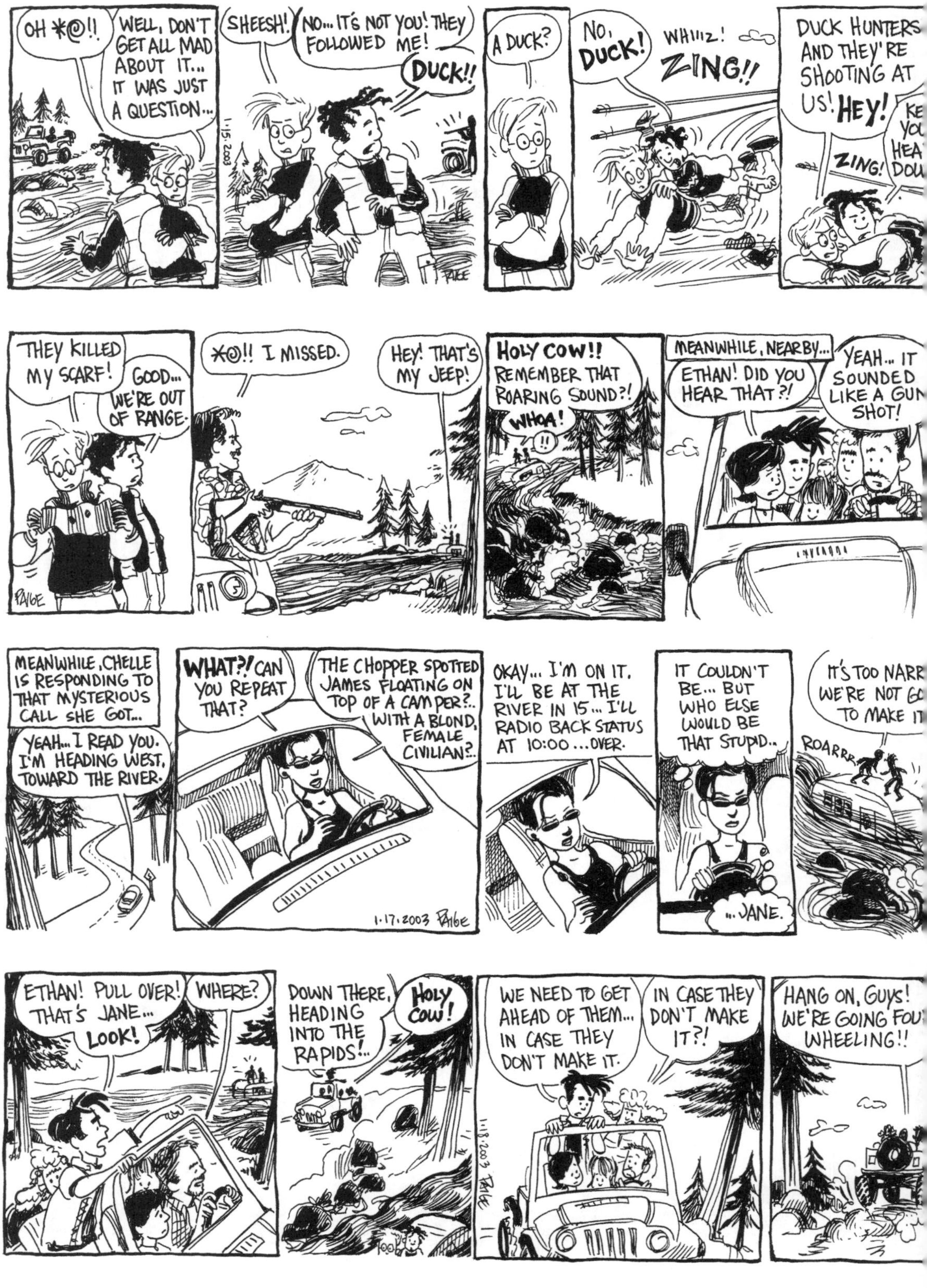
OH *@!!
WELL, DON'T GET ALL MAD ABOUT IT... IT WAS JUST A QUESTION...
SHEESH!
NO... IT'S NOT YOU! THEY FOLLOWED ME!
DUCK!!
1.15.2003
A DUCK?
NO, DUCK!
WHIIZ!
ZING!!
DUCK HUNTERS AND THEY'RE SHOOTING AT US!
HEY!
ZING!
THEY KILLED MY SCARF!
GOOD... WE'RE OUT OF RANGE.
*@!! I MISSED.
HEY! THAT'S MY JEEP!
HOLY COW!! REMEMBER THAT ROARING SOUND?!
WHOA!
!!
MEANWHILE, NEARBY...
ETHAN! DID YOU HEAR THAT?!
YEAH... IT SOUNDED LIKE A GUN SHOT!
MEANWHILE, CHELLE IS RESPONDING TO THAT MYSTERIOUS CALL SHE GOT...
YEAH... I READ YOU. I'M HEADING WEST, TOWARD THE RIVER.
WHAT?! CAN YOU REPEAT THAT?
THE CHOPPER SPOTTED JAMES FLOATING ON TOP OF A CAMPER?.. WITH A BLOND, FEMALE CIVILIAN?..
1.17.2003
OKAY... I'M ON IT. I'LL BE AT THE RIVER IN 15... I'LL RADIO BACK STATUS AT 10:00... OVER.
IT COULDN'T BE... BUT WHO ELSE WOULD BE THAT STUPID..
...JANE.
ROARRR
ETHAN! PULL OVER! THAT'S JANE... LOOK!
WHERE?
DOWN THERE, HEADING INTO THE RAPIDS!..
HOLY COW!
1.18.2003
WE NEED TO GET AHEAD OF THEM... IN CASE THEY DON'T MAKE IT.
IN CASE THEY DON'T MAKE IT?!
HANG ON, GUYS! WE'RE GOING FOU WHEELING!!

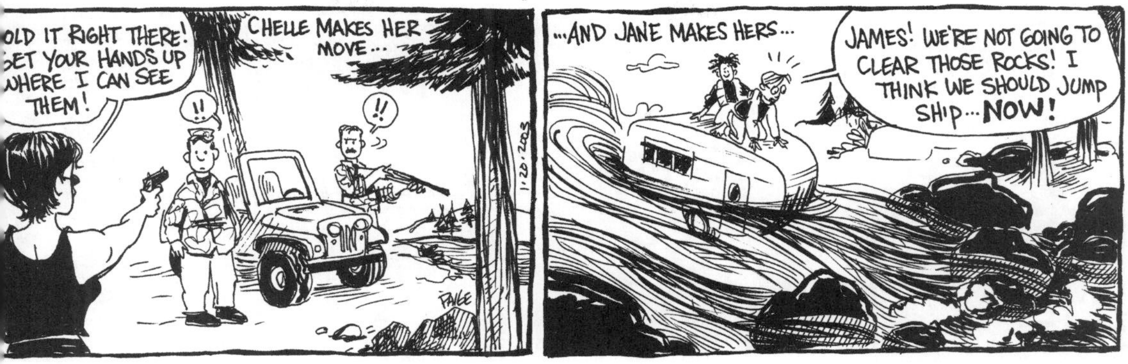
OLD IT RIGHT THERE! ET YOUR HANDS UP HERE I CAN SEE THEM!
CHELLE MAKES HER MOVE...
!!
!!
1.20.2003
PAIGE
...AND JANE MAKES HERS...
JAMES! WE'RE NOT GOING TO CLEAR THOSE ROCKS! I THINK WE SHOULD JUMP SHIP... NOW!

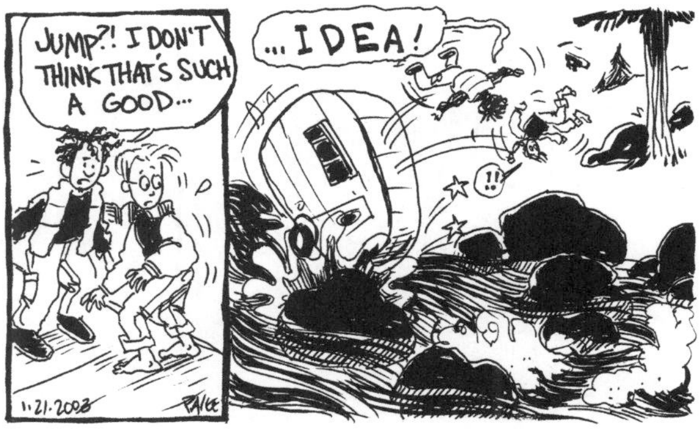
JUMP?! I DON'T THINK THAT'S SUCH A GOOD...
...IDEA!
!!
1.21.2003
PAIGE

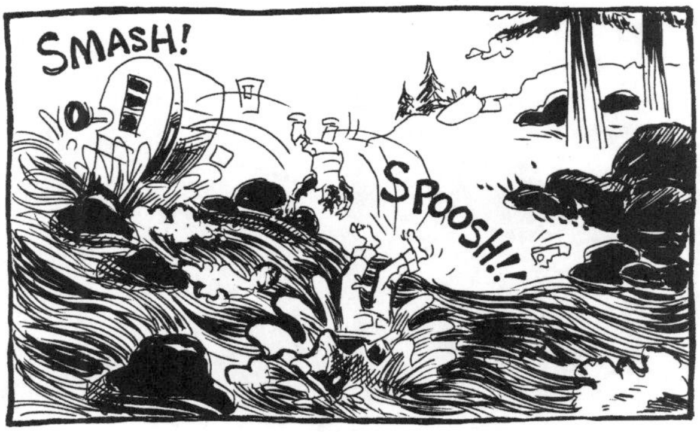
SMASH!
SPOOSH!!

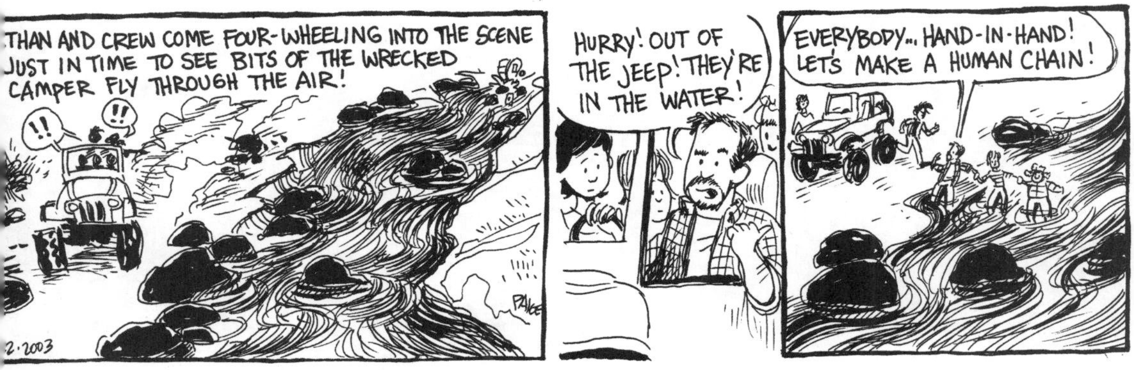
THAN AND CREW COME FOUR-WHEELING INTO THE SCENE JUST IN TIME TO SEE BITS OF THE WRECKED CAMPER FLY THROUGH THE AIR!
!!
!!
2.2003
PAIGE
HURRY! OUT OF THE JEEP! THEY'RE IN THE WATER!
EVERYBODY... HAND-IN-HAND! LET'S MAKE A HUMAN CHAIN!

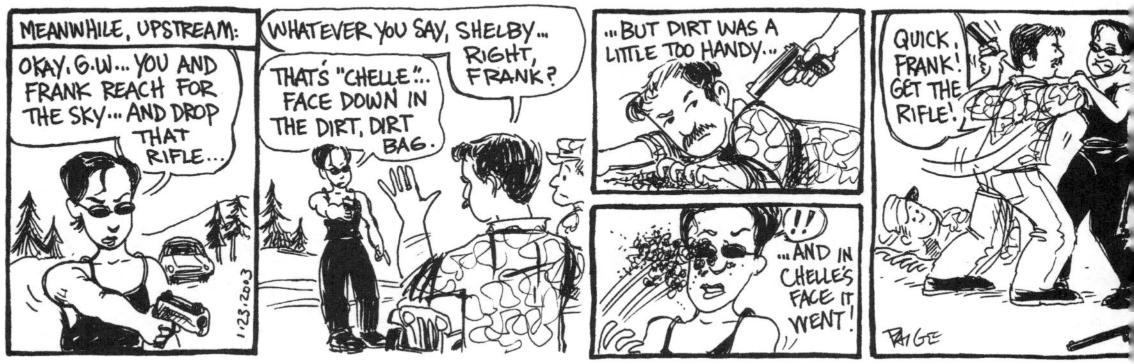
MEANWHILE, UPSTREAM:
OKAY, G.W... YOU AND FRANK REACH FOR THE SKY... AND DROP THAT RIFLE...
1·23·2003
WHATEVER YOU SAY, SHELBY... RIGHT, FRANK?
THAT'S "CHELLE"... FACE DOWN IN THE DIRT, DIRT BAG.
...BUT DIRT WAS A LITTLE TOO HANDY...
!!
...AND IN CHELLE'S FACE IT WENT!
QUICK, FRANK! GET THE RIFLE!
PAIGE

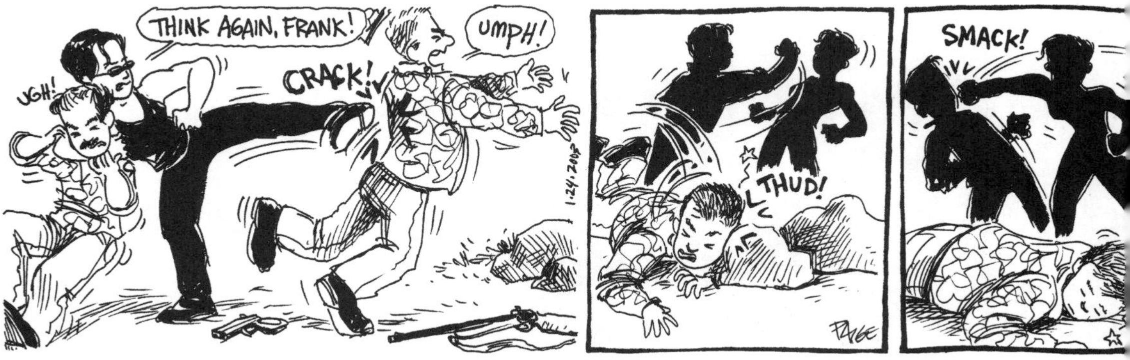
THINK AGAIN, FRANK!
UMPH!
UGH!
CRACK!
1·24·2003
THUD!
PAIGE
SMACK!

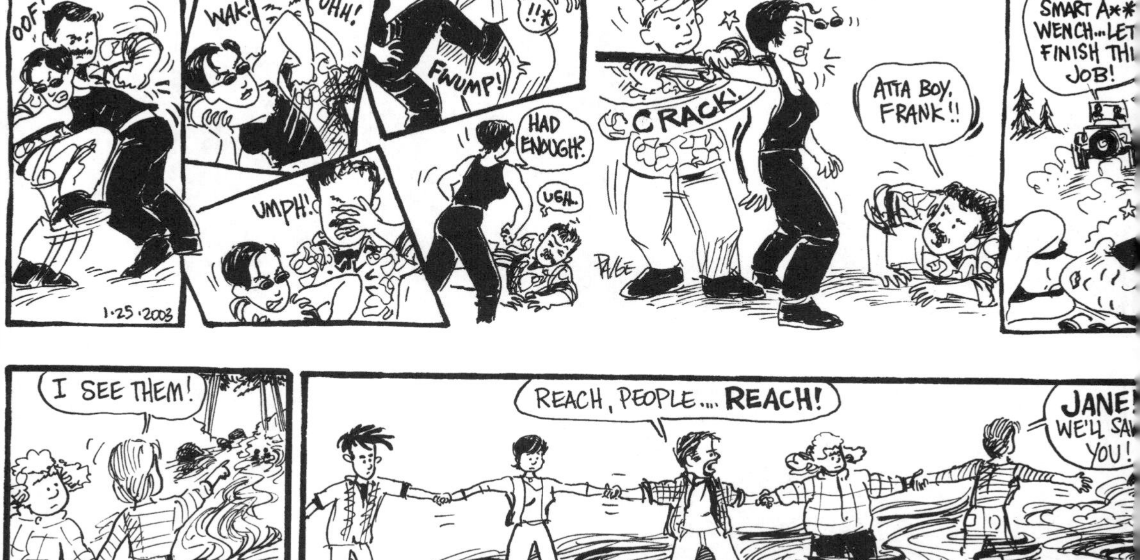
OOF!
WAK!
OHH!
!!*
FWUMP!
HAD ENOUGH?
UMPH!
UGH
1·25·2003
CRACK!
ATTA BOY, FRANK!!
PAIGE
SMART A** WENCH...LET FINISH THI JOB!

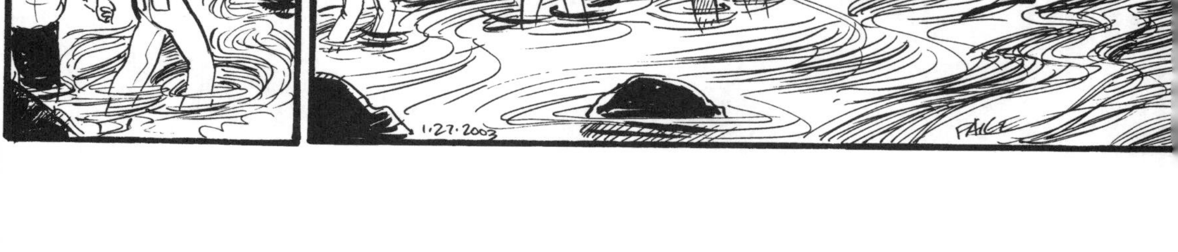
I SEE THEM!
REACH, PEOPLE.... REACH!
JANE! WE'LL SAV YOU!
1·27·2003
PAIGE

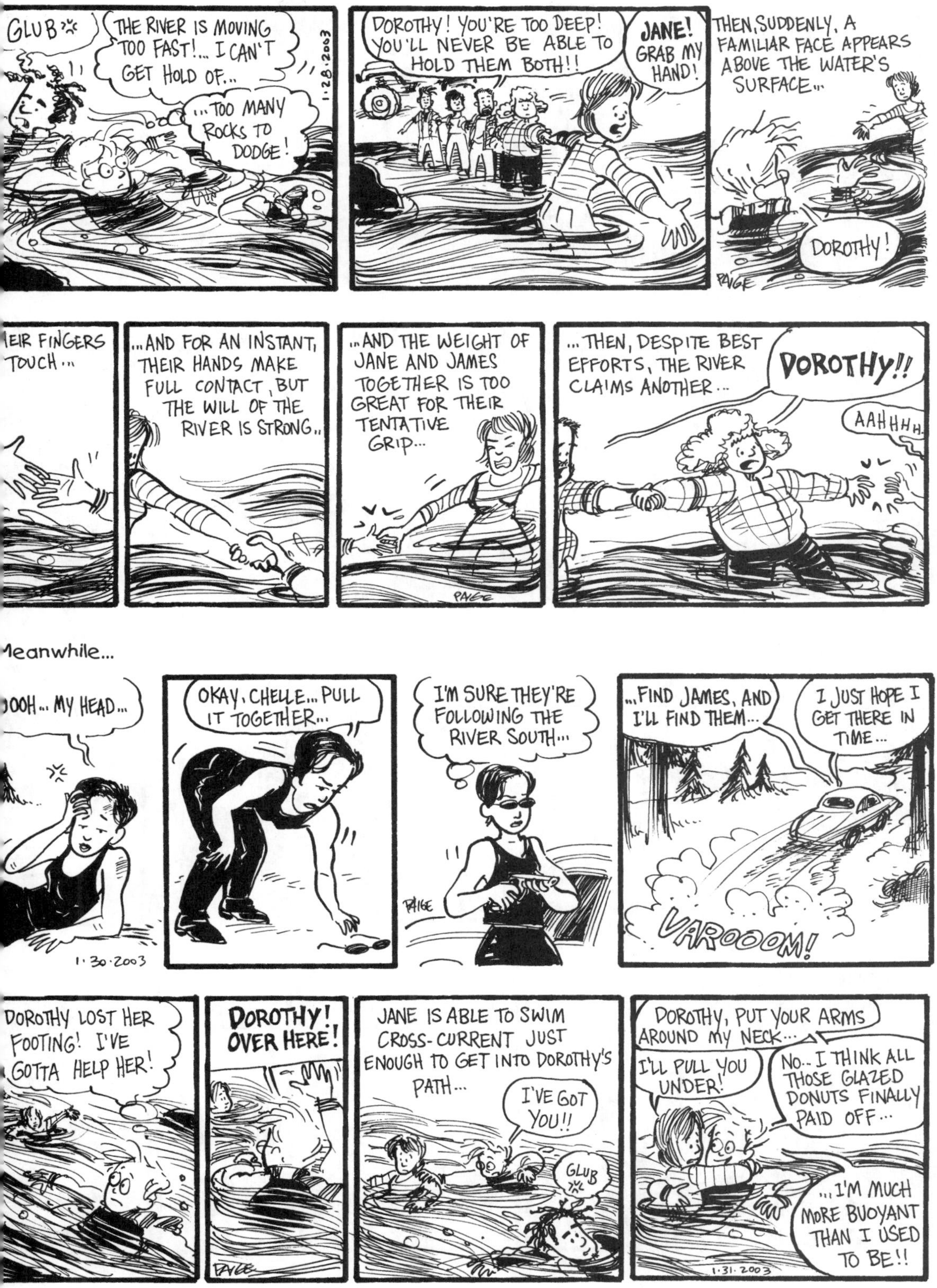
GLUB
THE RIVER IS MOVING TOO FAST!... I CAN'T GET HOLD OF...
...TOO MANY ROCKS TO DODGE!
1·28·2003
DOROTHY! YOU'RE TOO DEEP! YOU'LL NEVER BE ABLE TO HOLD THEM BOTH!!
JANE! GRAB MY HAND!
THEN, SUDDENLY, A FAMILIAR FACE APPEARS ABOVE THE WATER'S SURFACE...
DOROTHY!
PAIGE
EIR FINGERS TOUCH...
...AND FOR AN INSTANT, THEIR HANDS MAKE FULL CONTACT, BUT THE WILL OF THE RIVER IS STRONG..
...AND THE WEIGHT OF JANE AND JAMES TOGETHER IS TOO GREAT FOR THEIR TENTATIVE GRIP...
PAIGE
... THEN, DESPITE BEST EFFORTS, THE RIVER CLAIMS ANOTHER...
DOROTHY!!
AAHHHH..
Meanwhile...
OOH... MY HEAD...
OKAY, CHELLE... PULL IT TOGETHER...
I'M SURE THEY'RE FOLLOWING THE RIVER SOUTH...
PAIGE
...FIND JAMES, AND I'LL FIND THEM...
I JUST HOPE I GET THERE IN TIME...
VAROOOM!
1·30·2003
DOROTHY LOST HER FOOTING! I'VE GOTTA HELP HER!
DOROTHY! OVER HERE!
JANE IS ABLE TO SWIM CROSS-CURRENT JUST ENOUGH TO GET INTO DOROTHY'S PATH...
I'VE GOT YOU!!
GLUB
PAIGE
DOROTHY, PUT YOUR ARMS AROUND MY NECK...
I'LL PULL YOU UNDER!
NO.. I THINK ALL THOSE GLAZED DONUTS FINALLY PAID OFF...
...I'M MUCH MORE BUOYANT THAN I USED TO BE!!
1·31·2003

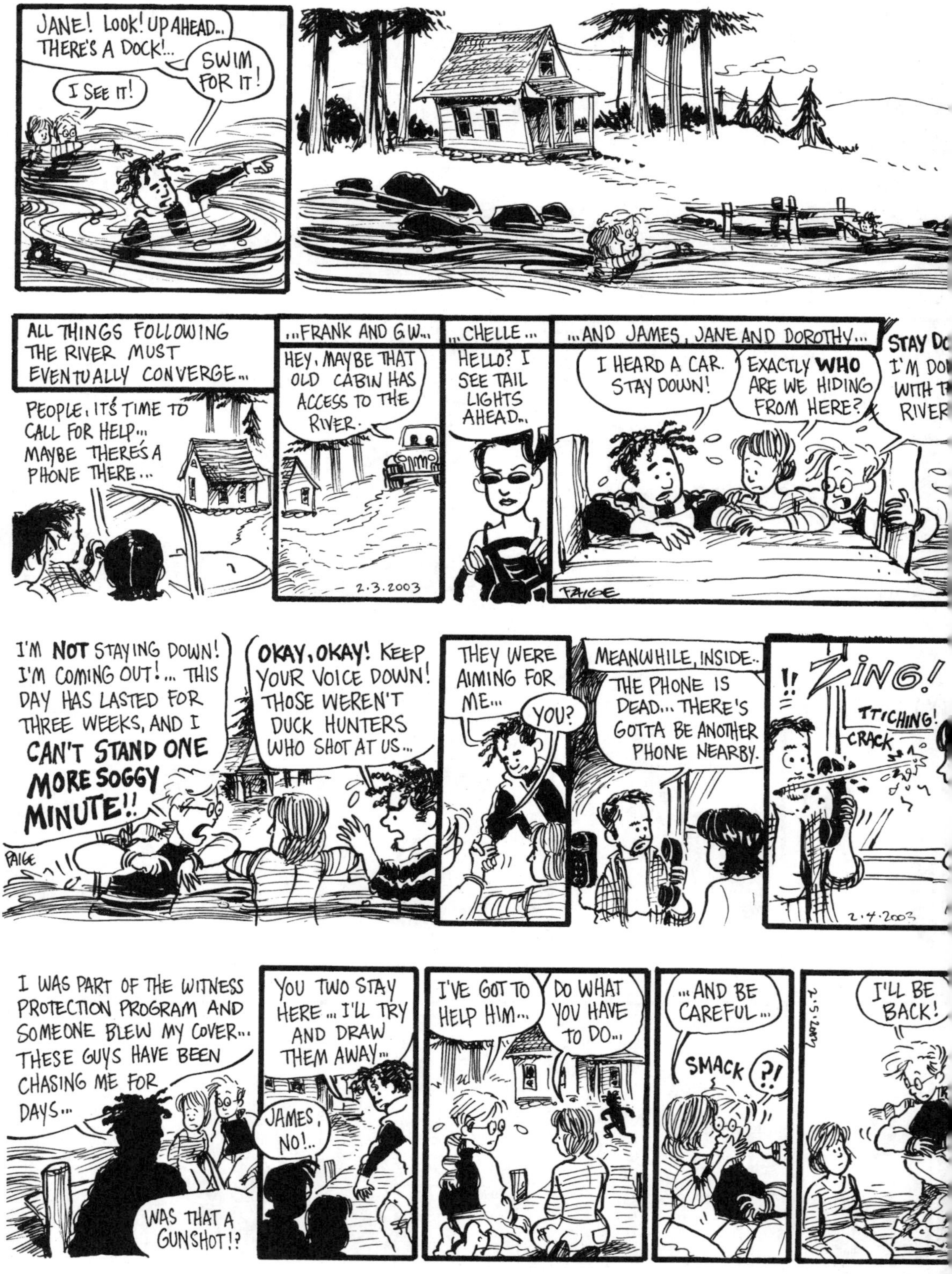
JANE! LOOK! UP AHEAD.. THERE'S A DOCK!..
SWIM FOR IT!
I SEE IT!
ALL THINGS FOLLOWING THE RIVER MUST EVENTUALLY CONVERGE...
PEOPLE, IT'S TIME TO CALL FOR HELP... MAYBE THERE'S A PHONE THERE...
...FRANK AND G.W...
HEY, MAYBE THAT OLD CABIN HAS ACCESS TO THE RIVER.
...CHELLE...
HELLO? I SEE TAIL LIGHTS AHEAD..
...AND JAMES, JANE AND DOROTHY...
I HEARD A CAR. STAY DOWN!
EXACTLY WHO ARE WE HIDING FROM HERE?
PAIGE
2.3.2003
I'M NOT STAYING DOWN! I'M COMING OUT!... THIS DAY HAS LASTED FOR THREE WEEKS, AND I CAN'T STAND ONE MORE SOGGY MINUTE!!
OKAY, OKAY! KEEP YOUR VOICE DOWN! THOSE WEREN'T DUCK HUNTERS WHO SHOT AT US...
THEY WERE AIMING FOR ME...
YOU?
MEANWHILE, INSIDE..
THE PHONE IS DEAD... THERE'S GOTTA BE ANOTHER PHONE NEARBY.
ZING!
TTICHING!
CRACK
PAIGE
2.4.2003
I WAS PART OF THE WITNESS PROTECTION PROGRAM AND SOMEONE BLEW MY COVER... THESE GUYS HAVE BEEN CHASING ME FOR DAYS...
WAS THAT A GUNSHOT!?
YOU TWO STAY HERE... I'LL TRY AND DRAW THEM AWAY...
JAMES, NO!..
I'VE GOT TO HELP HIM...
DO WHAT YOU HAVE TO DO...
...AND BE CAREFUL...
SMACK
?!
I'LL BE BACK!

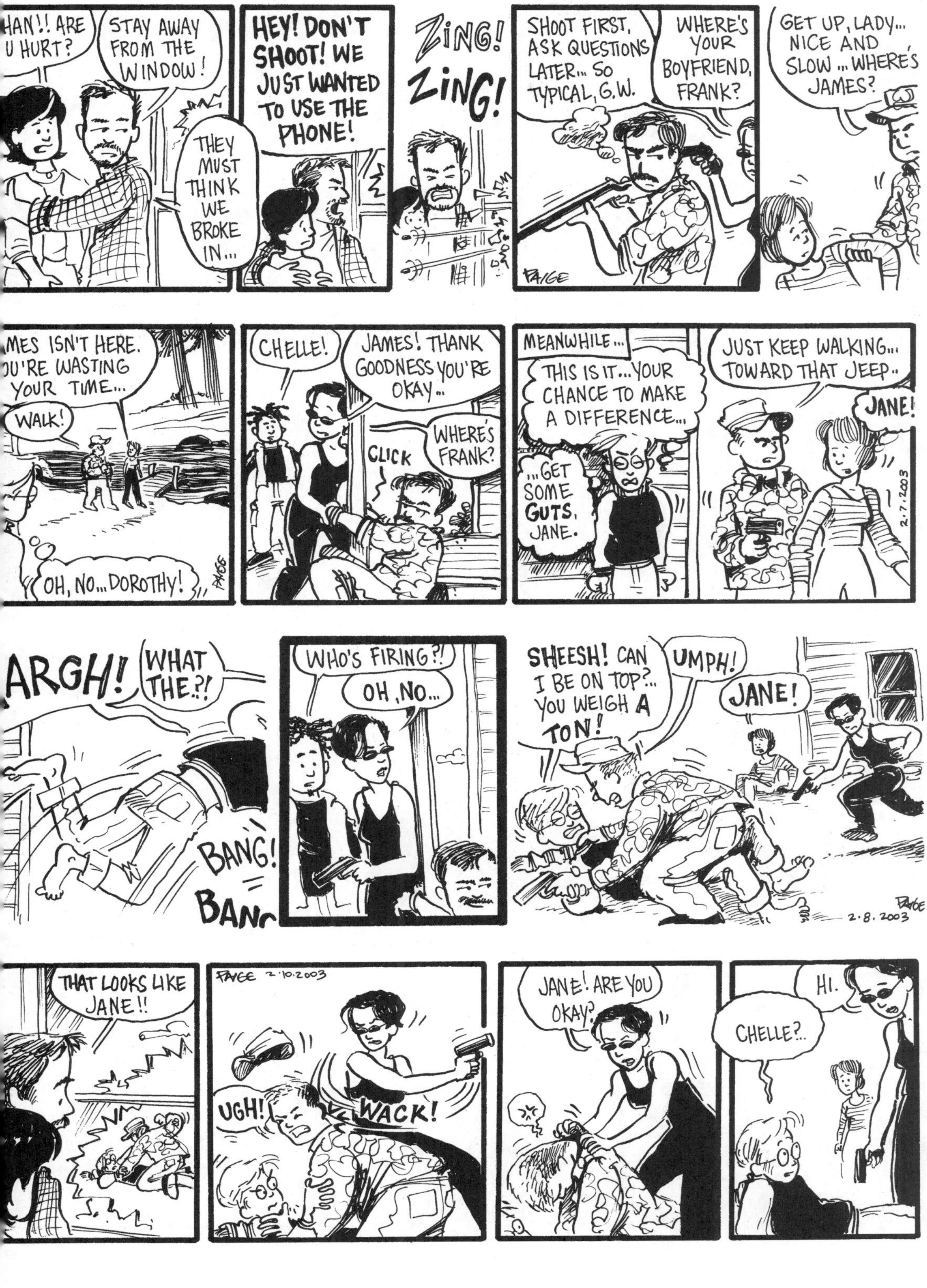

HAN!! ARE
U HURT?
STAY AWAY FROM THE WINDOW!
THEY MUST THINK WE BROKE IN...
HEY! DON'T SHOOT! WE JUST WANTED TO USE THE PHONE!
ZING!
ZING!
SHOOT FIRST, ASK QUESTIONS LATER... SO TYPICAL, G.W.
WHERE'S YOUR BOYFRIEND, FRANK?
PAIGE
GET UP, LADY... NICE AND SLOW ... WHERE'S JAMES?
MES ISN'T HERE.
OU'RE WASTING YOUR TIME...
WALK!
OH, NO... DOROTHY!
PAIGE
CHELLE!
JAMES! THANK GOODNESS YOU'RE OKAY..
WHERE'S FRANK?
CLICK
MEANWHILE...
THIS IS IT... YOUR CHANCE TO MAKE A DIFFERENCE...
...GET SOME GUTS, JANE.
JUST KEEP WALKING... TOWARD THAT JEEP..
JANE!
2.7.2003
ARGH!
WHAT THE?!
BANG!
BANG
WHO'S FIRING?!
OH, NO...
SHEESH! CAN I BE ON TOP?... YOU WEIGH A TON!
UMPH!
JANE!
PAIGE
2.8.2003
THAT LOOKS LIKE JANE!!
PAIGE 2.10.2003
UGH!
WACK!
JANE! ARE YOU OKAY?
HI.
CHELLE?..

THE LONGEST DAY IN THE HISTORY OF COMIC ART HAS FINALLY COME TO AN END... AND THINGS IN JANE'S WORLD MAY NEVER BE QUITE THE SAME... ALL THAT SPECULATION ABOUT CHELLE'S SECRET LIFE CONTAINED A BIT OF TRUTH... AS IS SOMETIMES THE CASE... SHE **DID** HAVE A SECRET LIFE AFTER ALL!... BUT WHAT EXACTLY DOES ANY OF THIS MEAN?....

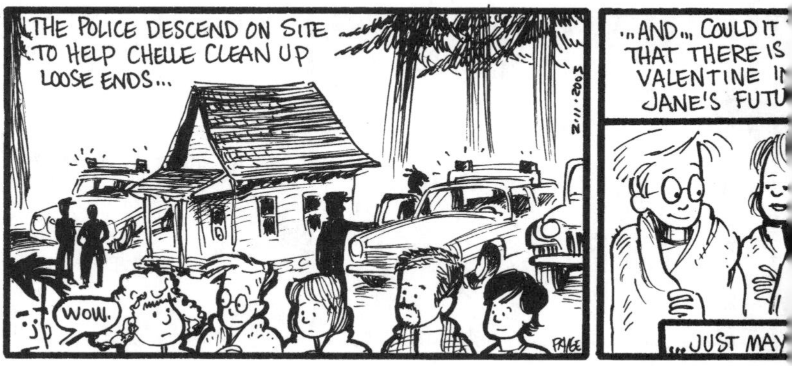

THE POLICE DESCEND ON SITE TO HELP CHELLE CLEAN UP LOOSE ENDS...
WOW.
2.11.2003
PAIGE
...AND... COULD IT
THAT THERE IS
VALENTINE I
JANE'S FUTU
...JUST MAY

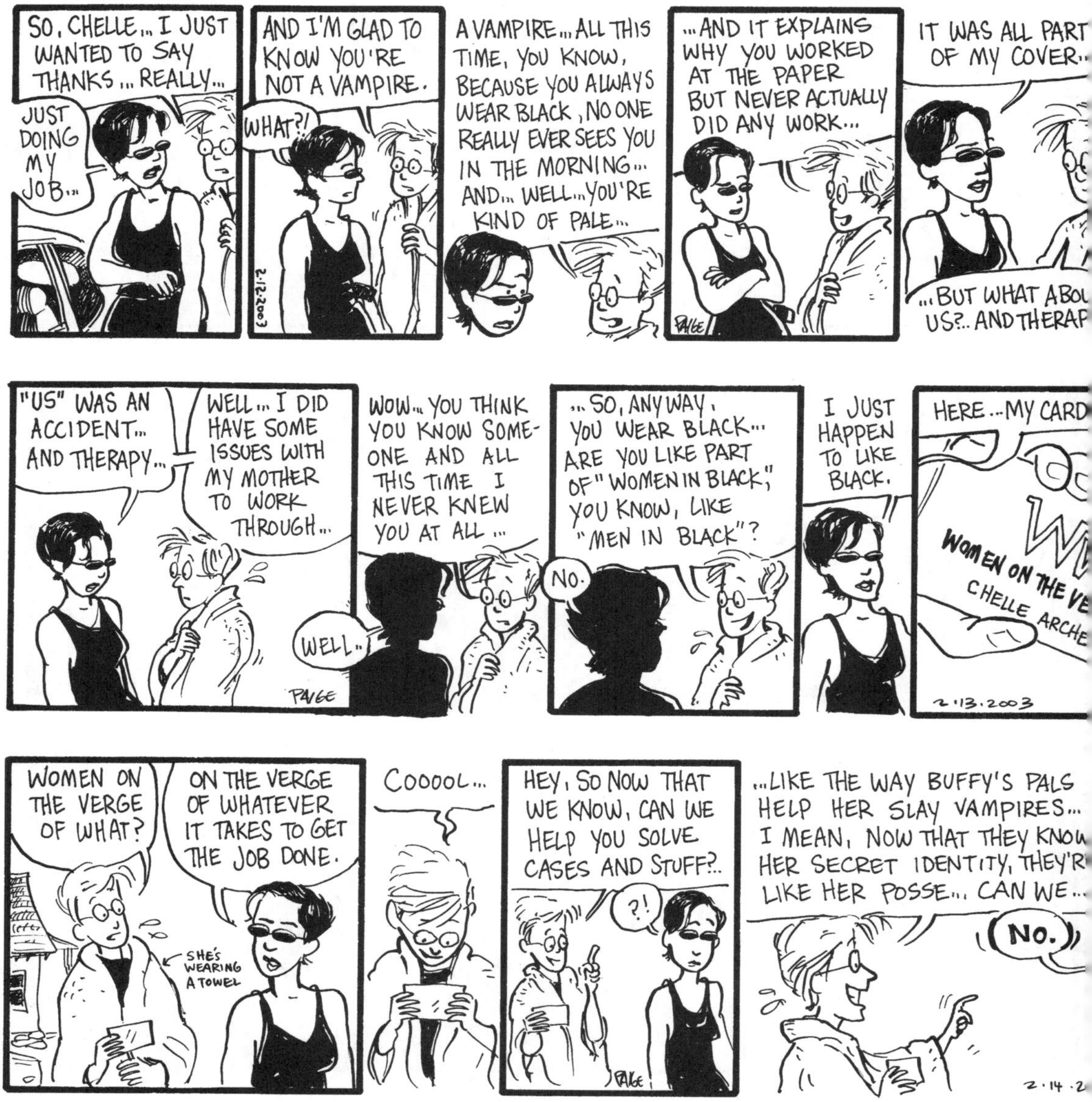

SO, CHELLE... I JUST WANTED TO SAY THANKS... REALLY...
JUST DOING MY JOB...
AND I'M GLAD TO KNOW YOU'RE NOT A VAMPIRE.
WHAT?!
2.12.2003
A VAMPIRE... ALL THIS TIME, YOU KNOW, BECAUSE YOU ALWAYS WEAR BLACK, NO ONE REALLY EVER SEES YOU IN THE MORNING... AND... WELL... YOU'RE KIND OF PALE...
...AND IT EXPLAINS WHY YOU WORKED AT THE PAPER BUT NEVER ACTUALLY DID ANY WORK...
PAIGE
IT WAS ALL PART OF MY COVER...
...BUT WHAT ABOU US?.. AND THERAP
"US" WAS AN ACCIDENT... AND THERAPY...
WELL... I DID HAVE SOME ISSUES WITH MY MOTHER TO WORK THROUGH...
PAIGE
WOW... YOU THINK YOU KNOW SOMEONE AND ALL THIS TIME I NEVER KNEW YOU AT ALL...
WELL..
...SO, ANYWAY, YOU WEAR BLACK... ARE YOU LIKE PART OF "WOMEN IN BLACK," YOU KNOW, LIKE "MEN IN BLACK"?
NO.
I JUST HAPPEN TO LIKE BLACK.
HERE...MY CARD
WOMEN ON THE VE
CHELLE ARCHE
2.13.2003
WOMEN ON THE VERGE OF WHAT?
ON THE VERGE OF WHATEVER IT TAKES TO GET THE JOB DONE.
SHE'S WEARING A TOWEL
COOOOL...
HEY, SO NOW THAT WE KNOW, CAN WE HELP YOU SOLVE CASES AND STUFF?..
?!
PAIGE
...LIKE THE WAY BUFFY'S PALS HELP HER SLAY VAMPIRES... I MEAN, NOW THAT THEY KNOW HER SECRET IDENTITY, THEY'R LIKE HER POSSE... CAN WE...
(NO.)
2.14.2

he next day, at Jane's...

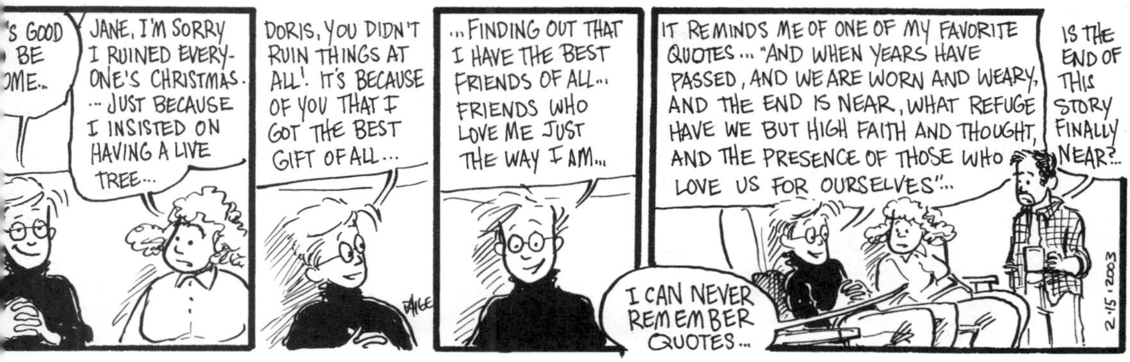

'S GOOD BE ME..
JANE, I'M SORRY I RUINED EVERY-ONE'S CHRISTMAS. ... JUST BECAUSE I INSISTED ON HAVING A LIVE TREE...
DORIS, YOU DIDN'T RUIN THINGS AT ALL! IT'S BECAUSE OF YOU THAT I GOT THE BEST GIFT OF ALL...
...FINDING OUT THAT I HAVE THE BEST FRIENDS OF ALL... FRIENDS WHO LOVE ME JUST THE WAY I AM...
IT REMINDS ME OF ONE OF MY FAVORITE QUOTES... "AND WHEN YEARS HAVE PASSED, AND WE ARE WORN AND WEARY, AND THE END IS NEAR, WHAT REFUGE HAVE WE BUT HIGH FAITH AND THOUGHT, AND THE PRESENCE OF THOSE WHO LOVE US FOR OURSELVES"...
IS THE END OF THIS STORY FINALLY NEAR?...
I CAN NEVER REMEMBER QUOTES...
PAIGE
2.15.2003

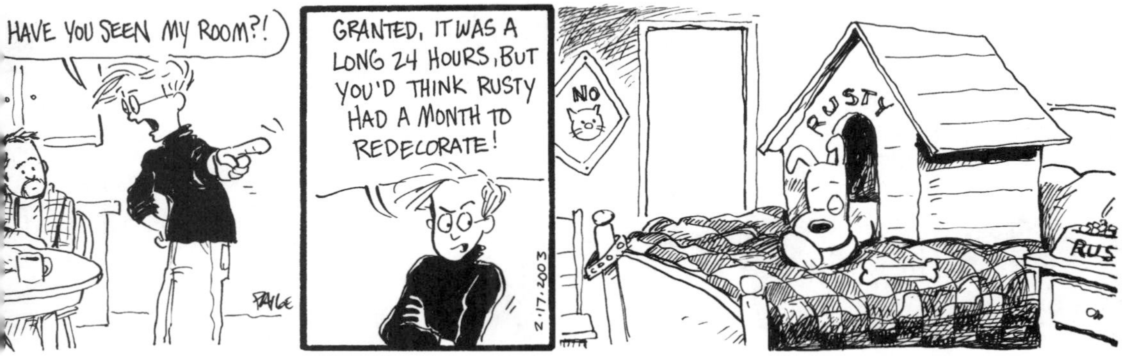

HAVE YOU SEEN MY ROOM?!
PAIGE
GRANTED, IT WAS A LONG 24 HOURS, BUT YOU'D THINK RUSTY HAD A MONTH TO REDECORATE!
2.17.2003
NO
RUSTY
RUS

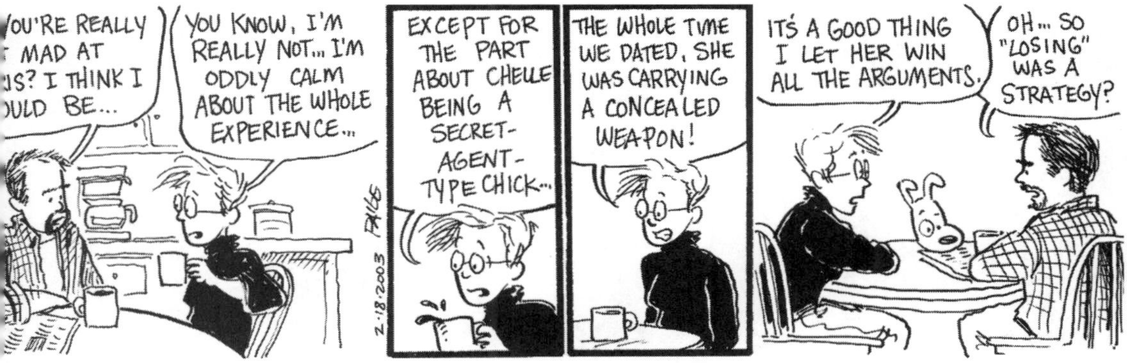

OU'RE REALLY MAD AT US? I THINK I ULD BE...
YOU KNOW, I'M REALLY NOT... I'M ODDLY CALM ABOUT THE WHOLE EXPERIENCE...
EXCEPT FOR THE PART ABOUT CHELLE BEING A SECRET-AGENT-TYPE CHICK...
PAIGE
2.18.2003
THE WHOLE TIME WE DATED, SHE WAS CARRYING A CONCEALED WEAPON!
IT'S A GOOD THING I LET HER WIN ALL THE ARGUMENTS.
OH... SO "LOSING" WAS A STRATEGY?

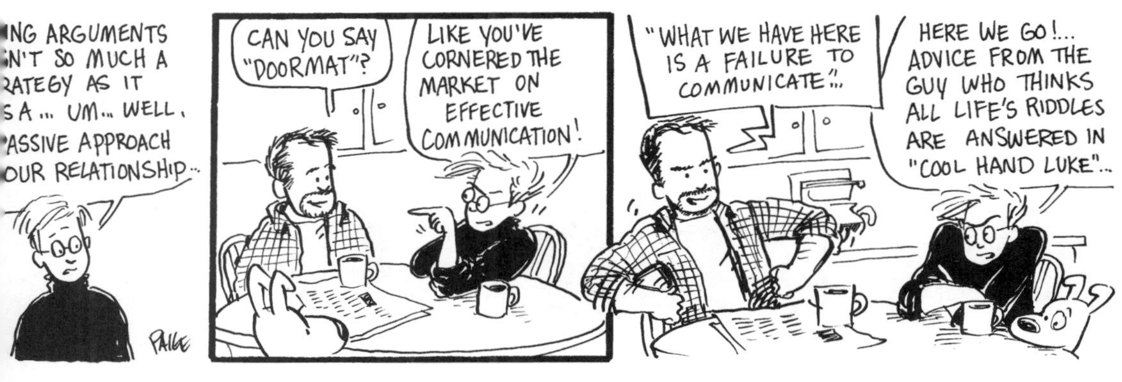

NG ARGUMENTS N'T SO MUCH A RATEGY AS IT S A... UM... WELL, ASSIVE APPROACH OUR RELATIONSHIP...
PAIGE
CAN YOU SAY "DOORMAT"?
LIKE YOU'VE CORNERED THE MARKET ON EFFECTIVE COMMUNICATION!
"WHAT WE HAVE HERE IS A FAILURE TO COMMUNICATE"...
HERE WE GO!... ADVICE FROM THE GUY WHO THINKS ALL LIFE'S RIDDLES ARE ANSWERED IN "COOL HAND LUKE"...

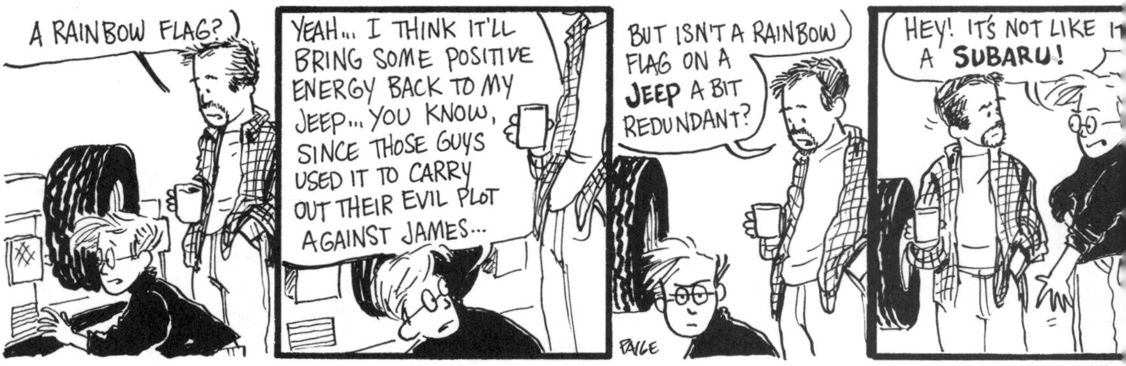
A RAINBOW FLAG?
YEAH... I THINK IT'LL BRING SOME POSITIVE ENERGY BACK TO MY JEEP... YOU KNOW, SINCE THOSE GUYS USED IT TO CARRY OUT THEIR EVIL PLOT AGAINST JAMES...
BUT ISN'T A RAINBOW FLAG ON A **JEEP** A BIT REDUNDANT?
PAIGE
HEY! IT'S NOT LIKE I
A **SUBARU**!

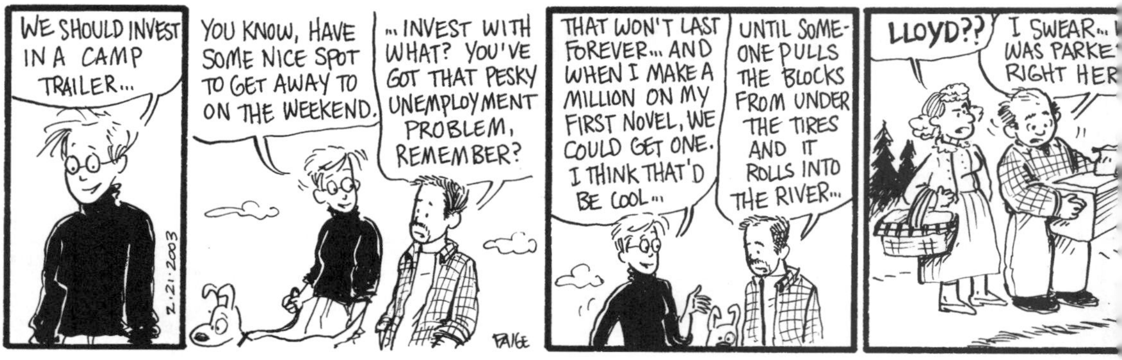
WE SHOULD INVEST IN A CAMP TRAILER...
2.21.2003
YOU KNOW, HAVE SOME NICE SPOT TO GET AWAY TO ON THE WEEKEND.
...INVEST WITH WHAT? YOU'VE GOT THAT PESKY UNEMPLOYMENT PROBLEM, REMEMBER?
PAIGE
THAT WON'T LAST FOREVER... AND WHEN I MAKE A MILLION ON MY FIRST NOVEL, WE COULD GET ONE. I THINK THAT'D BE COOL...
UNTIL SOME-ONE PULLS THE BLOCKS FROM UNDER THE TIRES AND IT ROLLS INTO THE RIVER...
LLOYD??
I SWEAR... WAS PARKE RIGHT HER

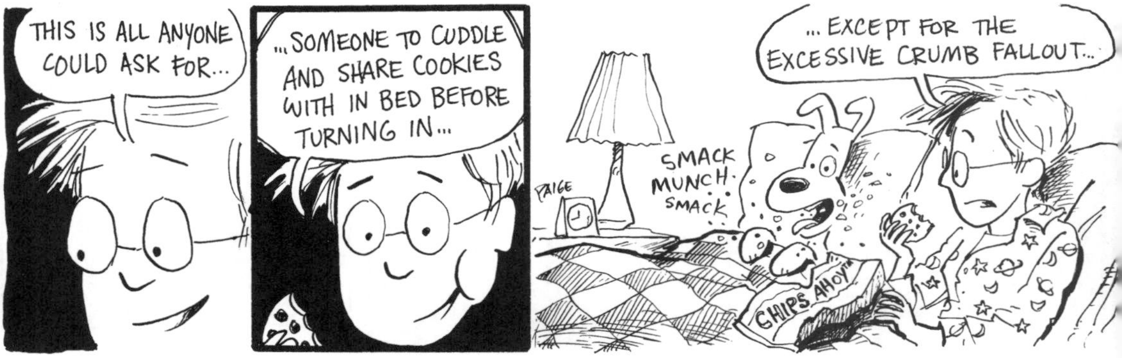
THIS IS ALL ANYONE COULD ASK FOR...
...SOMEONE TO CUDDLE AND SHARE COOKIES WITH IN BED BEFORE TURNING IN...
PAIGE
SMACK MUNCH SMACK
CHIPS AHOY!
...EXCEPT FOR THE EXCESSIVE CRUMB FALLOUT...

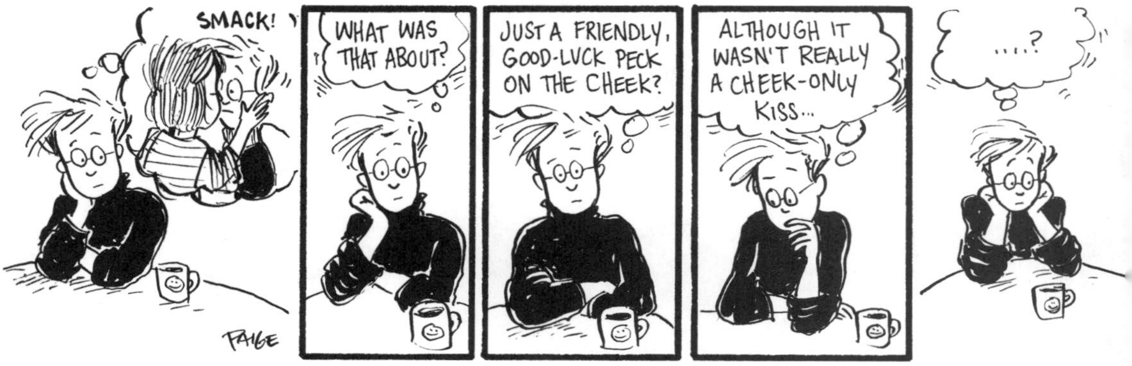
SMACK!
PAIGE
WHAT WAS THAT ABOUT?
JUST A FRIENDLY, GOOD-LUCK PECK ON THE CHEEK?
ALTHOUGH IT WASN'T REALLY A CHEEK-ONLY KISS...
....?

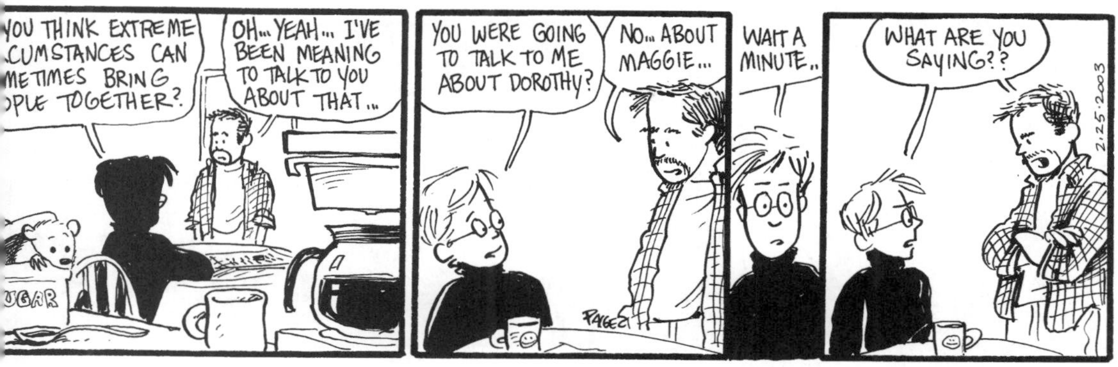
YOU THINK EXTREME
CUMSTANCES CAN
METIMES BRING
OPLE TOGETHER?
OH... YEAH... I'VE BEEN MEANING TO TALK TO YOU ABOUT THAT...
SUGAR
YOU WERE GOING TO TALK TO ME ABOUT DOROTHY?
NO... ABOUT MAGGIE...
PAIGE
WAIT A MINUTE..
WHAT ARE YOU SAYING??
2.25.2003

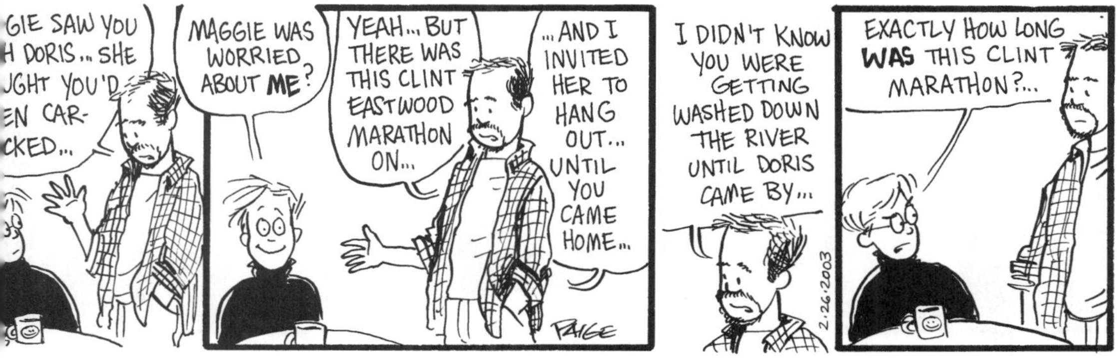
GIE SAW YOU
H DORIS... SHE
UGHT YOU'D
EN CAR-
CKED...
MAGGIE WAS WORRIED ABOUT ME?
YEAH... BUT THERE WAS THIS CLINT EASTWOOD MARATHON ON...
...AND I INVITED HER TO HANG OUT... UNTIL YOU CAME HOME...
PAIGE
I DIDN'T KNOW YOU WERE GETTING WASHED DOWN THE RIVER UNTIL DORIS CAME BY...
2.26.2003
EXACTLY HOW LONG WAS THIS CLINT MARATHON?...

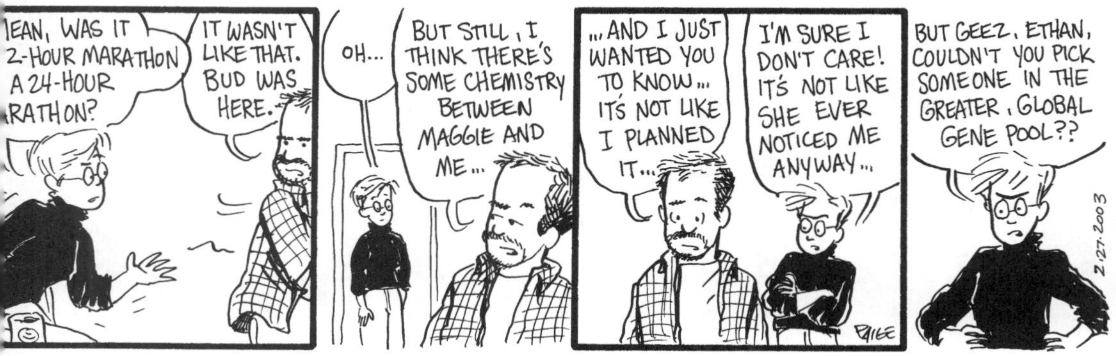
EAN, WAS IT
2-HOUR MARATHON
A 24-HOUR
RATHON?
IT WASN'T LIKE THAT. BUD WAS HERE.
OH...
BUT STILL, I THINK THERE'S SOME CHEMISTRY BETWEEN MAGGIE AND ME...
...AND I JUST WANTED YOU TO KNOW... IT'S NOT LIKE I PLANNED IT...
I'M SURE I DON'T CARE! IT'S NOT LIKE SHE EVER NOTICED ME ANYWAY...
PAIGE
BUT GEEZ, ETHAN, COULDN'T YOU PICK SOMEONE IN THE GREATER, GLOBAL GENE POOL??
2.27.2003

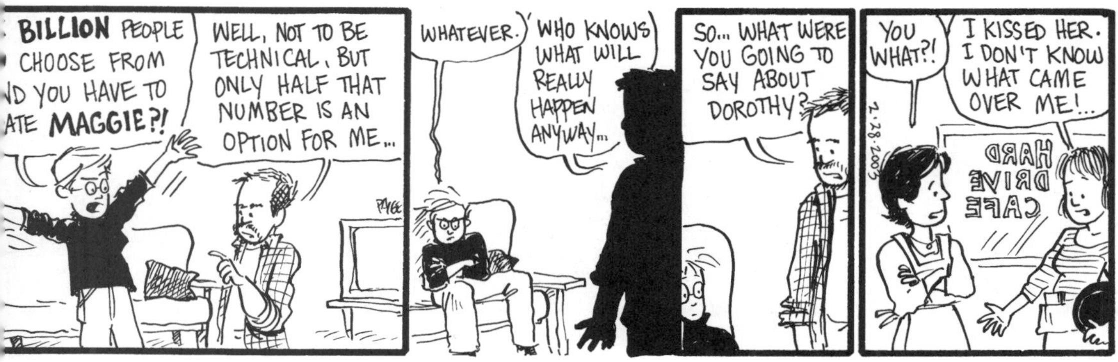
BILLION PEOPLE
CHOOSE FROM
ND YOU HAVE TO
ATE MAGGIE?!
WELL, NOT TO BE TECHNICAL, BUT ONLY HALF THAT NUMBER IS AN OPTION FOR ME...
PAIGE
WHATEVER.
WHO KNOWS WHAT WILL REALLY HAPPEN ANYWAY...
SO... WHAT WERE YOU GOING TO SAY ABOUT DOROTHY?
YOU WHAT?!
I KISSED HER. I DON'T KNOW WHAT CAME OVER ME!...
2.28.2003
HARD DRIVE CAFE

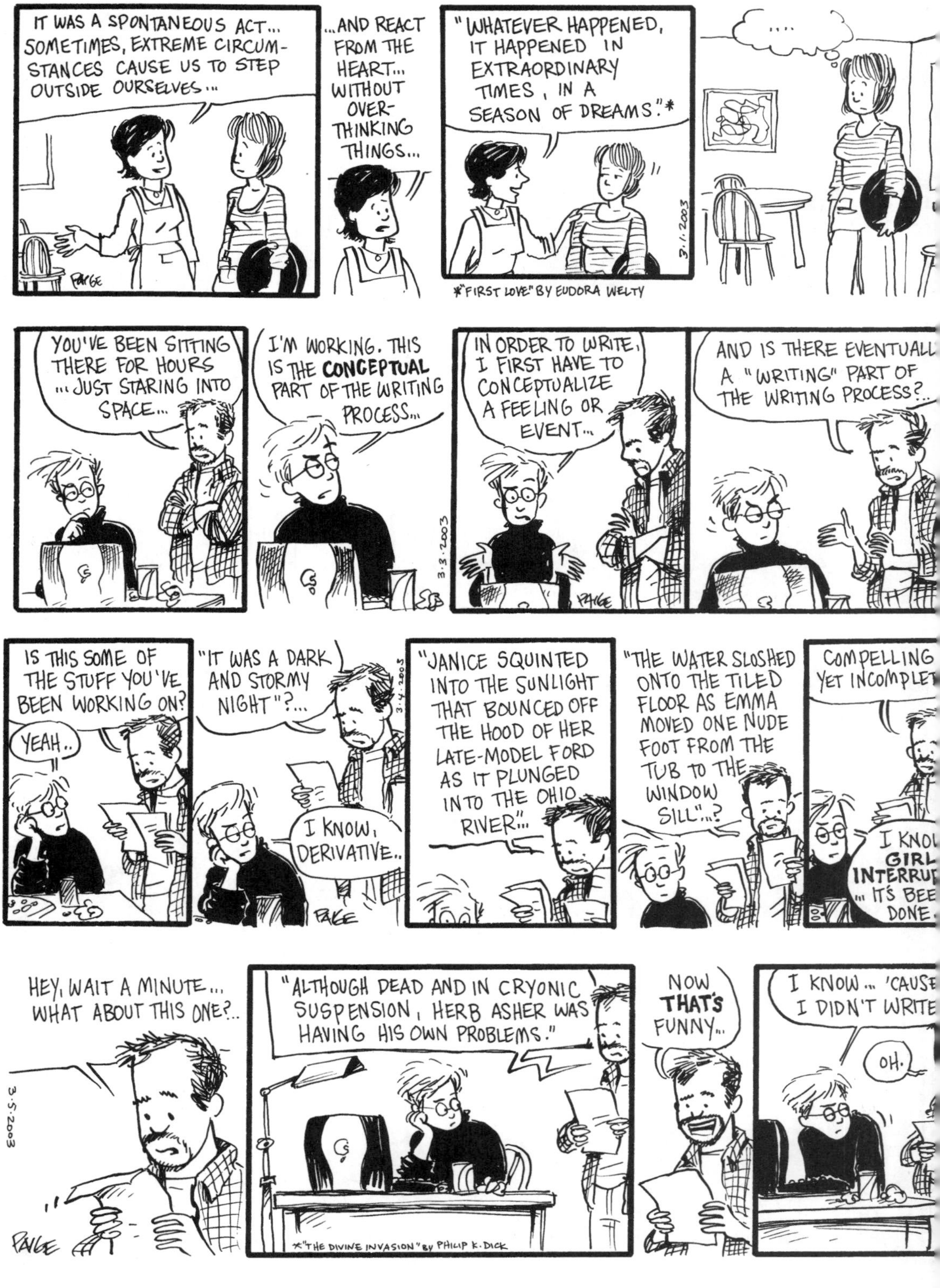
IT WAS A SPONTANEOUS ACT... SOMETIMES, EXTREME CIRCUMSTANCES CAUSE US TO STEP OUTSIDE OURSELVES...
...AND REACT FROM THE HEART... WITHOUT OVER-THINKING THINGS...
"WHATEVER HAPPENED, IT HAPPENED IN EXTRAORDINARY TIMES, IN A SEASON OF DREAMS."*
3.1.2003
PAIGE
....
*"FIRST LOVE" BY EUDORA WELTY
YOU'VE BEEN SITTING THERE FOR HOURS ...JUST STARING INTO SPACE...
I'M WORKING. THIS IS THE **CONCEPTUAL** PART OF THE WRITING PROCESS...
3.3.2003
IN ORDER TO WRITE, I FIRST HAVE TO CONCEPTUALIZE A FEELING OR EVENT...
PAIGE
AND IS THERE EVENTUALL A "WRITING" PART OF THE WRITING PROCESS?...
IS THIS SOME OF THE STUFF YOU'VE BEEN WORKING ON?
YEAH..
"IT WAS A DARK AND STORMY NIGHT"?...
3.4.2003
I KNOW, DERIVATIVE..
PAIGE
"JANICE SQUINTED INTO THE SUNLIGHT THAT BOUNCED OFF THE HOOD OF HER LATE-MODEL FORD AS IT PLUNGED INTO THE OHIO RIVER"...
"THE WATER SLOSHED ONTO THE TILED FLOOR AS EMMA MOVED ONE NUDE FOOT FROM THE TUB TO THE WINDOW SILL"...?
COMPELLING YET INCOMPLET
I KNOW **GIRL INTERRUP** ...IT'S BEE DONE
3.5.2003
HEY, WAIT A MINUTE... WHAT ABOUT THIS ONE?...
PAIGE
"ALTHOUGH DEAD AND IN CRYONIC SUSPENSION, HERB ASHER WAS HAVING HIS OWN PROBLEMS."
*"THE DIVINE INVASION" BY PHILIP K. DICK
NOW **THAT'S** FUNNY...
I KNOW... 'CAUSE I DIDN'T WRITE
OH.

KNOW I'M IN **RUT** HERE... I JUST CAN'T SEEM TO GET PAST THE FIRST LINE...

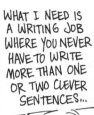

WHAT I NEED IS A WRITING JOB WHERE YOU NEVER HAVE TO WRITE MORE THAN ONE OR TWO CLEVER SENTENCES...

EVERY DAY, ALL I'D HAVE TO DO IS COME UP WITH A CLEVER COMMENT OR TWO...

...A DIFFERENT TOPIC EACH DAY... THAT WAY I'D NEVER GET BORED...

SOUNDS LIKE "SHORT-ATTENTION-SPAN THEATER"...

THINK, THINK...

THAN! I'VE GOT IT! LL DO A COMIC STRIP!

?!

BUT YOU CAN'T DRAW...

SAYS YOU...

CHECK THIS OUT...

UH... IS THAT A RABBIT?

NO!... IT'S AN AIRPLANE!

THIS IS GREAT! A FEW SHORT HOURS AGO I WAS COMPLETELY STALLED... IN A RUT...

NOW I'M IN A RUT WITH A VIEW!

CHECK IT OUT...

WHAT IS IT?

WHAT D'YA MEAN, "WHAT IS IT?"...

IT'S A RUT WITH A VIEW!

IT LOOKS LIKE A CABBAGE THAT GOT RUN OVER...

, JANE. HI, DOROTHY.

LISTEN, I MEANT TO SAY THANKS FOR TRYING TO PULL ME OUT OF THE RIVER...

...AND, WELL, I'M SORRY YOU ENDED UP FALLING IN.

ETHAN WAS THE MASTERMIND BEHIND THE RESCUE... I JUST HAPPENED TO BE THE ONE WITH SLIPPERY FOOTING.

WHY IS JANE ACTING SO NERVOUS AROUND DOROTHY?...

YEAH... HEH, HEH...

27

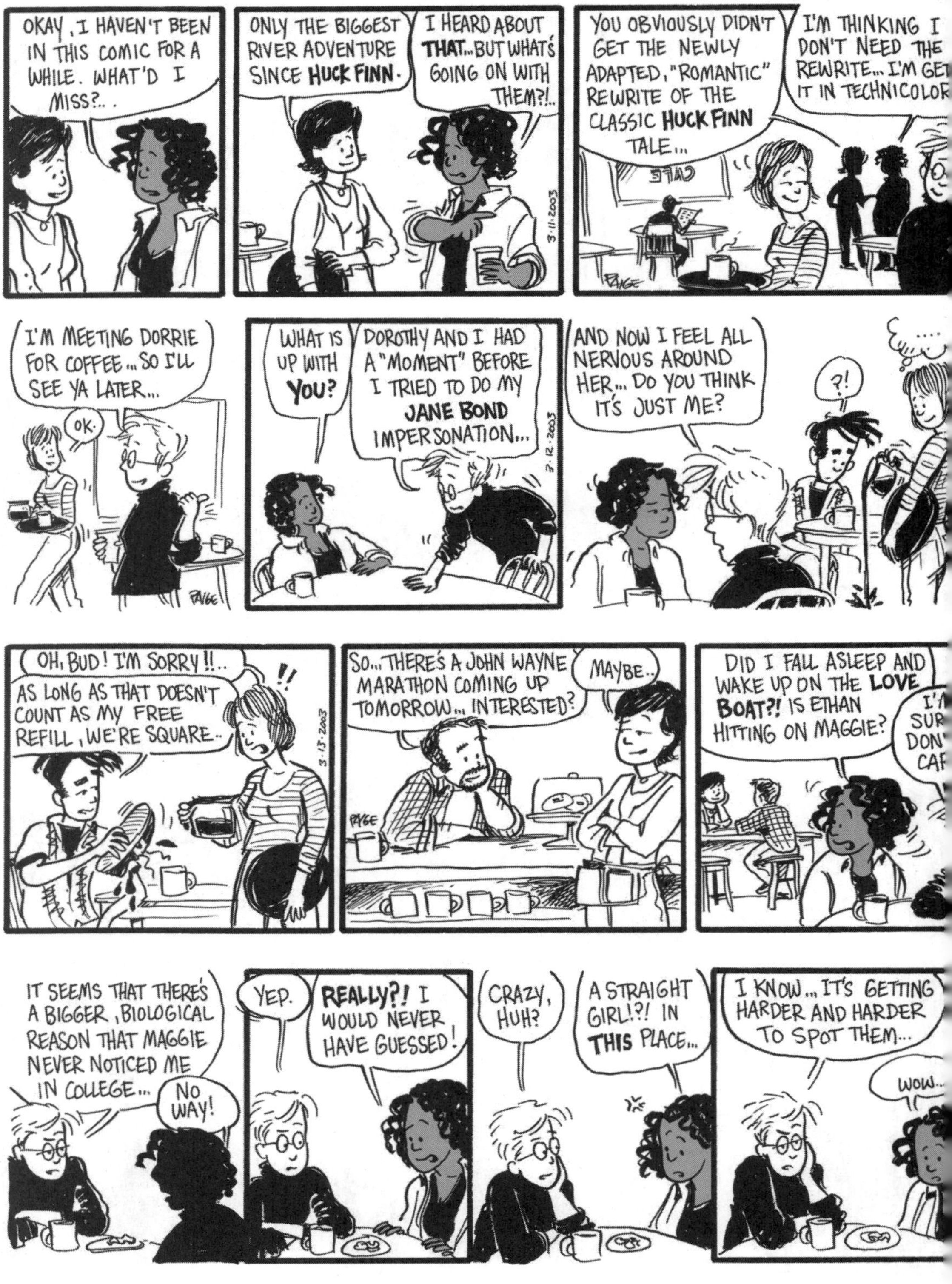
OKAY, I HAVEN'T BEEN IN THIS COMIC FOR A WHILE. WHAT'D I MISS?..
ONLY THE BIGGEST RIVER ADVENTURE SINCE HUCK FINN.
I HEARD ABOUT THAT... BUT WHAT'S GOING ON WITH THEM?!..
3·11·2003
YOU OBVIOUSLY DIDN'T GET THE NEWLY ADAPTED, "ROMANTIC" REWRITE OF THE CLASSIC HUCK FINN TALE...
I'M THINKING I DON'T NEED THE REWRITE... I'M GE
IT IN TECHNICOLOR
PAIGE
I'M MEETING DORRIE FOR COFFEE... SO I'LL SEE YA LATER...
OK.
PAIGE
WHAT IS UP WITH YOU?
DOROTHY AND I HAD A "MOMENT" BEFORE I TRIED TO DO MY JANE BOND IMPERSONATION...
3·12·2003
AND NOW I FEEL ALL NERVOUS AROUND HER... DO YOU THINK IT'S JUST ME?
?!
....
OH, BUD! I'M SORRY!!..
AS LONG AS THAT DOESN'T COUNT AS MY FREE REFILL, WE'RE SQUARE..
!!
3·13·2003
SO... THERE'S A JOHN WAYNE MARATHON COMING UP TOMORROW... INTERESTED?
MAYBE..
PAIGE
DID I FALL ASLEEP AND WAKE UP ON THE LOVE BOAT?! IS ETHAN HITTING ON MAGGIE?
IT SEEMS THAT THERE'S A BIGGER, BIOLOGICAL REASON THAT MAGGIE NEVER NOTICED ME IN COLLEGE...
NO WAY!
YEP.
REALLY?! I WOULD NEVER HAVE GUESSED!
CRAZY, HUH?
A STRAIGHT GIRL!?! IN THIS PLACE...
I KNOW... IT'S GETTING HARDER AND HARDER TO SPOT THEM...
WOW...

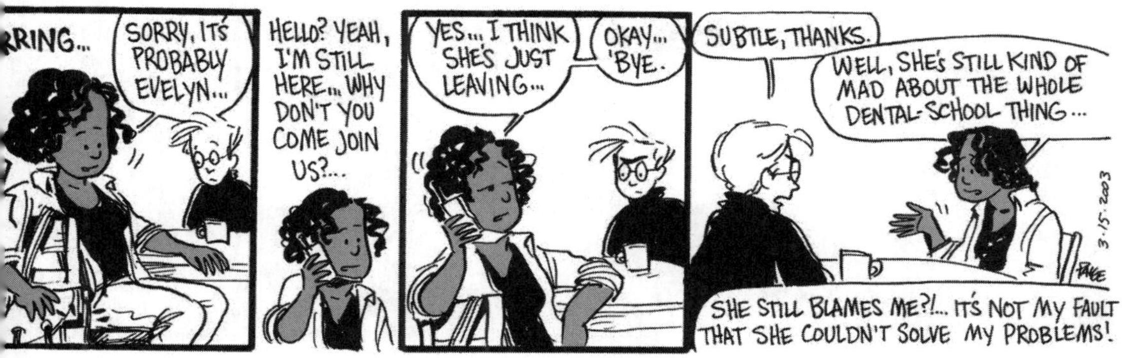
RRING...
SORRY, IT'S PROBABLY EVELYN...
HELLO? YEAH, I'M STILL HERE... WHY DON'T YOU COME JOIN US?...
YES... I THINK SHE'S JUST LEAVING...
OKAY... 'BYE.
SUBTLE, THANKS.
WELL, SHE'S STILL KIND OF MAD ABOUT THE WHOLE DENTAL-SCHOOL THING...
SHE STILL BLAMES ME?!... IT'S NOT MY FAULT THAT SHE COULDN'T SOLVE MY PROBLEMS!
3-15-2003
PAIGE

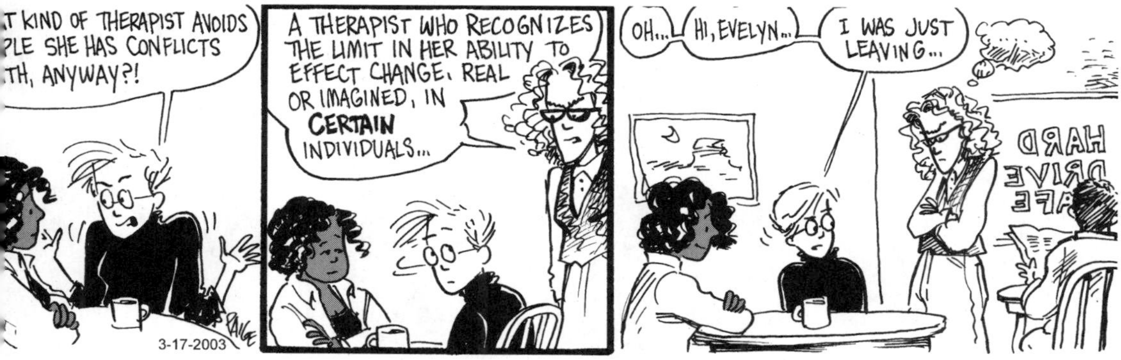
T KIND OF THERAPIST AVOIDS PLE SHE HAS CONFLICTS TH, ANYWAY?!
3-17-2003
PAIGE
A THERAPIST WHO RECOGNIZES THE LIMIT IN HER ABILITY TO EFFECT CHANGE, REAL OR IMAGINED, IN CERTAIN INDIVIDUALS...
OH...
HI, EVELYN...
I WAS JUST LEAVING...
HARD DRIVE AFE

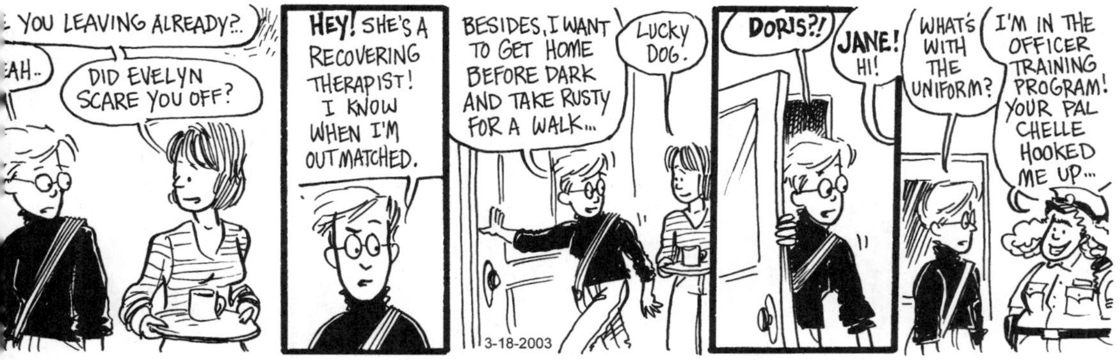
YOU LEAVING ALREADY?..
AH..
DID EVELYN SCARE YOU OFF?
HEY! SHE'S A RECOVERING THERAPIST! I KNOW WHEN I'M OUTMATCHED.
BESIDES, I WANT TO GET HOME BEFORE DARK AND TAKE RUSTY FOR A WALK...
LUCKY DOG.
3-18-2003
DORIS?!
JANE! HI!
WHAT'S WITH THE UNIFORM?
I'M IN THE OFFICER TRAINING PROGRAM! YOUR PAL CHELLE HOOKED ME UP...

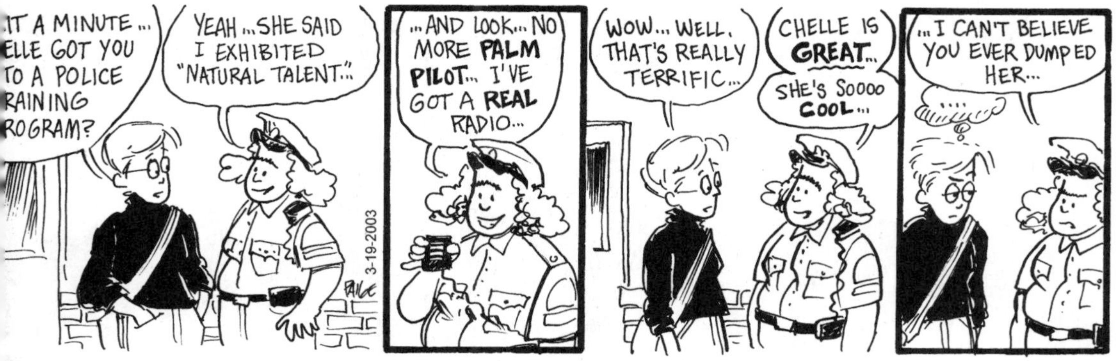
IT A MINUTE... ELLE GOT YOU TO A POLICE RAINING ROGRAM?
YEAH... SHE SAID I EXHIBITED "NATURAL TALENT."
3-19-2003
PAIGE
...AND LOOK... NO MORE PALM PILOT... I'VE GOT A REAL RADIO...
WOW... WELL, THAT'S REALLY TERRIFIC...
CHELLE IS GREAT...
SHE'S SOOOO COOL...
...I CAN'T BELIEVE YOU EVER DUMPED HER...

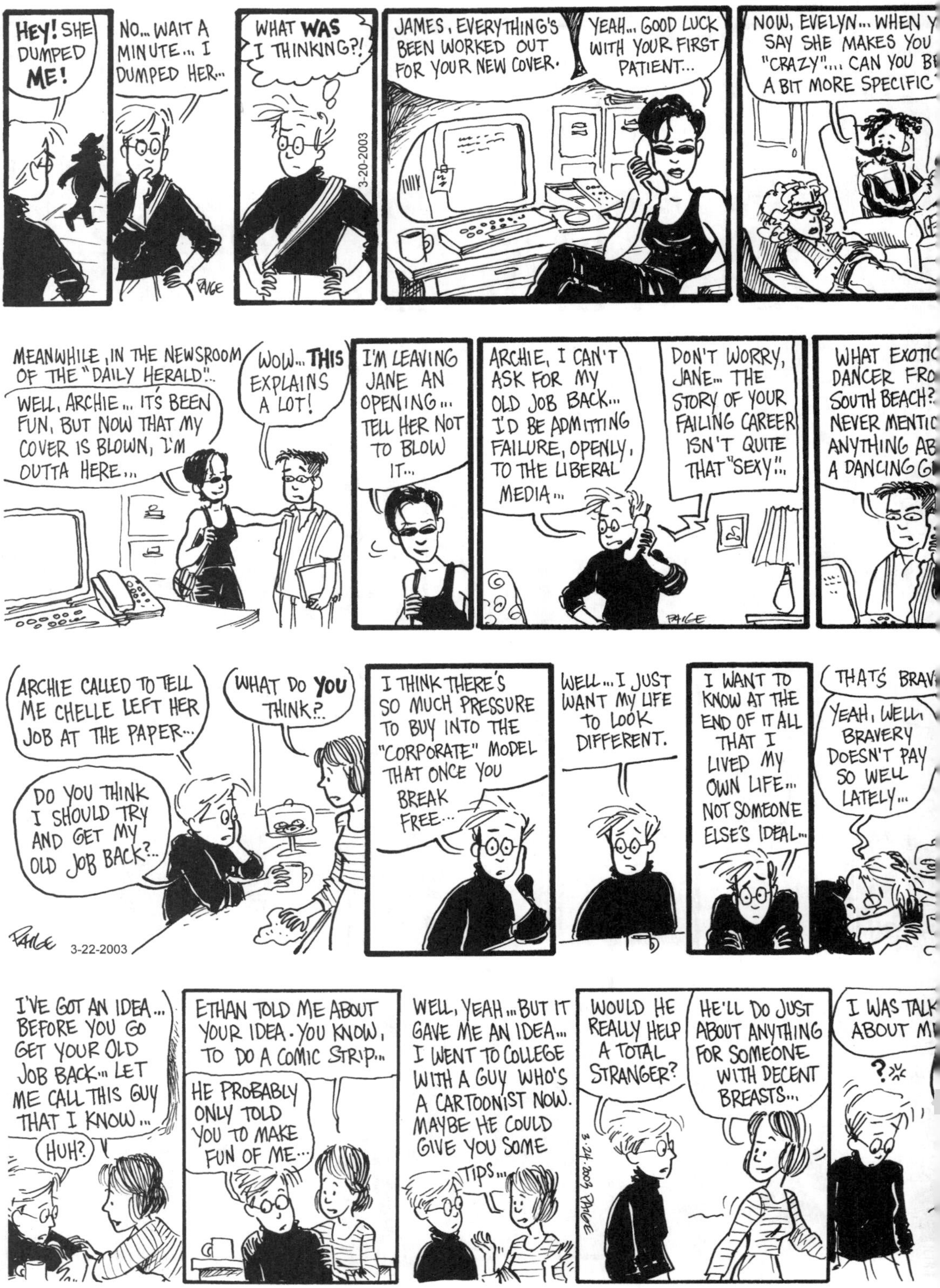
HEY! SHE DUMPED ME!
NO... WAIT A MINUTE... I DUMPED HER...
WHAT WAS I THINKING?!
3-20-2003
PAIGE
JAMES, EVERYTHING'S BEEN WORKED OUT FOR YOUR NEW COVER.
YEAH... GOOD LUCK WITH YOUR FIRST PATIENT...
MEANWHILE, IN THE NEWSROOM OF THE "DAILY HERALD"...
WELL, ARCHIE... IT'S BEEN FUN, BUT NOW THAT MY COVER IS BLOWN, I'M OUTTA HERE...
WOW... THIS EXPLAINS A LOT!
I'M LEAVING JANE AN OPENING... TELL HER NOT TO BLOW IT...
ARCHIE, I CAN'T ASK FOR MY OLD JOB BACK... I'D BE ADMITTING FAILURE, OPENLY, TO THE LIBERAL MEDIA...
DON'T WORRY, JANE... THE STORY OF YOUR FAILING CAREER ISN'T QUITE THAT "SEXY"...
PAIGE
ARCHIE CALLED TO TELL ME CHELLE LEFT HER JOB AT THE PAPER...
DO YOU THINK I SHOULD TRY AND GET MY OLD JOB BACK?...
WHAT DO YOU THINK?...
PAIGE
3-22-2003
I THINK THERE'S SO MUCH PRESSURE TO BUY INTO THE "CORPORATE" MODEL THAT ONCE YOU BREAK FREE...
WELL... I JUST WANT MY LIFE TO LOOK DIFFERENT.
I WANT TO KNOW AT THE END OF IT ALL THAT I LIVED MY OWN LIFE... NOT SOMEONE ELSE'S IDEAL...
YEAH, WELL, BRAVERY DOESN'T PAY SO WELL LATELY...
I'VE GOT AN IDEA... BEFORE YOU GO GET YOUR OLD JOB BACK... LET ME CALL THIS GUY THAT I KNOW...
HUH?
ETHAN TOLD ME ABOUT YOUR IDEA. YOU KNOW, TO DO A COMIC STRIP...
HE PROBABLY ONLY TOLD YOU TO MAKE FUN OF ME...
WELL, YEAH... BUT IT GAVE ME AN IDEA... I WENT TO COLLEGE WITH A GUY WHO'S A CARTOONIST NOW. MAYBE HE COULD GIVE YOU SOME TIPS...
WOULD HE REALLY HELP A TOTAL STRANGER?
HE'LL DO JUST ABOUT ANYTHING FOR SOMEONE WITH DECENT BREASTS...
3.24.2003 PAIGE
?

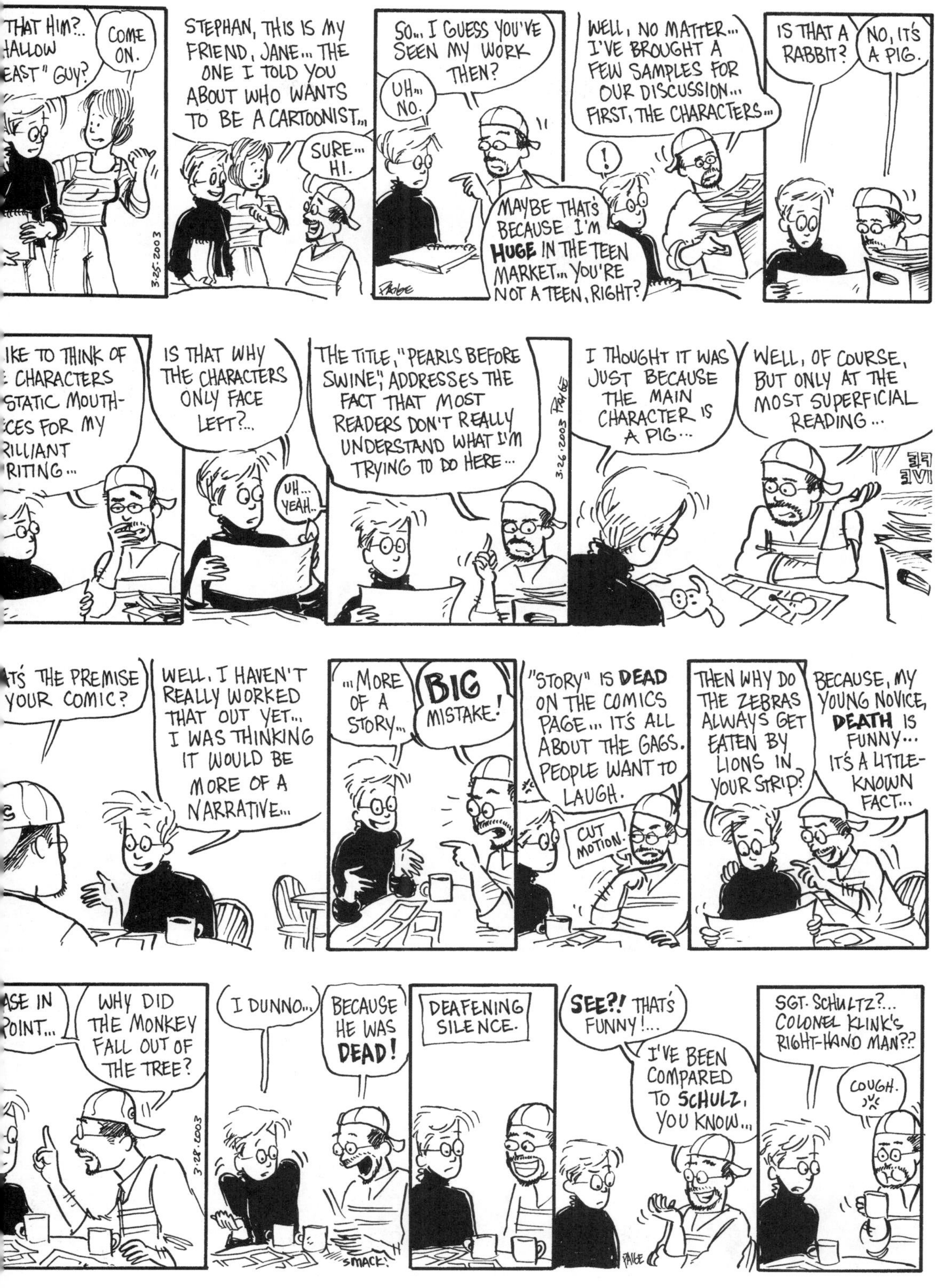
THAT HIM?... HALLOW EAST" GUY?
COME ON.
3.25.2003
STEPHAN, THIS IS MY FRIEND, JANE... THE ONE I TOLD YOU ABOUT WHO WANTS TO BE A CARTOONIST...
SURE... HI.
SO... I GUESS YOU'VE SEEN MY WORK THEN?
UH... NO.
MAYBE THAT'S BECAUSE I'M HUGE IN THE TEEN MARKET... YOU'RE NOT A TEEN, RIGHT?
WELL, NO MATTER... I'VE BROUGHT A FEW SAMPLES FOR OUR DISCUSSION... FIRST, THE CHARACTERS...
!
IS THAT A RABBIT?
NO, IT'S A PIG.
IKE TO THINK OF CHARACTERS STATIC MOUTH-CES FOR MY RILLIANT RITING...
IS THAT WHY THE CHARACTERS ONLY FACE LEFT?...
UH... YEAH...
THE TITLE, "PEARLS BEFORE SWINE", ADDRESSES THE FACT THAT MOST READERS DON'T REALLY UNDERSTAND WHAT I'M TRYING TO DO HERE...
3.26.2003
I THOUGHT IT WAS JUST BECAUSE THE MAIN CHARACTER IS A PIG...
WELL, OF COURSE, BUT ONLY AT THE MOST SUPERFICIAL READING...
T'S THE PREMISE YOUR COMIC?
WELL, I HAVEN'T REALLY WORKED THAT OUT YET... I WAS THINKING IT WOULD BE MORE OF A NARRATIVE...
...MORE OF A STORY...
BIG MISTAKE!
"STORY" IS DEAD ON THE COMICS PAGE... IT'S ALL ABOUT THE GAGS. PEOPLE WANT TO LAUGH.
CUT MOTION.
THEN WHY DO THE ZEBRAS ALWAYS GET EATEN BY LIONS IN YOUR STRIP?
BECAUSE, MY YOUNG NOVICE, DEATH IS FUNNY... IT'S A LITTLE-KNOWN FACT...
ASE IN POINT...
WHY DID THE MONKEY FALL OUT OF THE TREE?
3.28.2003
I DUNNO...
BECAUSE HE WAS DEAD!
SMACK
DEAFENING SILENCE.
SEE?! THAT'S FUNNY!...
I'VE BEEN COMPARED TO SCHULZ, YOU KNOW...
SGT. SCHULTZ?... COLONEL KLINK'S RIGHT-HAND MAN??
COUGH.

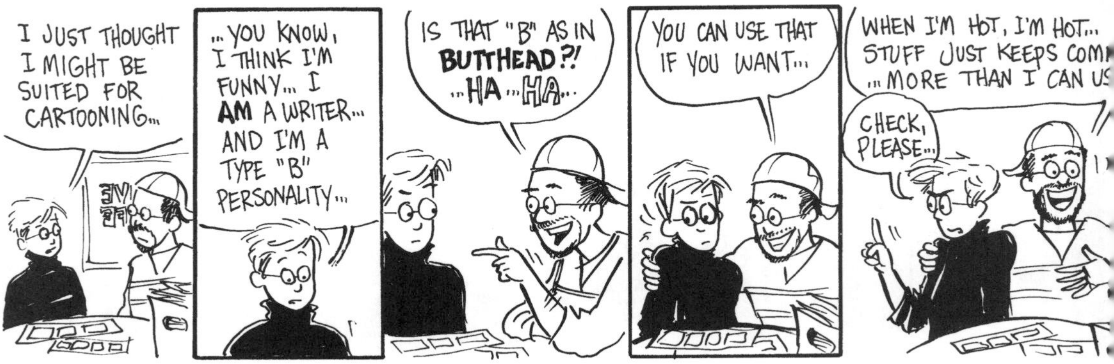
I JUST THOUGHT I MIGHT BE SUITED FOR CARTOONING...
...YOU KNOW, I THINK I'M FUNNY... I **AM** A WRITER... AND I'M A TYPE "B" PERSONALITY...
IS THAT "B" AS IN **BUTTHEAD?!** ..HA..HA..
YOU CAN USE THAT IF YOU WANT...
WHEN I'M HOT, I'M HOT... STUFF JUST KEEPS COM ...MORE THAN I CAN US
CHECK, PLEASE...

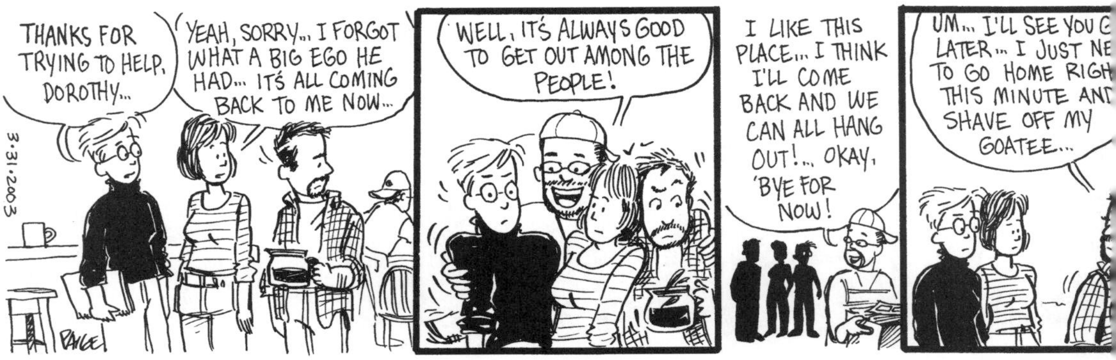
3.31.2003
THANKS FOR TRYING TO HELP, DOROTHY...
YEAH, SORRY... I FORGOT WHAT A BIG EGO HE HAD... IT'S ALL COMING BACK TO ME NOW...
PAIGE
WELL, IT'S ALWAYS GOOD TO GET OUT AMONG THE PEOPLE!
I LIKE THIS PLACE... I THINK I'LL COME BACK AND WE CAN ALL HANG OUT!... OKAY, 'BYE FOR NOW!
UM... I'LL SEE YOU LATER... I JUST NE TO GO HOME RIGH THIS MINUTE AND SHAVE OFF MY GOATEE...

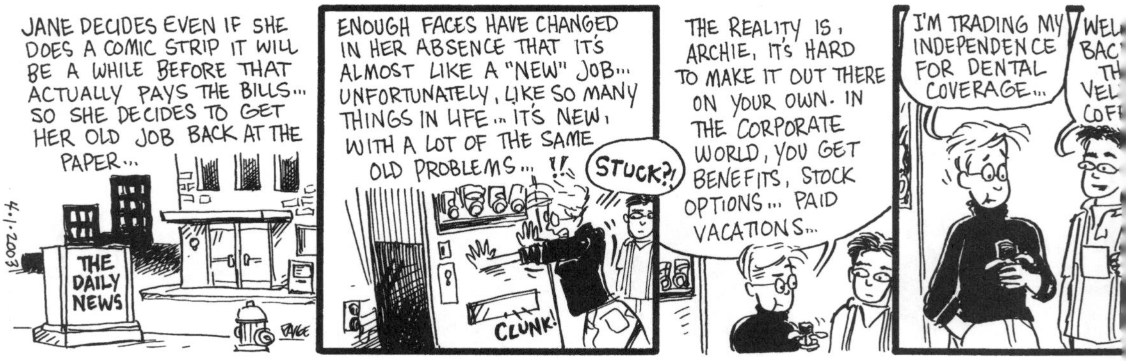
4.1.2003
JANE DECIDES EVEN IF SHE DOES A COMIC STRIP IT WILL BE A WHILE BEFORE THAT ACTUALLY PAYS THE BILLS... SO SHE DECIDES TO GET HER OLD JOB BACK AT THE PAPER...
THE DAILY NEWS
PAIGE
ENOUGH FACES HAVE CHANGED IN HER ABSENCE THAT IT'S ALMOST LIKE A "NEW" JOB... UNFORTUNATELY, LIKE SO MANY THINGS IN LIFE... IT'S NEW, WITH A LOT OF THE SAME OLD PROBLEMS...
!!
STUCK?!
CLUNK!
THE REALITY IS, ARCHIE, IT'S HARD TO MAKE IT OUT THERE ON YOUR OWN. IN THE CORPORATE WORLD, YOU GET BENEFITS, STOCK OPTIONS... PAID VACATIONS...
I'M TRADING MY INDEPENDENCE FOR DENTAL COVERAGE...

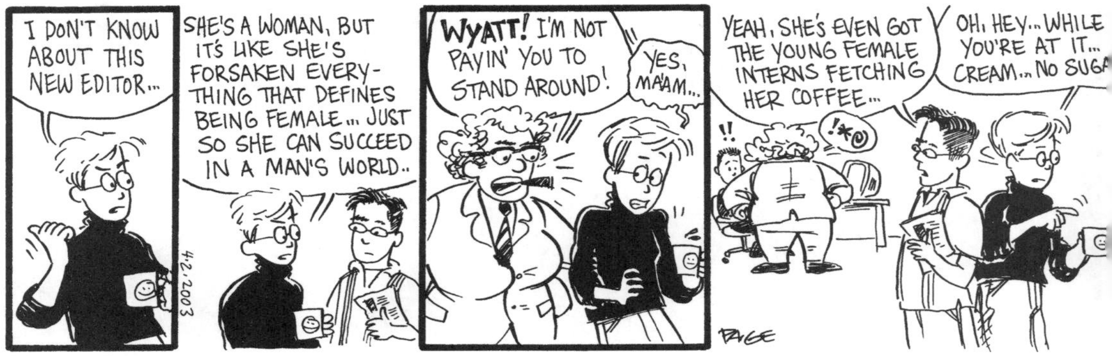
I DON'T KNOW ABOUT THIS NEW EDITOR...
4.2.2003
SHE'S A WOMAN, BUT IT'S LIKE SHE'S FORSAKEN EVERY-THING THAT DEFINES BEING FEMALE... JUST SO SHE CAN SUCCEED IN A MAN'S WORLD..
WYATT! I'M NOT PAYIN' YOU TO STAND AROUND!
YES, MA'AM...
YEAH, SHE'S EVEN GOT THE YOUNG FEMALE INTERNS FETCHING HER COFFEE...
!!
!*@
OH, HEY.. WHILE YOU'RE AT IT... CREAM... NO SUGA
PAIGE

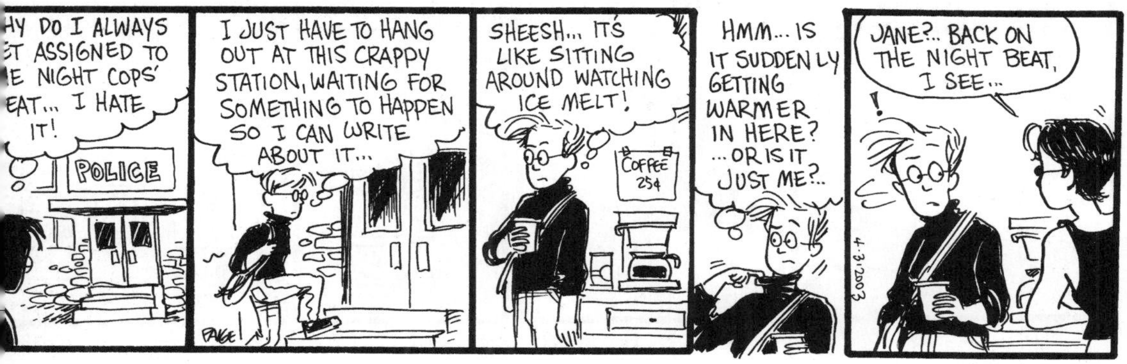
HY DO I ALWAYS
T ASSIGNED TO
E NIGHT COPS'
EAT... I HATE
IT!
POLICE
I JUST HAVE TO HANG OUT AT THIS CRAPPY STATION, WAITING FOR SOMETHING TO HAPPEN SO I CAN WRITE ABOUT IT...
SHEESH... IT'S LIKE SITTING AROUND WATCHING ICE MELT!
COFFEE 25¢
HMM... IS IT SUDDENLY GETTING WARMER IN HERE? ...OR IS IT JUST ME?..
4-3-2003
JANE?.. BACK ON THE NIGHT BEAT, I SEE...
!

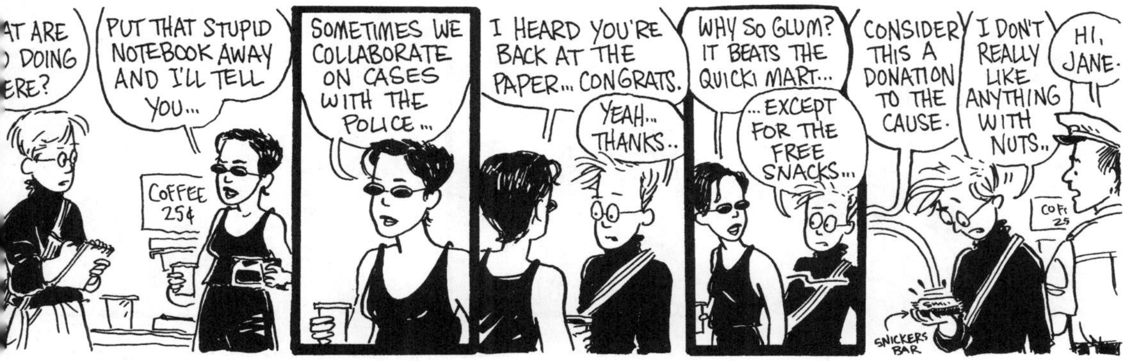
AT ARE
DOING
ERE?
PUT THAT STUPID NOTEBOOK AWAY AND I'LL TELL YOU...
COFFEE 25¢
SOMETIMES WE COLLABORATE ON CASES WITH THE POLICE...
I HEARD YOU'RE BACK AT THE PAPER... CONGRATS.
YEAH... THANKS..
WHY SO GLUM? IT BEATS THE QUICKI MART...
...EXCEPT FOR THE FREE SNACKS...
CONSIDER THIS A DONATION TO THE CAUSE.
I DON'T REALLY LIKE ANYTHING WITH NUTS..
HI, JANE.
SNICKERS BAR

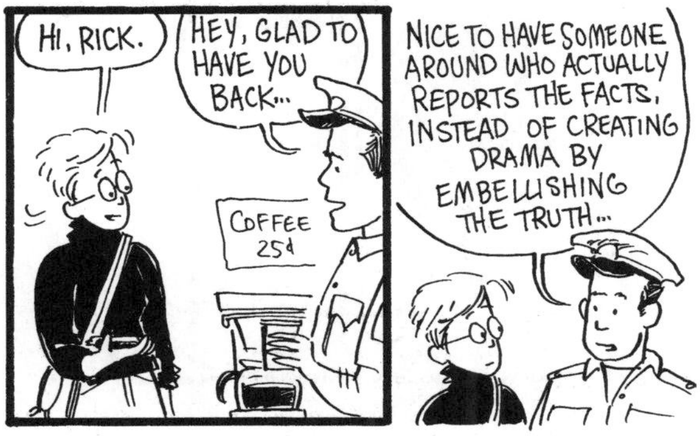
HI, RICK.
HEY, GLAD TO HAVE YOU BACK...
COFFEE 25¢
NICE TO HAVE SOMEONE AROUND WHO ACTUALLY REPORTS THE FACTS, INSTEAD OF CREATING DRAMA BY EMBELLISHING THE TRUTH...

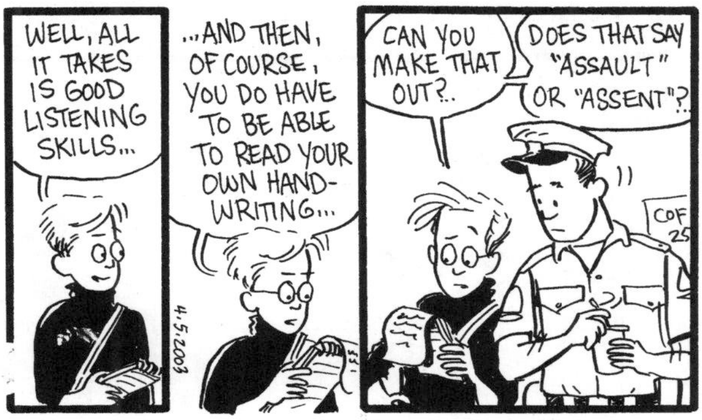
WELL, ALL IT TAKES IS GOOD LISTENING SKILLS...
...AND THEN, OF COURSE, YOU DO HAVE TO BE ABLE TO READ YOUR OWN HAND-WRITING...
4-5-2003
CAN YOU MAKE THAT OUT?..
DOES THAT SAY "ASSAULT" OR "ASSENT"?..

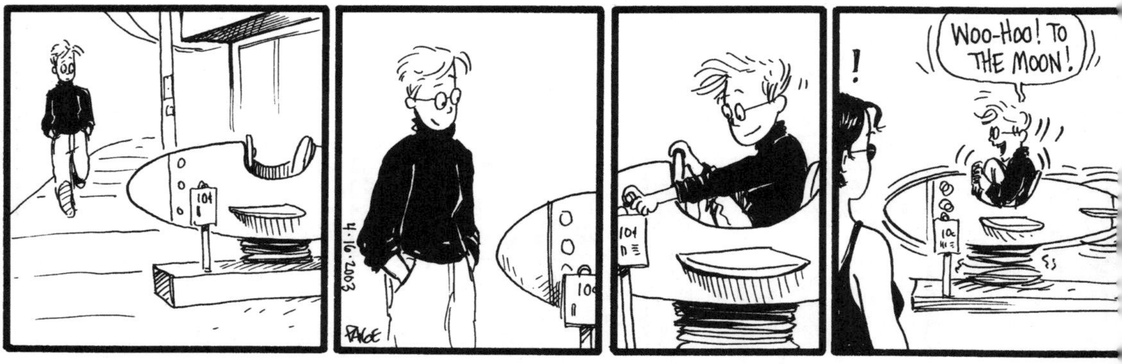
4.16.2003
PAIGE
!
WOO-HOO! TO THE MOON!

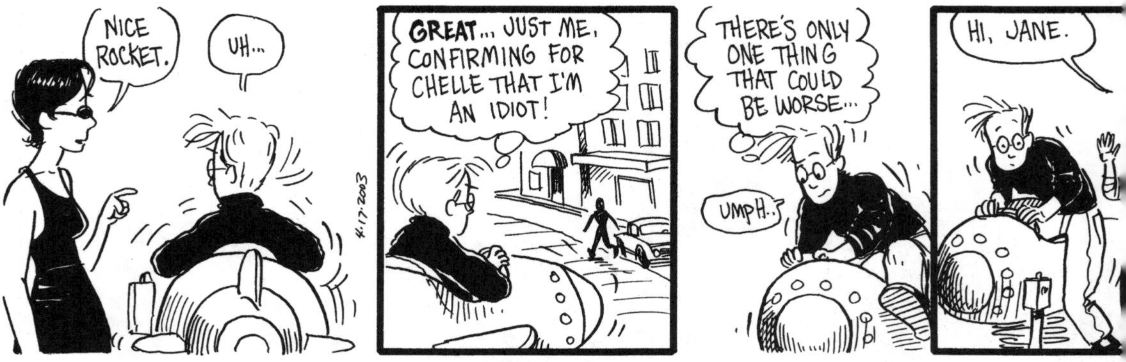
NICE ROCKET.
UH...
4.17.2003
GREAT... JUST ME, CONFIRMING FOR CHELLE THAT I'M AN IDIOT!
THERE'S ONLY ONE THING THAT COULD BE WORSE...
UMPH..
HI, JANE.

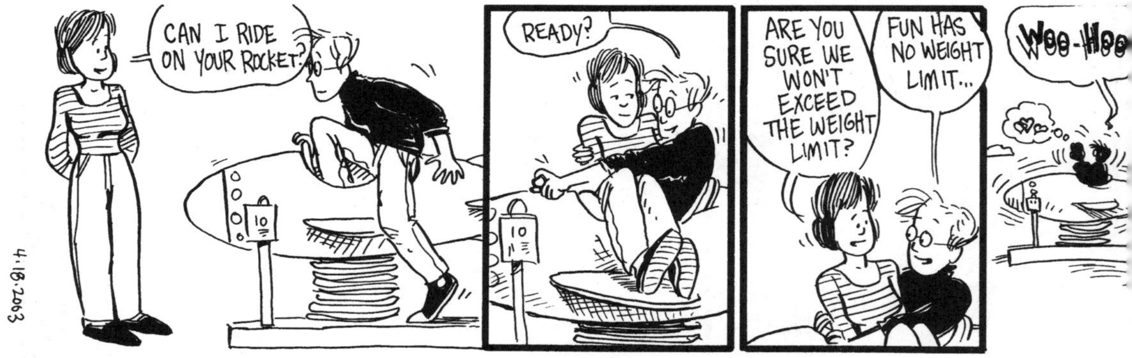
4.18.2003
CAN I RIDE ON YOUR ROCKET?
READY?
ARE YOU SURE WE WON'T EXCEED THE WEIGHT LIMIT?
FUN HAS NO WEIGHT LIMIT...
WOO-HOO

Later, Jane and Ethan settle in for a little video relaxation...

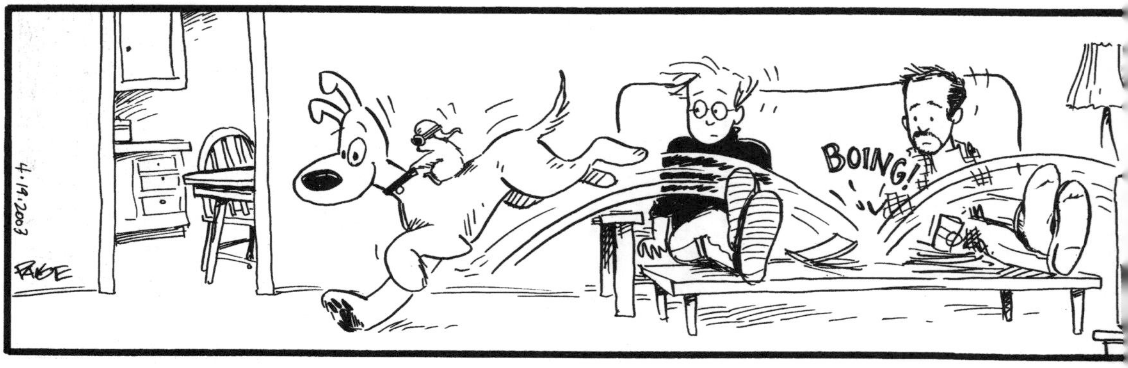
4.19.2003
PAIGE
BOING!

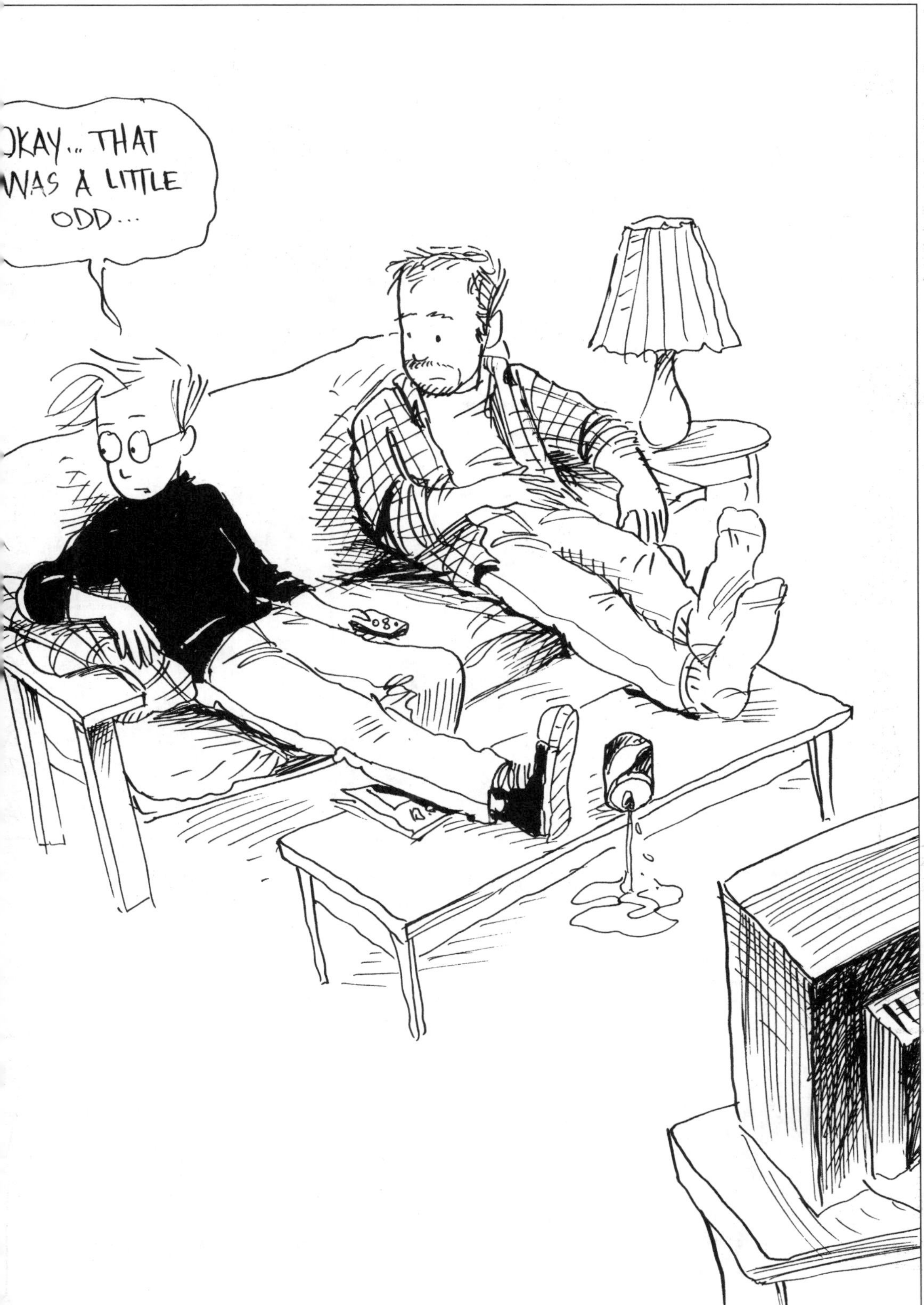
OKAY... THAT WAS A LITTLE ODD...

007
MARATHON
WHEN THEY SAY "MARATHON," THEY MUST BE TALKING ABOUT THE COMMERCIALS...
DO YOU EVER WISH YOU WERE JAMES BOND?
IS THAT A RHETORICAL QUESTION?
PAIGE

I SUPPOSE..
4.21.2003
A LITTLE LOWER, YES... RIGHT THERE...
I SEE YOU'RE IN GOOD HANDS JAMES.

ZZZZ
PAIGE
4.22.2003

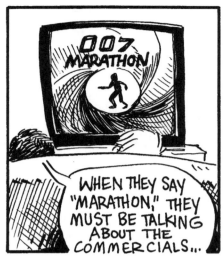

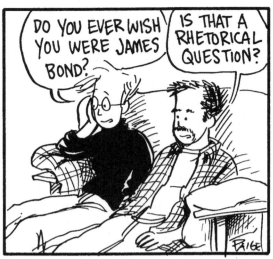

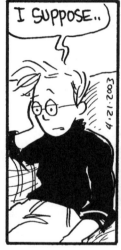

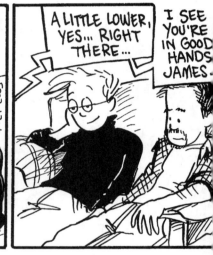

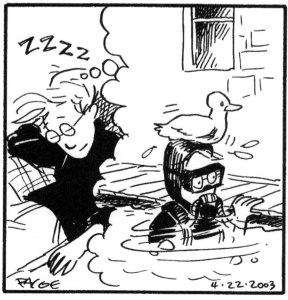

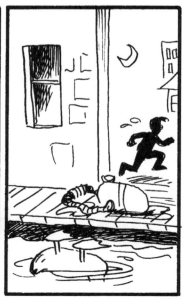

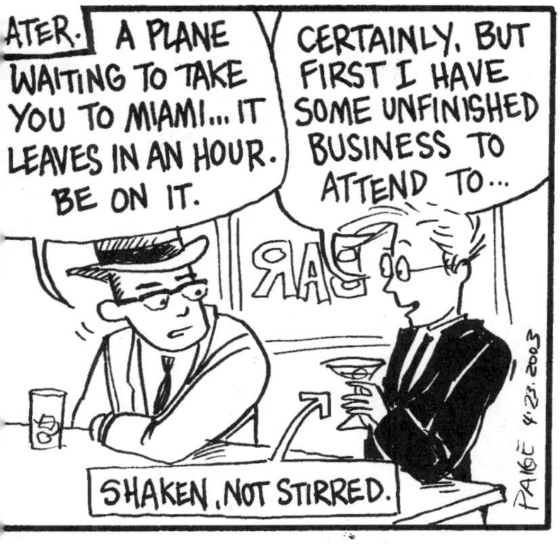
ATER.
A PLANE WAITING TO TAKE YOU TO MIAMI... IT LEAVES IN AN HOUR. BE ON IT.
CERTAINLY. BUT FIRST I HAVE SOME UNFINISHED BUSINESS TO ATTEND TO...
SHAKEN, NOT STIRRED.
PAIGE 4.23.2003

Moments later, in Jane Bond's room...

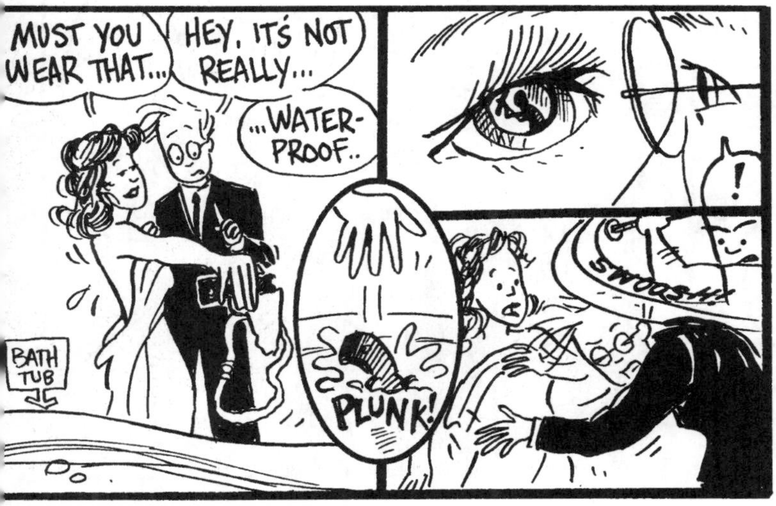
MUST YOU WEAR THAT...
HEY, IT'S NOT REALLY...
...WATER-PROOF..
BATH TUB
PLUNK!
!
SWOOSH!!
FLIP!

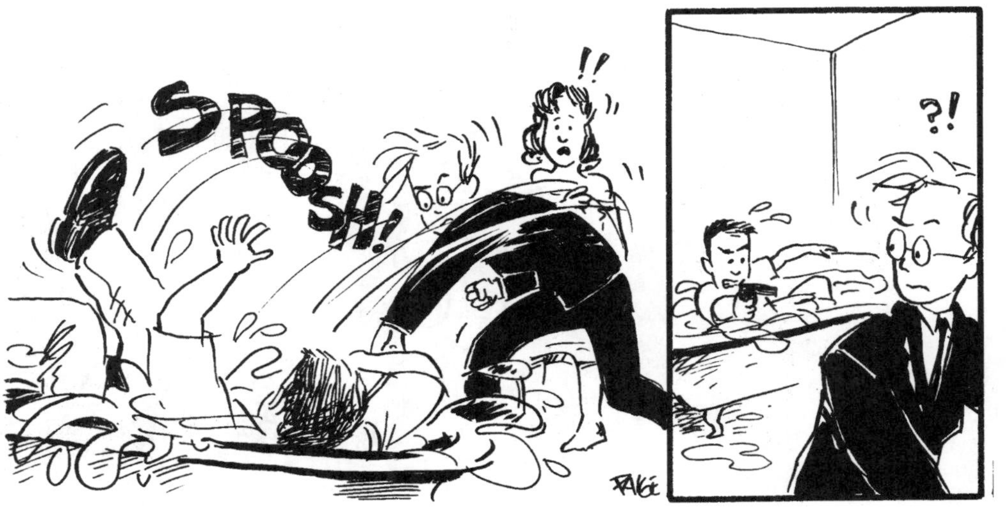
SPOOSH!
!!
?!
PAIGE

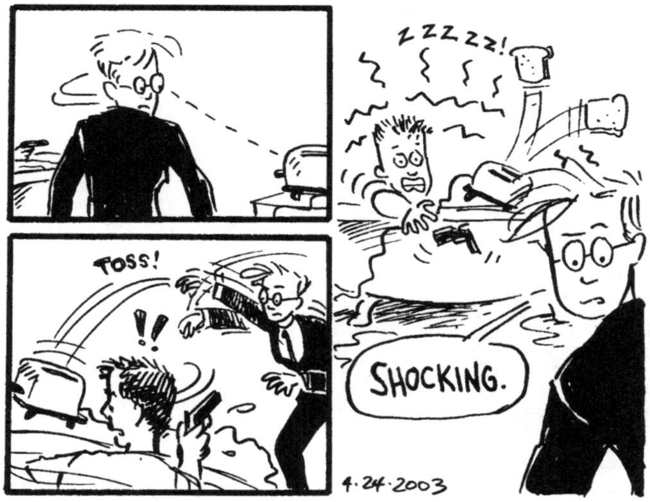
TOSS!
!!
ZZZZZ!
SHOCKING.
4·24·2003

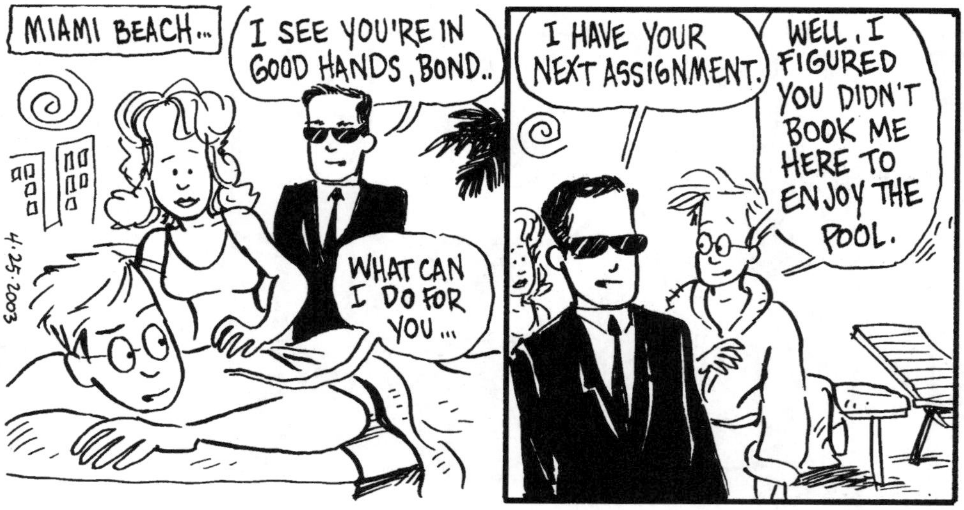
MIAMI BEACH...
I SEE YOU'RE IN GOOD HANDS, BOND..
WHAT CAN I DO FOR YOU...
4·25·2003
I HAVE YOUR NEXT ASSIGNMENT.
WELL, I FIGURED YOU DIDN'T BOOK ME HERE TO ENJOY THE POOL.

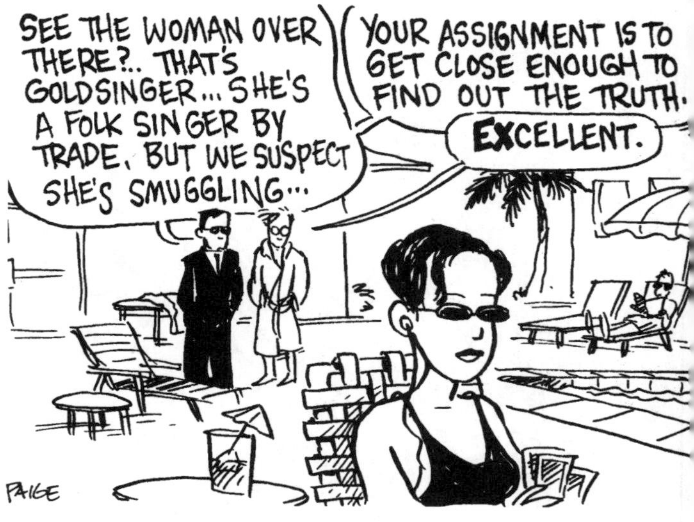
SEE THE WOMAN OVER THERE?.. THAT'S GOLDSINGER... SHE'S A FOLK SINGER BY TRADE, BUT WE SUSPECT SHE'S SMUGGLING...
YOUR ASSIGNMENT IS TO GET CLOSE ENOUGH TO FIND OUT THE TRUTH.
EXCELLENT.
PAIGE

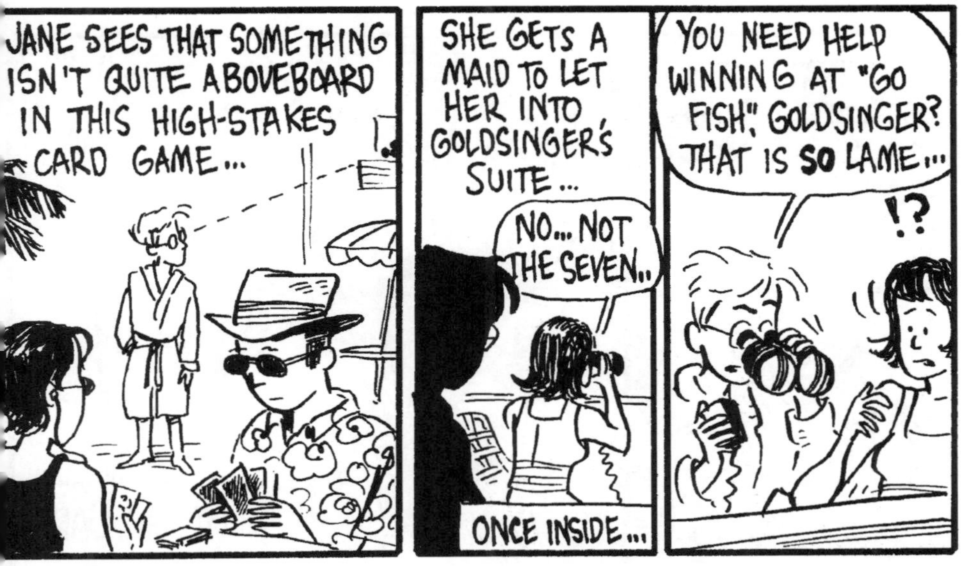
JANE SEES THAT SOMETHING ISN'T QUITE ABOVEBOARD IN THIS HIGH-STAKES CARD GAME...
SHE GETS A MAID TO LET HER INTO GOLDSINGER'S SUITE...
NO... NOT THE SEVEN..
ONCE INSIDE...
YOU NEED HELP WINNING AT "GO FISH", GOLDSINGER? THAT IS SO LAME...
!?

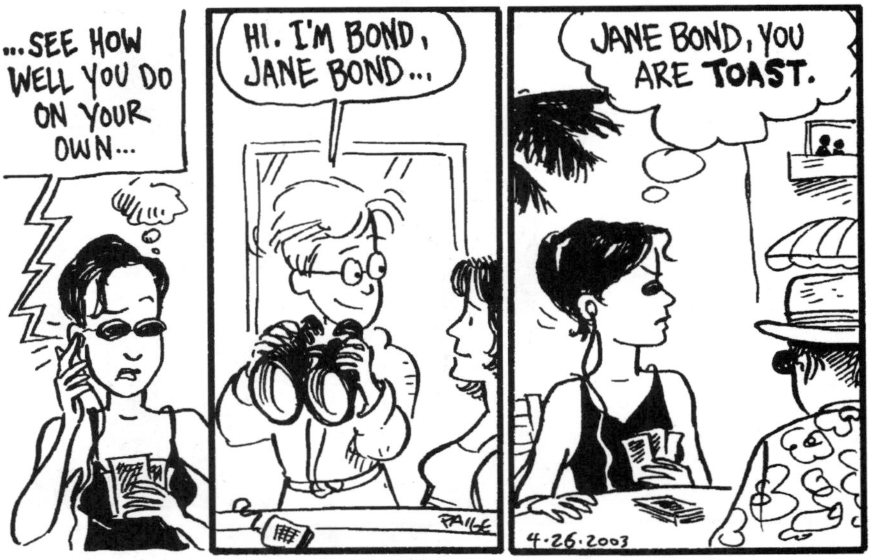
...SEE HOW WELL YOU DO ON YOUR OWN...
HI. I'M BOND, JANE BOND...
PAIGE
JANE BOND, YOU ARE TOAST.
4-26-2003

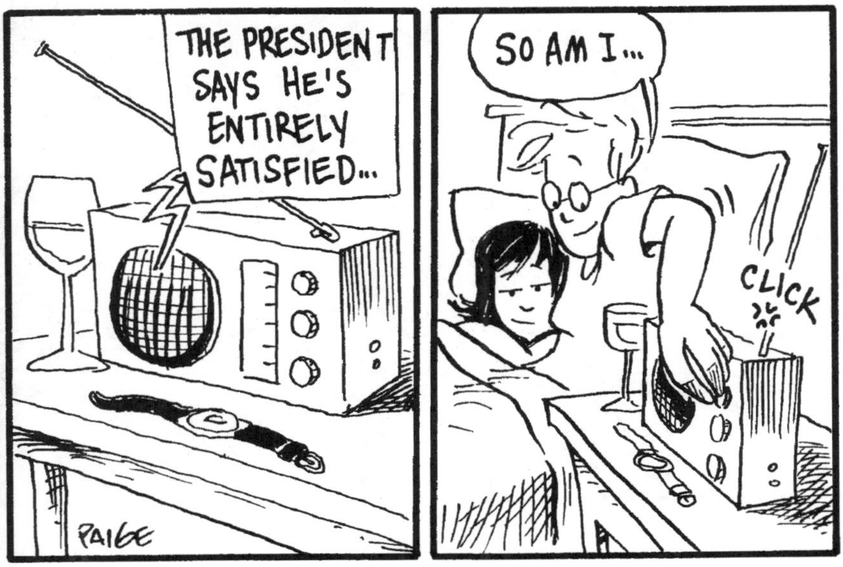
THE PRESIDENT SAYS HE'S ENTIRELY SATISFIED...
PAIGE
SO AM I...
CLICK

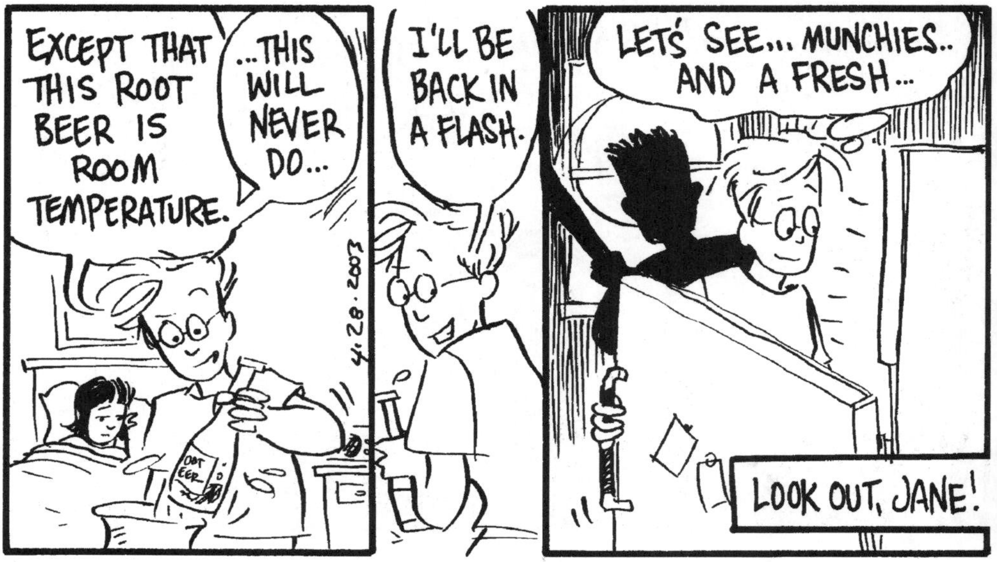
EXCEPT THAT THIS ROOT BEER IS ROOM TEMPERATURE.
...THIS WILL NEVER DO...
4.28.2003
I'LL BE BACK IN A FLASH.
LET'S SEE... MUNCHIES.. AND A FRESH...
LOOK OUT, JANE!

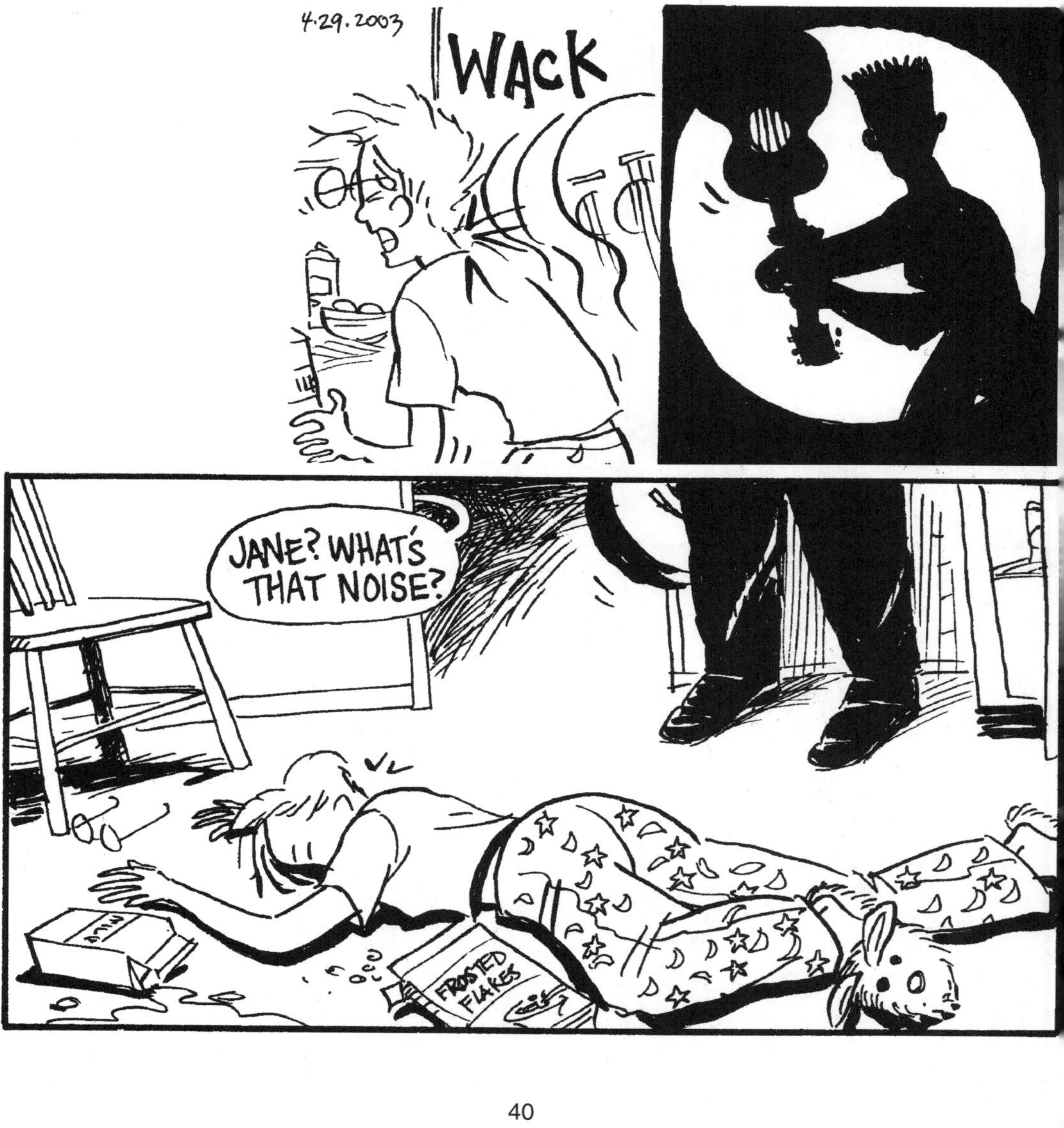
4.29.2003
WACK
JANE? WHAT'S THAT NOISE?
MILK
FROSTED FLAKES

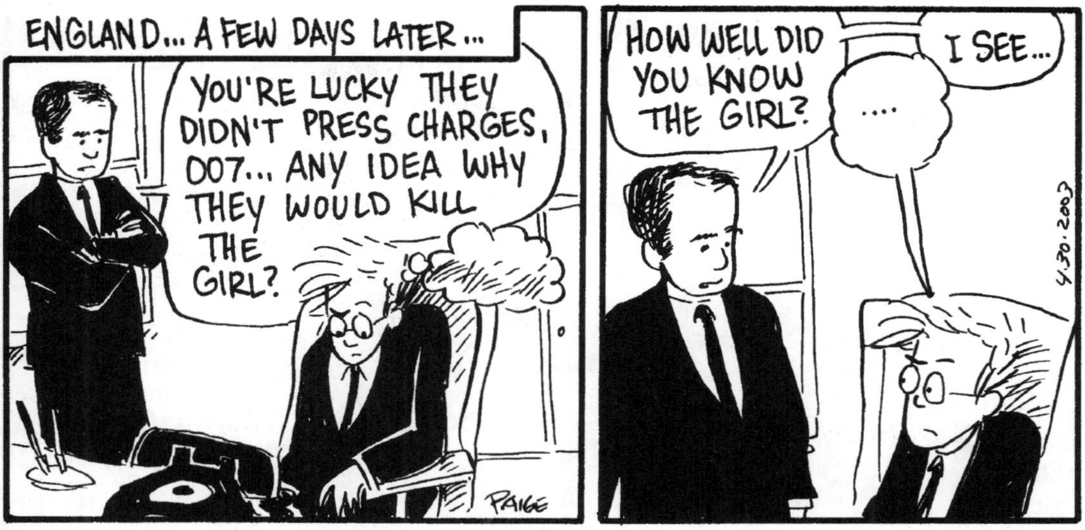
ENGLAND... A FEW DAYS LATER...
YOU'RE LUCKY THEY DIDN'T PRESS CHARGES, 007... ANY IDEA WHY THEY WOULD KILL THE GIRL?
PAIGE
HOW WELL DID YOU KNOW THE GIRL?
....
I SEE...
4.30.2003

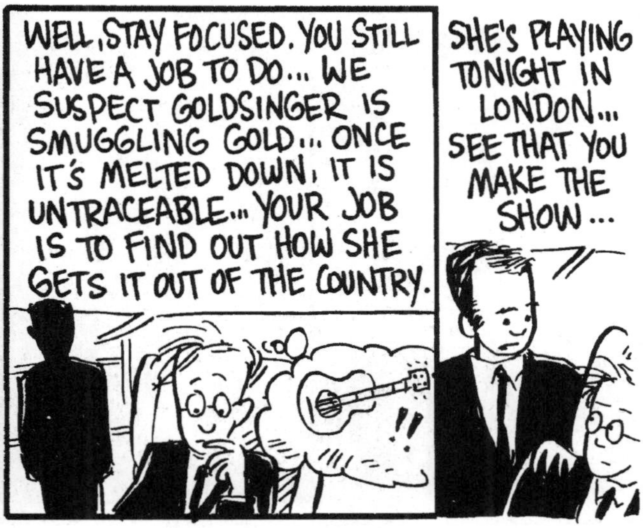
WELL, STAY FOCUSED. YOU STILL HAVE A JOB TO DO... WE SUSPECT GOLDSINGER IS SMUGGLING GOLD... ONCE IT'S MELTED DOWN, IT IS UNTRACEABLE... YOUR JOB IS TO FIND OUT HOW SHE GETS IT OUT OF THE COUNTRY.
!!
SHE'S PLAYING TONIGHT IN LONDON... SEE THAT YOU MAKE THE SHOW...

Moments later...

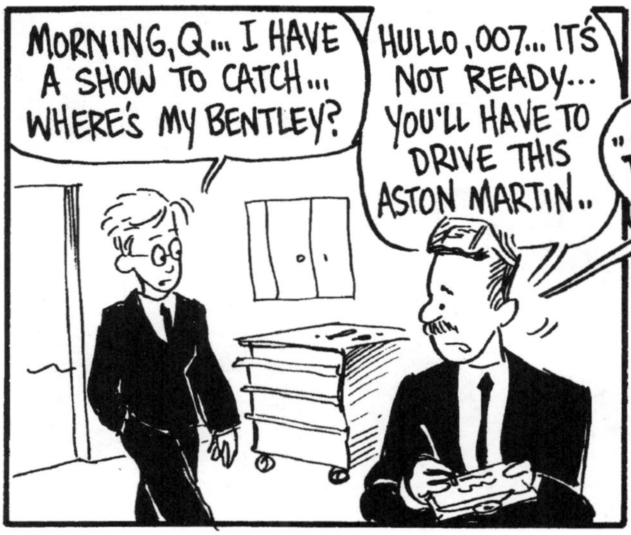
MORNING, Q... I HAVE A SHOW TO CATCH... WHERE'S MY BENTLEY?
HULLO, 007... IT'S NOT READY... YOU'LL HAVE TO DRIVE THIS ASTON MARTIN..
.. AND I'D LIKE THIS ONE BACK IN ONE PIECE!

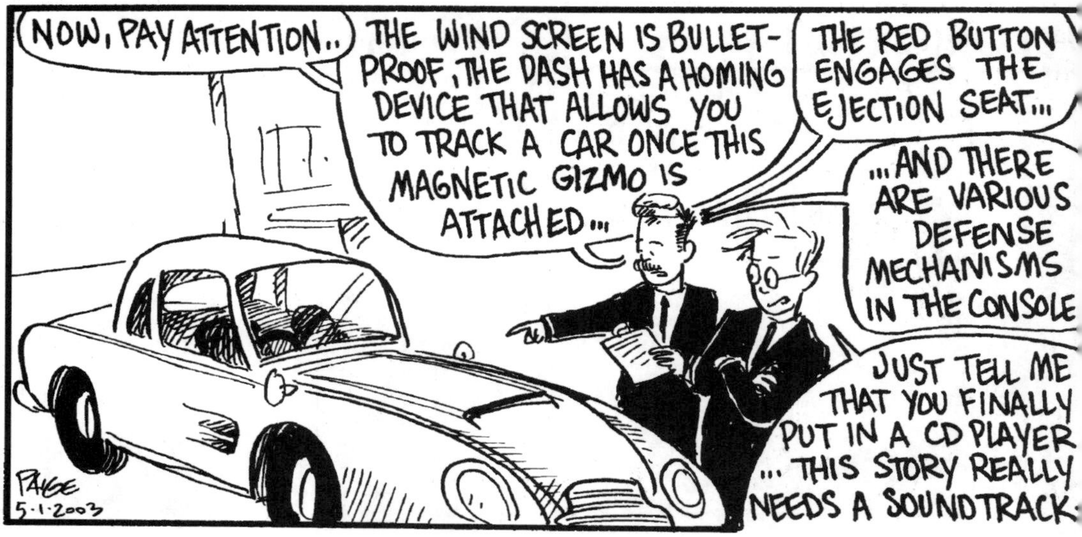
NOW, PAY ATTENTION..
THE WIND SCREEN IS BULLET-PROOF, THE DASH HAS A HOMING DEVICE THAT ALLOWS YOU TO TRACK A CAR ONCE THIS MAGNETIC GIZMO IS ATTACHED...
THE RED BUTTON ENGAGES THE EJECTION SEAT...
...AND THERE ARE VARIOUS DEFENSE MECHANISMS IN THE CONSOLE
JUST TELL ME THAT YOU FINALLY PUT IN A CD PLAYER ... THIS STORY REALLY NEEDS A SOUNDTRACK.
PAIGE
5-1-2003

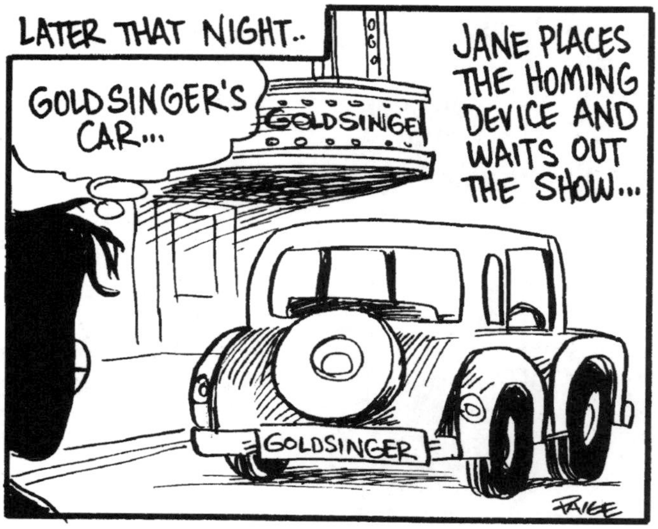
LATER THAT NIGHT..
GOLDSINGER'S CAR...
GOLDSINGE
JANE PLACES THE HOMING DEVICE AND WAITS OUT THE SHOW...
GOLDSINGER
PAIGE

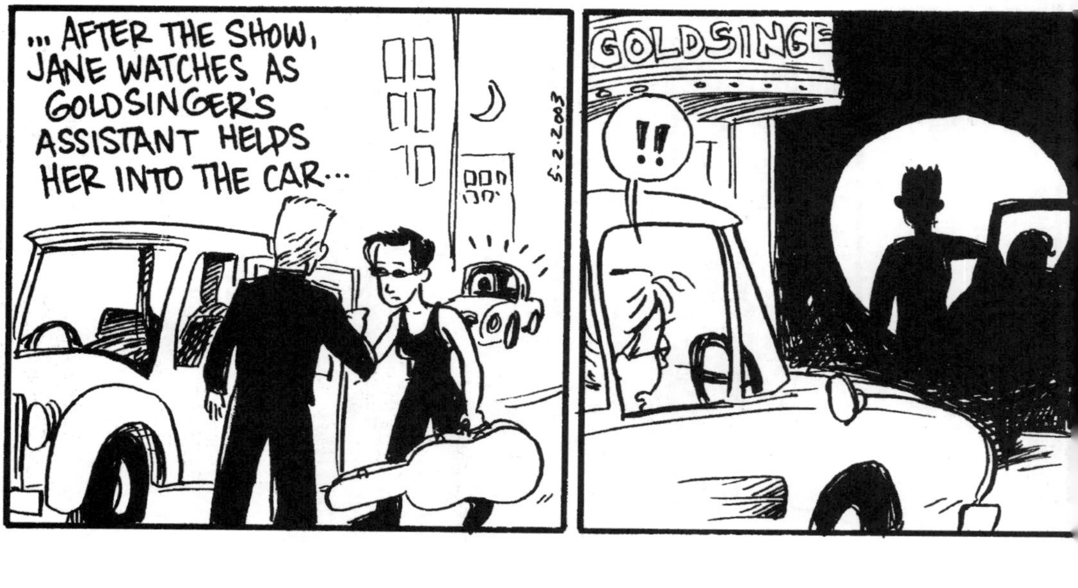
... AFTER THE SHOW, JANE WATCHES AS GOLDSINGER'S ASSISTANT HELPS HER INTO THE CAR...
5.2.2003
GOLDSINGE
!!

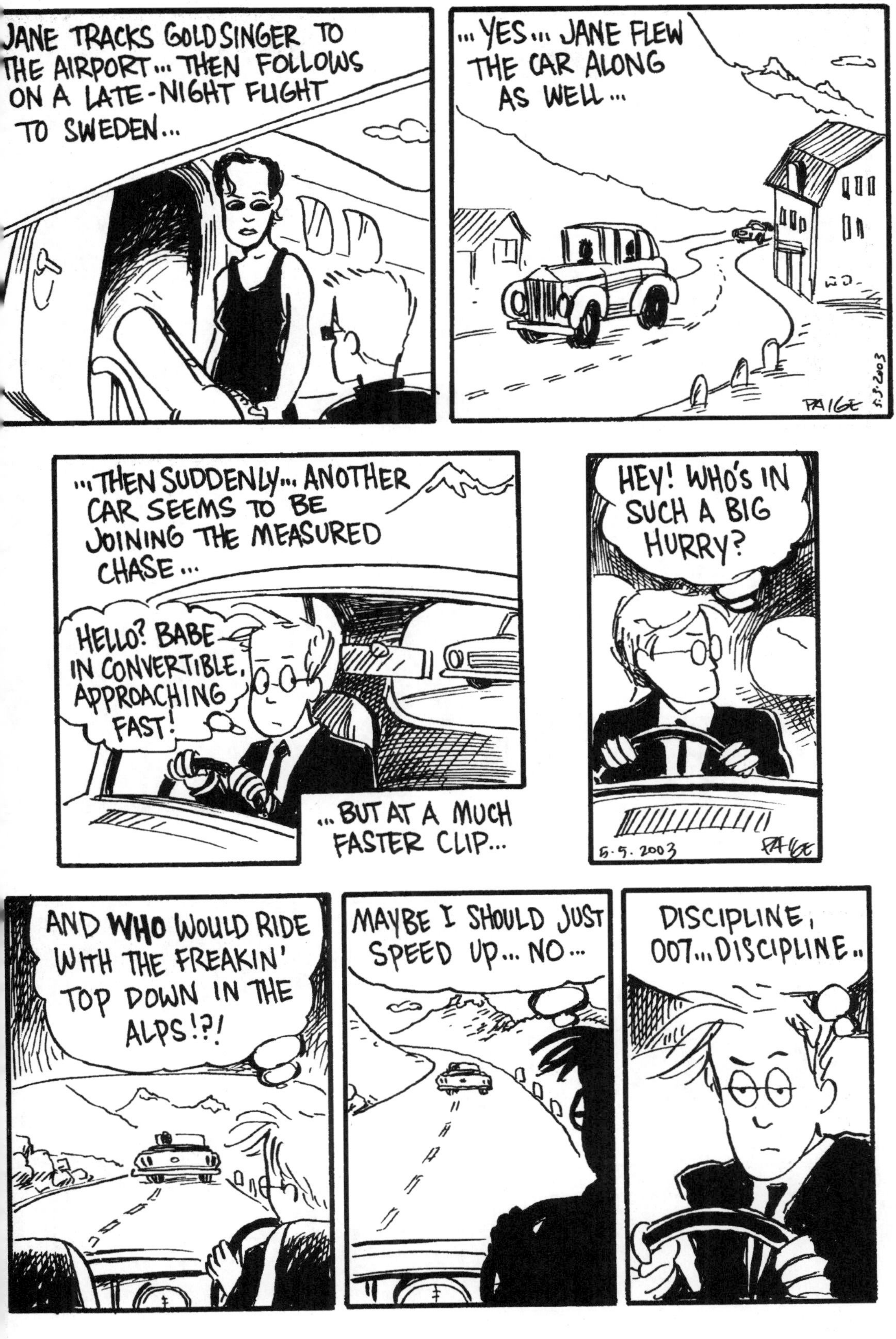
JANE TRACKS GOLDSINGER TO THE AIRPORT... THEN FOLLOWS ON A LATE-NIGHT FLIGHT TO SWEDEN...
...YES... JANE FLEW THE CAR ALONG AS WELL...
PAIGE 5.5.2003
...THEN SUDDENLY... ANOTHER CAR SEEMS TO BE JOINING THE MEASURED CHASE...
HELLO? BABE IN CONVERTIBLE, APPROACHING FAST!
...BUT AT A MUCH FASTER CLIP...
HEY! WHO'S IN SUCH A BIG HURRY?
5.5.2003
PAIGE
AND WHO WOULD RIDE WITH THE FREAKIN' TOP DOWN IN THE ALPS!?!
MAYBE I SHOULD JUST SPEED UP... NO...
DISCIPLINE, 007... DISCIPLINE..

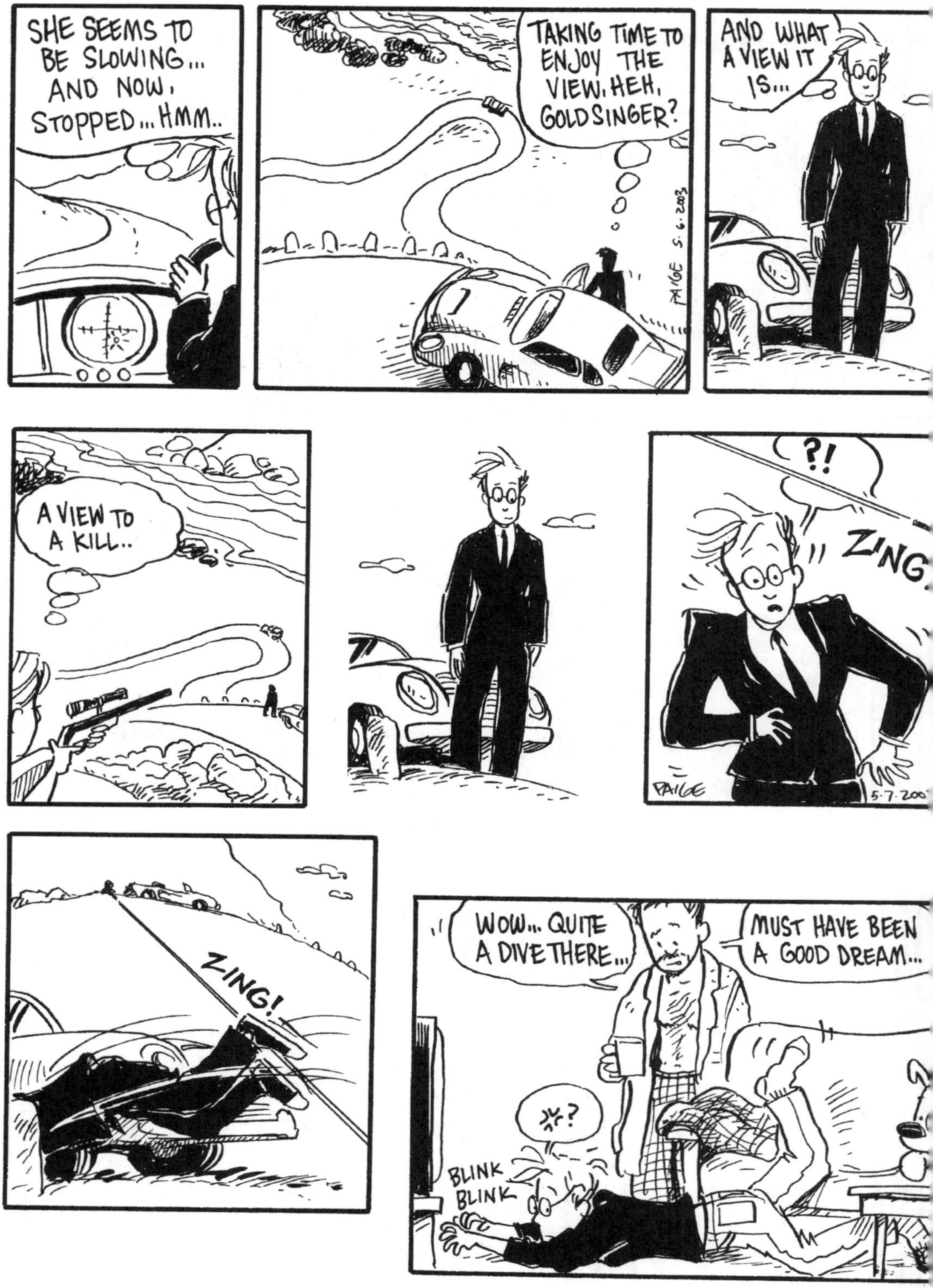
SHE SEEMS TO BE SLOWING... AND NOW, STOPPED... HMM..
TAKING TIME TO ENJOY THE VIEW, HEH, GOLDSINGER?
AND WHAT A VIEW IT IS...
A VIEW TO A KILL..
?!
ZING
ZING!
WOW... QUITE A DIVE THERE...
MUST HAVE BEEN A GOOD DREAM...
?
BLINK BLINK

IT WAS A GREAT DREAM...I WAS **JANE BOND**... AND I WAS AMAZINGLY COOL...
..DEFINITELY A DREAM THEN..
5·8·2003
HEY! WHY DIDN'T YOU WAKE ME UP?.. YOU LET ME SLEEP ON THE FUTON ALL NIGHT AND NOW MY NECK IS KILLING ME!
PAIGE

OOOH... BUT NOTHING IS KILLING ME AS MUCH AS CHEST HAIR BEFORE COFFEE... PULEEZE... DO I HAVE TO SEE THAT?!
ALL PART OF THE PACKAGE, 007... NO EXTRA CHARGE..

WELL, I'LL LEAVE YOU ALONE WITH YOUR PACKAGE...
5·9·2003

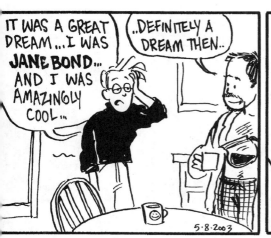

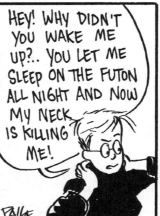

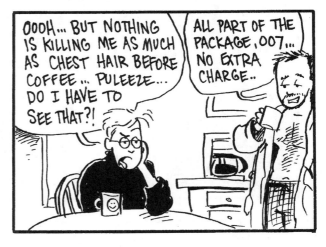

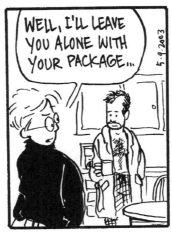

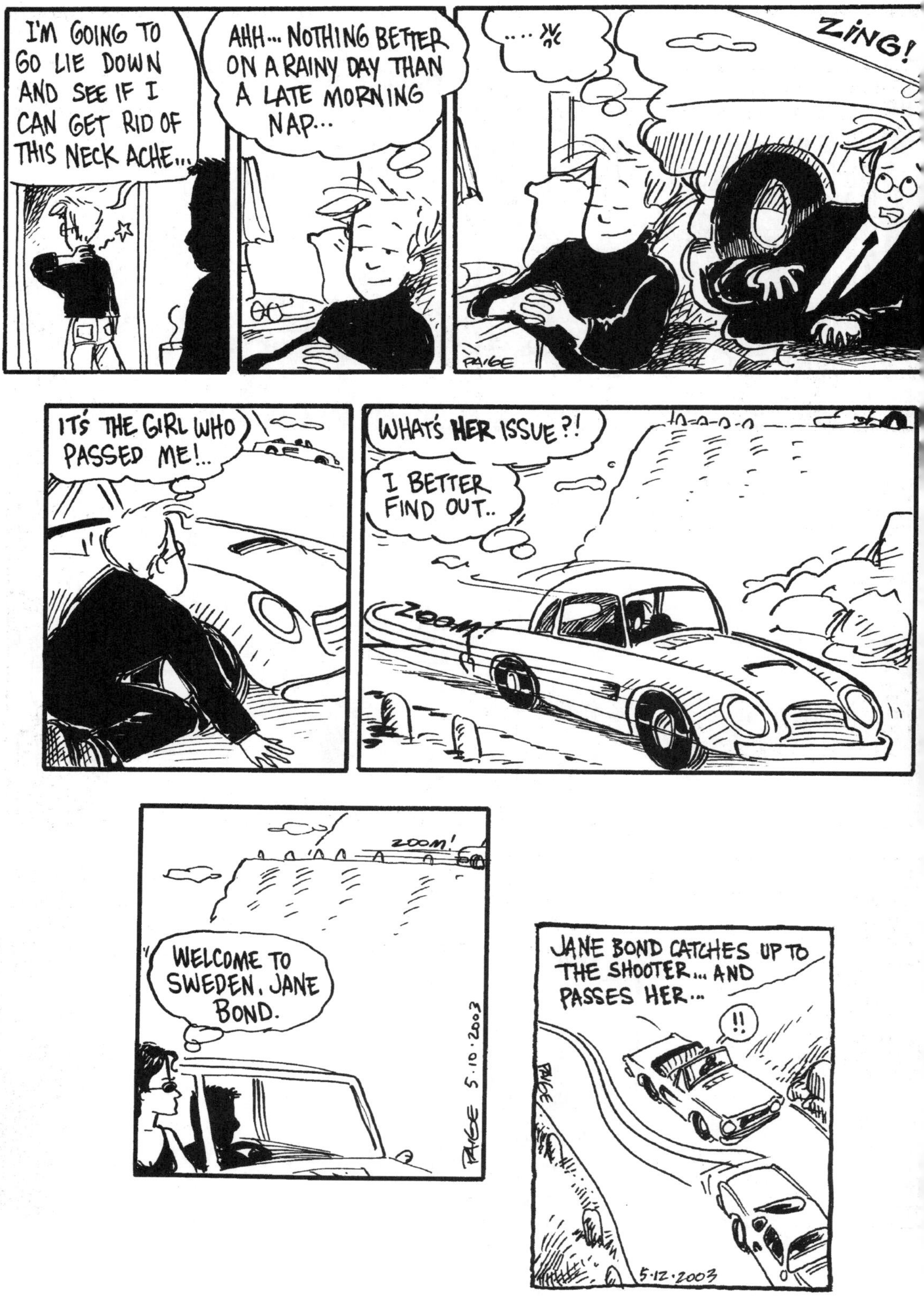
I'M GOING TO GO LIE DOWN AND SEE IF I CAN GET RID OF THIS NECK ACHE...
AHH... NOTHING BETTER ON A RAINY DAY THAN A LATE MORNING NAP...
ZING!
PAIGE
IT'S THE GIRL WHO PASSED ME!..
WHAT'S **HER** ISSUE?!
I BETTER FIND OUT..
ZOOM!
ZOOM!
WELCOME TO SWEDEN, JANE BOND.
PAIGE 5.10.2003
JANE BOND CATCHES UP TO THE SHOOTER... AND PASSES HER...
!!
PAIGE
5.12.2003

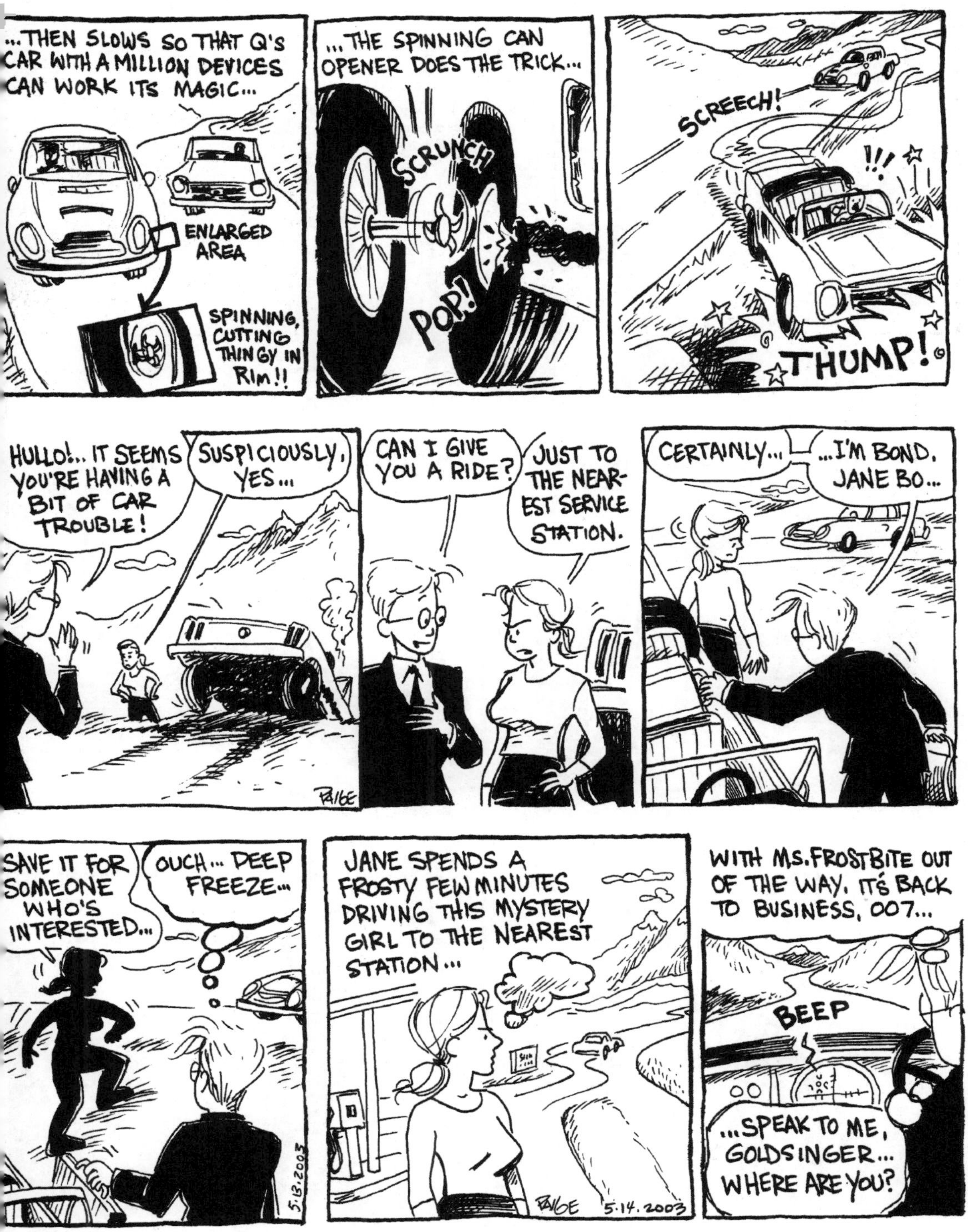
...THEN SLOWS SO THAT Q'S CAR WITH A MILLION DEVICES CAN WORK ITS MAGIC...
ENLARGED AREA
SPINNING, CUTTING THINGY IN RIM!!
...THE SPINNING CAN OPENER DOES THE TRICK...
SCRUNCH!
POP!
SCREECH!
!!!
THUMP!
HULLO!... IT SEEMS YOU'RE HAVING A BIT OF CAR TROUBLE!
SUSPICIOUSLY, YES...
PAIGE
CAN I GIVE YOU A RIDE?
JUST TO THE NEAREST SERVICE STATION.
CERTAINLY...
...I'M BOND. JANE BO...
SAVE IT FOR SOMEONE WHO'S INTERESTED...
OUCH... DEEP FREEZE...
5.13.2003
JANE SPENDS A FROSTY FEW MINUTES DRIVING THIS MYSTERY GIRL TO THE NEAREST STATION...
PAIGE
5.14.2003
WITH MS. FROSTBITE OUT OF THE WAY, IT'S BACK TO BUSINESS, 007...
BEEP
...SPEAK TO ME, GOLDSINGER... WHERE ARE YOU?

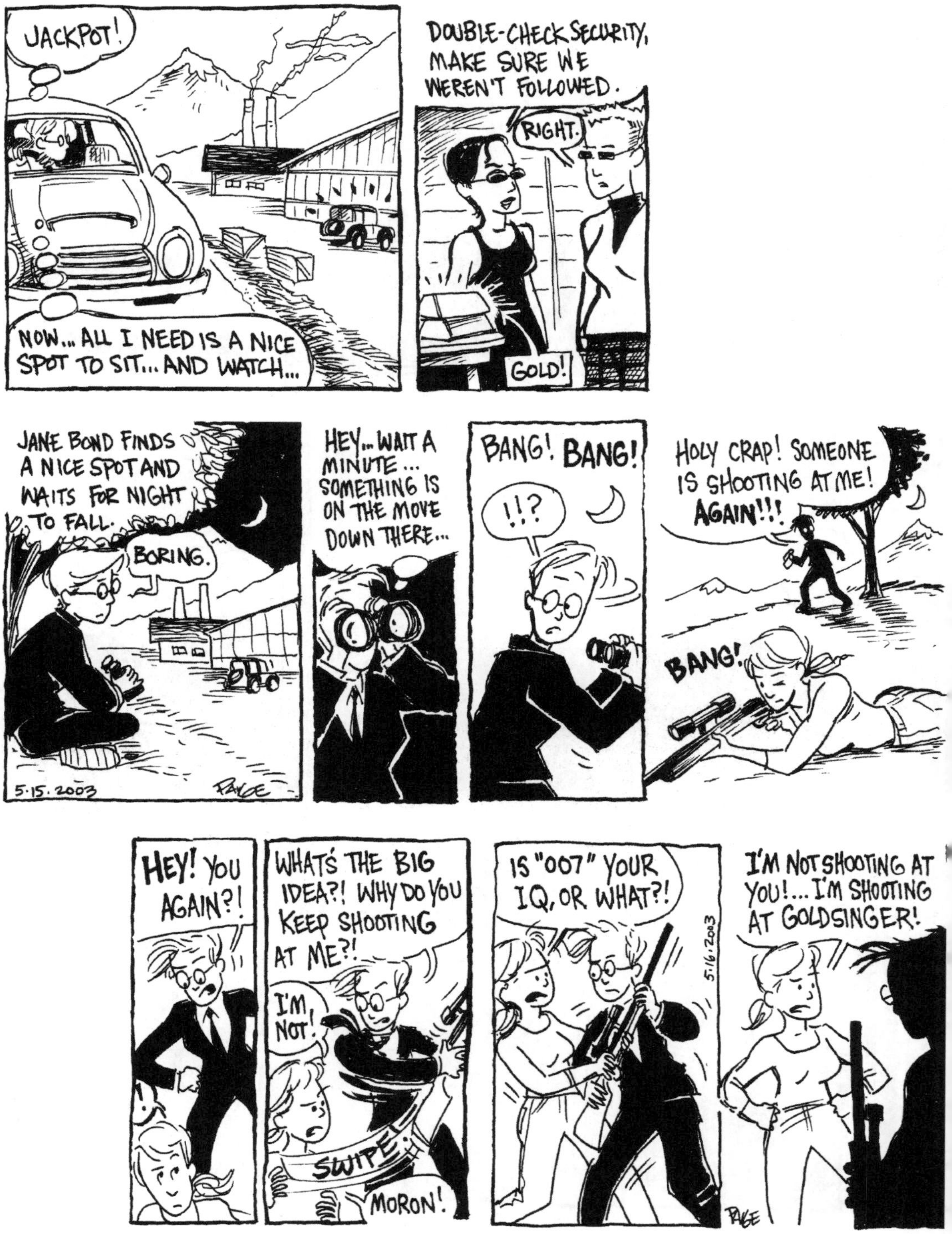
JACKPOT!
NOW... ALL I NEED IS A NICE SPOT TO SIT... AND WATCH...
DOUBLE-CHECK SECURITY, MAKE SURE WE WEREN'T FOLLOWED.
RIGHT.
GOLD!
JANE BOND FINDS A NICE SPOT AND WAITS FOR NIGHT TO FALL.
BORING.
5.15.2003
PAIGE
HEY... WAIT A MINUTE... SOMETHING IS ON THE MOVE DOWN THERE...
BANG! BANG!
!!?
HOLY CRAP! SOMEONE IS SHOOTING AT ME! AGAIN!!!
BANG!
HEY! YOU AGAIN?!
WHAT'S THE BIG IDEA?! WHY DO YOU KEEP SHOOTING AT ME?!
I'M NOT!
SWIPE!
MORON!
IS "007" YOUR IQ, OR WHAT?!
5.16.2003
I'M NOT SHOOTING AT YOU!... I'M SHOOTING AT GOLDSINGER!
PAIGE

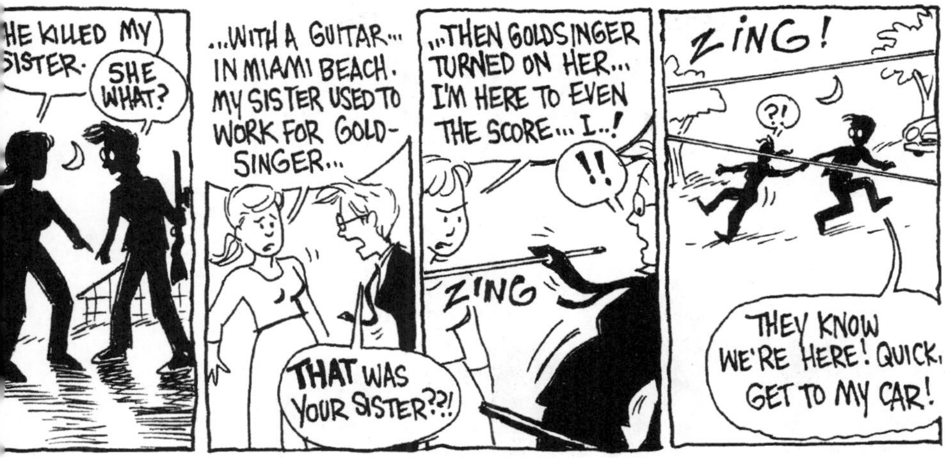
HE KILLED MY SISTER.
SHE WHAT?
...WITH A GUITAR... IN MIAMI BEACH. MY SISTER USED TO WORK FOR GOLD-SINGER...
THAT WAS YOUR SISTER??!
...THEN GOLDSINGER TURNED ON HER... I'M HERE TO EVEN THE SCORE... I..!
!!
ZING
ZING!
?!
THEY KNOW WE'RE HERE! QUICK, GET TO MY CAR!

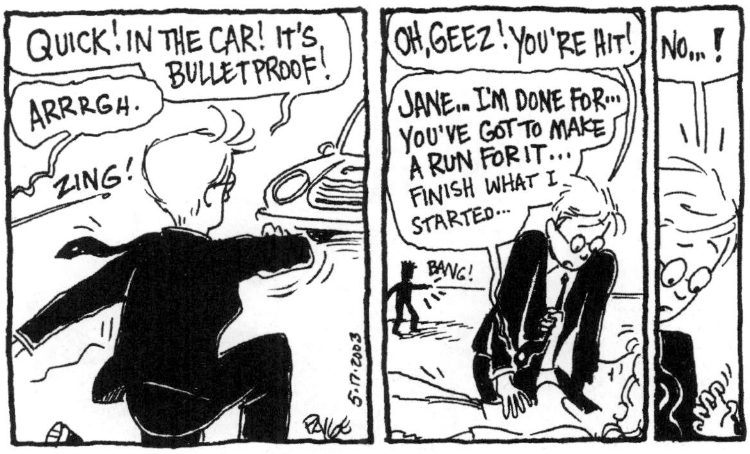
QUICK! IN THE CAR! IT'S BULLETPROOF!
ARRRGH.
ZING!
5.17.2003
OH, GEEZ! YOU'RE HIT!
JANE... I'M DONE FOR... YOU'VE GOT TO MAKE A RUN FOR IT... FINISH WHAT I STARTED...
BANG!
NO...!

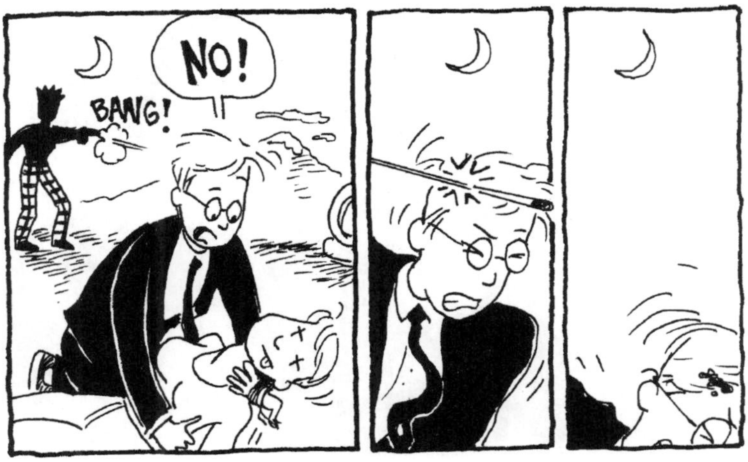
NO!
BANG!

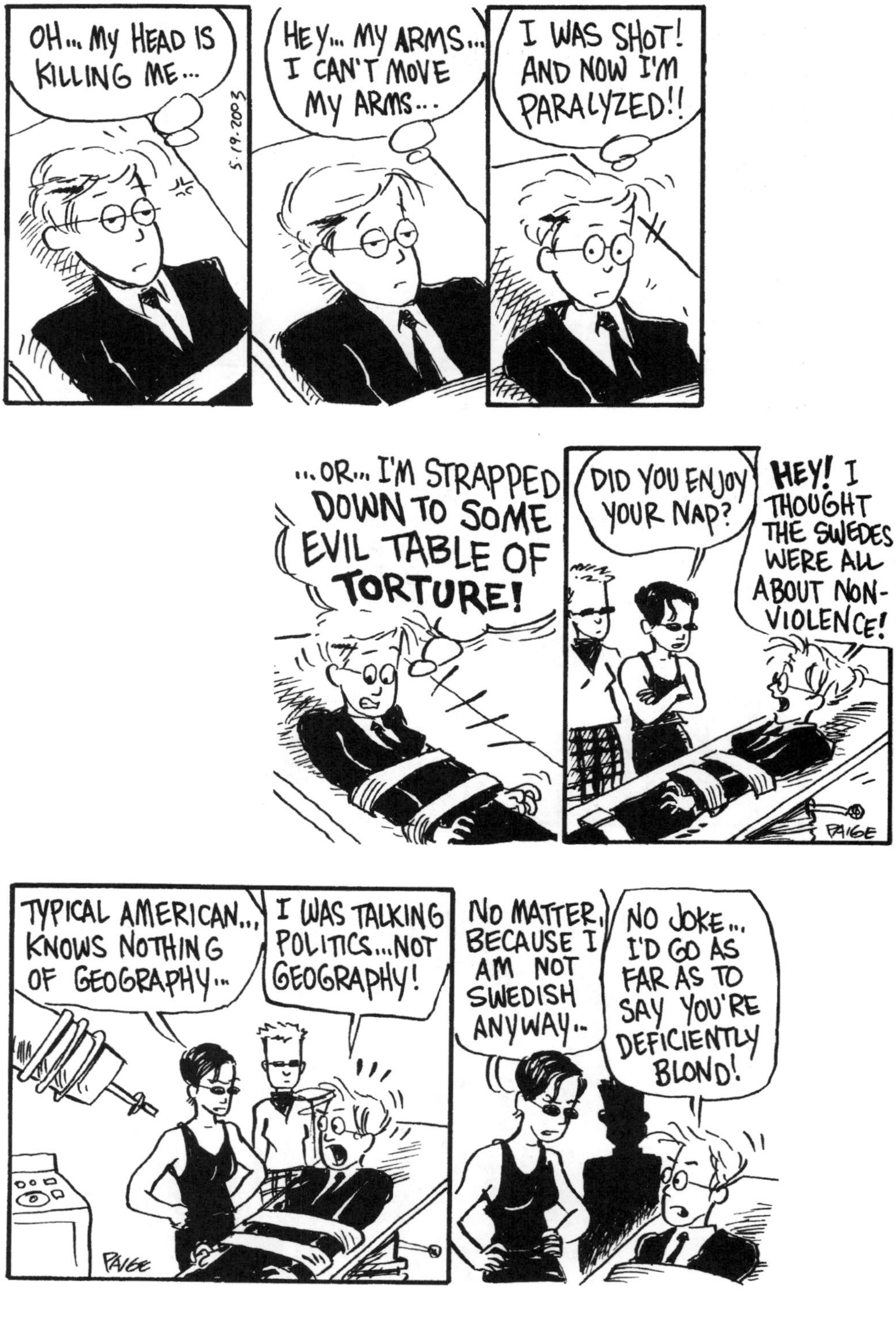
OH... MY HEAD IS KILLING ME...
5.19.2003
HEY... MY ARMS... I CAN'T MOVE MY ARMS...
I WAS SHOT! AND NOW I'M PARALYZED!!
...OR... I'M STRAPPED DOWN TO SOME EVIL TABLE OF TORTURE!
DID YOU ENJOY YOUR NAP?
HEY! I THOUGHT THE SWEDES WERE ALL ABOUT NON-VIOLENCE!
PAIGE
TYPICAL AMERICAN... KNOWS NOTHING OF GEOGRAPHY...
I WAS TALKING POLITICS...NOT GEOGRAPHY!
PAIGE
NO MATTER, BECAUSE I AM NOT SWEDISH ANYWAY..
NO JOKE... I'D GO AS FAR AS TO SAY YOU'RE DEFICIENTLY BLOND!

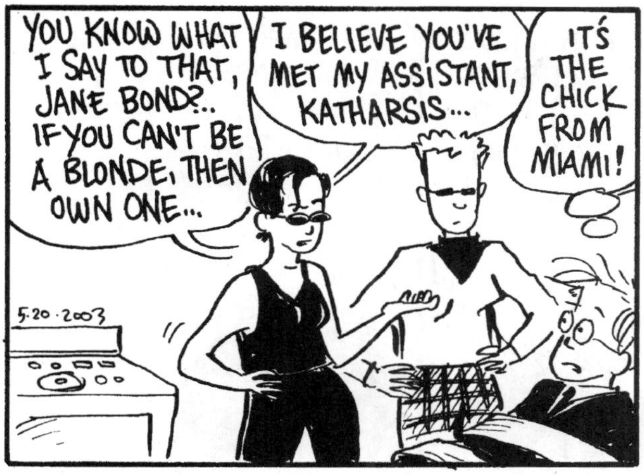
YOU KNOW WHAT I SAY TO THAT, JANE BOND?.. IF YOU CAN'T BE A BLONDE, THEN OWN ONE...
I BELIEVE YOU'VE MET MY ASSISTANT, KATHARSIS...
IT'S THE CHICK FROM MIAMI!
5.20.2003

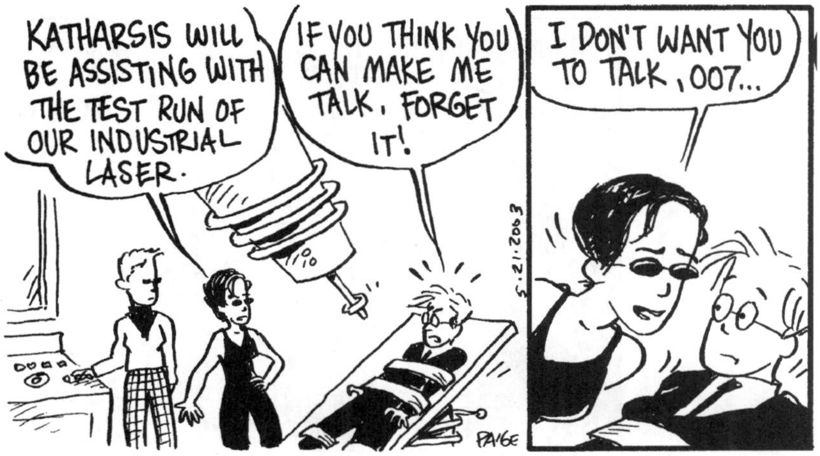
KATHARSIS WILL BE ASSISTING WITH THE TEST RUN OF OUR INDUSTRIAL LASER.
IF YOU THINK YOU CAN MAKE ME TALK, FORGET IT!
5.21.2003
PAIGE
I DON'T WANT YOU TO TALK, 007...

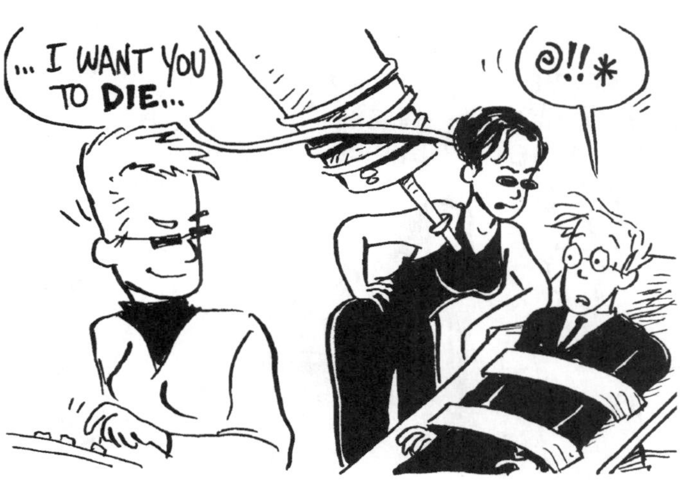
... I WANT YOU TO **DIE**...
@!!*

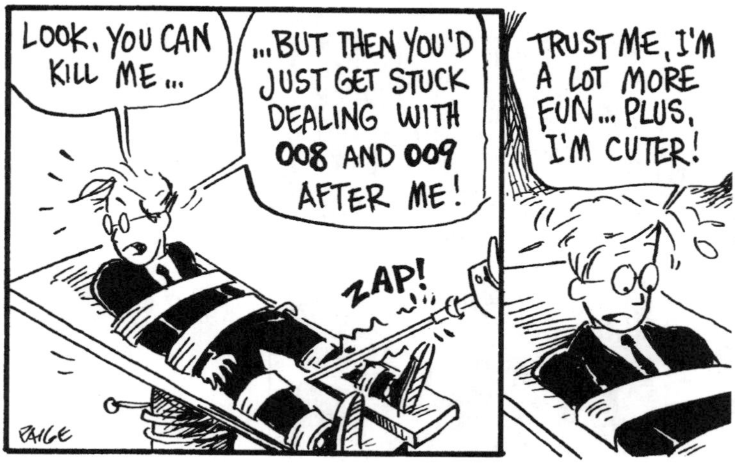
LOOK, YOU CAN KILL ME...
...BUT THEN YOU'D JUST GET STUCK DEALING WITH 008 AND 009 AFTER ME!
ZAP!
TRUST ME, I'M A LOT MORE FUN... PLUS, I'M CUTER!
PAIGE

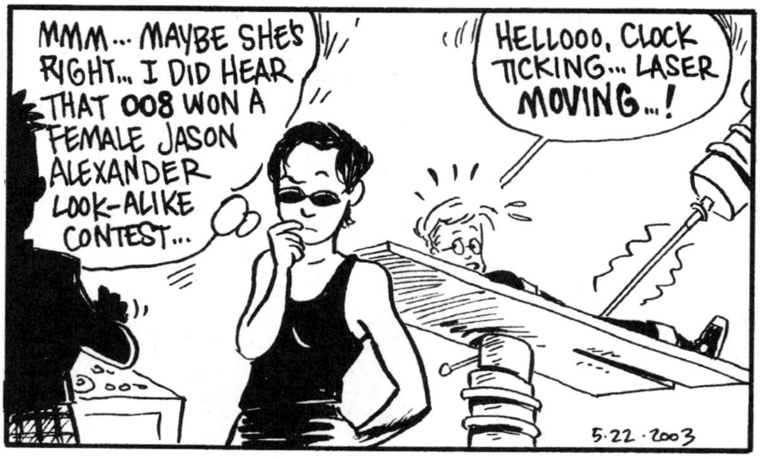
MMM... MAYBE SHE'S RIGHT... I DID HEAR THAT 008 WON A FEMALE JASON ALEXANDER LOOK-ALIKE CONTEST...
HELLOOO, CLOCK TICKING... LASER MOVING...!
5.22.2003

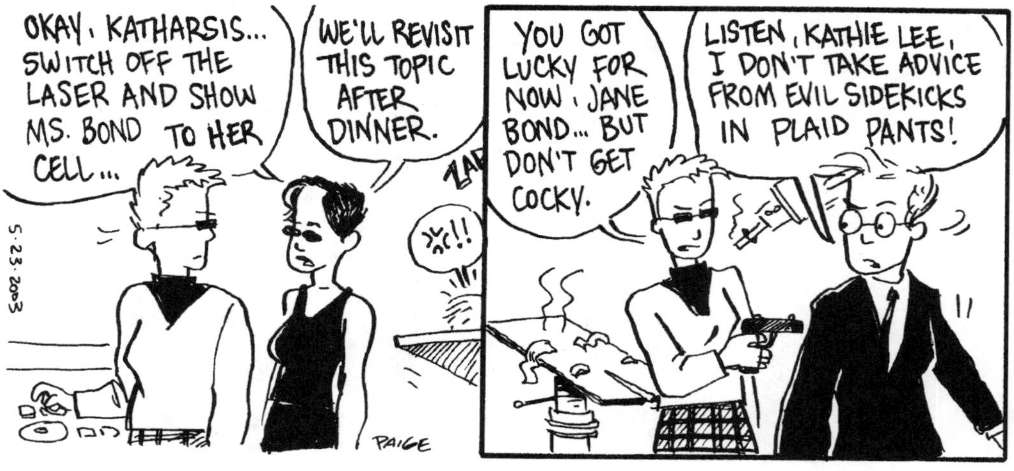
OKAY, KATHARSIS... SWITCH OFF THE LASER AND SHOW MS. BOND TO HER CELL...
WE'LL REVISIT THIS TOPIC AFTER DINNER.
5.23.2003
PAIGE
YOU GOT LUCKY FOR NOW, JANE BOND... BUT DON'T GET COCKY.
LISTEN, KATHIE LEE, I DON'T TAKE ADVICE FROM EVIL SIDEKICKS IN PLAID PANTS!

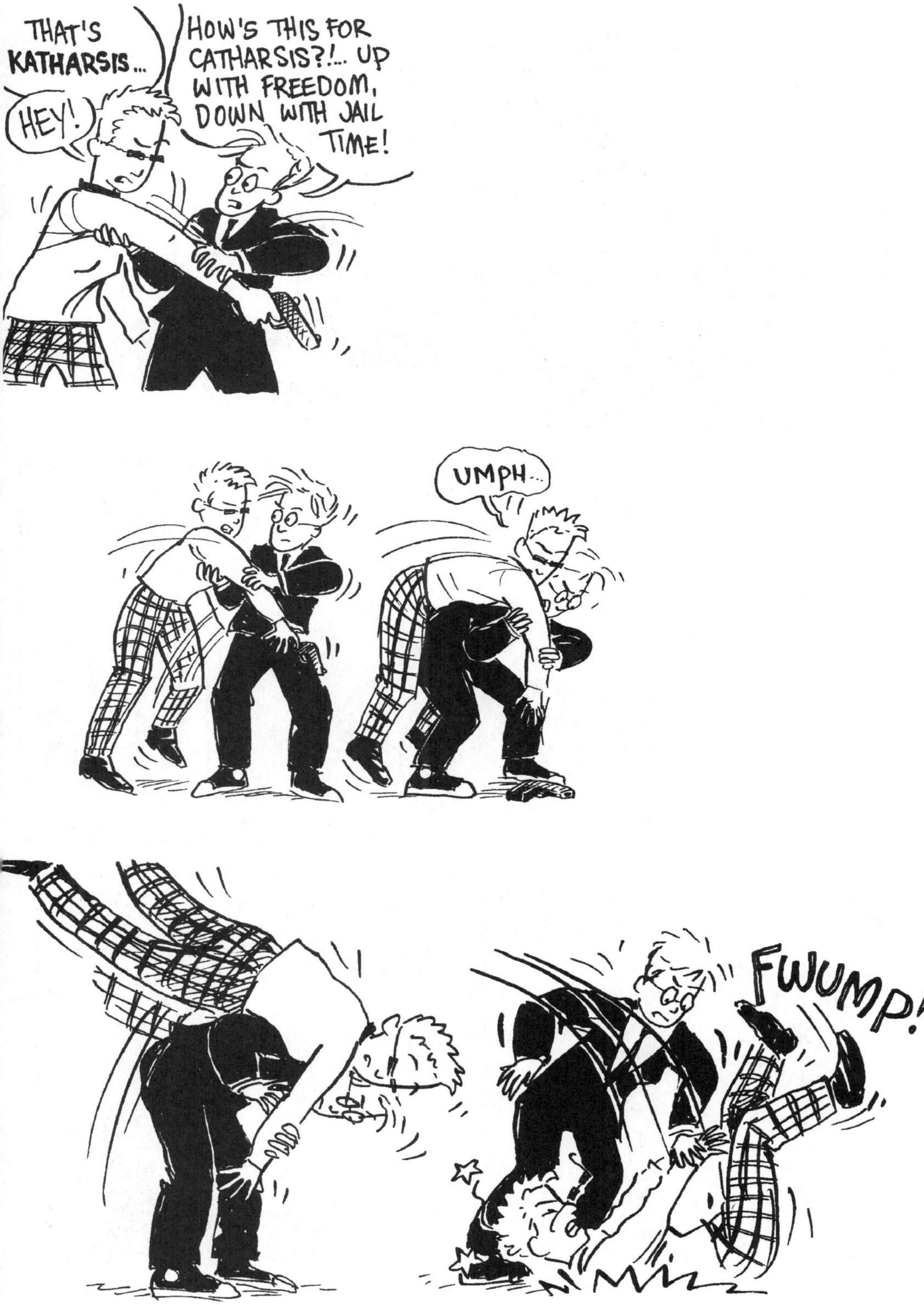
THAT'S KATHARSIS...
HEY!
HOW'S THIS FOR CATHARSIS?!... UP WITH FREEDOM, DOWN WITH JAIL TIME!
UMPH...
FWUMP!

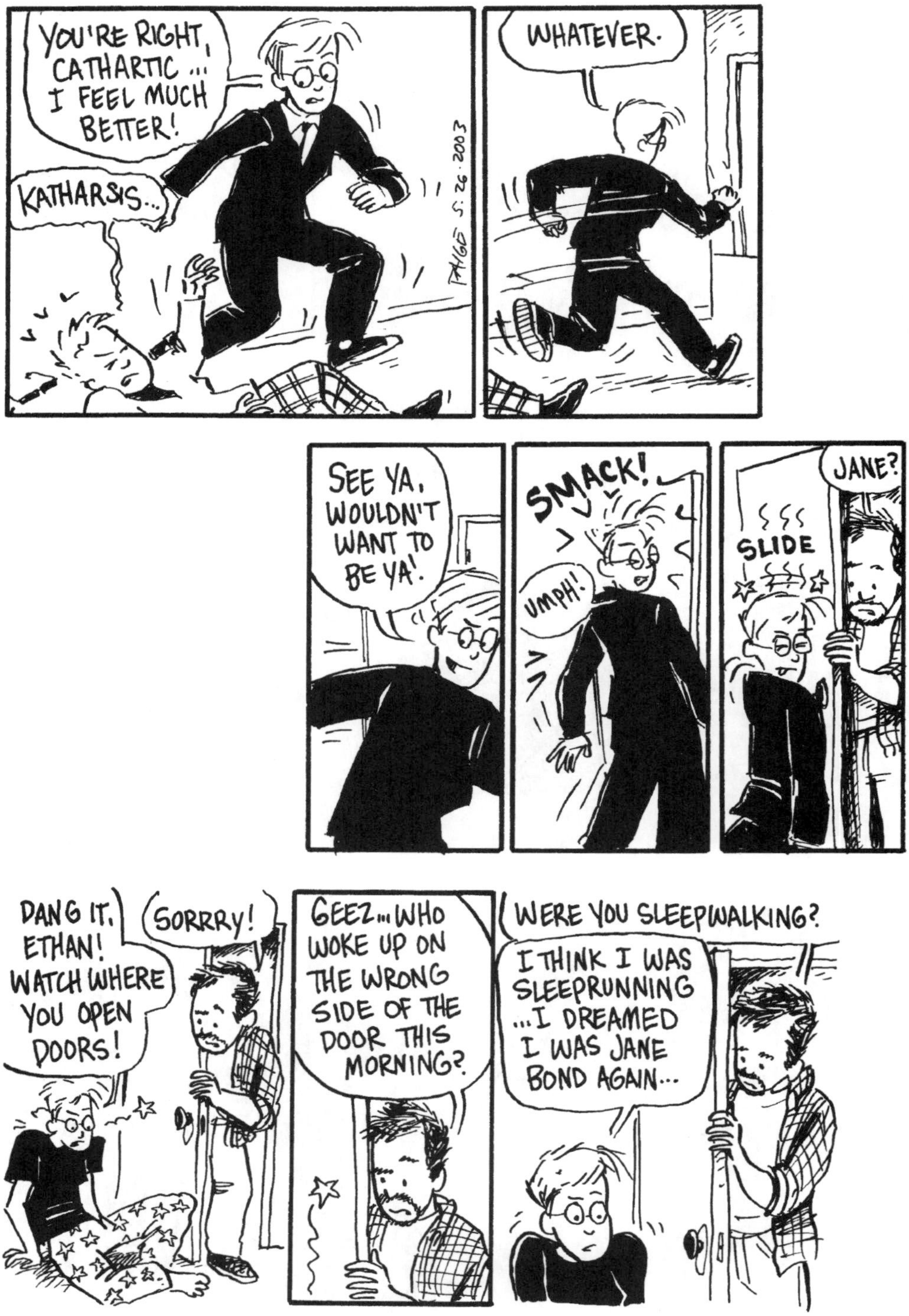
YOU'RE RIGHT, CATHARTIC... I FEEL MUCH BETTER!
KATHARSIS...
WHATEVER.
SEE YA, WOULDN'T WANT TO BE YA!
SMACK!
UMPH!
JANE?
SLIDE
DANG IT, ETHAN! WATCH WHERE YOU OPEN DOORS!
SORRRY!
GEEZ... WHO WOKE UP ON THE WRONG SIDE OF THE DOOR THIS MORNING?
WERE YOU SLEEPWALKING?
I THINK I WAS SLEEPRUNNING ...I DREAMED I WAS JANE BOND AGAIN...

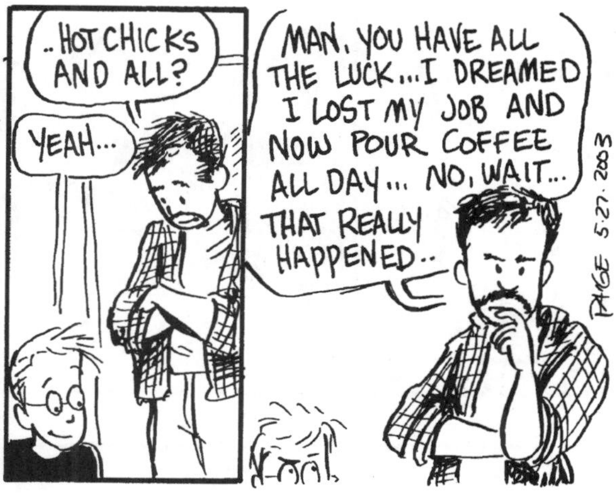
..HOT CHICKS AND ALL?
YEAH...
MAN, YOU HAVE ALL THE LUCK...I DREAMED I LOST MY JOB AND NOW POUR COFFEE ALL DAY... NO, WAIT... THAT REALLY HAPPENED..
PAIGE 5.27.2003

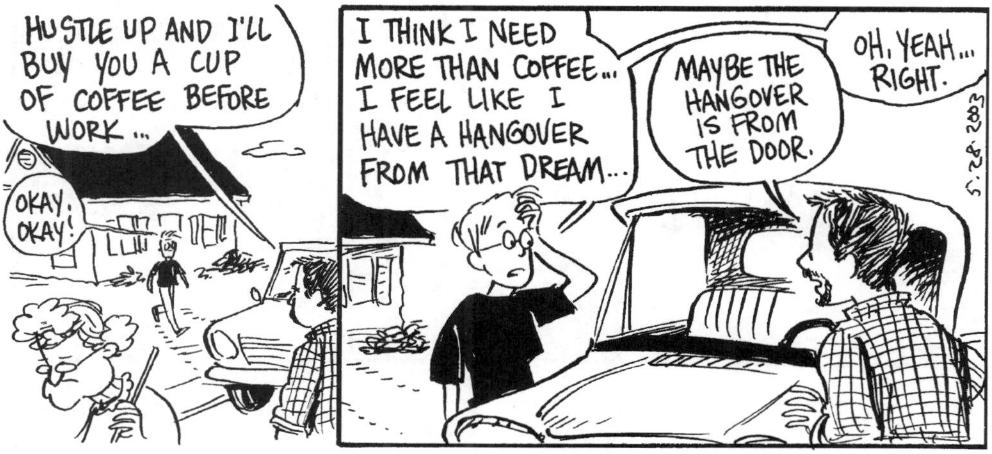
HUSTLE UP AND I'LL BUY YOU A CUP OF COFFEE BEFORE WORK...
OKAY, OKAY!
I THINK I NEED MORE THAN COFFEE... I FEEL LIKE I HAVE A HANGOVER FROM THAT DREAM...
MAYBE THE HANGOVER IS FROM THE DOOR.
OH, YEAH... RIGHT.
5.28.2003

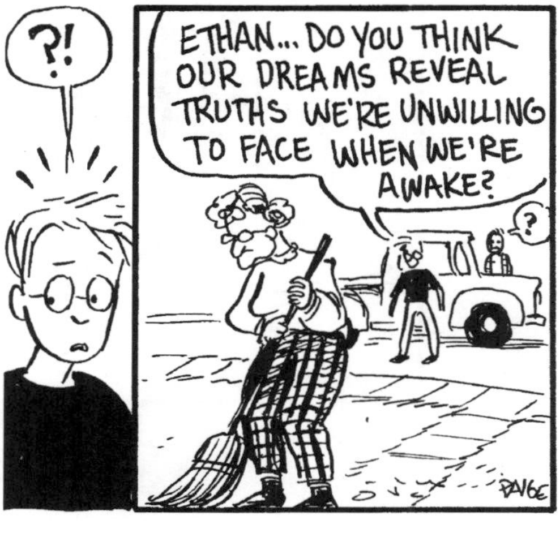
?!
ETHAN... DO YOU THINK OUR DREAMS REVEAL TRUTHS WE'RE UNWILLING TO FACE WHEN WE'RE AWAKE?
?
PAIGE

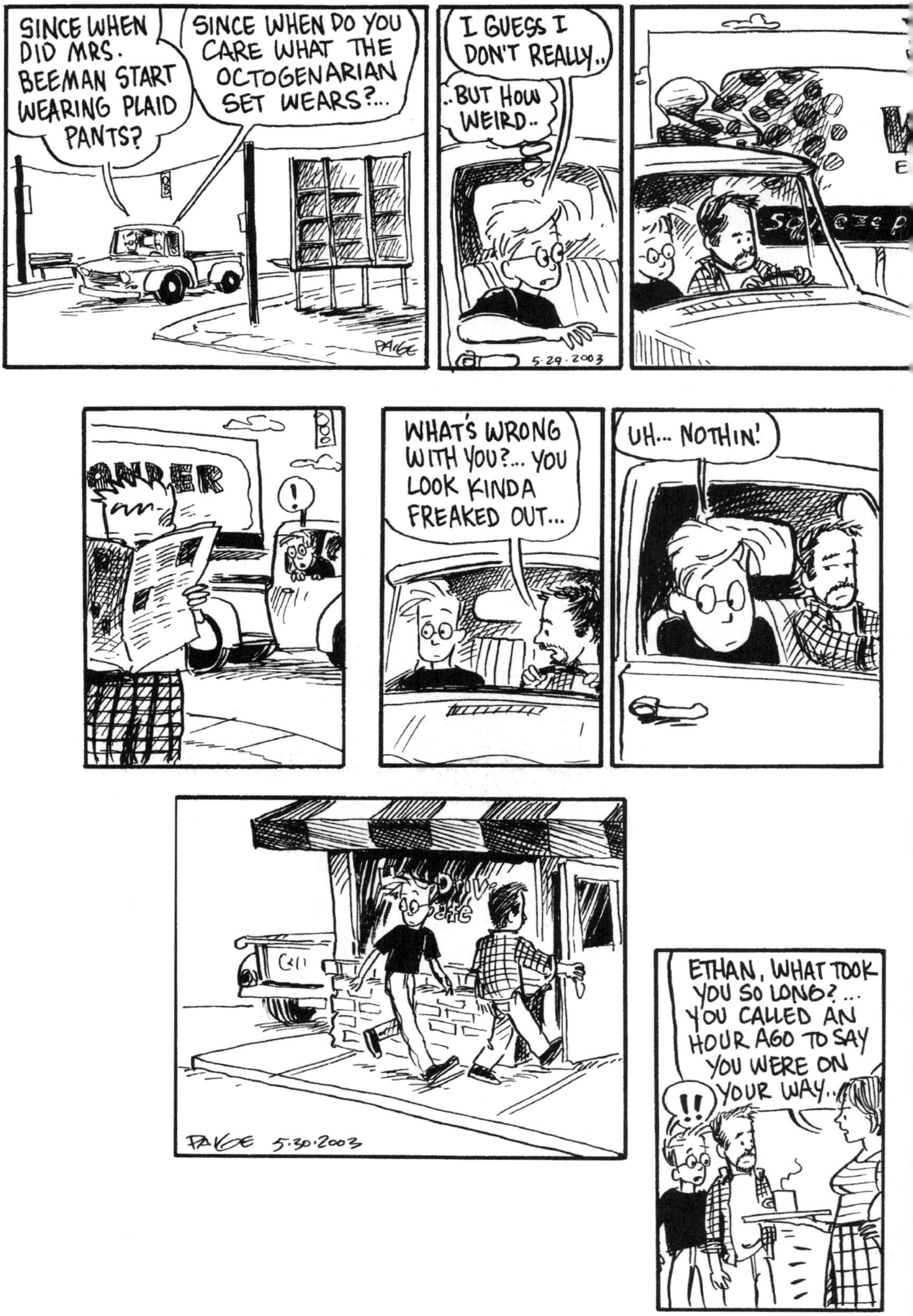
SINCE WHEN DID MRS. BEEMAN START WEARING PLAID PANTS?
SINCE WHEN DO YOU CARE WHAT THE OCTOGENARIAN SET WEARS?...
I GUESS I DON'T REALLY..
..BUT HOW WEIRD..
WHAT'S WRONG WITH YOU?... YOU LOOK KINDA FREAKED OUT...
UH... NOTHIN'!
ETHAN, WHAT TOOK YOU SO LONG?... YOU CALLED AN HOUR AGO TO SAY YOU WERE ON YOUR WAY..

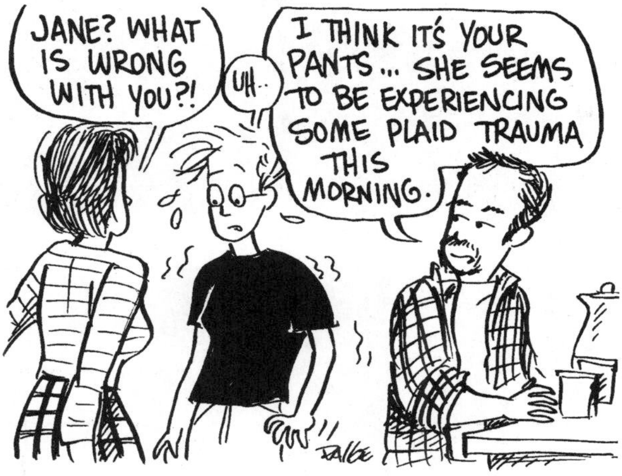
JANE? WHAT IS WRONG WITH YOU?!
UH..
I THINK IT'S YOUR PANTS... SHE SEEMS TO BE EXPERIENCING SOME PLAID TRAUMA THIS MORNING.

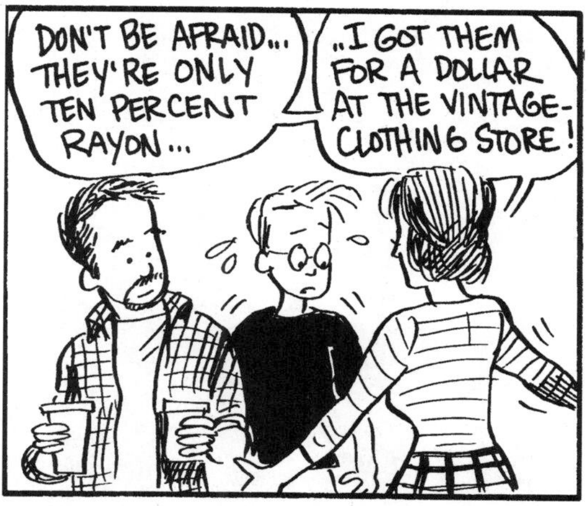
DON'T BE AFRAID... THEY'RE ONLY TEN PERCENT RAYON...
..I GOT THEM FOR A DOLLAR AT THE VINTAGE-CLOTHING STORE!

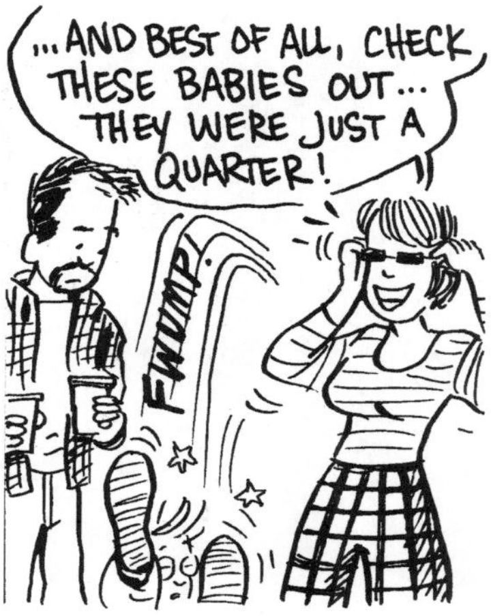
...AND BEST OF ALL, CHECK THESE BABIES OUT... THEY WERE JUST A QUARTER!
FWUMP!

Chapter 2

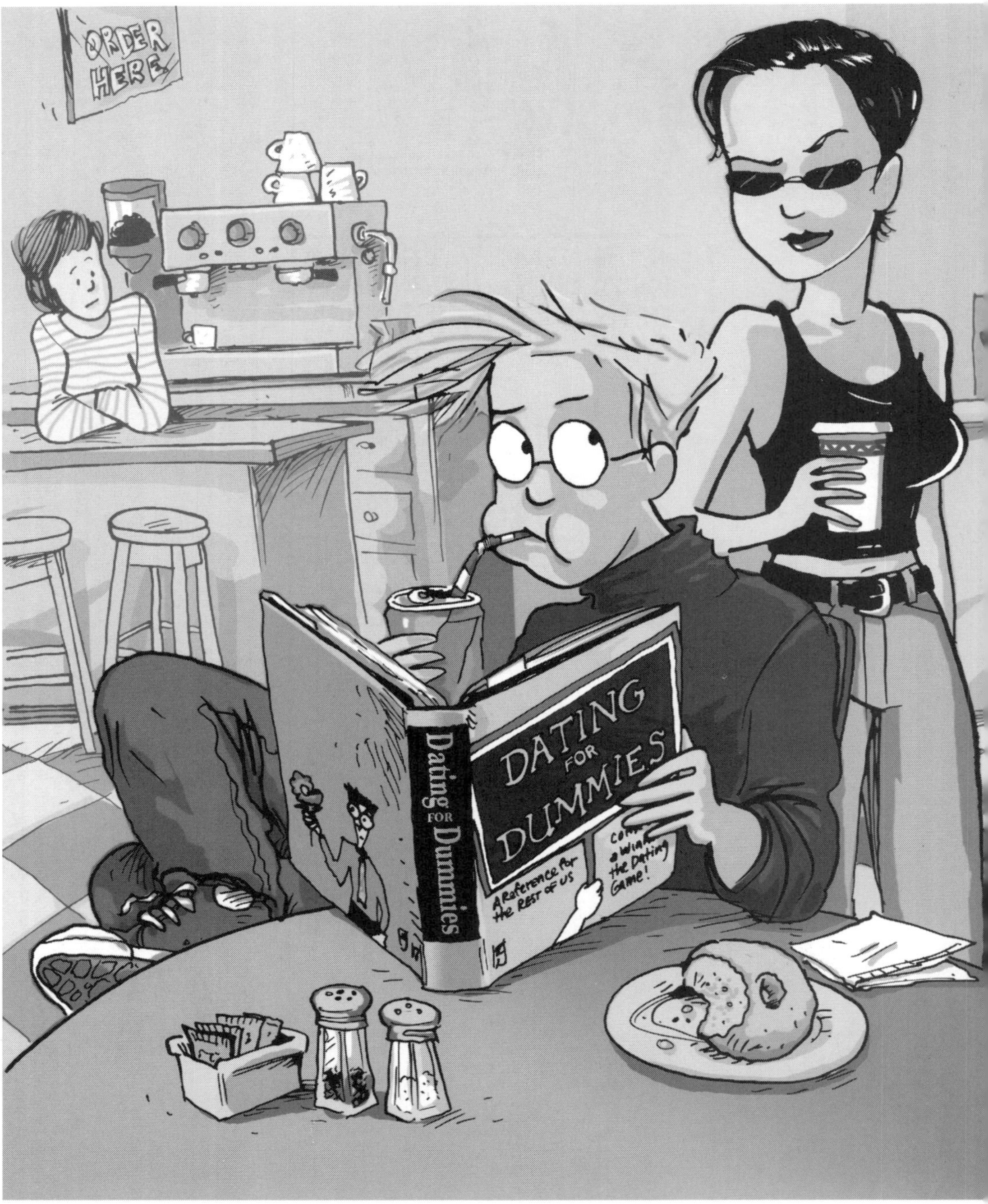

ORDER HERE
DATING FOR DUMMIES
Dating FOR Dummies
A Reference for the Rest of Us
the Dating Game!

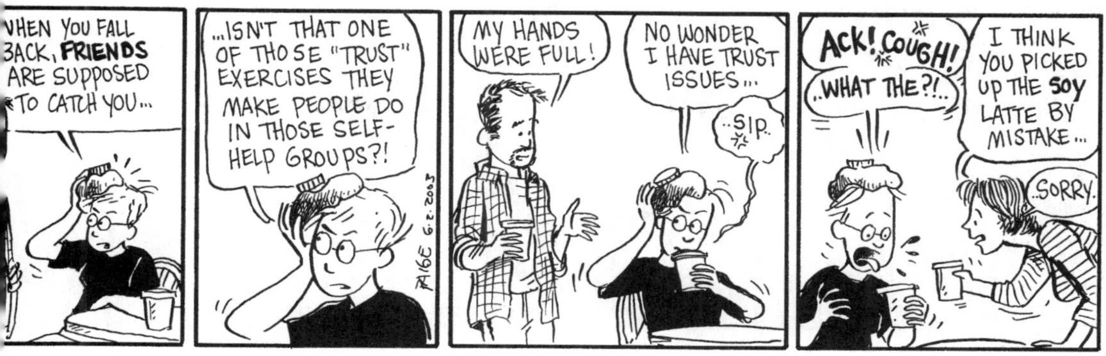
WHEN YOU FALL BACK, FRIENDS ARE SUPPOSED TO CATCH YOU...
...ISN'T THAT ONE OF THOSE "TRUST" EXERCISES THEY MAKE PEOPLE DO IN THOSE SELF-HELP GROUPS?!
PAIGE 6.2.2003
MY HANDS WERE FULL!
NO WONDER I HAVE TRUST ISSUES...
..SIP.
ACK! COUGH!
..WHAT THE?!..
I THINK YOU PICKED UP THE SOY LATTE BY MISTAKE...
..SORRY.

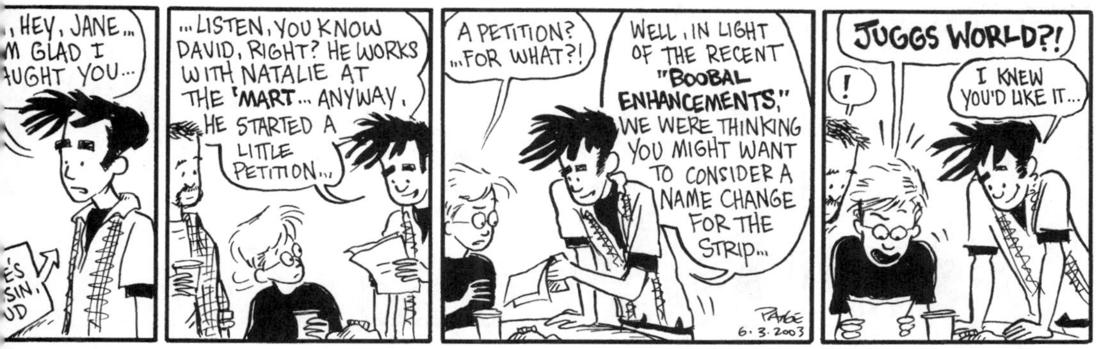
..HEY, JANE... I'M GLAD I CAUGHT YOU...
...LISTEN, YOU KNOW DAVID, RIGHT? HE WORKS WITH NATALIE AT THE 'MART... ANYWAY, HE STARTED A LITTLE PETITION...
A PETITION? ...FOR WHAT?!
WELL, IN LIGHT OF THE RECENT "BOOBAL ENHANCEMENTS," WE WERE THINKING YOU MIGHT WANT TO CONSIDER A NAME CHANGE FOR THE STRIP...
PAIGE 6.3.2003
JUGGS WORLD?!
!
I KNEW YOU'D LIKE IT...

*Note to readers: You aren't losing it, this one strip is a repeat... sorry. It was originally printed out of order for effect.

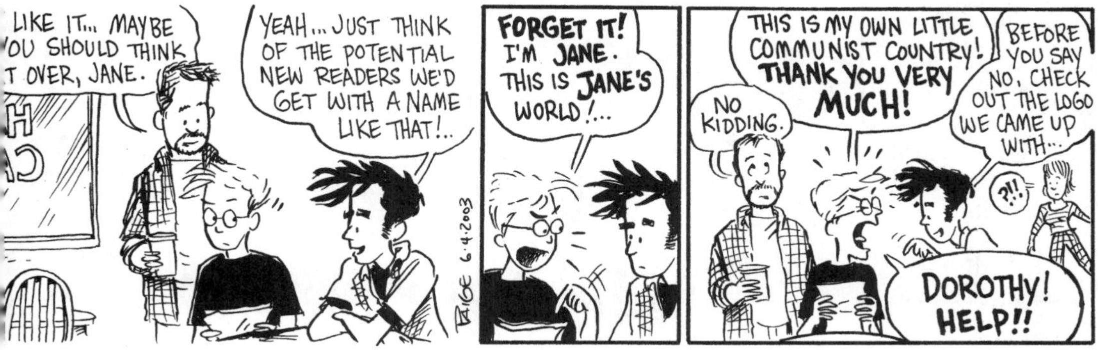
..LIKE IT... MAYBE YOU SHOULD THINK IT OVER, JANE.
YEAH... JUST THINK OF THE POTENTIAL NEW READERS WE'D GET WITH A NAME LIKE THAT!..
PAIGE 6.4.2003
FORGET IT! I'M JANE. THIS IS JANE'S WORLD!...
THIS IS MY OWN LITTLE COMMUNIST COUNTRY! THANK YOU VERY MUCH!
NO KIDDING.
BEFORE YOU SAY NO, CHECK OUT THE LOGO WE CAME UP WITH...
?!!
DOROTHY! HELP!!

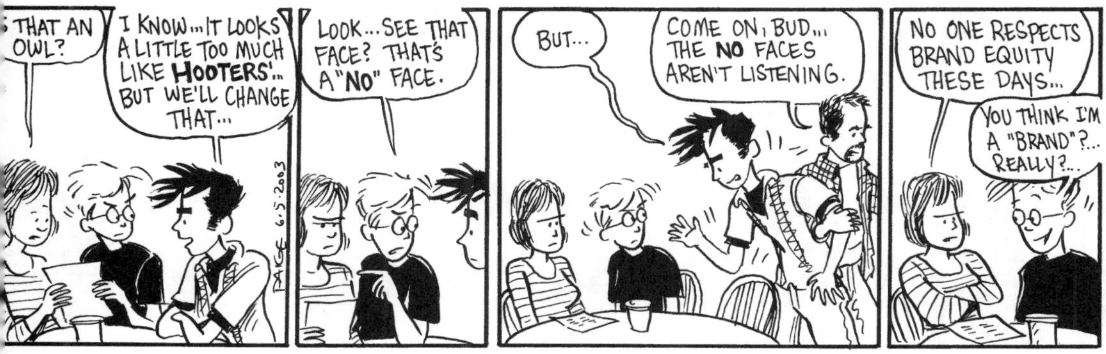
..IS THAT AN OWL?
I KNOW... IT LOOKS A LITTLE TOO MUCH LIKE HOOTERS'... BUT WE'LL CHANGE THAT...
PAIGE 6.5.2003
LOOK... SEE THAT FACE? THAT'S A "NO" FACE.
BUT...
COME ON, BUD... THE NO FACES AREN'T LISTENING.
NO ONE RESPECTS BRAND EQUITY THESE DAYS...
YOU THINK I'M A "BRAND"?... REALLY?...

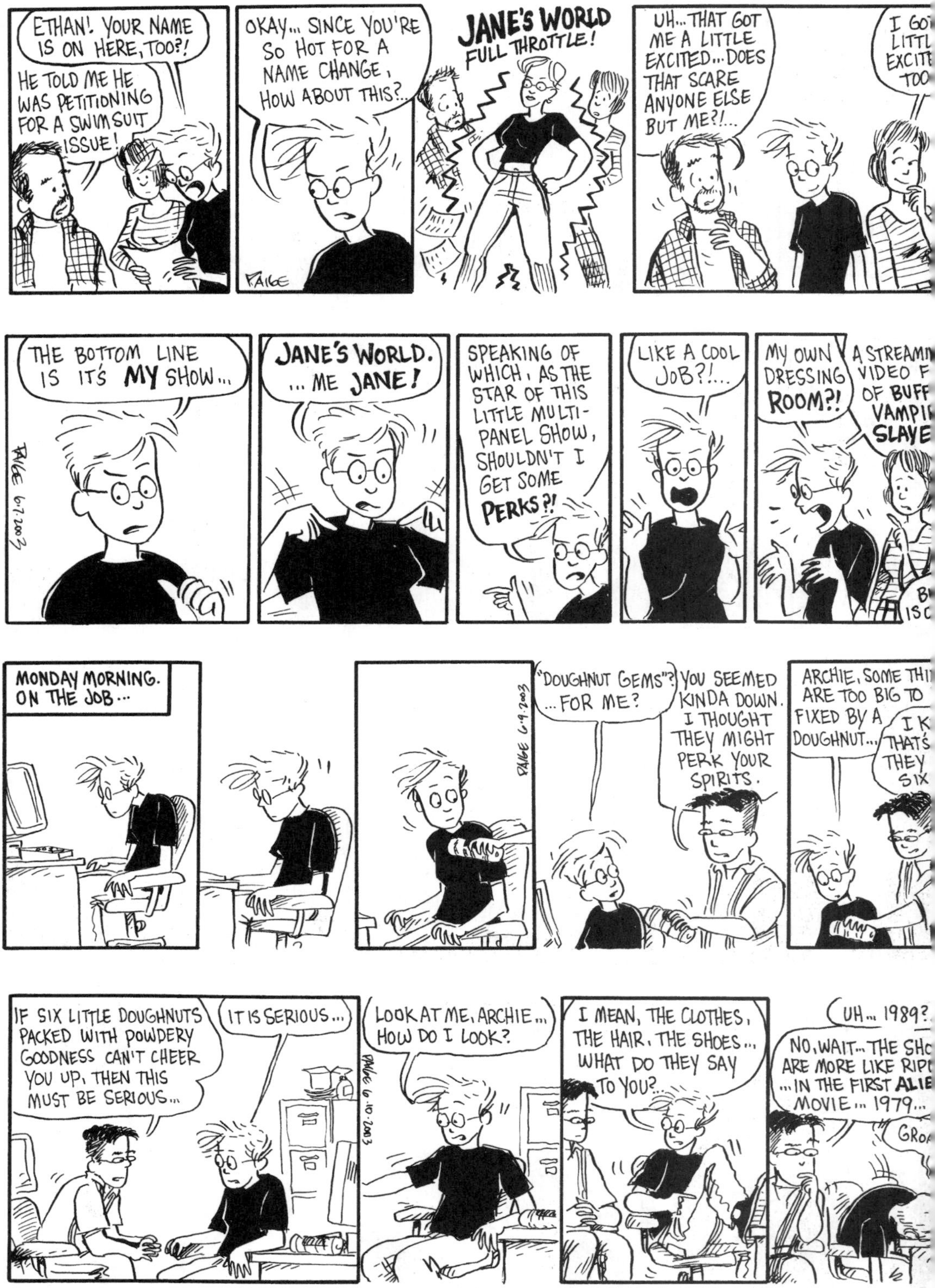

ETHAN! YOUR NAME IS ON HERE, TOO?!
HE TOLD ME HE WAS PETITIONING FOR A SWIMSUIT ISSUE!
OKAY... SINCE YOU'RE SO HOT FOR A NAME CHANGE, HOW ABOUT THIS?..
PAIGE
JANE'S WORLD FULL THROTTLE!
UH... THAT GOT ME A LITTLE EXCITED... DOES THAT SCARE ANYONE ELSE BUT ME?!..
I GOT LITTL EXCITE TOO
THE BOTTOM LINE IS IT'S MY SHOW...
PAIGE 6·7·2003
JANE'S WORLD. ... ME JANE!
SPEAKING OF WHICH, AS THE STAR OF THIS LITTLE MULTI-PANEL SHOW, SHOULDN'T I GET SOME PERKS?!
LIKE A COOL JOB?!...
MY OWN DRESSING ROOM?!
A STREAMI VIDEO F OF BUFF VAMPI SLAYE
MONDAY MORNING. ON THE JOB...
PAIGE 6·9·2003
"DOUGHNUT GEMS"?! ... FOR ME?
YOU SEEMED KINDA DOWN. I THOUGHT THEY MIGHT PERK YOUR SPIRITS.
ARCHIE, SOME THI ARE TOO BIG TO FIXED BY A DOUGHNUT...
I K THAT'S THEY SIX
IF SIX LITTLE DOUGHNUTS PACKED WITH POWDERY GOODNESS CAN'T CHEER YOU UP, THEN THIS MUST BE SERIOUS...
IT IS SERIOUS...
LOOK AT ME, ARCHIE... HOW DO I LOOK?
PAIGE 6·10·2003
I MEAN, THE CLOTHES, THE HAIR, THE SHOES... WHAT DO THEY SAY TO YOU?..
UH... 1989?
NO, WAIT... THE SH ARE MORE LIKE RIP ...IN THE FIRST ALIE MOVIE... 1979...
GRO

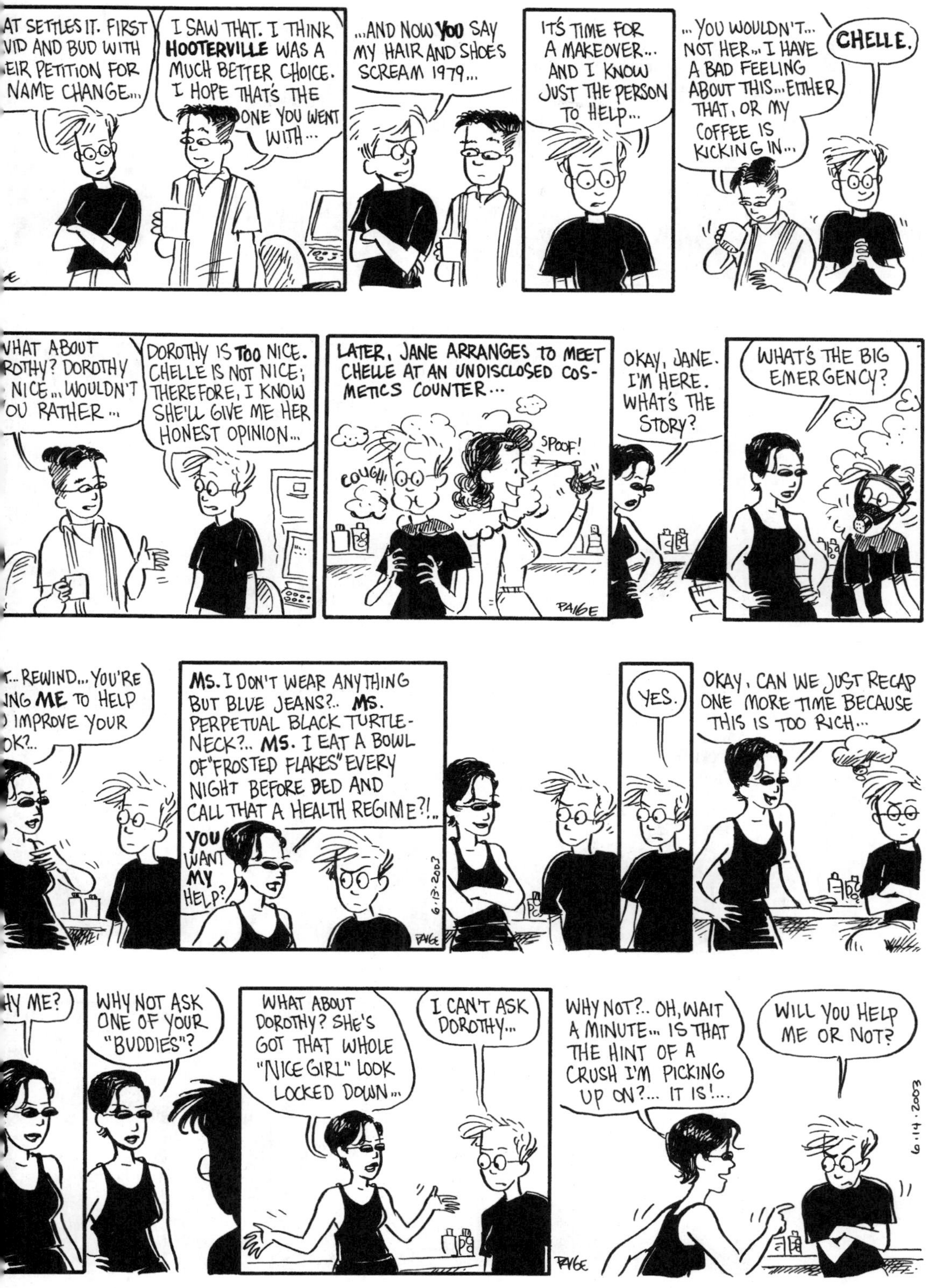
AT SETTLES IT. FIRST VID AND BUD WITH EIR PETITION FOR NAME CHANGE...
I SAW THAT. I THINK HOOTERVILLE WAS A MUCH BETTER CHOICE. I HOPE THAT'S THE ONE YOU WENT WITH...
...AND NOW YOU SAY MY HAIR AND SHOES SCREAM 1979...
IT'S TIME FOR A MAKEOVER... AND I KNOW JUST THE PERSON TO HELP...
...YOU WOULDN'T... NOT HER... I HAVE A BAD FEELING ABOUT THIS... EITHER THAT, OR MY COFFEE IS KICKING IN...
CHELLE.
VHAT ABOUT ROTHY? DOROTHY NICE... WOULDN'T OU RATHER...
DOROTHY IS TOO NICE. CHELLE IS NOT NICE; THEREFORE, I KNOW SHE'LL GIVE ME HER HONEST OPINION...
LATER, JANE ARRANGES TO MEET CHELLE AT AN UNDISCLOSED COSMETICS COUNTER...
COUGH!
SPOOF!
PAIGE
OKAY, JANE. I'M HERE. WHAT'S THE STORY?
WHAT'S THE BIG EMERGENCY?
T... REWIND... YOU'RE NG ME TO HELP IMPROVE YOUR OK?..
MS. I DON'T WEAR ANYTHING BUT BLUE JEANS?.. MS. PERPETUAL BLACK TURTLE-NECK?.. MS. I EAT A BOWL OF "FROSTED FLAKES" EVERY NIGHT BEFORE BED AND CALL THAT A HEALTH REGIME?!..
YOU WANT MY HELP?
6·13·2003
PAIGE
YES.
OKAY, CAN WE JUST RECAP ONE MORE TIME BECAUSE THIS IS TOO RICH...
HY ME?
WHY NOT ASK ONE OF YOUR "BUDDIES"?
WHAT ABOUT DOROTHY? SHE'S GOT THAT WHOLE "NICE GIRL" LOOK LOCKED DOWN...
I CAN'T ASK DOROTHY...
PAIGE
WHY NOT?.. OH, WAIT A MINUTE... IS THAT THE HINT OF A CRUSH I'M PICKING UP ON?... IT IS!...
WILL YOU HELP ME OR NOT?
6·14·2003

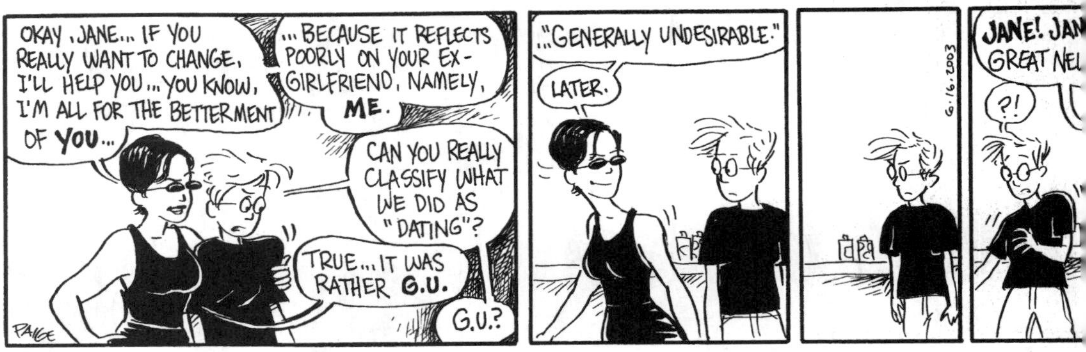
OKAY, JANE... IF YOU REALLY WANT TO CHANGE, I'LL HELP YOU... YOU KNOW, I'M ALL FOR THE BETTERMENT OF **YOU**...
... BECAUSE IT REFLECTS POORLY ON YOUR EX-GIRLFRIEND, NAMELY, **ME**.
CAN YOU REALLY CLASSIFY WHAT WE DID AS "DATING"?
TRUE... IT WAS RATHER **G.U.**
G.U.?
PAIGE
..."GENERALLY UNDESIRABLE."
LATER.
6·16·2003
JANE! JAN
GREAT NE
?!

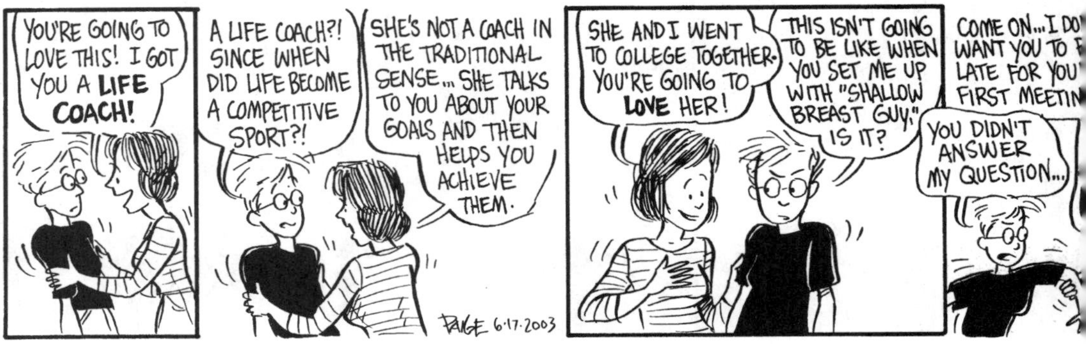
YOU'RE GOING TO LOVE THIS! I GOT YOU A **LIFE COACH!**
A LIFE COACH?! SINCE WHEN DID LIFE BECOME A COMPETITIVE SPORT?!
SHE'S NOT A COACH IN THE TRADITIONAL SENSE... SHE TALKS TO YOU ABOUT YOUR GOALS AND THEN HELPS YOU ACHIEVE THEM.
PAIGE 6·17·2003
SHE AND I WENT TO COLLEGE TOGETHER. YOU'RE GOING TO **LOVE** HER!
THIS ISN'T GOING TO BE LIKE WHEN YOU SET ME UP WITH "SHALLOW BREAST GUY," IS IT?
COME ON... I DO WANT YOU TO LATE FOR YOU FIRST MEETIN
YOU DIDN'T ANSWER MY QUESTION...

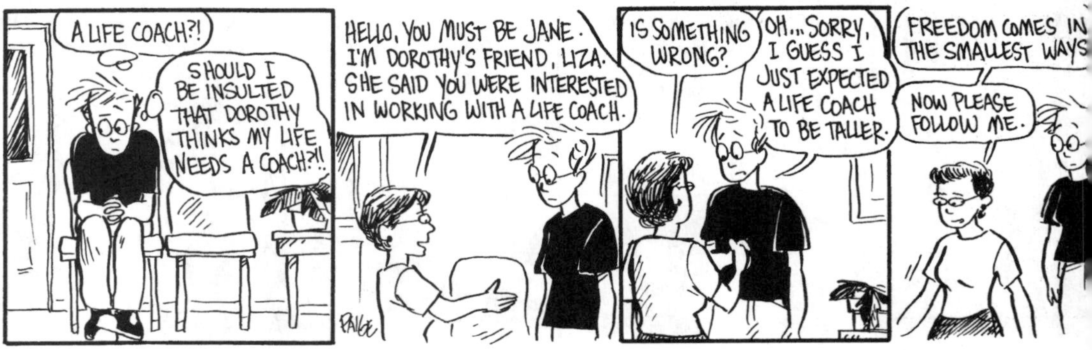
A LIFE COACH?!
SHOULD I BE INSULTED THAT DOROTHY THINKS MY LIFE NEEDS A COACH?!
HELLO, YOU MUST BE JANE. I'M DOROTHY'S FRIEND, LIZA. SHE SAID YOU WERE INTERESTED IN WORKING WITH A LIFE COACH.
PAIGE
IS SOMETHING WRONG?
OH... SORRY, I GUESS I JUST EXPECTED A LIFE COACH TO BE TALLER.
FREEDOM COMES IN THE SMALLEST WAYS
NOW PLEASE FOLLOW ME.

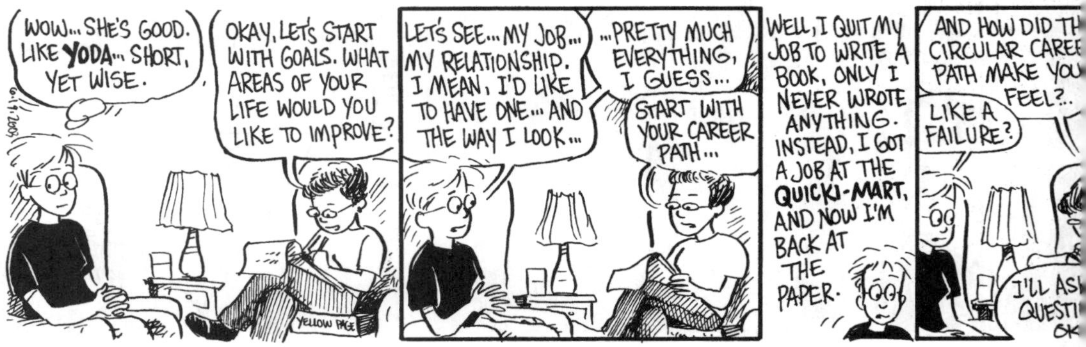
WOW... SHE'S GOOD. LIKE **YODA**... SHORT, YET WISE.
6·19·2003
OKAY, LET'S START WITH GOALS. WHAT AREAS OF YOUR LIFE WOULD YOU LIKE TO IMPROVE?
YELLOW PAGE
LET'S SEE... MY JOB... MY RELATIONSHIP. I MEAN, I'D LIKE TO HAVE ONE... AND THE WAY I LOOK...
...PRETTY MUCH EVERYTHING, I GUESS...
START WITH YOUR CAREER PATH...
WELL, I QUIT MY JOB TO WRITE A BOOK, ONLY I NEVER WROTE ANYTHING. INSTEAD, I GOT A JOB AT THE **QUICKI-MART**, AND NOW I'M BACK AT THE PAPER.
AND HOW DID TH CIRCULAR CARE PATH MAKE YOU FEEL?...
LIKE A FAILURE?
I'LL AS QUESTI OK

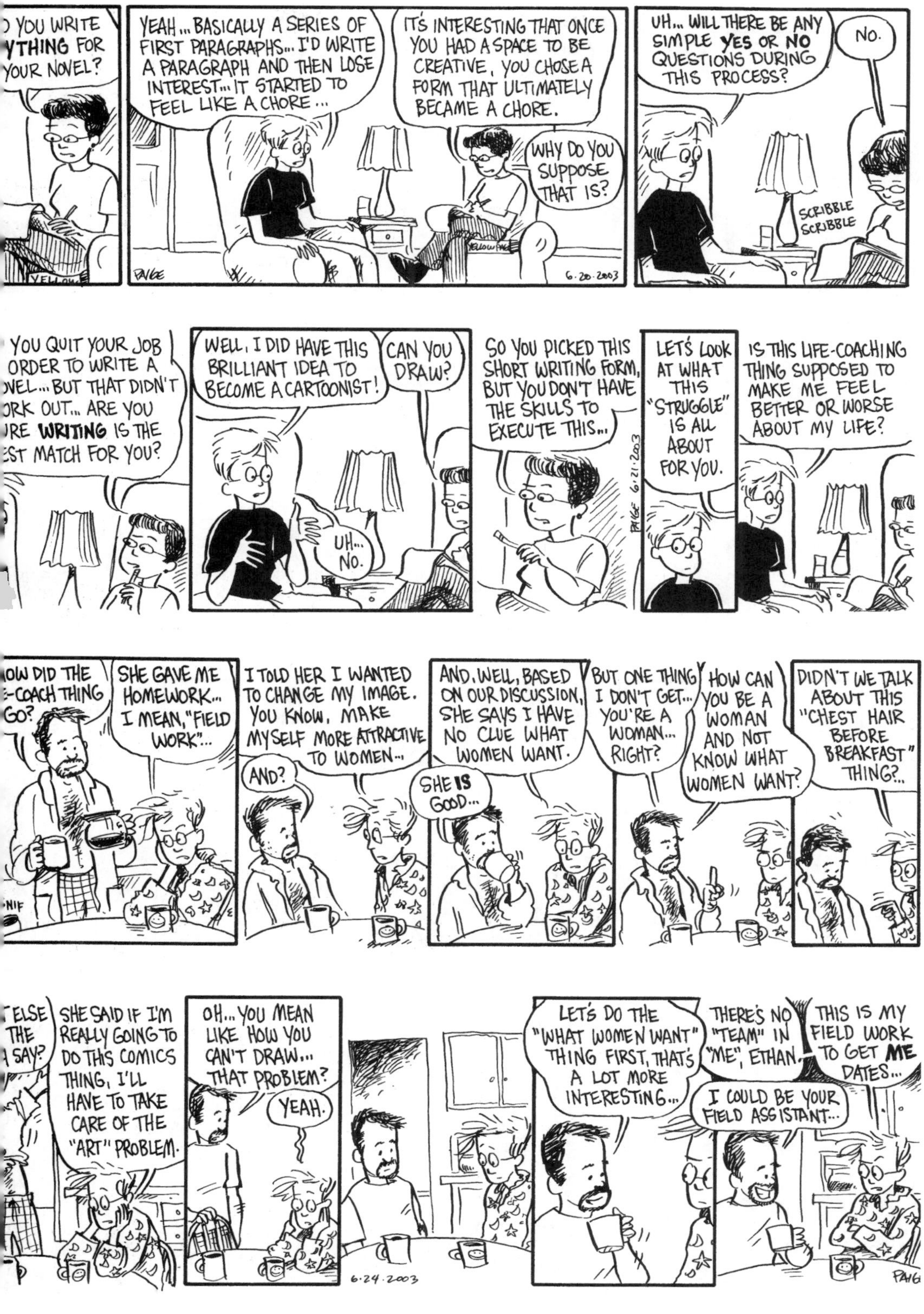

O YOU WRITE YTHING FOR YOUR NOVEL?
YEAH... BASICALLY A SERIES OF FIRST PARAGRAPHS... I'D WRITE A PARAGRAPH AND THEN LOSE INTEREST... IT STARTED TO FEEL LIKE A CHORE...
IT'S INTERESTING THAT ONCE YOU HAD A SPACE TO BE CREATIVE, YOU CHOSE A FORM THAT ULTIMATELY BECAME A CHORE.
WHY DO YOU SUPPOSE THAT IS?
UH... WILL THERE BE ANY SIMPLE **YES** OR **NO** QUESTIONS DURING THIS PROCESS?
NO.
SCRIBBLE SCRIBBLE
PAIGE
6·20·2003
YOU QUIT YOUR JOB ORDER TO WRITE A VEL... BUT THAT DIDN'T ORK OUT... ARE YOU RE **WRITING** IS THE ST MATCH FOR YOU?
WELL, I DID HAVE THIS BRILLIANT IDEA TO BECOME A CARTOONIST!
CAN YOU DRAW?
UH... NO.
SO YOU PICKED THIS SHORT WRITING FORM, BUT YOU DON'T HAVE THE SKILLS TO EXECUTE THIS...
PAIGE 6·21·2003
LET'S LOOK AT WHAT THIS "STRUGGLE" IS ALL ABOUT FOR YOU.
IS THIS LIFE-COACHING THING SUPPOSED TO MAKE ME FEEL BETTER OR WORSE ABOUT MY LIFE?
OW DID THE -COACH THING GO?
SHE GAVE ME HOMEWORK... I MEAN, "FIELD WORK"...
I TOLD HER I WANTED TO CHANGE MY IMAGE. YOU KNOW, MAKE MYSELF MORE ATTRACTIVE TO WOMEN...
AND?
AND, WELL, BASED ON OUR DISCUSSION, SHE SAYS I HAVE NO CLUE WHAT WOMEN WANT.
SHE **IS** GOOD...
BUT ONE THING I DON'T GET... YOU'RE A WOMAN... RIGHT?
HOW CAN YOU BE A WOMAN AND NOT KNOW WHAT WOMEN WANT?
DIDN'T WE TALK ABOUT THIS "CHEST HAIR BEFORE BREAKFAST" THING?...
ELSE THE SAY?
SHE SAID IF I'M REALLY GOING TO DO THIS COMICS THING, I'LL HAVE TO TAKE CARE OF THE "ART" PROBLEM.
OH... YOU MEAN LIKE HOW YOU CAN'T DRAW... THAT PROBLEM?
YEAH.
6·24·2003
LET'S DO THE "WHAT WOMEN WANT" THING FIRST, THAT'S A LOT MORE INTERESTING...
THERE'S NO "TEAM" IN "ME", ETHAN.
THIS IS MY FIELD WORK TO GET **ME** DATES...
I COULD BE YOUR FIELD ASSISTANT...

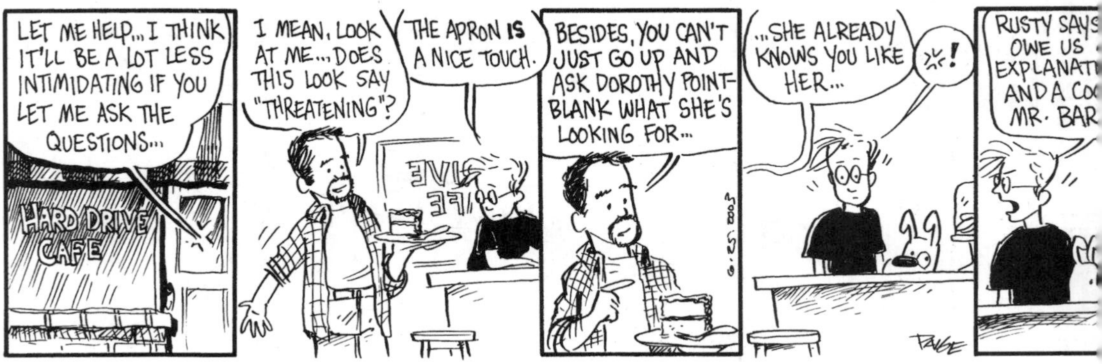

LET ME HELP... I THINK IT'LL BE A LOT LESS INTIMIDATING IF YOU LET ME ASK THE QUESTIONS...
HARD DRIVE CAFE
I MEAN, LOOK AT ME... DOES THIS LOOK SAY "THREATENING"?
THE APRON IS A NICE TOUCH.
BESIDES, YOU CAN'T JUST GO UP AND ASK DOROTHY POINT-BLANK WHAT SHE'S LOOKING FOR...
6·25·2003
...SHE ALREADY KNOWS YOU LIKE HER...
!
PAIGE
RUSTY SAYS OWE US EXPLANAT AND A CO MR. BAR

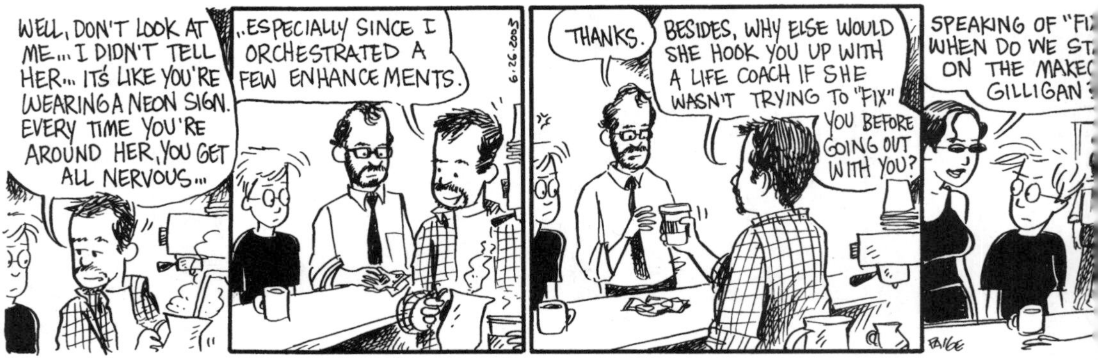

WELL, DON'T LOOK AT ME... I DIDN'T TELL HER... IT'S LIKE YOU'RE WEARING A NEON SIGN. EVERY TIME YOU'RE AROUND HER, YOU GET ALL NERVOUS...
...ESPECIALLY SINCE I ORCHESTRATED A FEW ENHANCEMENTS.
6·26·2003
THANKS.
BESIDES, WHY ELSE WOULD SHE HOOK YOU UP WITH A LIFE COACH IF SHE WASN'T TRYING TO "FIX" YOU BEFORE GOING OUT WITH YOU?
SPEAKING OF "FI WHEN DO WE ST ON THE MAKE GILLIGAN
PAIGE

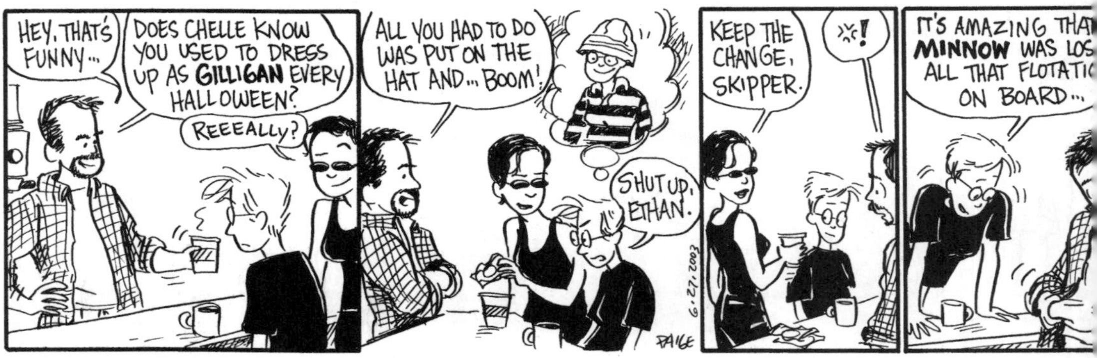

HEY, THAT'S FUNNY...
DOES CHELLE KNOW YOU USED TO DRESS UP AS GILLIGAN EVERY HALLOWEEN?
REEEALLY?
ALL YOU HAD TO DO WAS PUT ON THE HAT AND... BOOM!
SHUT UP, ETHAN.
6·27·2003
PAIGE
KEEP THE CHANGE, SKIPPER.
!
IT'S AMAZING THA MINNOW WAS LOS ALL THAT FLOTATI ON BOARD...

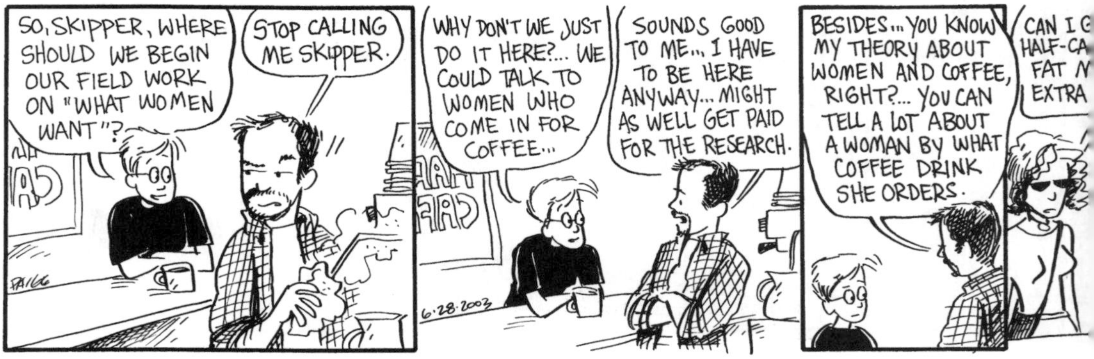

SO, SKIPPER, WHERE SHOULD WE BEGIN OUR FIELD WORK ON "WHAT WOMEN WANT"?
STOP CALLING ME SKIPPER.
PAIGE
WHY DON'T WE JUST DO IT HERE?... WE COULD TALK TO WOMEN WHO COME IN FOR COFFEE...
6·28·2003
SOUNDS GOOD TO ME... I HAVE TO BE HERE ANYWAY... MIGHT AS WELL GET PAID FOR THE RESEARCH.
BESIDES... YOU KNOW MY THEORY ABOUT WOMEN AND COFFEE, RIGHT?... YOU CAN TELL A LOT ABOUT A WOMAN BY WHAT COFFEE DRINK SHE ORDERS.
CAN I G HALF-CA FAT N EXTRA

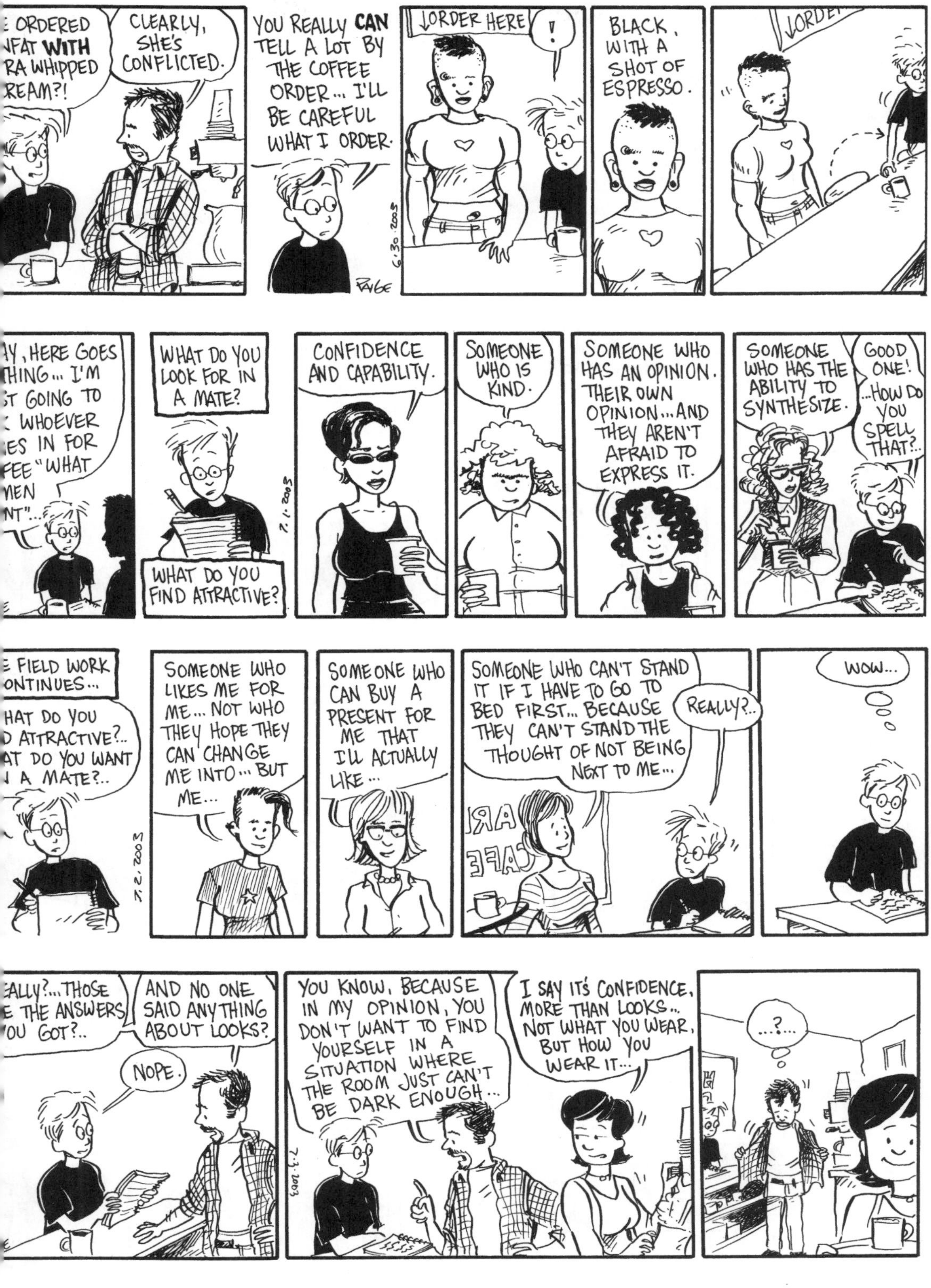

E ORDERED
NFAT WITH
RA WHIPPED
REAM?!
CLEARLY, SHE'S CONFLICTED.
YOU REALLY CAN TELL A LOT BY THE COFFEE ORDER... I'LL BE CAREFUL WHAT I ORDER.
6.30.2003
PAIGE
ORDER HERE
!
BLACK, WITH A SHOT OF ESPRESSO.
ORDER
AY, HERE GOES
THING... I'M
ST GOING TO
WHOEVER
ES IN FOR
FEE "WHAT
MEN
NT"...
WHAT DO YOU LOOK FOR IN A MATE?
WHAT DO YOU FIND ATTRACTIVE?
7.1.2003
CONFIDENCE AND CAPABILITY.
SOMEONE WHO IS KIND.
SOMEONE WHO HAS AN OPINION. THEIR OWN OPINION... AND THEY AREN'T AFRAID TO EXPRESS IT.
SOMEONE WHO HAS THE ABILITY TO SYNTHESIZE.
GOOD ONE! ...HOW DO YOU SPELL THAT?..
E FIELD WORK
ONTINUES...
HAT DO YOU
D ATTRACTIVE?..
AT DO YOU WANT
N A MATE?..
7.2.2003
SOMEONE WHO LIKES ME FOR ME... NOT WHO THEY HOPE THEY CAN CHANGE ME INTO... BUT ME...
SOMEONE WHO CAN BUY A PRESENT FOR ME THAT I'LL ACTUALLY LIKE...
SOMEONE WHO CAN'T STAND IT IF I HAVE TO GO TO BED FIRST... BECAUSE THEY CAN'T STAND THE THOUGHT OF NOT BEING NEXT TO ME...
REALLY?..
WOW...
EALLY?... THOSE
E THE ANSWERS
OU GOT?..
AND NO ONE SAID ANYTHING ABOUT LOOKS?
NOPE.
YOU KNOW, BECAUSE IN MY OPINION, YOU DON'T WANT TO FIND YOURSELF IN A SITUATION WHERE THE ROOM JUST CAN'T BE DARK ENOUGH...
I SAY IT'S CONFIDENCE, MORE THAN LOOKS... NOT WHAT YOU WEAR, BUT HOW YOU WEAR IT...
7.3.2003
...?...

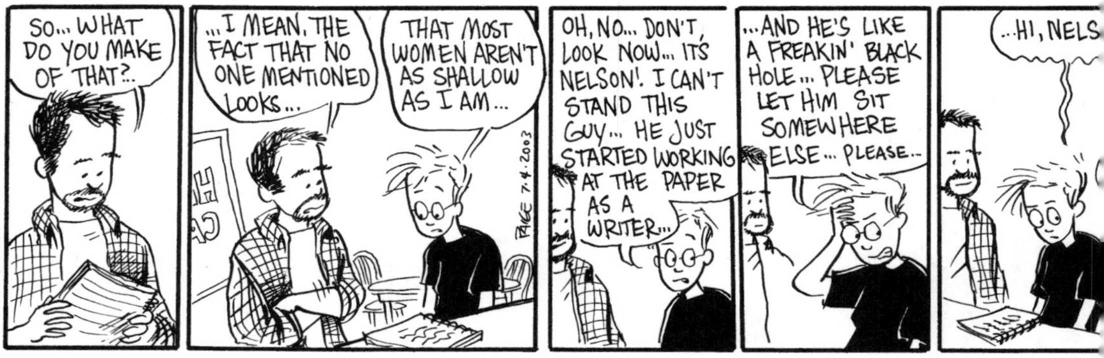
SO... WHAT DO YOU MAKE OF THAT?..
...I MEAN, THE FACT THAT NO ONE MENTIONED LOOKS...
THAT MOST WOMEN AREN'T AS SHALLOW AS I AM...
PAIGE 7.4.2003
OH, NO... DON'T, LOOK NOW... IT'S NELSON! I CAN'T STAND THIS GUY... HE JUST STARTED WORKING AT THE PAPER AS A WRITER...
...AND HE'S LIKE A FREAKIN' BLACK HOLE... PLEASE LET HIM SIT SOMEWHERE ELSE... PLEASE...
...HI, NELS

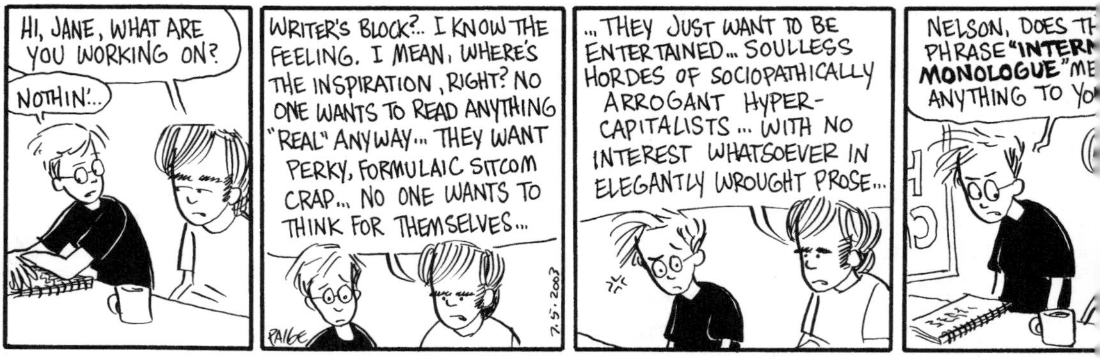
HI, JANE, WHAT ARE YOU WORKING ON?
NOTHIN'...
WRITER'S BLOCK?.. I KNOW THE FEELING. I MEAN, WHERE'S THE INSPIRATION, RIGHT? NO ONE WANTS TO READ ANYTHING "REAL" ANYWAY... THEY WANT PERKY, FORMULAIC SITCOM CRAP... NO ONE WANTS TO THINK FOR THEMSELVES...
PAIGE 7.5.2003
...THEY JUST WANT TO BE ENTERTAINED... SOULLESS HORDES OF SOCIOPATHICALLY ARROGANT HYPER-CAPITALISTS... WITH NO INTEREST WHATSOEVER IN ELEGANTLY WROUGHT PROSE...
NELSON, DOES TH PHRASE "INTERN MONOLOGUE" ME ANYTHING TO YO

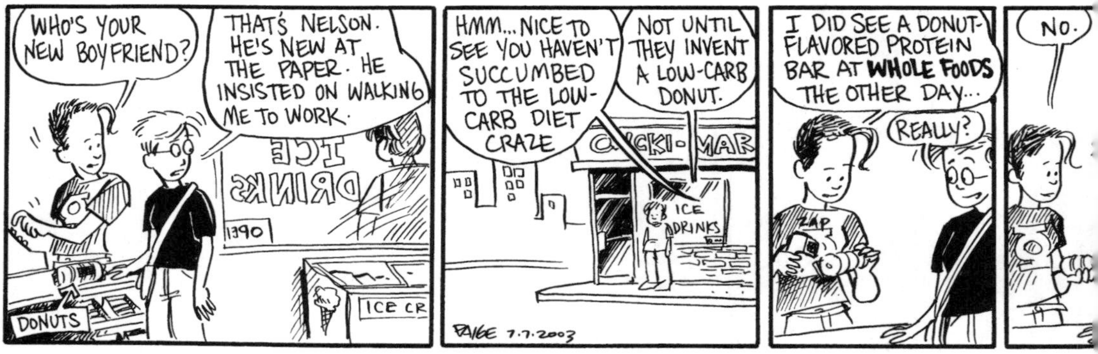
WHO'S YOUR NEW BOYFRIEND?
THAT'S NELSON. HE'S NEW AT THE PAPER. HE INSISTED ON WALKING ME TO WORK.
DONUTS
ICE CR
HMM... NICE TO SEE YOU HAVEN'T SUCCUMBED TO THE LOW-CARB DIET CRAZE
NOT UNTIL THEY INVENT A LOW-CARB DONUT.
ICE DRINKS
PAIGE 7.7.2003
I DID SEE A DONUT-FLAVORED PROTEIN BAR AT **WHOLE FOODS** THE OTHER DAY...
REALLY?
ZAP
NO.

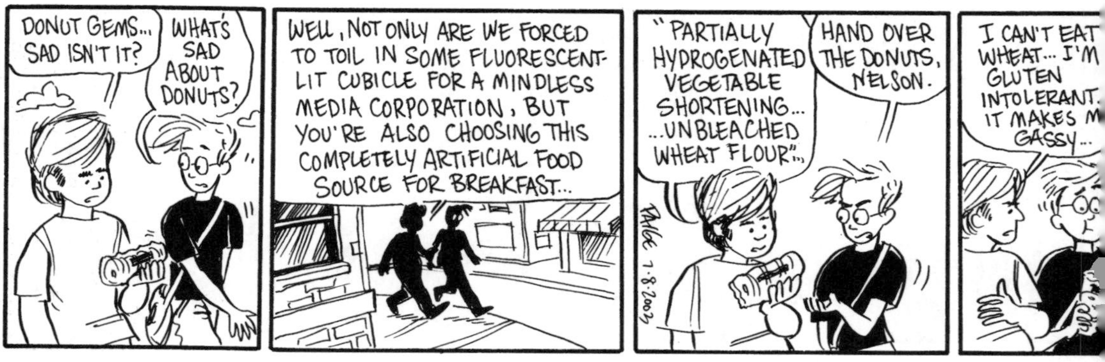
DONUT GEMS... SAD ISN'T IT?
WHAT'S SAD ABOUT DONUTS?
WELL, NOT ONLY ARE WE FORCED TO TOIL IN SOME FLUORESCENT-LIT CUBICLE FOR A MINDLESS MEDIA CORPORATION, BUT YOU'RE ALSO CHOOSING THIS COMPLETELY ARTIFICIAL FOOD SOURCE FOR BREAKFAST...
"PARTIALLY HYDROGENATED VEGETABLE SHORTENING... ...UNBLEACHED WHEAT FLOUR"...
HAND OVER THE DONUTS, NELSON.
PAIGE 7.8.2003
I CAN'T EAT WHEAT... I'M GLUTEN INTOLERANT. IT MAKES M GASSY...

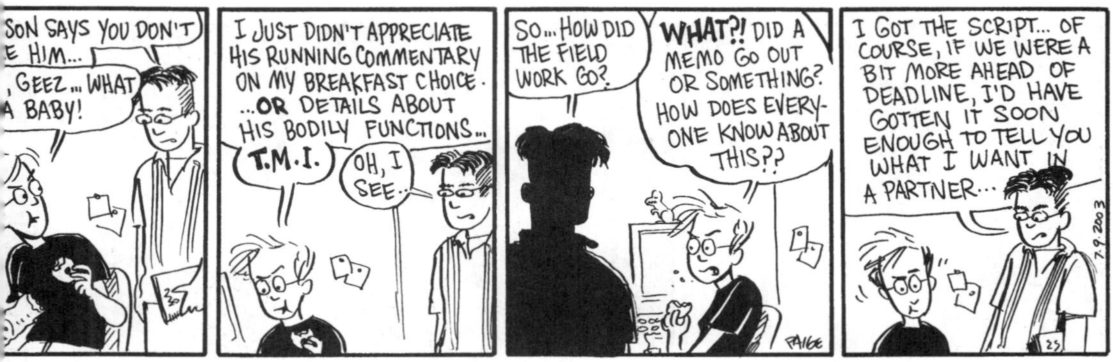
SON SAYS YOU DON'T
E HIM...
, GEEZ... WHAT
A BABY!
I JUST DIDN'T APPRECIATE HIS RUNNING COMMENTARY ON MY BREAKFAST CHOICE. ...OR DETAILS ABOUT HIS BODILY FUNCTIONS...
T.M.I.
OH, I SEE...
SO... HOW DID THE FIELD WORK GO?
WHAT?! DID A MEMO GO OUT OR SOMETHING? HOW DOES EVERYONE KNOW ABOUT THIS??
PAIGE
I GOT THE SCRIPT... OF COURSE, IF WE WERE A BIT MORE AHEAD OF DEADLINE, I'D HAVE GOTTEN IT SOON ENOUGH TO TELL YOU WHAT I WANT IN A PARTNER...
7.9.2003

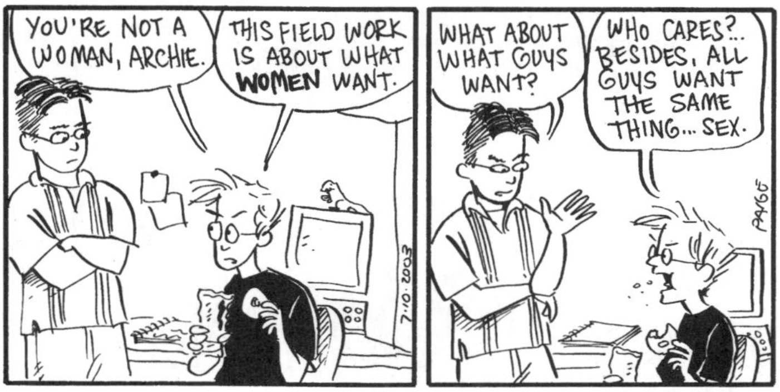
YOU'RE NOT A WOMAN, ARCHIE.
THIS FIELD WORK IS ABOUT WHAT WOMEN WANT.
7.10.2003
WHAT ABOUT WHAT GUYS WANT?
WHO CARES?.. BESIDES, ALL GUYS WANT THE SAME THING... SEX.
PAIGE

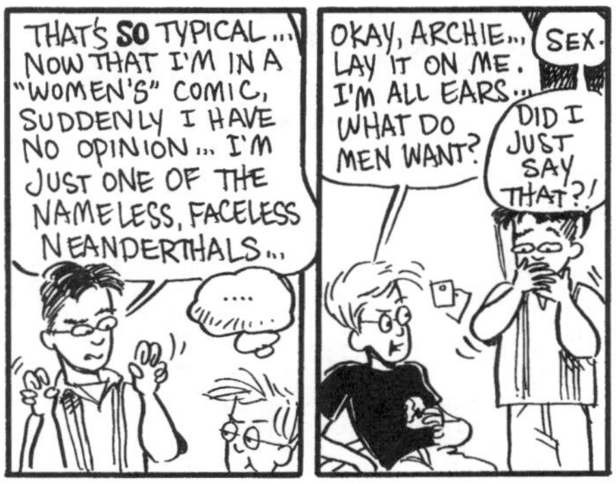
THAT'S SO TYPICAL... NOW THAT I'M IN A "WOMEN'S" COMIC, SUDDENLY I HAVE NO OPINION... I'M JUST ONE OF THE NAMELESS, FACELESS NEANDERTHALS...
....
OKAY, ARCHIE... LAY IT ON ME. I'M ALL EARS... WHAT DO MEN WANT?
SEX.
DID I JUST SAY THAT?!

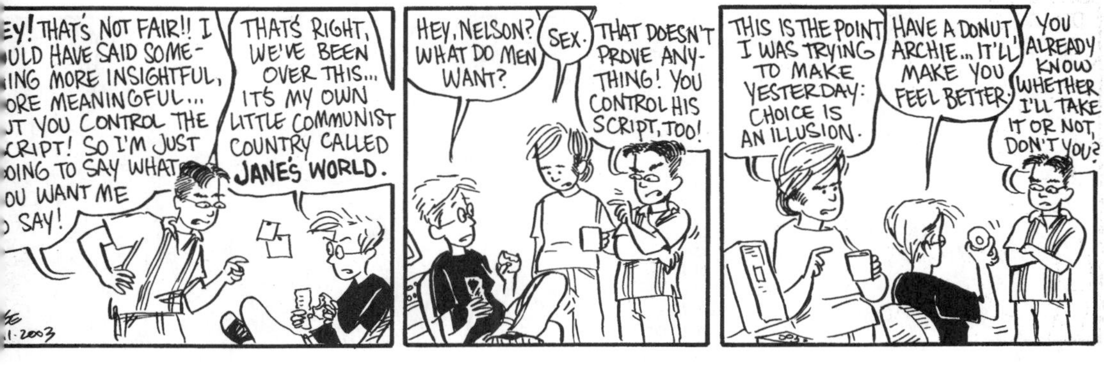
EY! THAT'S NOT FAIR!! I
ULD HAVE SAID SOME-
ING MORE INSIGHTFUL,
ORE MEANINGFUL...
UT YOU CONTROL THE
CRIPT! SO I'M JUST
OING TO SAY WHAT
OU WANT ME
SAY!
THAT'S RIGHT, WE'VE BEEN OVER THIS... IT'S MY OWN LITTLE COMMUNIST COUNTRY CALLED JANE'S WORLD.
HEY, NELSON? WHAT DO MEN WANT?
SEX.
THAT DOESN'T PROVE ANYTHING! YOU CONTROL HIS SCRIPT, TOO!
THIS IS THE POINT I WAS TRYING TO MAKE YESTERDAY: CHOICE IS AN ILLUSION.
HAVE A DONUT, ARCHIE... IT'LL MAKE YOU FEEL BETTER.
YOU ALREADY KNOW WHETHER I'LL TAKE IT OR NOT, DON'T YOU?

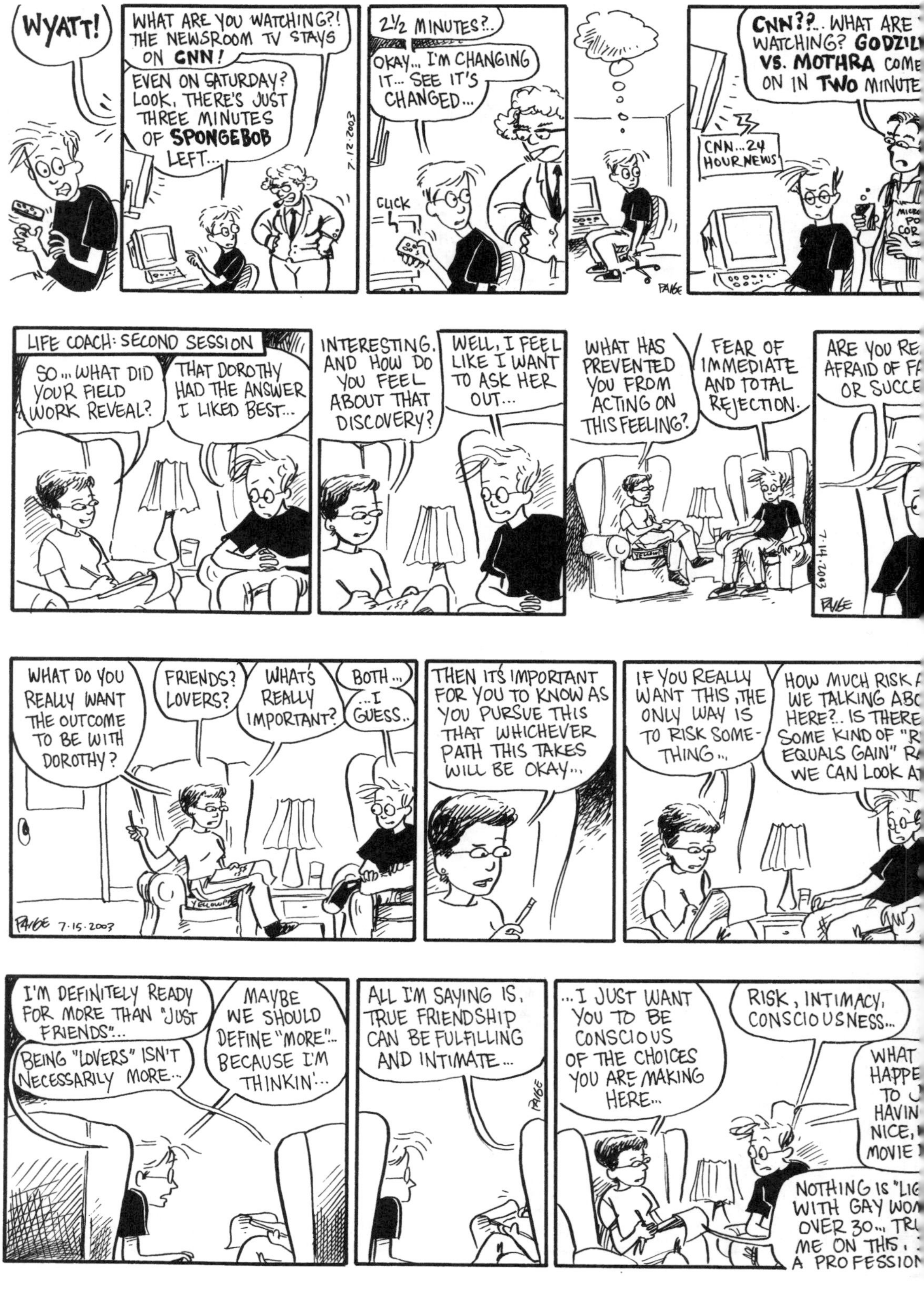
WYATT!
WHAT ARE YOU WATCHING?! THE NEWSROOM TV STAYS ON CNN!
EVEN ON SATURDAY? LOOK, THERE'S JUST THREE MINUTES OF SPONGEBOB LEFT...
7.12.2003
2½ MINUTES?..
OKAY... I'M CHANGING IT... SEE IT'S CHANGED...
CLICK
CNN...24 HOUR NEWS
CNN??.. WHAT ARE
WATCHING? GODZIL
VS. MOTHRA COME
ON IN TWO MINUTE
PAIGE
LIFE COACH: SECOND SESSION
SO... WHAT DID YOUR FIELD WORK REVEAL?
THAT DOROTHY HAD THE ANSWER I LIKED BEST...
INTERESTING. AND HOW DO YOU FEEL ABOUT THAT DISCOVERY?
WELL, I FEEL LIKE I WANT TO ASK HER OUT...
WHAT HAS PREVENTED YOU FROM ACTING ON THIS FEELING?
FEAR OF IMMEDIATE AND TOTAL REJECTION.
7.14.2003
ARE YOU RE
AFRAID OF F
OR SUCCE
PAIGE
WHAT DO YOU REALLY WANT THE OUTCOME TO BE WITH DOROTHY?
FRIENDS? LOVERS?
WHAT'S REALLY IMPORTANT?
BOTH... ...I GUESS..
PAIGE 7.15.2003
THEN IT'S IMPORTANT FOR YOU TO KNOW AS YOU PURSUE THIS THAT WHICHEVER PATH THIS TAKES WILL BE OKAY...
IF YOU REALLY WANT THIS, THE ONLY WAY IS TO RISK SOMETHING...
HOW MUCH RISK A
WE TALKING ABO
HERE?.. IS THERE
SOME KIND OF "R
EQUALS GAIN" R
WE CAN LOOK A
I'M DEFINITELY READY FOR MORE THAN "JUST FRIENDS"...
BEING "LOVERS" ISN'T NECESSARILY MORE...
MAYBE WE SHOULD DEFINE "MORE"... BECAUSE I'M THINKIN'...
ALL I'M SAYING IS, TRUE FRIENDSHIP CAN BE FULFILLING AND INTIMATE...
PAIGE
...I JUST WANT YOU TO BE CONSCIOUS OF THE CHOICES YOU ARE MAKING HERE...
RISK, INTIMACY, CONSCIOUSNESS...
WHAT
HAPPE
TO
HAVIN
NICE,
MOVIE
NOTHING IS "LIG
WITH GAY WOM
OVER 30... TRU
ME ON THIS.
A PROFESSION

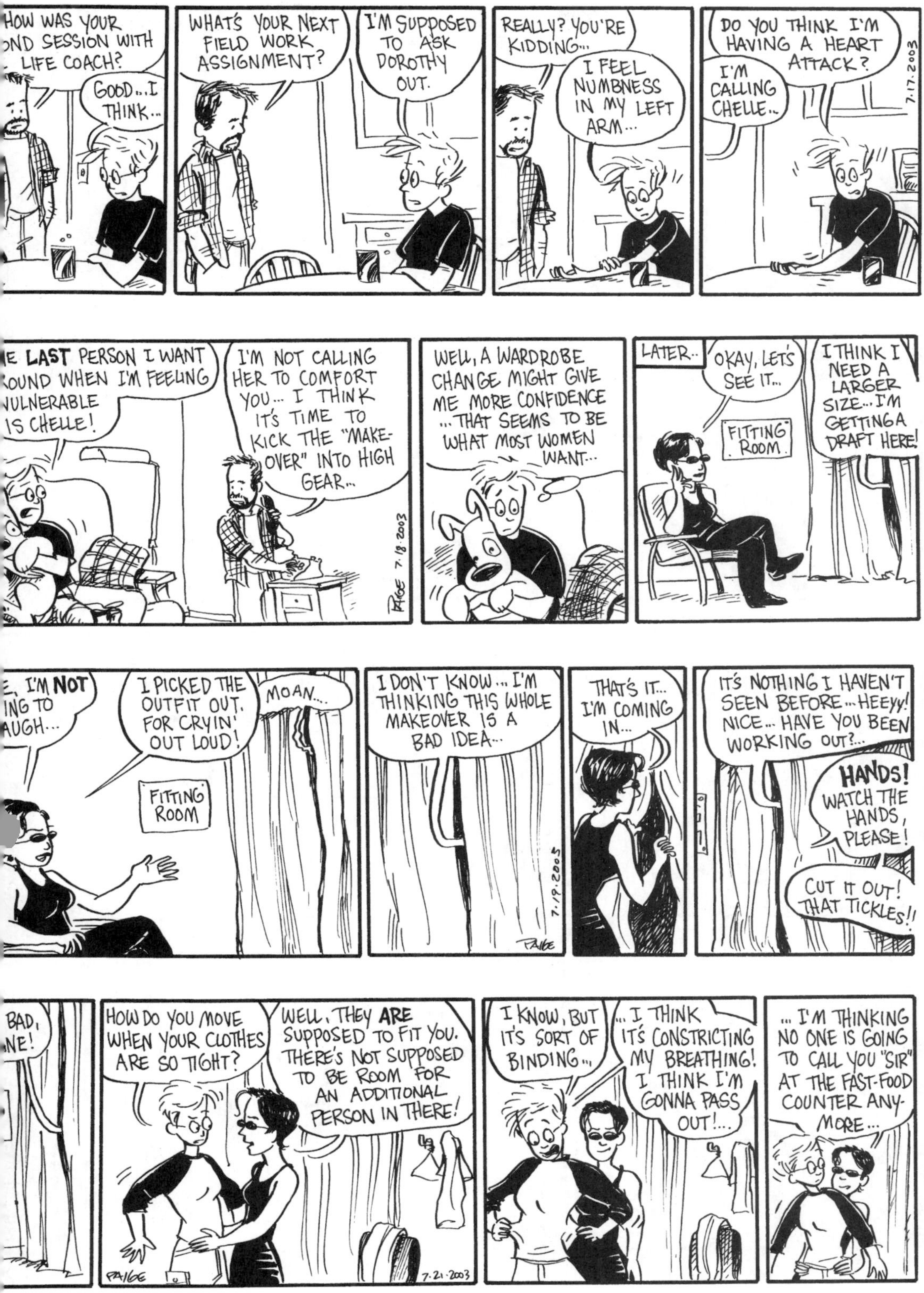
HOW WAS YOUR
OND SESSION WITH
LIFE COACH?
GOOD... I THINK...
WHAT'S YOUR NEXT FIELD WORK ASSIGNMENT?
I'M SUPPOSED TO ASK DOROTHY OUT.
REALLY? YOU'RE KIDDING...
I FEEL NUMBNESS IN MY LEFT ARM...
DO YOU THINK I'M HAVING A HEART ATTACK?
I'M CALLING CHELLE...
7.17.2003
E LAST PERSON I WANT
OUND WHEN I'M FEELING
ULNERABLE
IS CHELLE!
I'M NOT CALLING HER TO COMFORT YOU... I THINK IT'S TIME TO KICK THE "MAKE-OVER" INTO HIGH GEAR...
7.18.2003
PAIGE
WELL, A WARDROBE CHANGE MIGHT GIVE ME MORE CONFIDENCE ...THAT SEEMS TO BE WHAT MOST WOMEN WANT...
LATER..
OKAY, LET'S SEE IT...
FITTING ROOM
I THINK I NEED A LARGER SIZE... I'M GETTING A DRAFT HERE!
, I'M NOT
ING TO
AUGH...
I PICKED THE OUTFIT OUT. FOR CRYIN' OUT LOUD!
FITTING ROOM
MOAN...
I DON'T KNOW... I'M THINKING THIS WHOLE MAKEOVER IS A BAD IDEA...
7.19.2003
PAIGE
THAT'S IT... I'M COMING IN...
IT'S NOTHING I HAVEN'T SEEN BEFORE... HEEYY! NICE... HAVE YOU BEEN WORKING OUT?...
HANDS! WATCH THE HANDS, PLEASE!
CUT IT OUT! THAT TICKLES!!
BAD,
NE!
HOW DO YOU MOVE WHEN YOUR CLOTHES ARE SO TIGHT?
WELL, THEY ARE SUPPOSED TO FIT YOU. THERE'S NOT SUPPOSED TO BE ROOM FOR AN ADDITIONAL PERSON IN THERE!
PAIGE
7.21.2003
I KNOW, BUT IT'S SORT OF BINDING...
...I THINK IT'S CONSTRICTING MY BREATHING! I THINK I'M GONNA PASS OUT!...
... I'M THINKING NO ONE IS GOING TO CALL YOU "SIR" AT THE FAST-FOOD COUNTER ANY-MORE...

WOW... AND YOU HAVE HIPS!... WHO KNEW?

CAN WE GO NOW? I'M FEELING A BIT INVADED IN THE PERSONAL SPACE DEPARTMENT.

YOU CAN THANK ME LATER, JANE. I MANAGED TO MAKE YOU LOOK BETTER, BUT STILL LOOK LIKE YOURSELF.

I MEAN, IT'S NO EASY TASK TO PICK AN OUTFIT THAT WORKS WITH THOSE SHOES...

7.22.2003

YEAH, YEAH... YOU'RE A FREAKIN' GENIUS... NOW CAN WE GO?

LET M... HEAR T... GENIUS... PART O... MORE T... WITH CONVIC...

YOU'RE A GENIUS... YOU'RE SOOOO SMART ...WOOOO

OKAY, ENOUGH WITH THE MOCKING... WE CAN GO.

?!

WAIT!

WHAT?

THIS WOMAN I'VE BEEN TRACKING IS HERE...

...WAIT, SHE'S AT THE CHECKOUT...

PAIGE 7.23.2003

...COME O...

HURRY... PUT THIS ON.

PUNCH CLOTHING · SHOES

PUNCH CLOTHING · SHOES

Z·oom!

HMM... LOOKS LIKE CHELLE HAS FOUND HERSELF A CUTE NEW GIRL...

PAIGE 7·24·2...

CAR! LOOK OUT FOR THE CAR!

7·25·2003

*@!

SCREECH

I THINK ... LOST HE...

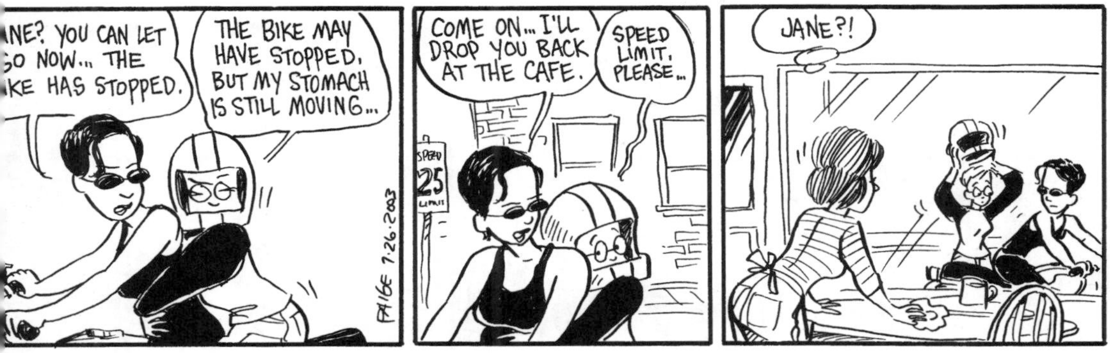

NE? YOU CAN LET
GO NOW... THE
KE HAS STOPPED.
THE BIKE MAY HAVE STOPPED, BUT MY STOMACH IS STILL MOVING...
PAIGE 7·26·2003
COME ON... I'LL DROP YOU BACK AT THE CAFE.
SPEED LIMIT, PLEASE...
SPEED 25 LIMIT
JANE?!

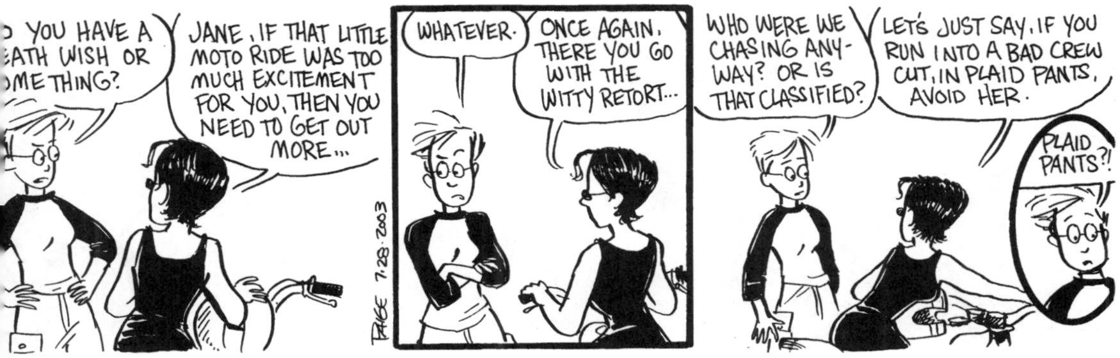

D YOU HAVE A
EATH WISH OR
OMETHING?
JANE, IF THAT LITTLE MOTO RIDE WAS TOO MUCH EXCITEMENT FOR YOU, THEN YOU NEED TO GET OUT MORE...
PAIGE 7·28·2003
WHATEVER.
ONCE AGAIN, THERE YOU GO WITH THE WITTY RETORT...
WHO WERE WE CHASING ANYWAY? OR IS THAT CLASSIFIED?
LET'S JUST SAY, IF YOU RUN INTO A BAD CREW CUT, IN PLAID PANTS, AVOID HER.
PLAID PANTS?!

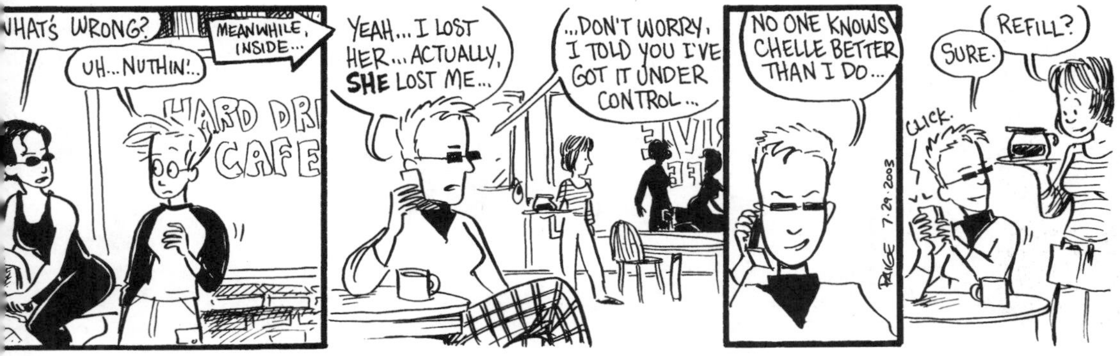

WHAT'S WRONG?
UH... NUTHIN'...
MEANWHILE, INSIDE...
HARD DRI CAFE
YEAH... I LOST HER... ACTUALLY, SHE LOST ME...
...DON'T WORRY, I TOLD YOU I'VE GOT IT UNDER CONTROL...
NO ONE KNOWS CHELLE BETTER THAN I DO...
PAIGE 7·29·2003
CLICK.
SURE.
REFILL?

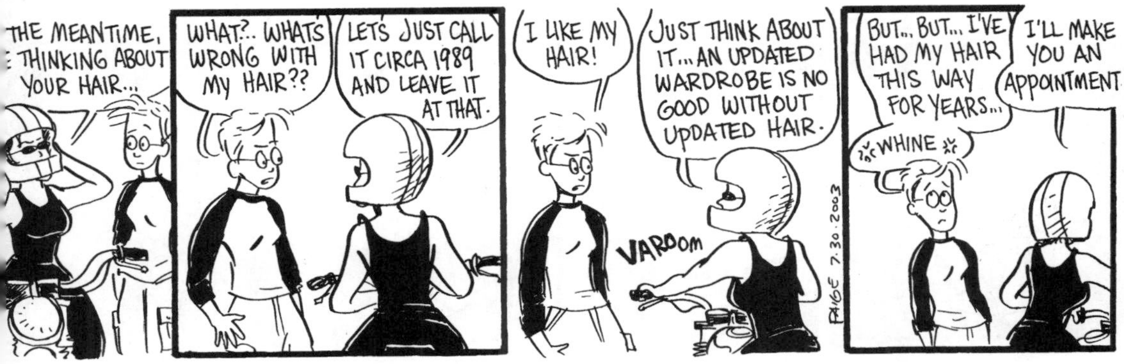

THE MEANTIME,
THINKING ABOUT
YOUR HAIR...
WHAT?.. WHATS WRONG WITH MY HAIR??
LET'S JUST CALL IT CIRCA 1989 AND LEAVE IT AT THAT.
I LIKE MY HAIR!
JUST THINK ABOUT IT... AN UPDATED WARDROBE IS NO GOOD WITHOUT UPDATED HAIR.
VAROOM
PAIGE 7·30·2003
BUT... BUT... I'VE HAD MY HAIR THIS WAY FOR YEARS...
WHINE
I'LL MAKE YOU AN APPOINTMENT.

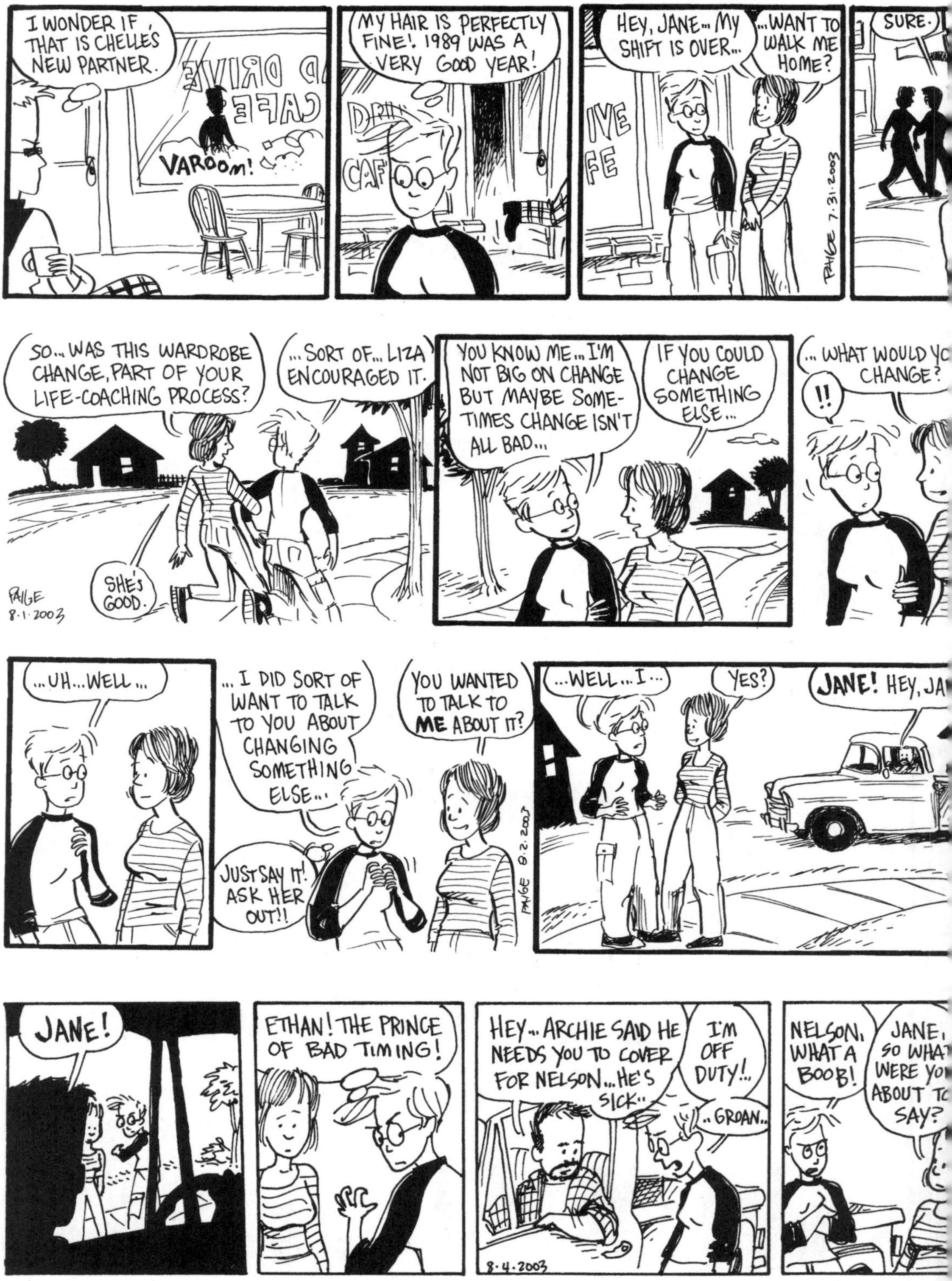
I WONDER IF THAT IS CHELLE'S NEW PARTNER.
VAROOM!
MY HAIR IS PERFECTLY FINE! 1989 WAS A VERY GOOD YEAR!
HEY, JANE... MY SHIFT IS OVER...
...WANT TO WALK ME HOME?
PAIGE 7.31.2003
SURE.
SO... WAS THIS WARDROBE CHANGE, PART OF YOUR LIFE-COACHING PROCESS?
...SORT OF... LIZA ENCOURAGED IT.
SHE'S GOOD.
PAIGE 8.1.2003
YOU KNOW ME... I'M NOT BIG ON CHANGE BUT MAYBE SOMETIMES CHANGE ISN'T ALL BAD...
IF YOU COULD CHANGE SOMETHING ELSE...
...WHAT WOULD YO CHANGE?
!!
...UH...WELL...
...I DID SORT OF WANT TO TALK TO YOU ABOUT CHANGING SOMETHING ELSE...
JUST SAY IT! ASK HER OUT!!
YOU WANTED TO TALK TO **ME** ABOUT IT?
PAIGE 8.2.2003
...WELL...I...
YES?
JANE! HEY, JA
JANE!
ETHAN! THE PRINCE OF BAD TIMING!
HEY... ARCHIE SAID HE NEEDS YOU TO COVER FOR NELSON... HE'S SICK...
I'M OFF DUTY!..
..GROAN..
8.4.2003
NELSON, WHAT A BOOB!
JANE, SO WHA WERE YO ABOUT T SAY?

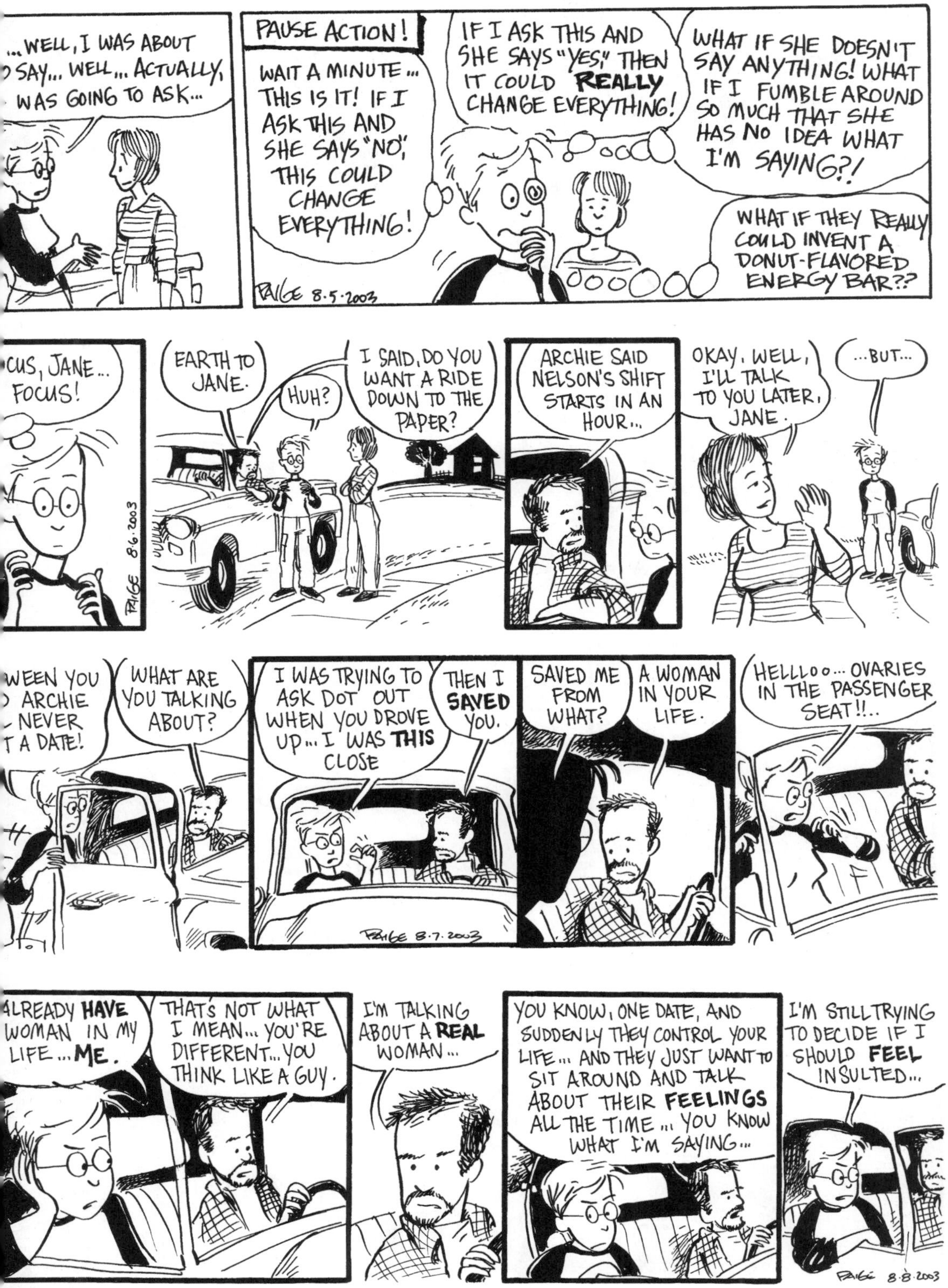
...WELL, I WAS ABOUT
SAY... WELL... ACTUALLY,
WAS GOING TO ASK...
PAUSE ACTION!
WAIT A MINUTE... THIS IS IT! IF I ASK THIS AND SHE SAYS "NO," THIS COULD CHANGE EVERYTHING!
IF I ASK THIS AND SHE SAYS "YES," THEN IT COULD **REALLY** CHANGE EVERYTHING!
WHAT IF SHE DOESN'T SAY ANYTHING! WHAT IF I FUMBLE AROUND SO MUCH THAT SHE HAS NO IDEA WHAT I'M SAYING?!
WHAT IF THEY REALLY COULD INVENT A DONUT-FLAVORED ENERGY BAR??
PAIGE 8.5.2003
CUS, JANE... FOCUS!
PAIGE 8.6.2003
EARTH TO JANE.
HUH?
I SAID, DO YOU WANT A RIDE DOWN TO THE PAPER?
ARCHIE SAID NELSON'S SHIFT STARTS IN AN HOUR...
OKAY. WELL, I'LL TALK TO YOU LATER, JANE.
...BUT...
WEEN YOU
ARCHIE
NEVER
A DATE!
WHAT ARE YOU TALKING ABOUT?
I WAS TRYING TO ASK DOT OUT WHEN YOU DROVE UP... I WAS **THIS** CLOSE
THEN I **SAVED** YOU.
SAVED ME FROM WHAT?
A WOMAN IN YOUR LIFE.
HELLLOO... OVARIES IN THE PASSENGER SEAT!!...
PAIGE 8.7.2003
LREADY **HAVE** WOMAN IN MY LIFE... **ME**.
THAT'S NOT WHAT I MEAN... YOU'RE DIFFERENT... YOU THINK LIKE A GUY.
I'M TALKING ABOUT A **REAL** WOMAN...
YOU KNOW, ONE DATE, AND SUDDENLY THEY CONTROL YOUR LIFE... AND THEY JUST WANT TO SIT AROUND AND TALK ABOUT THEIR **FEELINGS** ALL THE TIME... YOU KNOW WHAT I'M SAYING...
I'M STILL TRYING TO DECIDE IF I SHOULD **FEEL** INSULTED...
PAIGE 8.8.2003

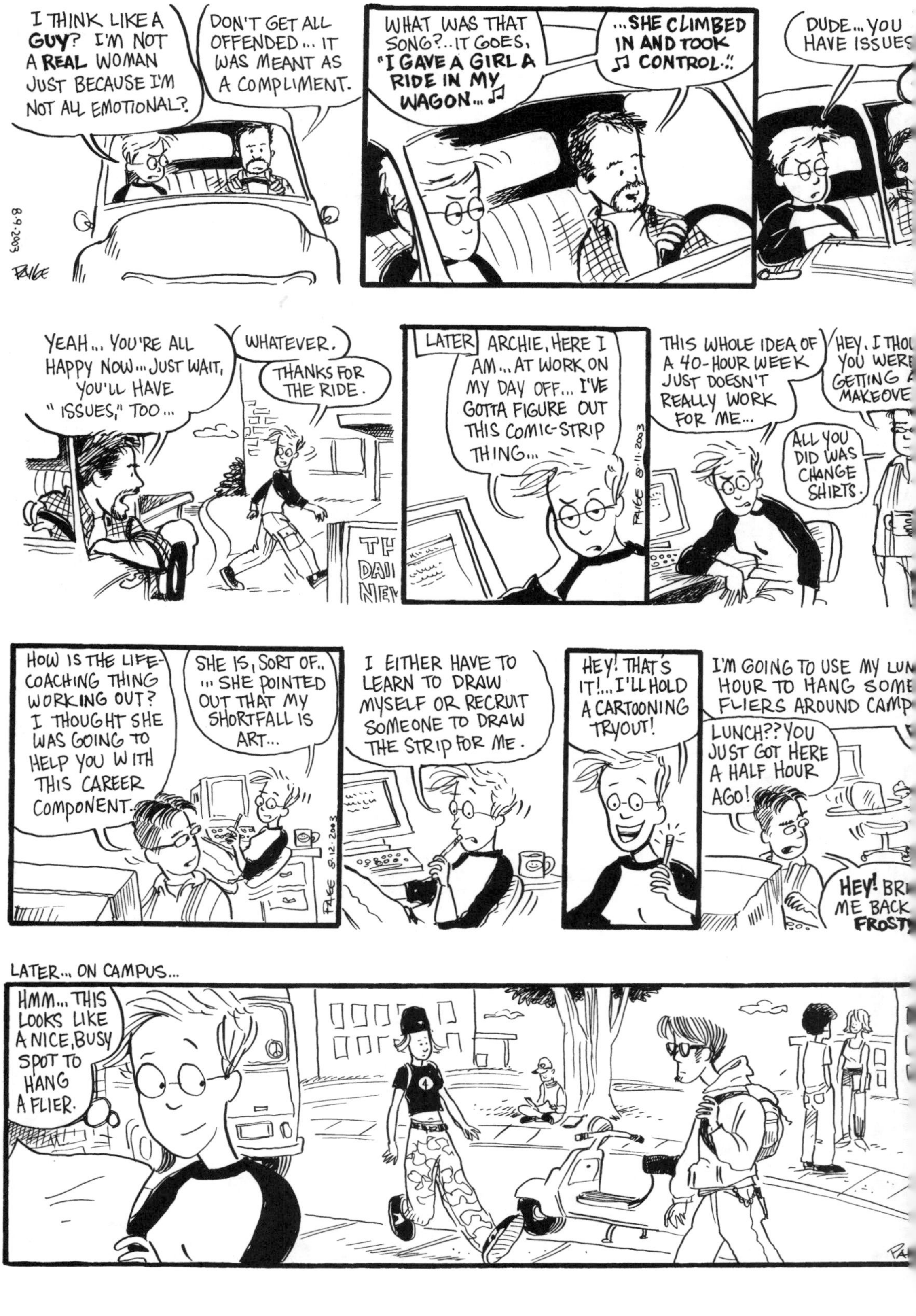
I THINK LIKE A GUY? I'M NOT A REAL WOMAN JUST BECAUSE I'M NOT ALL EMOTIONAL?
DON'T GET ALL OFFENDED... IT WAS MEANT AS A COMPLIMENT.
8.9.2003
PAIGE
WHAT WAS THAT SONG?...IT GOES, "I GAVE A GIRL A RIDE IN MY WAGON...♫
...SHE CLIMBED IN AND TOOK ♫ CONTROL."
DUDE... YOU HAVE ISSUES
YEAH... YOU'RE ALL HAPPY NOW... JUST WAIT, YOU'LL HAVE "ISSUES," TOO...
WHATEVER.
THANKS FOR THE RIDE.
LATER
ARCHIE, HERE I AM... AT WORK ON MY DAY OFF... I'VE GOTTA FIGURE OUT THIS COMIC-STRIP THING...
PAIGE 8.11.2003
THIS WHOLE IDEA OF A 40-HOUR WEEK JUST DOESN'T REALLY WORK FOR ME...
HEY, I THOU YOU WERE GETTING A MAKEOVE
ALL YOU DID WAS CHANGE SHIRTS.
HOW IS THE LIFE-COACHING THING WORKING OUT? I THOUGHT SHE WAS GOING TO HELP YOU WITH THIS CAREER COMPONENT.
SHE IS, SORT OF... ...SHE POINTED OUT THAT MY SHORTFALL IS ART...
PAIGE 8.12.2003
I EITHER HAVE TO LEARN TO DRAW MYSELF OR RECRUIT SOMEONE TO DRAW THE STRIP FOR ME.
HEY! THAT'S IT!... I'LL HOLD A CARTOONING TRYOUT!
I'M GOING TO USE MY LUN HOUR TO HANG SOME FLIERS AROUND CAMP
LUNCH?? YOU JUST GOT HERE A HALF HOUR AGO!
HEY! BRI ME BACK FROSTY
LATER... ON CAMPUS...
HMM... THIS LOOKS LIKE A NICE, BUSY SPOT TO HANG A FLIER.

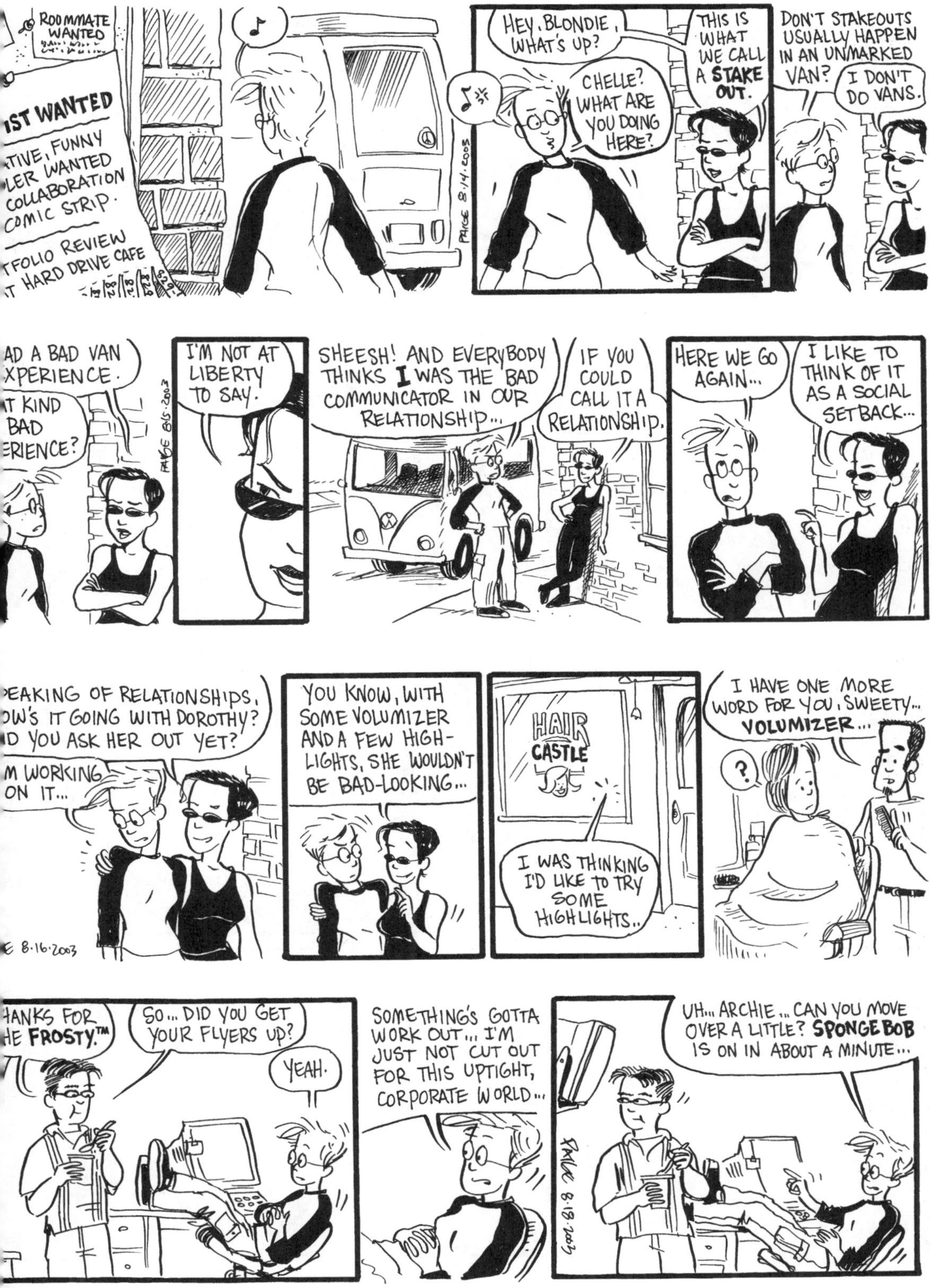
ROOMMATE WANTED
...IST WANTED
...ATIVE, FUNNY ...LER WANTED COLLABORATION COMIC STRIP.
...TFOLIO REVIEW ...T HARD DRIVE CAFE
PAIGE 8.14.2003
HEY, BLONDIE, WHAT'S UP?
CHELLE? WHAT ARE YOU DOING HERE?
THIS IS WHAT WE CALL A **STAKE OUT**.
DON'T STAKEOUTS USUALLY HAPPEN IN AN UNMARKED VAN?
I DON'T DO VANS.
...AD A BAD VAN ...XPERIENCE.
...T KIND ...BAD ...ERIENCE?
PAIGE 8.15.2003
I'M NOT AT LIBERTY TO SAY.
SHEESH! AND EVERYBODY THINKS **I** WAS THE BAD COMMUNICATOR IN OUR RELATIONSHIP...
IF YOU COULD CALL IT A RELATIONSHIP.
HERE WE GO AGAIN...
I LIKE TO THINK OF IT AS A SOCIAL SETBACK...
...EAKING OF RELATIONSHIPS, ...OW'S IT GOING WITH DOROTHY? ...D YOU ASK HER OUT YET?
...M WORKING ON IT...
...E 8.16.2003
YOU KNOW, WITH SOME VOLUMIZER AND A FEW HIGHLIGHTS, SHE WOULDN'T BE BAD-LOOKING...
HAIR CASTLE
I WAS THINKING I'D LIKE TO TRY SOME HIGHLIGHTS..
I HAVE ONE MORE WORD FOR YOU, SWEETY... **VOLUMIZER**...
?
...HANKS FOR ...HE **FROSTY**™
SO... DID YOU GET YOUR FLYERS UP?
YEAH.
SOMETHING'S GOTTA WORK OUT... I'M JUST NOT CUT OUT FOR THIS UPTIGHT, CORPORATE WORLD...
PAIGE 8.18.2003
UH... ARCHIE... CAN YOU MOVE OVER A LITTLE? **SPONGE BOB** IS ON IN ABOUT A MINUTE...

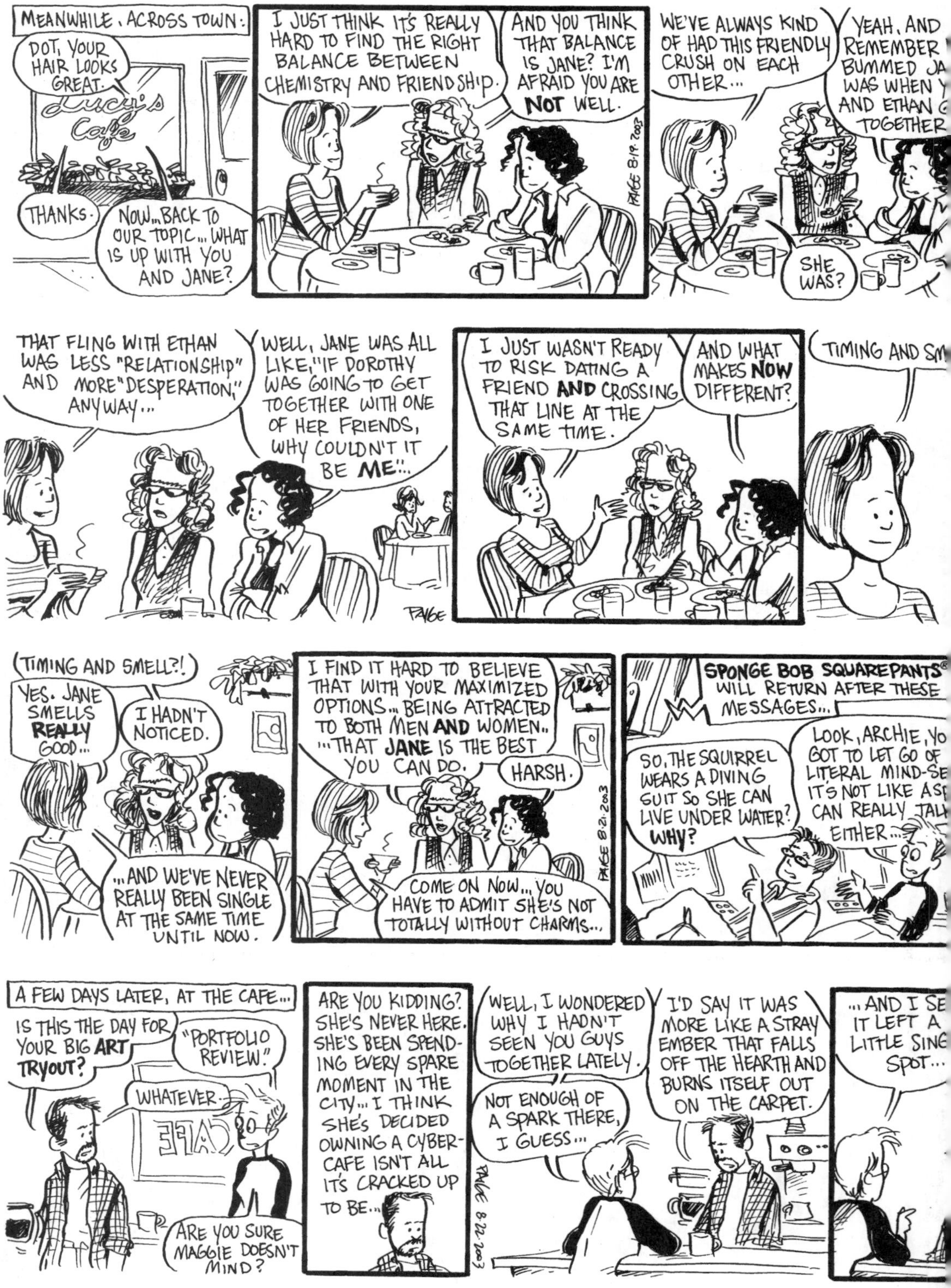
MEANWHILE, ACROSS TOWN:
DOT, YOUR HAIR LOOKS GREAT.
Lucy's Cafe
THANKS.
NOW... BACK TO OUR TOPIC... WHAT IS UP WITH YOU AND JANE?
I JUST THINK IT'S REALLY HARD TO FIND THE RIGHT BALANCE BETWEEN CHEMISTRY AND FRIENDSHIP.
AND YOU THINK THAT BALANCE IS JANE? I'M AFRAID YOU ARE **NOT** WELL.
PAIGE 8.19.2003
WE'VE ALWAYS KIND OF HAD THIS FRIENDLY CRUSH ON EACH OTHER...
YEAH, AND REMEMBER BUMMED JA WAS WHEN Y AND ETHAN G TOGETHER
SHE WAS?
THAT FLING WITH ETHAN WAS LESS "RELATIONSHIP" AND MORE "DESPERATION," ANYWAY...
WELL, JANE WAS ALL LIKE, "IF DOROTHY WAS GOING TO GET TOGETHER WITH ONE OF HER FRIENDS, WHY COULDN'T IT BE **ME**"...
PAIGE
I JUST WASN'T READY TO RISK DATING A FRIEND **AND** CROSSING THAT LINE AT THE SAME TIME.
AND WHAT MAKES **NOW** DIFFERENT?
TIMING AND SM
(TIMING AND SMELL?!)
YES. JANE SMELLS **REALLY** GOOD...
I HADN'T NOTICED.
...AND WE'VE NEVER REALLY BEEN SINGLE AT THE SAME TIME UNTIL NOW.
I FIND IT HARD TO BELIEVE THAT WITH YOUR MAXIMIZED OPTIONS... BEING ATTRACTED TO BOTH MEN **AND** WOMEN... ...THAT **JANE** IS THE BEST YOU CAN DO.
HARSH.
COME ON NOW... YOU HAVE TO ADMIT SHE'S NOT TOTALLY WITHOUT CHARMS...
PAIGE 8.21.2003
SPONGE BOB SQUAREPANTS® WILL RETURN AFTER THESE MESSAGES...
SO, THE SQUIRREL WEARS A DIVING SUIT SO SHE CAN LIVE UNDER WATER? **WHY?**
LOOK, ARCHIE, YO GOT TO LET GO OF LITERAL MIND-SE IT'S NOT LIKE A SP CAN REALLY TAL EITHER...
A FEW DAYS LATER, AT THE CAFE...
IS THIS THE DAY FOR YOUR BIG **ART TRYOUT?**
"PORTFOLIO REVIEW."
WHATEVER.
ARE YOU SURE MAGGIE DOESN'T MIND?
ARE YOU KIDDING? SHE'S NEVER HERE. SHE'S BEEN SPENDING EVERY SPARE MOMENT IN THE CITY... I THINK SHE'S DECIDED OWNING A CYBER-CAFE ISN'T ALL IT'S CRACKED UP TO BE...
PAIGE 8.22.2003
WELL, I WONDERED WHY I HADN'T SEEN YOU GUYS TOGETHER LATELY.
NOT ENOUGH OF A SPARK THERE, I GUESS...
I'D SAY IT WAS MORE LIKE A STRAY EMBER THAT FALLS OFF THE HEARTH AND BURNS ITSELF OUT ON THE CARPET.
...AND I SE IT LEFT A LITTLE SING SPOT...

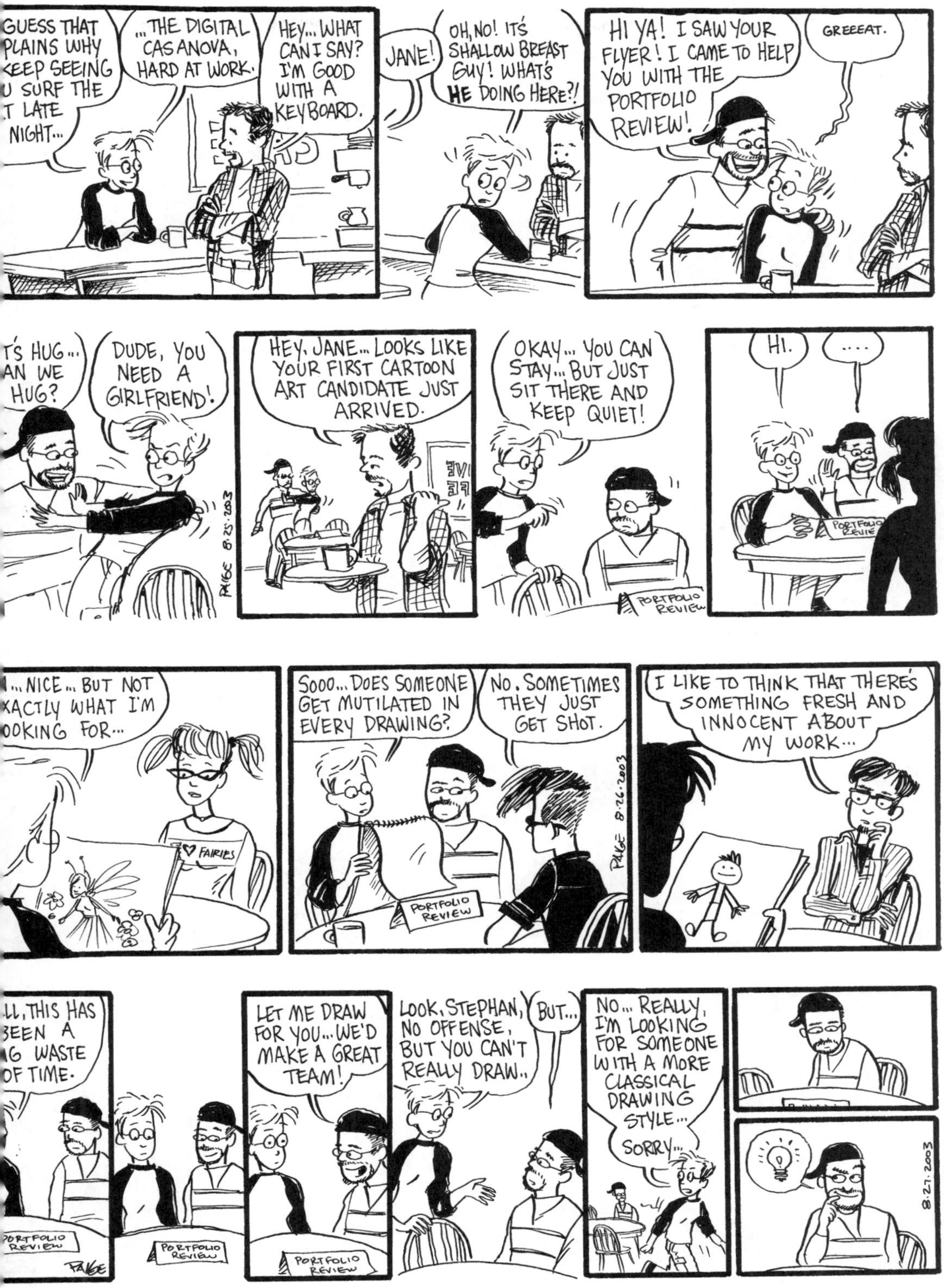

GUESS THAT PLAINS WHY KEEP SEEING U SURF THE T LATE NIGHT...
...THE DIGITAL CASANOVA, HARD AT WORK.
HEY... WHAT CAN I SAY? I'M GOOD WITH A KEYBOARD.
JANE!
OH, NO! IT'S SHALLOW BREAST GUY! WHAT'S HE DOING HERE?!
HI YA! I SAW YOUR FLYER! I CAME TO HELP YOU WITH THE PORTFOLIO REVIEW!
GREEEAT.
T'S HUG... AN WE HUG?
DUDE, YOU NEED A GIRLFRIEND!
PAIGE 8·25·2003
HEY, JANE... LOOKS LIKE YOUR FIRST CARTOON ART CANDIDATE JUST ARRIVED.
OKAY... YOU CAN STAY... BUT JUST SIT THERE AND KEEP QUIET!
PORTFOLIO REVIEW
HI.
....
PORTFOLIO REVIEW
...NICE... BUT NOT XACTLY WHAT I'M OOKING FOR...
♡ FAIRIES
SOOO... DOES SOMEONE GET MUTILATED IN EVERY DRAWING?
NO. SOMETIMES THEY JUST GET SHOT.
PORTFOLIO REVIEW
PAIGE 8·26·2003
I LIKE TO THINK THAT THERE'S SOMETHING FRESH AND INNOCENT ABOUT MY WORK...
LL, THIS HAS BEEN A G WASTE OF TIME.
PORTFOLIO REVIEW
PAIGE
PORTFOLIO REVIEW
LET ME DRAW FOR YOU... WE'D MAKE A GREAT TEAM!
PORTFOLIO REVIEW
LOOK, STEPHAN, NO OFFENSE, BUT YOU CAN'T REALLY DRAW.
BUT...
NO... REALLY, I'M LOOKING FOR SOMEONE WITH A MORE CLASSICAL DRAWING STYLE...
SORRY...
8·27·2003

....OKAY, I GIVE UP... WHY'D THE MONKEY FALL OUT OF THE TREE?
HE WAS DEAD!
HAHAHA HAHAHA!!
8.28.2003
WHAT THE?...
Y OW, CHELLE JOKE REALLY TURNS ME ON....
OH, DO ME, DOROTHY! DO ME! DO ME!
...WHAT HAPPENE TO MY COMIC
YES! YES! YES! YES! YEEEEEE
8.29.2003
SCRIBBLE
SCRIBBLE
AAAAAA
AAAAA
PAIGE
AUGH!
UMPH!!
WHAT THE *@ ARE YOU DOI
I WAS JUST GIVING YOU A LITTLE SAMPLE OF WHAT OUR COLLABORATION MIGHT LOOK LIKE...
YOU TURNED THIS COMIC INTO A GIRL-ON-GIRL ROMP!
8.30.2003
PAIGE
I KNOW! WASN'T IT GREAT?
ARGH!
UMPH!
HEY! I WAS JUST TRYIN TO HELP!
UMPH!
GRUNT!
PAIGE
SHOVE!
AUGH!
9.1.2003
OOF!

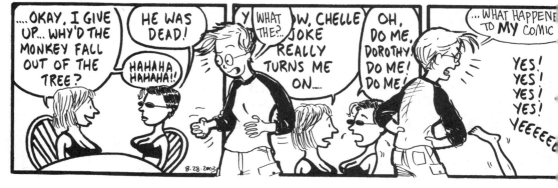

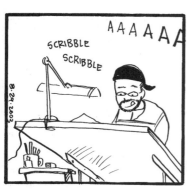

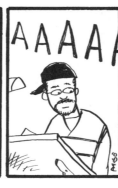

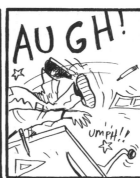

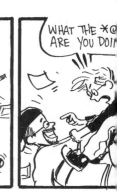

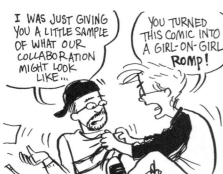

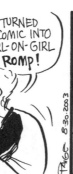

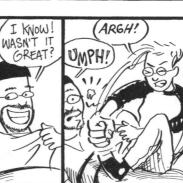

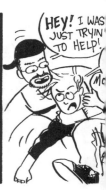

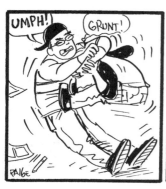

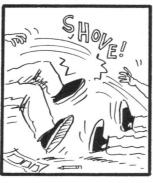

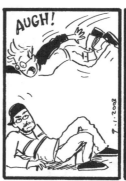

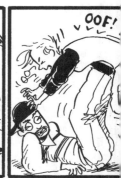

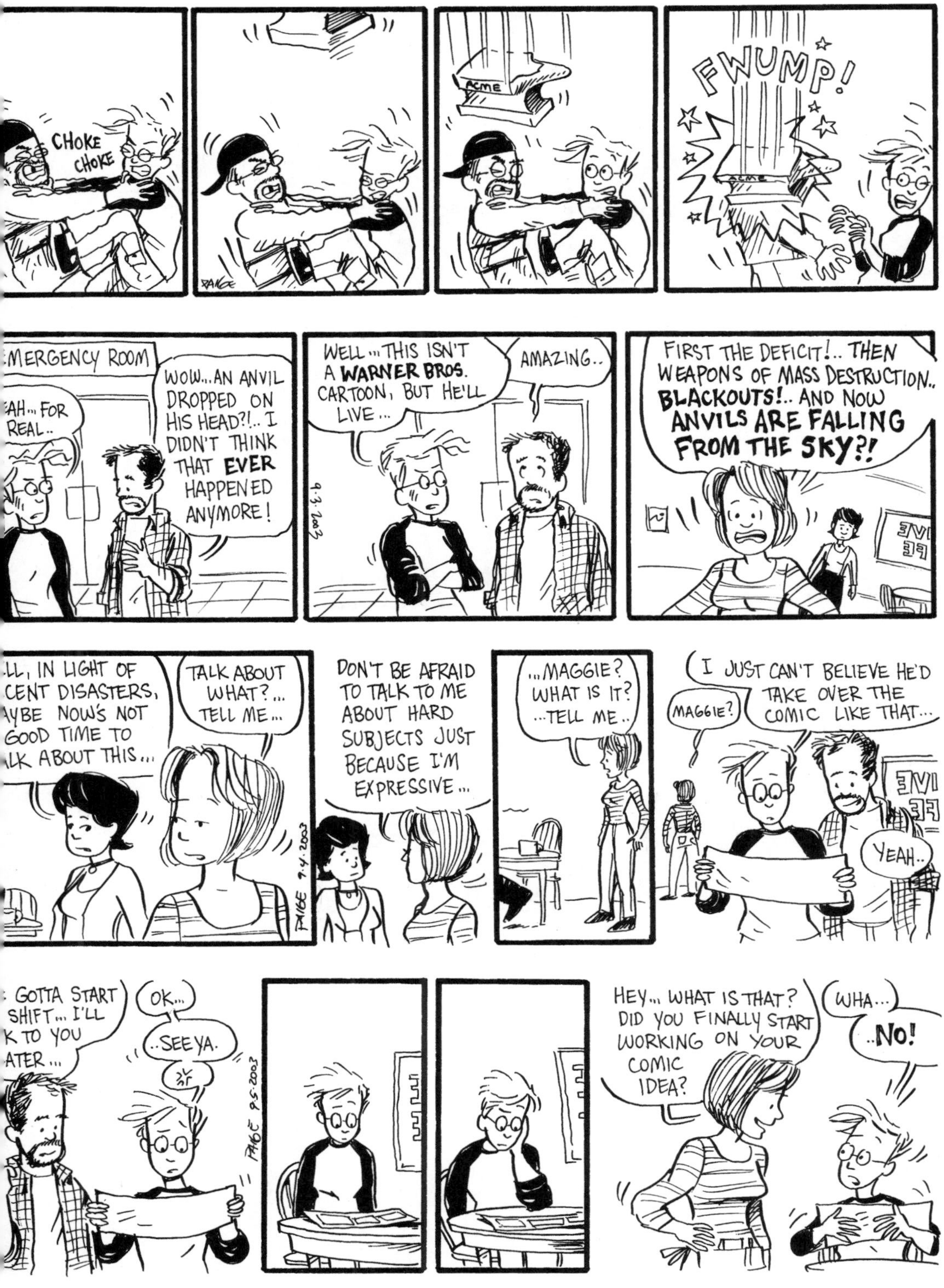
CHOKE CHOKE
ACME
FWUMP!
EMERGENCY ROOM
EAH... FOR REAL..
WOW... AN ANVIL DROPPED ON HIS HEAD?!.. I DIDN'T THINK THAT EVER HAPPENED ANYMORE!
WELL... THIS ISN'T A WARNER BROS. CARTOON, BUT HE'LL LIVE...
AMAZING..
FIRST THE DEFICIT!.. THEN WEAPONS OF MASS DESTRUCTION.. BLACKOUTS!.. AND NOW ANVILS ARE FALLING FROM THE SKY?!
LL, IN LIGHT OF CENT DISASTERS, AYBE NOW'S NOT GOOD TIME TO LK ABOUT THIS...
TALK ABOUT WHAT?... TELL ME...
DON'T BE AFRAID TO TALK TO ME ABOUT HARD SUBJECTS JUST BECAUSE I'M EXPRESSIVE...
...MAGGIE? WHAT IS IT? ...TELL ME..
I JUST CAN'T BELIEVE HE'D TAKE OVER THE COMIC LIKE THAT...
MAGGIE?
YEAH..
GOTTA START SHIFT... I'LL K TO YOU ATER...
OK...
..SEE YA.
HEY... WHAT IS THAT? DID YOU FINALLY START WORKING ON YOUR COMIC IDEA?
WHA...
..NO!

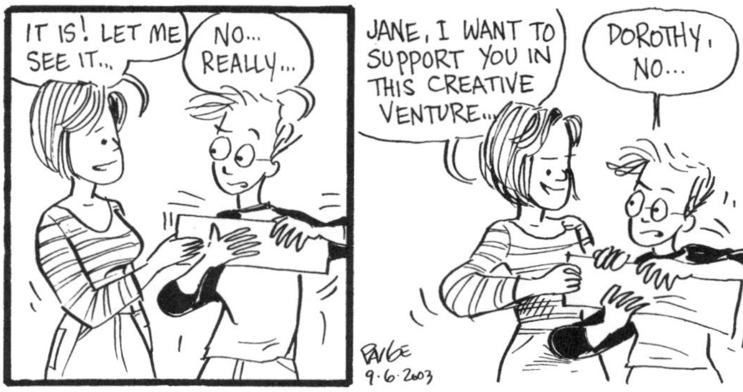
IT IS! LET ME SEE IT...
NO... REALLY...
JANE, I WANT TO SUPPORT YOU IN THIS CREATIVE VENTURE...
DOROTHY, NO...
PAIGE 9·6·2003

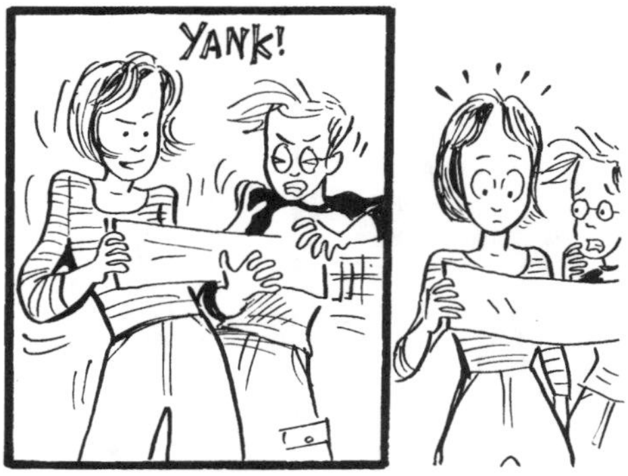
YANK!

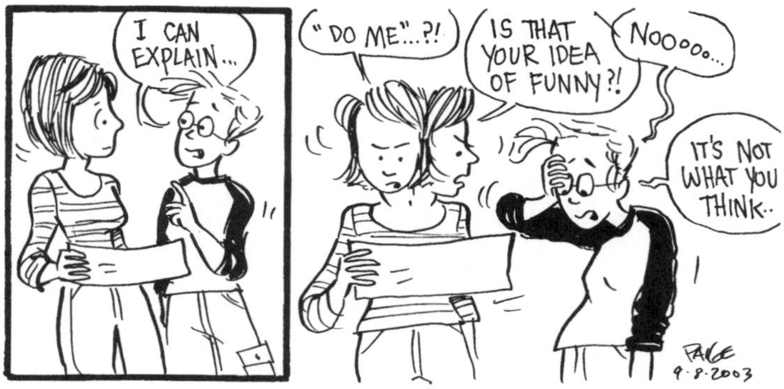
I CAN EXPLAIN...
"DO ME"...?!
IS THAT YOUR IDEA OF FUNNY?!
Nooooo...
IT'S NOT WHAT YOU THINK..
PAIGE 9·8·2003

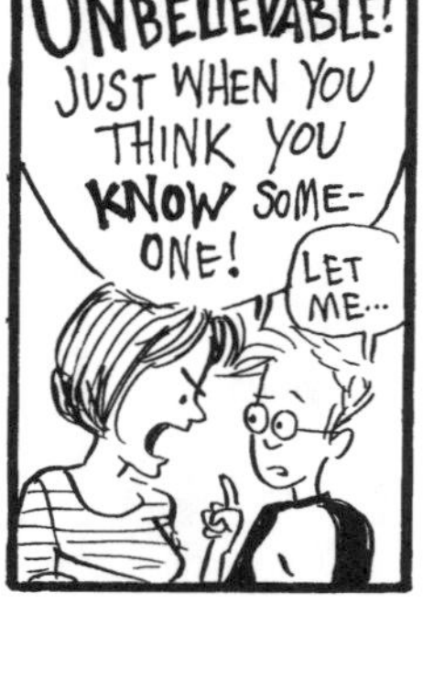
UNBELIEVABLE! JUST WHEN YOU THINK YOU KNOW SOME-ONE!
LET ME...

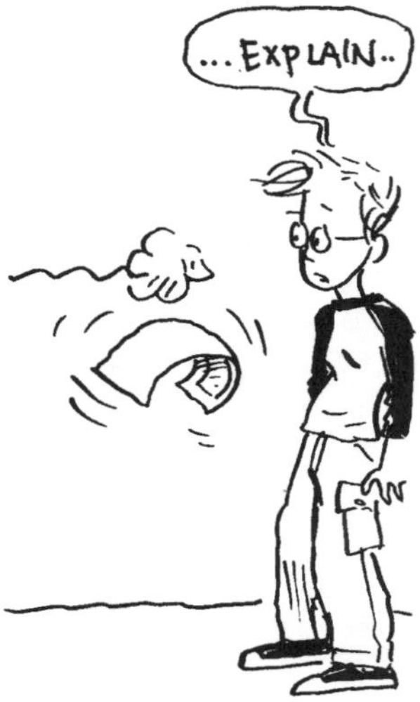
...EXPLAIN..

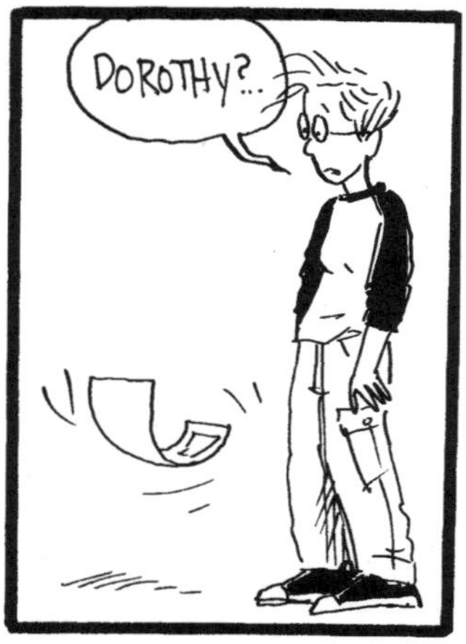
DOROTHY?...

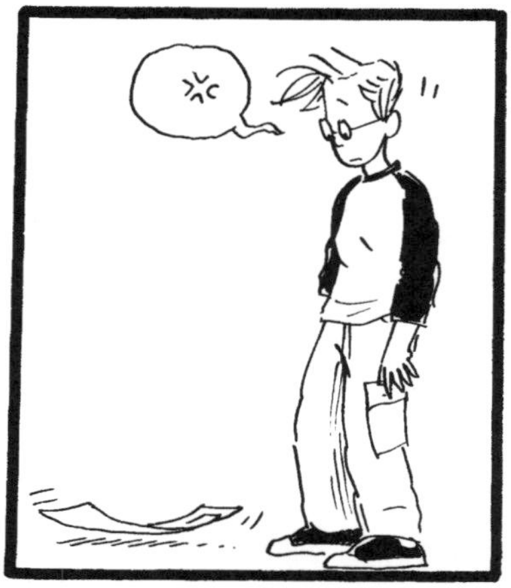

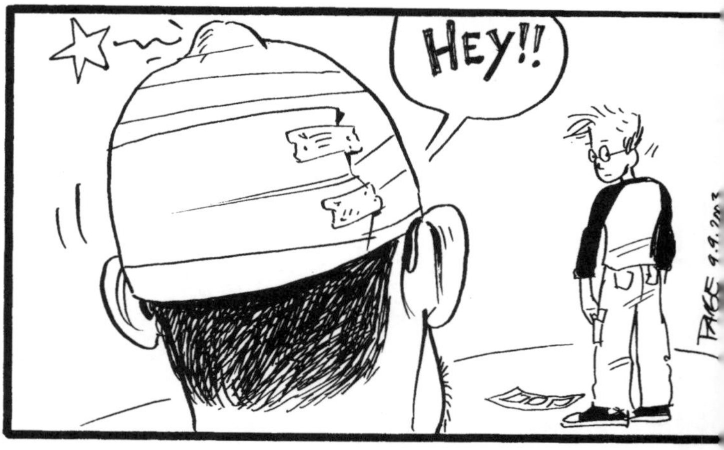
HEY!!

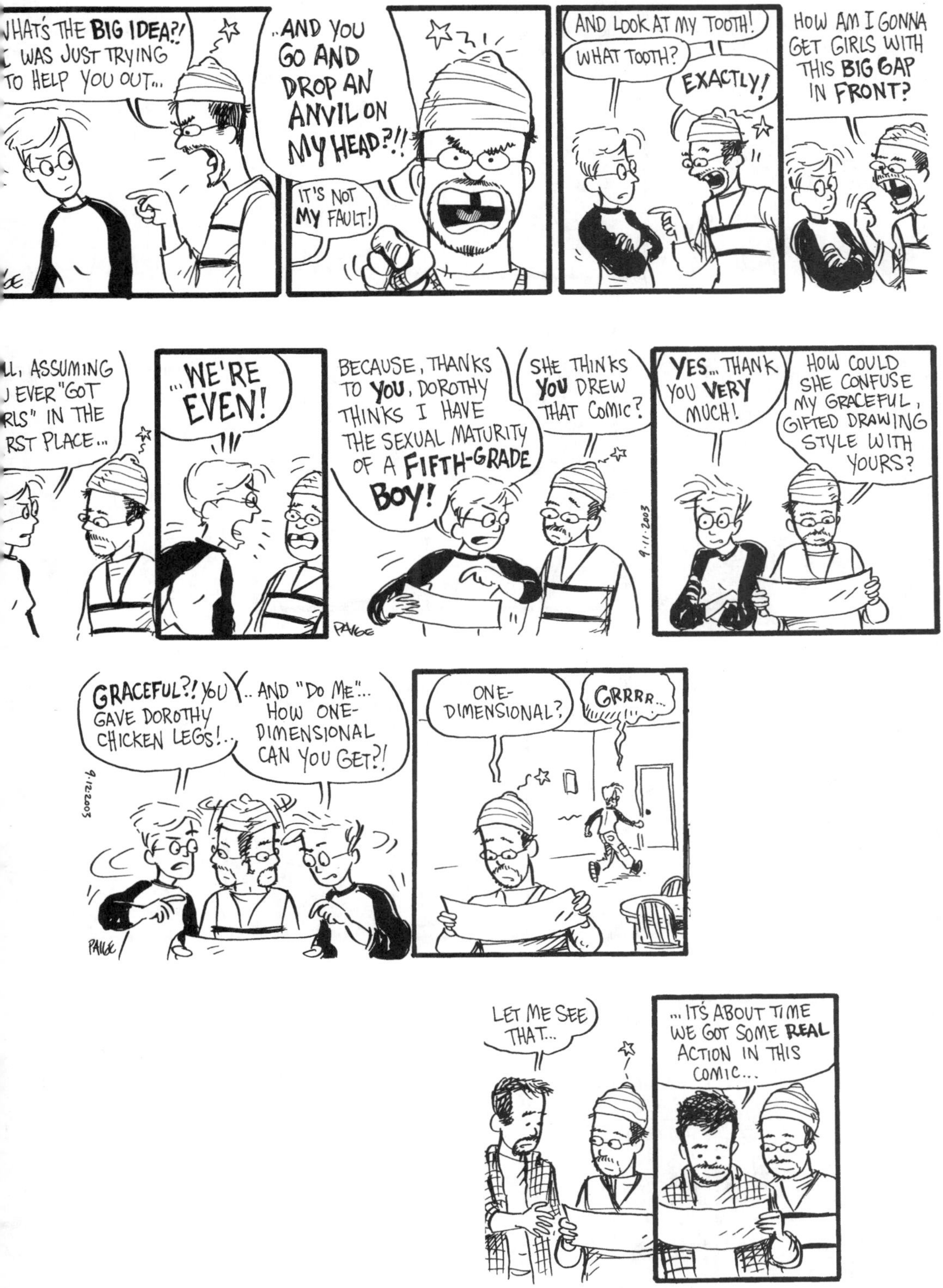

...HAT'S THE BIG IDEA?! ... WAS JUST TRYING TO HELP YOU OUT...
..AND YOU GO AND DROP AN ANVIL ON MY HEAD?!!
IT'S NOT MY FAULT!
AND LOOK AT MY TOOTH!
WHAT TOOTH?
EXACTLY!
HOW AM I GONNA GET GIRLS WITH THIS BIG GAP IN FRONT?
...LL, ASSUMING ...U EVER "GOT ...RLS" IN THE ...RST PLACE...
...WE'RE EVEN!
BECAUSE, THANKS TO YOU, DOROTHY THINKS I HAVE THE SEXUAL MATURITY OF A FIFTH-GRADE BOY!
SHE THINKS YOU DREW THAT COMIC?
9-11-2003
YES... THANK YOU VERY MUCH!
HOW COULD SHE CONFUSE MY GRACEFUL, GIFTED DRAWING STYLE WITH YOURS?
GRACEFUL?! YOU GAVE DOROTHY CHICKEN LEGS!..
..AND "DO ME"... HOW ONE-DIMENSIONAL CAN YOU GET?!
9-12-2003
ONE-DIMENSIONAL?
GRRRR...
LET ME SEE THAT...
...IT'S ABOUT TIME WE GOT SOME REAL ACTION IN THIS COMIC...

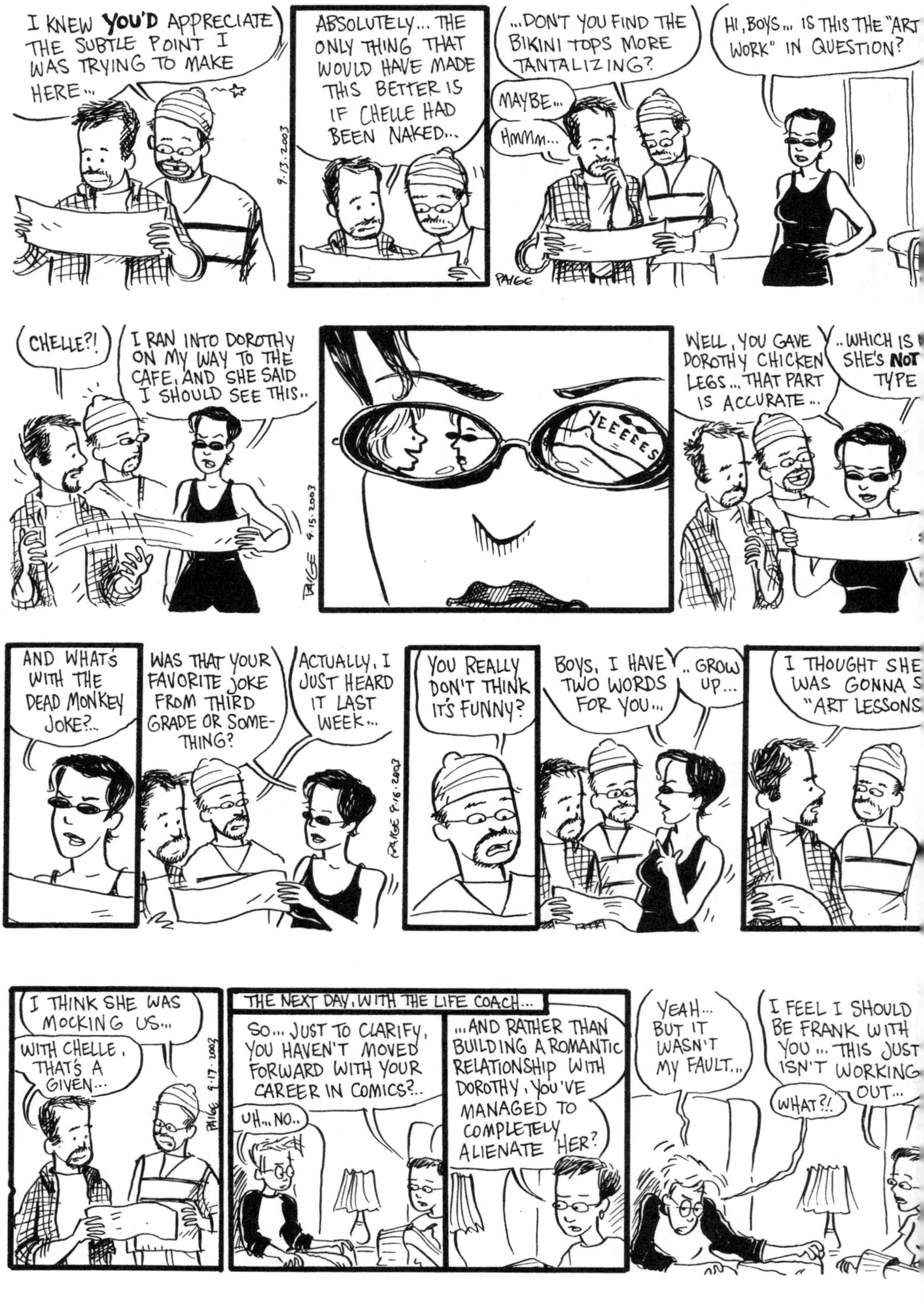

I KNEW YOU'D APPRECIATE THE SUBTLE POINT I WAS TRYING TO MAKE HERE...
ABSOLUTELY... THE ONLY THING THAT WOULD HAVE MADE THIS BETTER IS IF CHELLE HAD BEEN NAKED...
9.13.2003
...DON'T YOU FIND THE BIKINI TOPS MORE TANTALIZING?
MAYBE...
HMMM...
PAIGE
HI, BOYS... IS THIS THE "ART WORK" IN QUESTION?
CHELLE?!
I RAN INTO DOROTHY ON MY WAY TO THE CAFE, AND SHE SAID I SHOULD SEE THIS...
PAIGE 9.15.2003
YEEEEES
WELL, YOU GAVE DOROTHY CHICKEN LEGS... THAT PART IS ACCURATE...
..WHICH IS SHE'S NOT TYPE
AND WHAT'S WITH THE DEAD MONKEY JOKE?...
WAS THAT YOUR FAVORITE JOKE FROM THIRD GRADE OR SOMETHING?
ACTUALLY, I JUST HEARD IT LAST WEEK...
PAIGE 9.16.2003
YOU REALLY DON'T THINK IT'S FUNNY?
BOYS, I HAVE TWO WORDS FOR YOU...
.. GROW UP...
I THOUGHT SHE WAS GONNA S "ART LESSONS
I THINK SHE WAS MOCKING US...
WITH CHELLE, THAT'S A GIVEN...
PAIGE 9.17.2003
THE NEXT DAY, WITH THE LIFE COACH...
SO... JUST TO CLARIFY, YOU HAVEN'T MOVED FORWARD WITH YOUR CAREER IN COMICS?..
UH... NO..
...AND RATHER THAN BUILDING A ROMANTIC RELATIONSHIP WITH DOROTHY, YOU'VE MANAGED TO COMPLETELY ALIENATE HER?
YEAH... BUT IT WASN'T MY FAULT...
I FEEL I SHOULD BE FRANK WITH YOU... THIS JUST ISN'T WORKING OUT...
WHAT?!

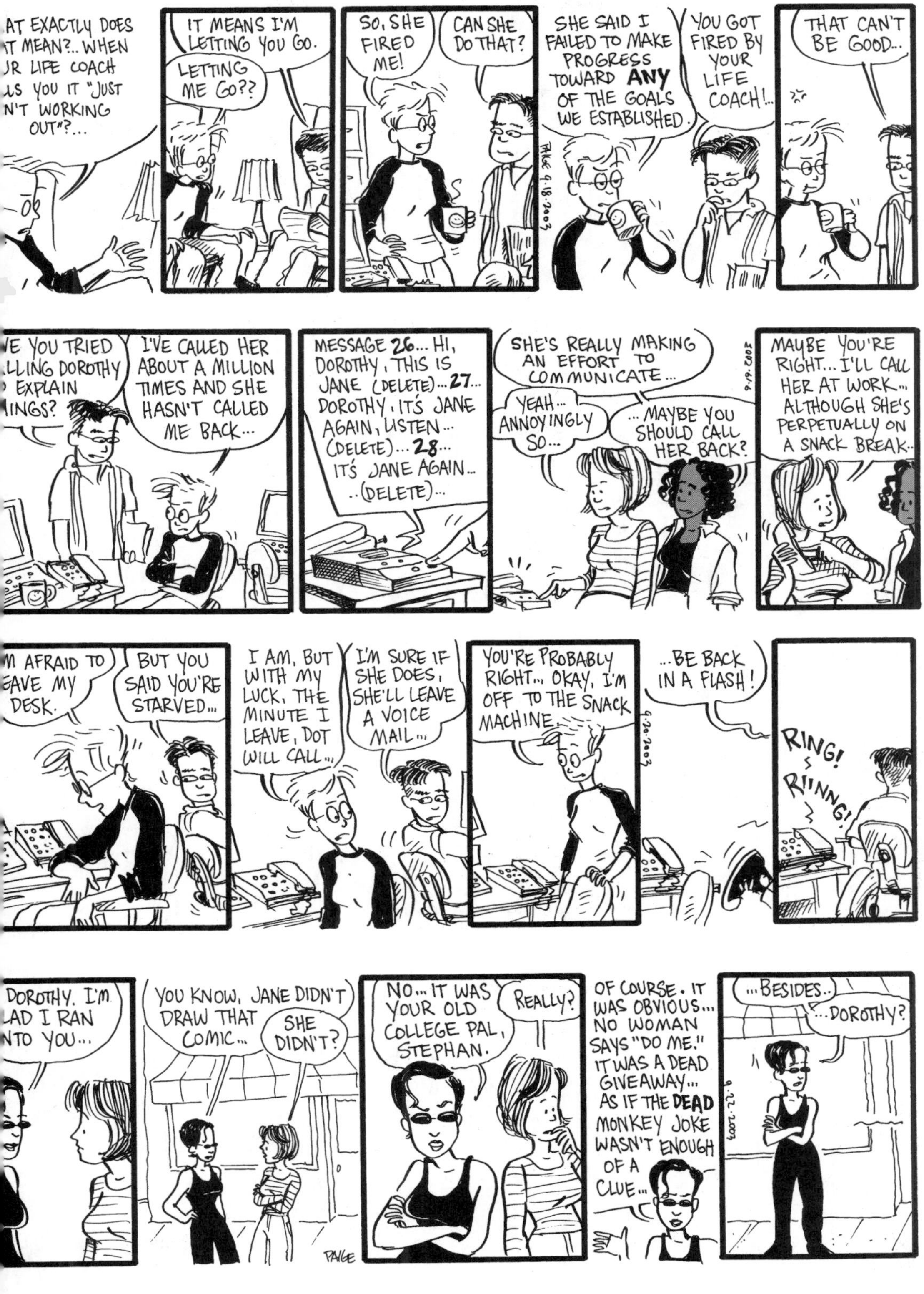

AT EXACTLY DOES T MEAN?.. WHEN R LIFE COACH LS YOU IT "JUST N'T WORKING OUT"?...
IT MEANS I'M LETTING YOU GO.
LETTING ME GO??
SO, SHE FIRED ME!
CAN SHE DO THAT?
PAIGE 9.18.2003
SHE SAID I FAILED TO MAKE PROGRESS TOWARD ANY OF THE GOALS WE ESTABLISHED.
YOU GOT FIRED BY YOUR LIFE COACH!..
THAT CAN'T BE GOOD...
VE YOU TRIED LLING DOROTHY EXPLAIN INGS?
I'VE CALLED HER ABOUT A MILLION TIMES AND SHE HASN'T CALLED ME BACK...
MESSAGE 26... HI, DOROTHY, THIS IS JANE (DELETE)...27... DOROTHY, IT'S JANE AGAIN, LISTEN... (DELETE)... 28... IT'S JANE AGAIN... ..(DELETE)...
SHE'S REALLY MAKING AN EFFORT TO COMMUNICATE...
YEAH... ANNOYINGLY SO...
...MAYBE YOU SHOULD CALL HER BACK?
9.19.2003
MAYBE YOU'RE RIGHT... I'LL CALL HER AT WORK... ALTHOUGH SHE'S PERPETUALLY ON A SNACK BREAK..
M AFRAID TO EAVE MY DESK.
BUT YOU SAID YOU'RE STARVED...
I AM, BUT WITH MY LUCK, THE MINUTE I LEAVE, DOT WILL CALL...
I'M SURE IF SHE DOES, SHE'LL LEAVE A VOICE MAIL...
YOU'RE PROBABLY RIGHT... OKAY, I'M OFF TO THE SNACK MACHINE.
9.20.2003
...BE BACK IN A FLASH!
RING!
RIINNG!
DOROTHY. I'M LAD I RAN NTO YOU...
YOU KNOW, JANE DIDN'T DRAW THAT COMIC...
SHE DIDN'T?
NO... IT WAS YOUR OLD COLLEGE PAL, STEPHAN.
REALLY?
PAIGE
OF COURSE. IT WAS OBVIOUS... NO WOMAN SAYS "DO ME." IT WAS A DEAD GIVEAWAY... AS IF THE DEAD MONKEY JOKE WASN'T ENOUGH OF A CLUE...
9.22.2003
...BESIDES..
..DOROTHY?

THE
DAIL
NEV
9·23·2003

THE
DAIL
NEV
9·23·2003
JANE...
DOROTHY?
LISTEN, I'M SO SORRY THAT I JUMPED TO CONCLUSIONS... CHELLE EXPLAINED THE WHOLE THING..
CHELLE?!

YOU KNOW, SOMETIMES I JUST HAVE AN EMOTION, AND IT GETS REALLY BIG..
DOROTHY, I WOULD NEVER...
I KNOW..
HEY! NO FAIR NOT IN FRONT OF THE SINGLE GUY! GET A ROOM!!

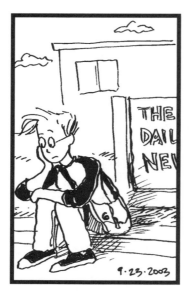

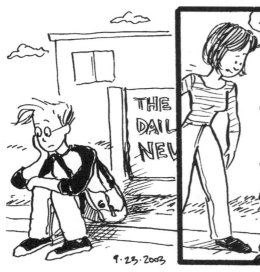

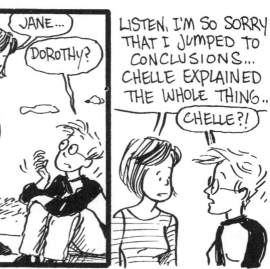

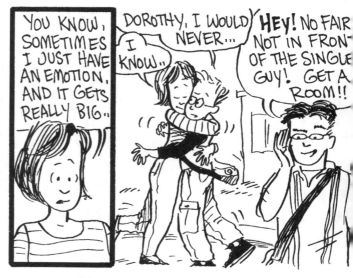

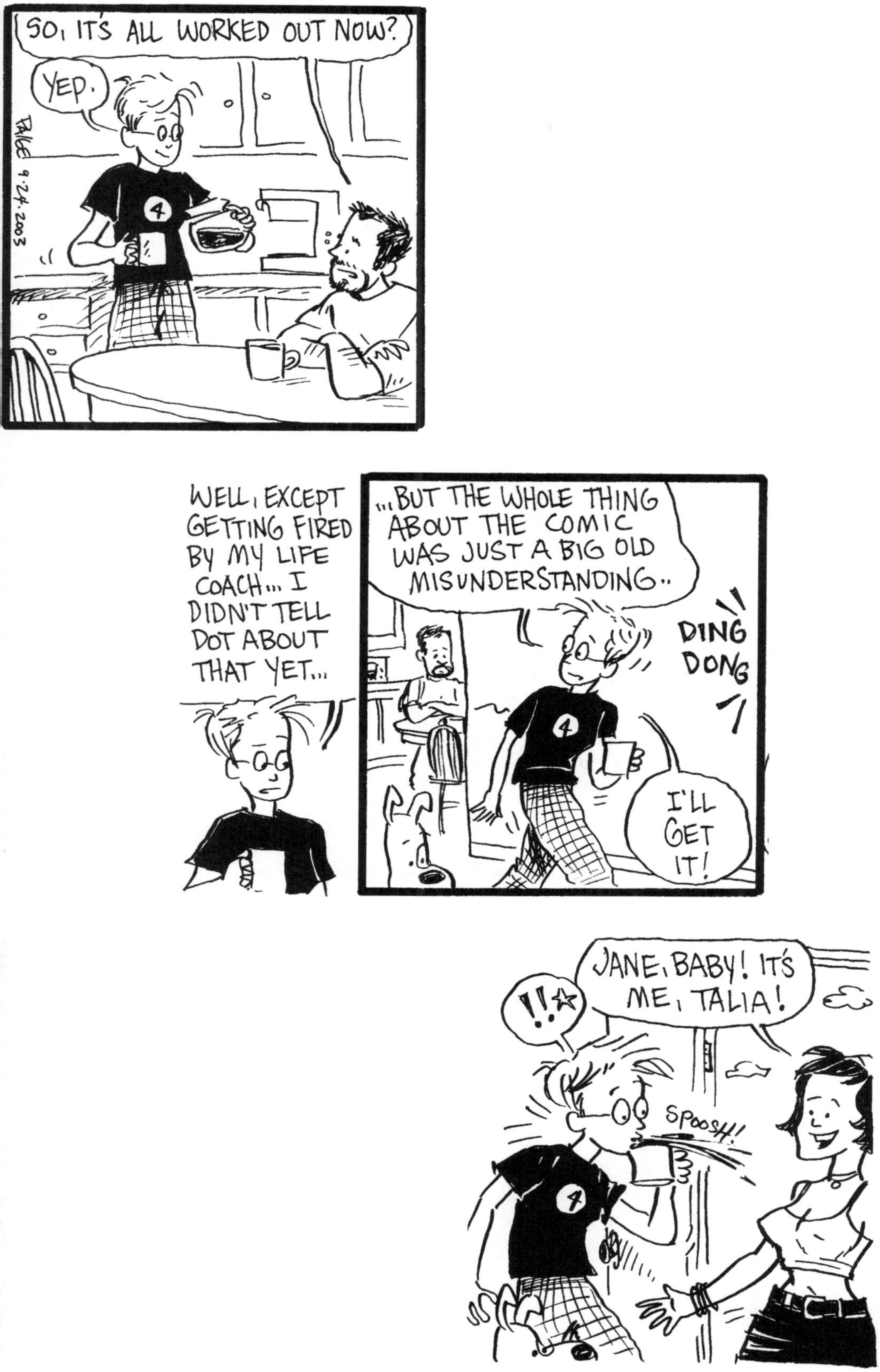

SO, IT'S ALL WORKED OUT NOW?
YEP.
PAIGE 9.24.2003
WELL, EXCEPT GETTING FIRED BY MY LIFE COACH... I DIDN'T TELL DOT ABOUT THAT YET...
...BUT THE WHOLE THING ABOUT THE COMIC WAS JUST A BIG OLD MISUNDERSTANDING..
DING DONG
I'LL GET IT!
JANE, BABY! IT'S ME, TALIA!
!!☆
SPOOSH!

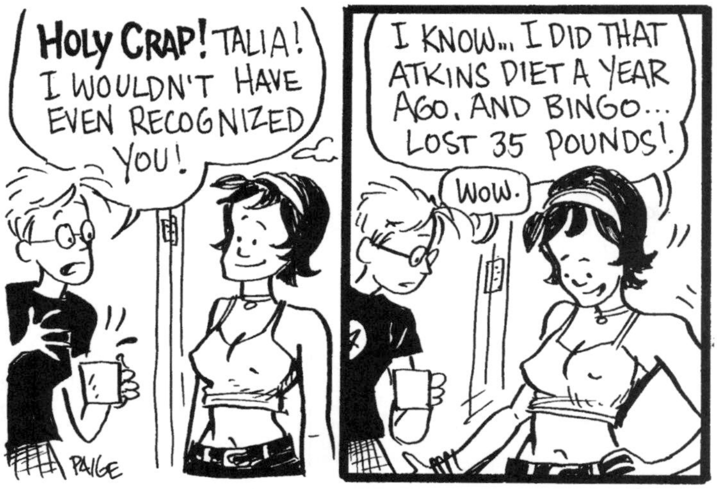
HOLY CRAP! TALIA! I WOULDN'T HAVE EVEN RECOGNIZED YOU!
PAIGE
I KNOW... I DID THAT ATKINS DIET A YEAR AGO, AND BINGO... LOST 35 POUNDS!
WOW.

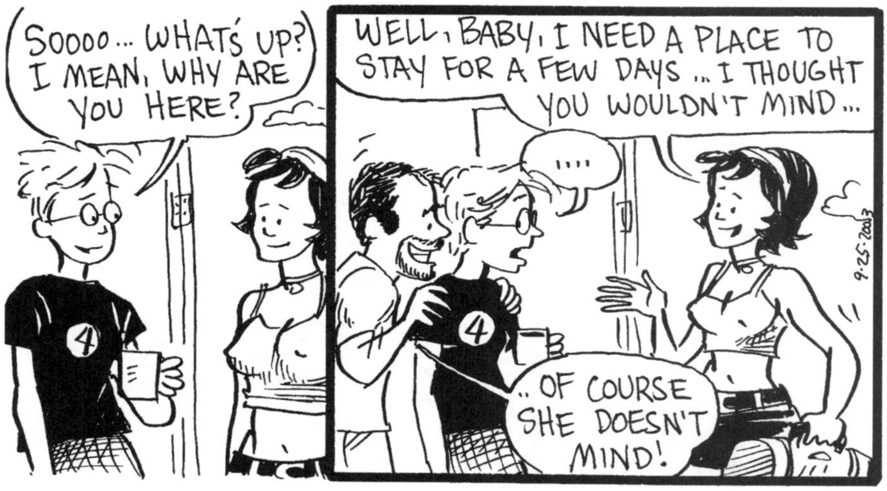
SOOOO... WHAT'S UP? I MEAN, WHY ARE YOU HERE?
WELL, BABY, I NEED A PLACE TO STAY FOR A FEW DAYS ... I THOUGHT YOU WOULDN'T MIND...
....
.. OF COURSE SHE DOESN'T MIND!
9·25·2003

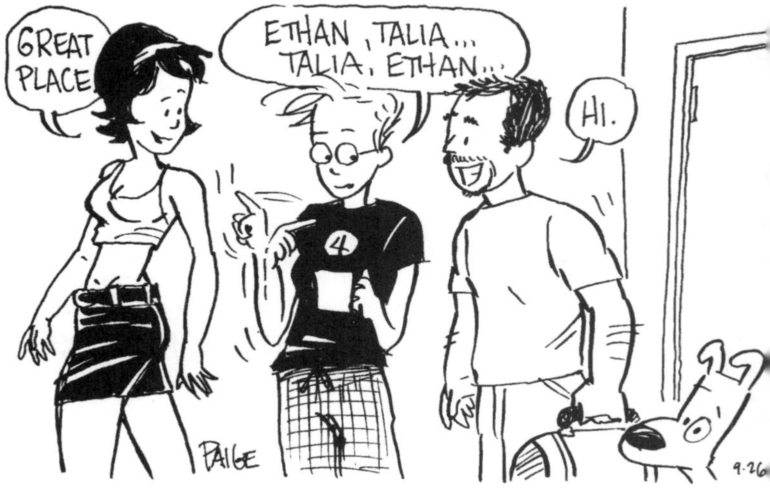
GREAT PLACE
ETHAN, TALIA... TALIA, ETHAN...
HI.
PAIGE

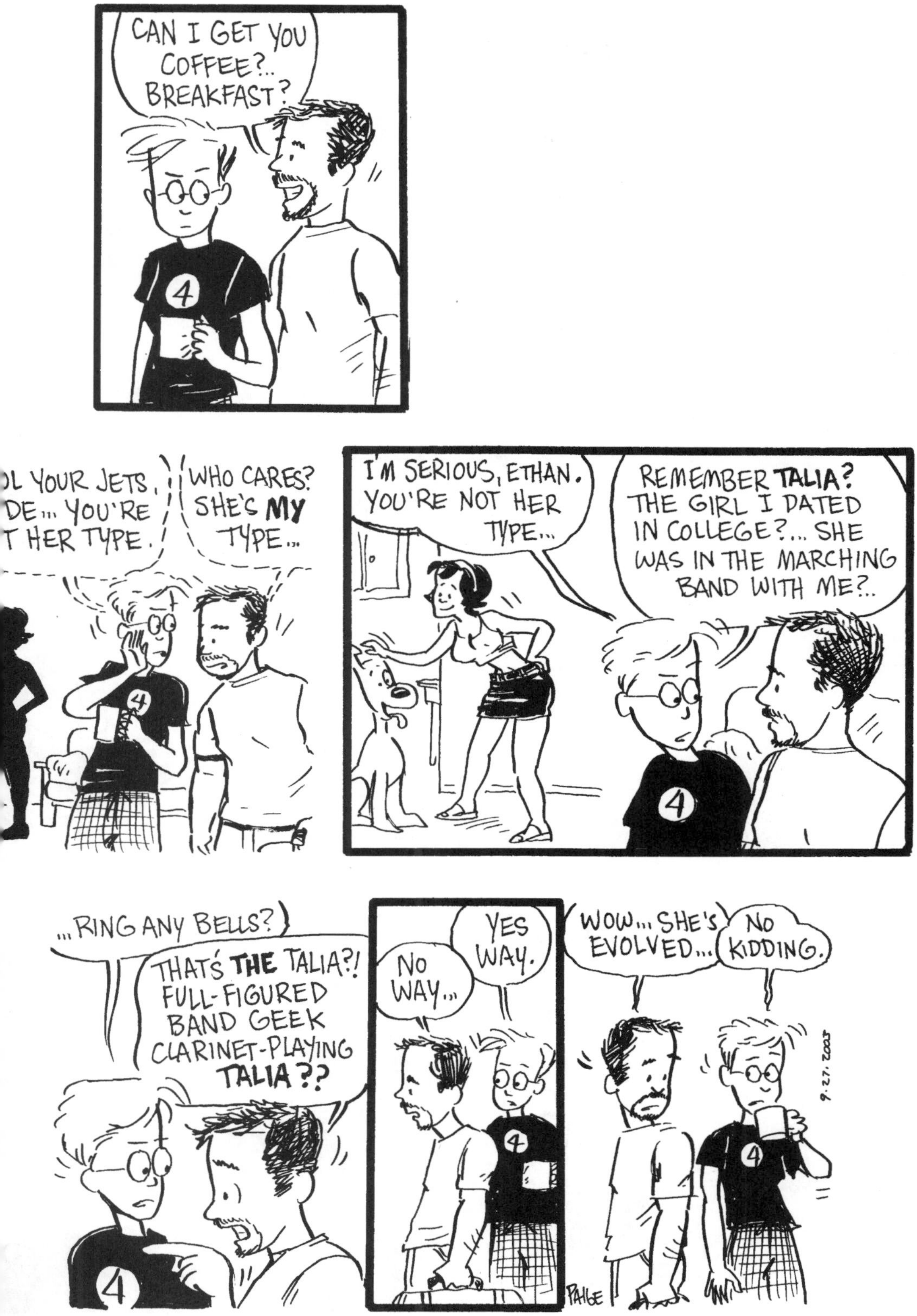
CAN I GET YOU COFFEE?.. BREAKFAST?
L YOUR JETS, DE... YOU'RE T HER TYPE.
WHO CARES? SHE'S **MY** TYPE...
I'M SERIOUS, ETHAN. YOU'RE NOT HER TYPE...
REMEMBER **TALIA?** THE GIRL I DATED IN COLLEGE?... SHE WAS IN THE MARCHING BAND WITH ME?..
...RING ANY BELLS?
THAT'S **THE** TALIA?! FULL-FIGURED BAND GEEK CLARINET-PLAYING **TALIA??**
NO WAY...
YES WAY.
WOW... SHE'S EVOLVED...
NO KIDDING.
9.27.2003
PAIGE

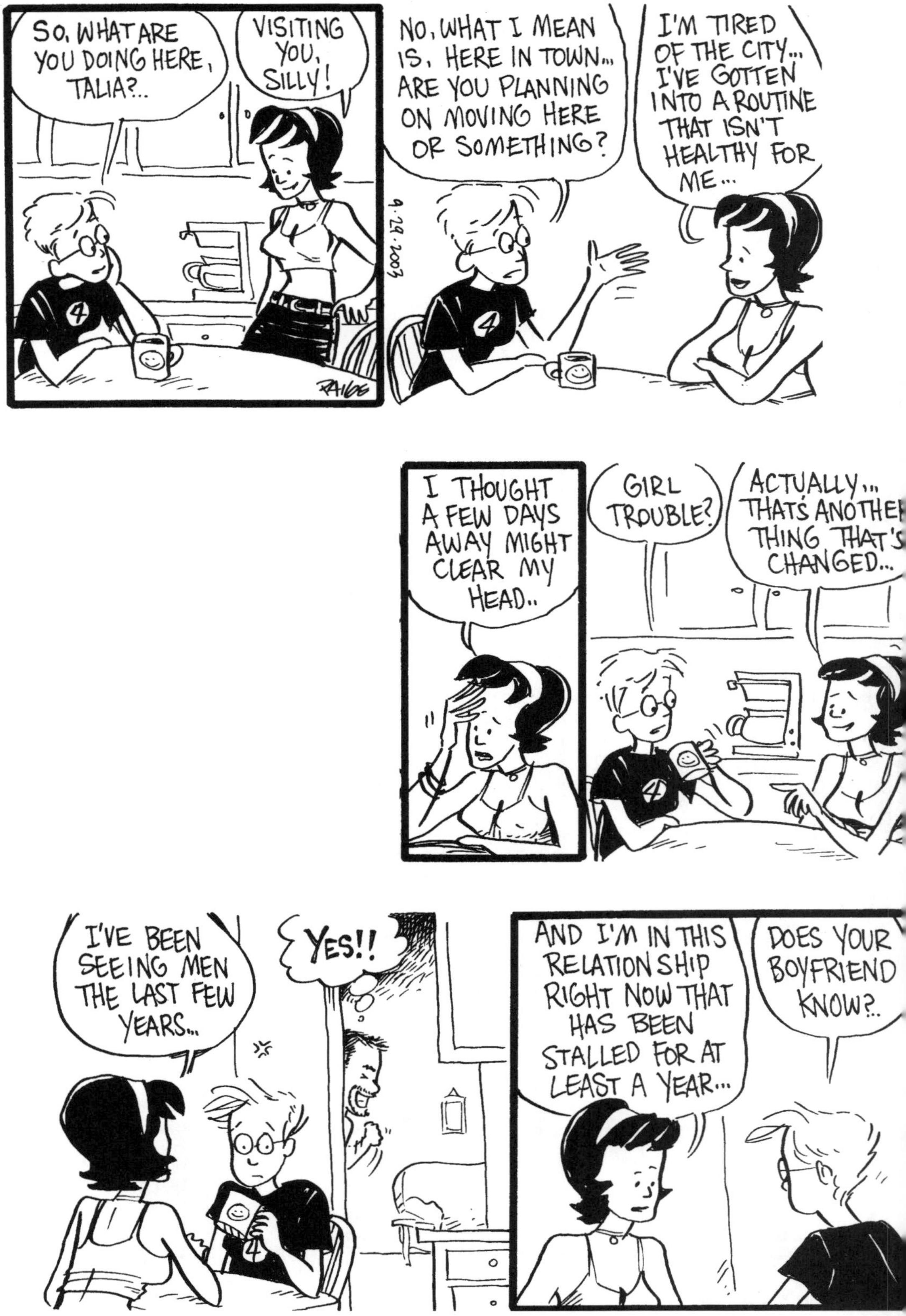
SO, WHAT ARE YOU DOING HERE, TALIA?..
VISITING YOU, SILLY!
9.29.2003
NO, WHAT I MEAN IS, HERE IN TOWN... ARE YOU PLANNING ON MOVING HERE OR SOMETHING?
I'M TIRED OF THE CITY... I'VE GOTTEN INTO A ROUTINE THAT ISN'T HEALTHY FOR ME...
I THOUGHT A FEW DAYS AWAY MIGHT CLEAR MY HEAD..
GIRL TROUBLE?
ACTUALLY... THAT'S ANOTHER THING THAT'S CHANGED...
I'VE BEEN SEEING MEN THE LAST FEW YEARS...
YES!!
AND I'M IN THIS RELATIONSHIP RIGHT NOW THAT HAS BEEN STALLED FOR AT LEAST A YEAR...
DOES YOUR BOYFRIEND KNOW?..

I DON'T KNOW... BUT I DON'T SEE THE RELATIONSHIP LASTING MUCH LONGER...
THANK YOU!
PAIGE 9.30.2003

, THIS IS ALL
ST A LOT FOR
E TO TAKE IN...
... I MEAN, LOOK AT US IN COLLEGE!
... LOOK AT YOU NOW...
... **AND** YOU HAVE A BOY-FRIEND!
PAIGE

YOU KNOW, A "TRANSITIONAL" LETTER WOULD HAVE BEEN NICE AT SOME POINT... BEFORE YOU JUST SHOW UP OUT OF THE BLUE!...
SOMETHING LIKE... "DEAR JANE, AFTER DATING YOU, I TURNED STRAIGHT...

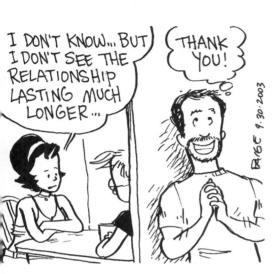

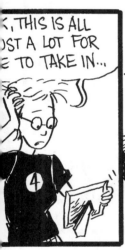

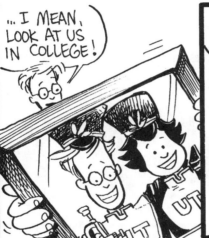

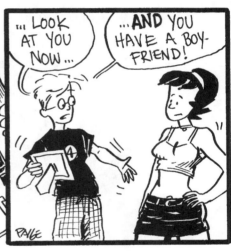

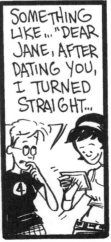

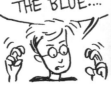

OR..."DEAR JANE, AFTER I DATED YOU, I GOT REALLY **HOT**, THEN TURNED STRAIGHT...
YOU REMEMBER YVETTE?..
YEAH... YOU GUYS DATED AFTER WE BROKE UP, RIGHT?
PAIGE

YEAH... WELL, SHE'S STRAIGHT NOW, TOO...
10.2.2003
THAT'S ME... JUST DOING MY PART TO DERAIL THE GAY AGENDA...
FINALLY, WE DISCOVER YOUR TRUE CALLING...

JANE, MY DATING JEFF HAS NOTHING TO DO WITH YOU ... OR US...
FRANKLY, IT'S JUST EASIER TO HAVE A MORE TRADITIONAL RELATIONSHIP WITH A GUY.

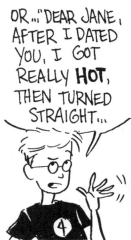

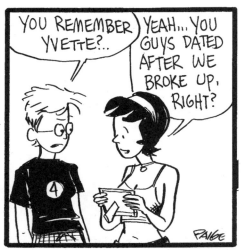

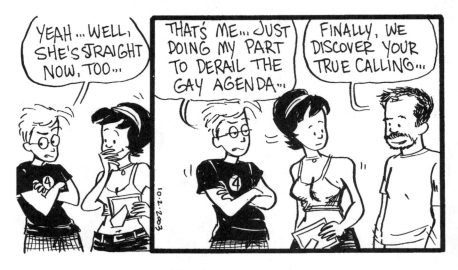

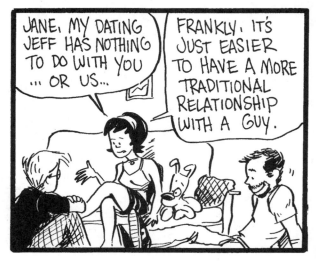

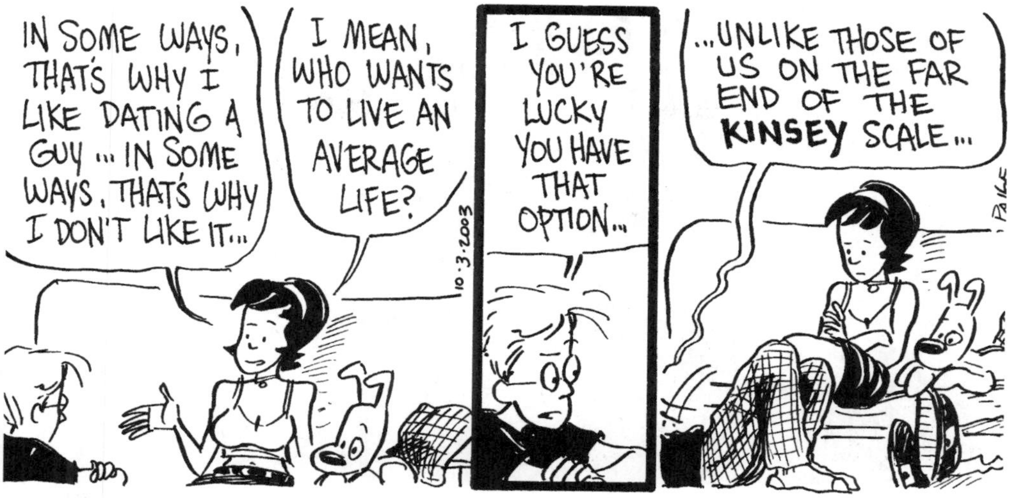
IN SOME WAYS, THAT'S WHY I LIKE DATING A GUY ... IN SOME WAYS, THAT'S WHY I DON'T LIKE IT...
I MEAN, WHO WANTS TO LIVE AN AVERAGE LIFE?
10·3·2003
I GUESS YOU'RE LUCKY YOU HAVE THAT OPTION...
...UNLIKE THOSE OF US ON THE FAR END OF THE **KINSEY** SCALE...
PAIGE

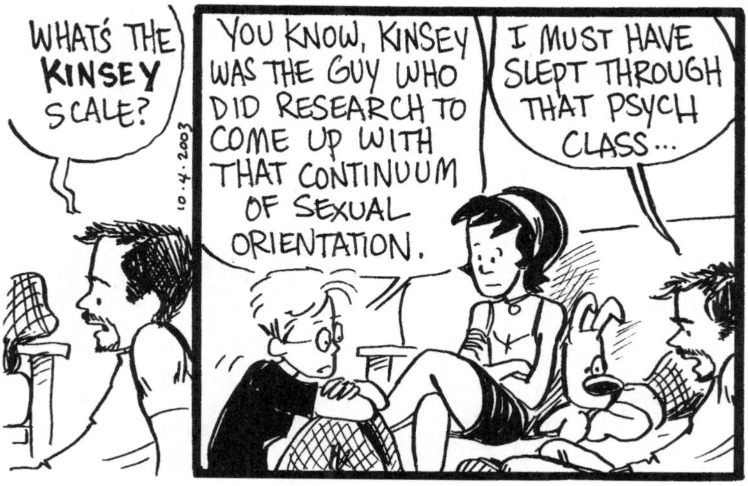
WHAT'S THE **KINSEY** SCALE?
10·4·2003
YOU KNOW, KINSEY WAS THE GUY WHO DID RESEARCH TO COME UP WITH THAT CONTINUUM OF SEXUAL ORIENTATION.
I MUST HAVE SLEPT THROUGH THAT PSYCH CLASS...

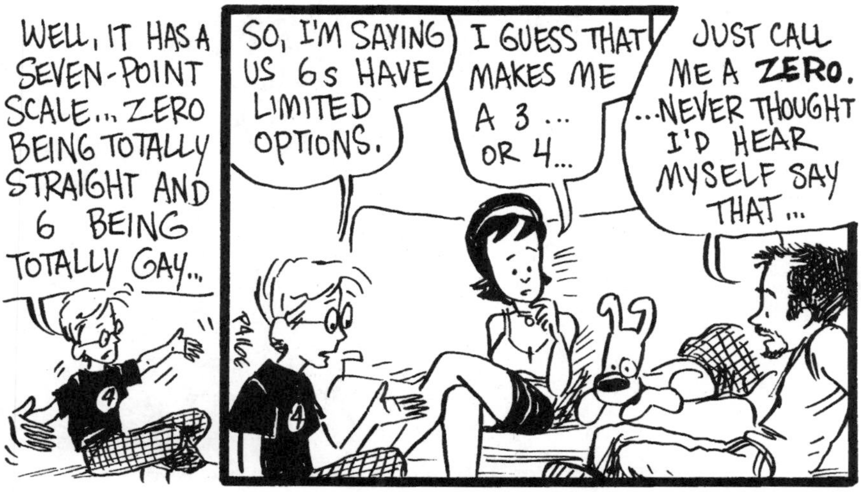
WELL, IT HAS A SEVEN-POINT SCALE... ZERO BEING TOTALLY STRAIGHT AND 6 BEING TOTALLY GAY...
PAIGE
SO, I'M SAYING US 6s HAVE LIMITED OPTIONS.
I GUESS THAT MAKES ME A 3 ... OR 4...
JUST CALL ME A **ZERO**. ...NEVER THOUGHT I'D HEAR MYSELF SAY THAT...

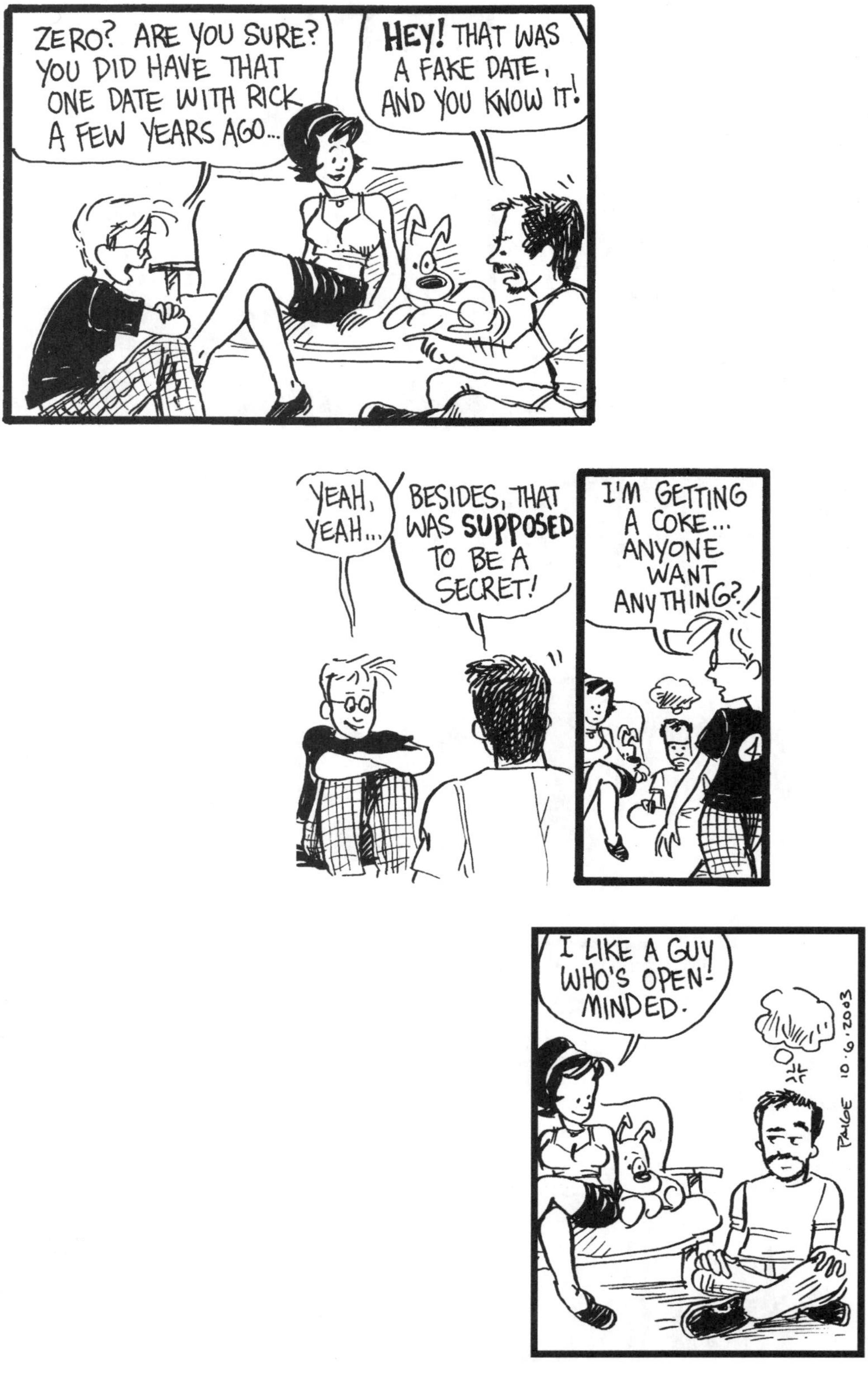
ZERO? ARE YOU SURE? YOU DID HAVE THAT ONE DATE WITH RICK A FEW YEARS AGO...
HEY! THAT WAS A FAKE DATE, AND YOU KNOW IT!
YEAH, YEAH...
BESIDES, THAT WAS SUPPOSED TO BE A SECRET!
I'M GETTING A COKE... ANYONE WANT ANYTHING?
I LIKE A GUY WHO'S OPEN-MINDED.
PAIGE 10·6·2003

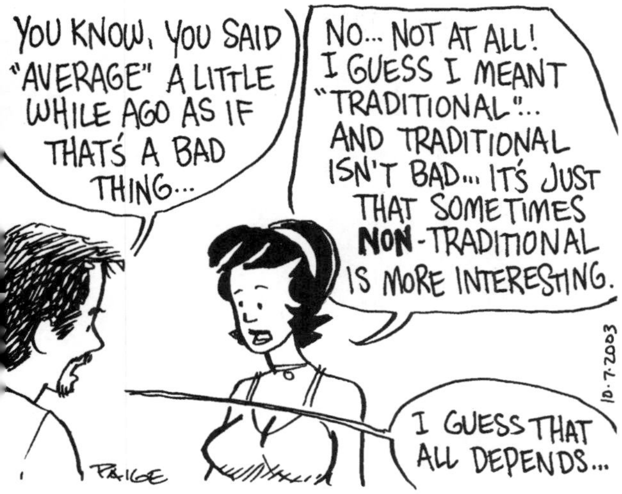
YOU KNOW, YOU SAID "AVERAGE" A LITTLE WHILE AGO AS IF THAT'S A BAD THING...
NO... NOT AT ALL! I GUESS I MEANT "TRADITIONAL"... AND TRADITIONAL ISN'T BAD... IT'S JUST THAT SOMETIMES **NON**-TRADITIONAL IS MORE INTERESTING.
I GUESS THAT ALL DEPENDS...
10-7-2003
PAIGE

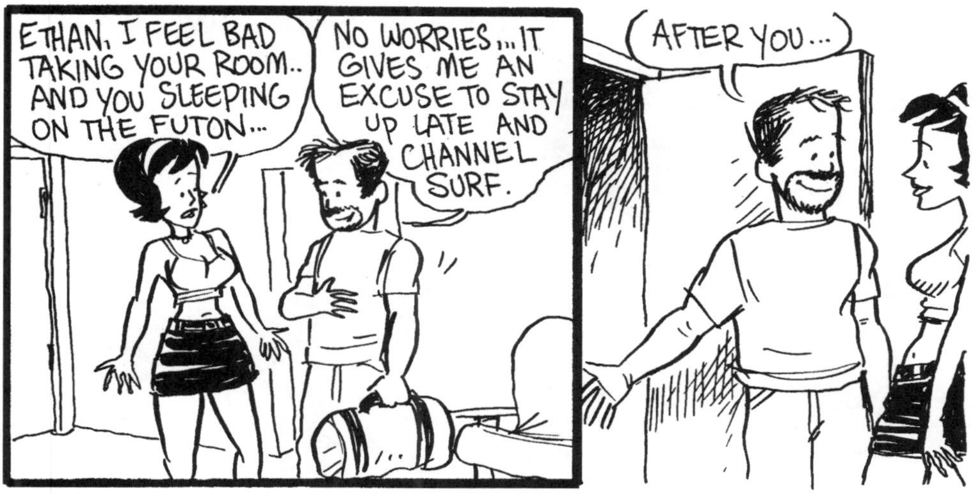
ETHAN, I FEEL BAD TAKING YOUR ROOM.. AND YOU SLEEPING ON THE FUTON...
NO WORRIES... IT GIVES ME AN EXCUSE TO STAY UP LATE AND CHANNEL SURF.
AFTER YOU...

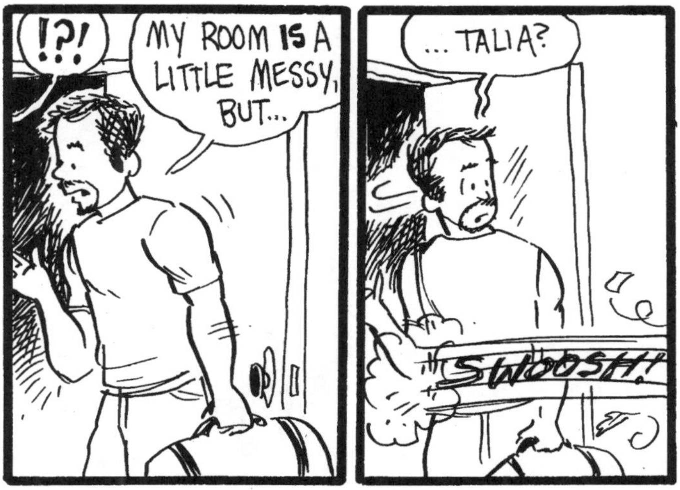
!?!
MY ROOM **IS** A LITTLE MESSY, BUT...
... TALIA?
SWOOSH!

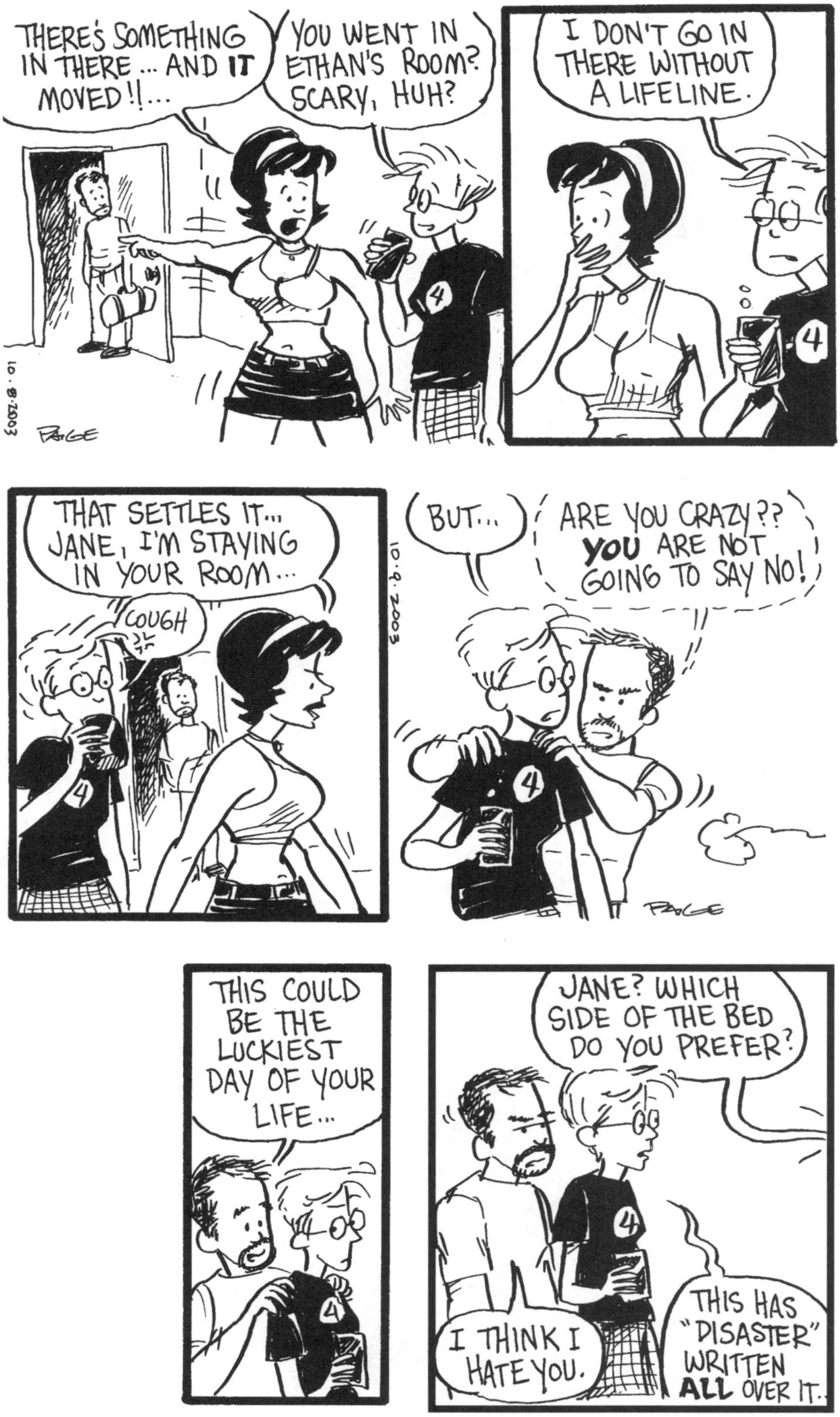
THERE'S SOMETHING IN THERE ... AND IT MOVED!!...
YOU WENT IN ETHAN'S ROOM? SCARY, HUH?
10·8·2003
PAIGE
I DON'T GO IN THERE WITHOUT A LIFELINE.
THAT SETTLES IT... JANE, I'M STAYING IN YOUR ROOM...
COUGH
10·8·2003
BUT...
ARE YOU CRAZY?? YOU ARE NOT GOING TO SAY NO!
PAIGE
THIS COULD BE THE LUCKIEST DAY OF YOUR LIFE...
JANE? WHICH SIDE OF THE BED DO YOU PREFER?
I THINK I HATE YOU.
THIS HAS "DISASTER" WRITTEN ALL OVER IT.

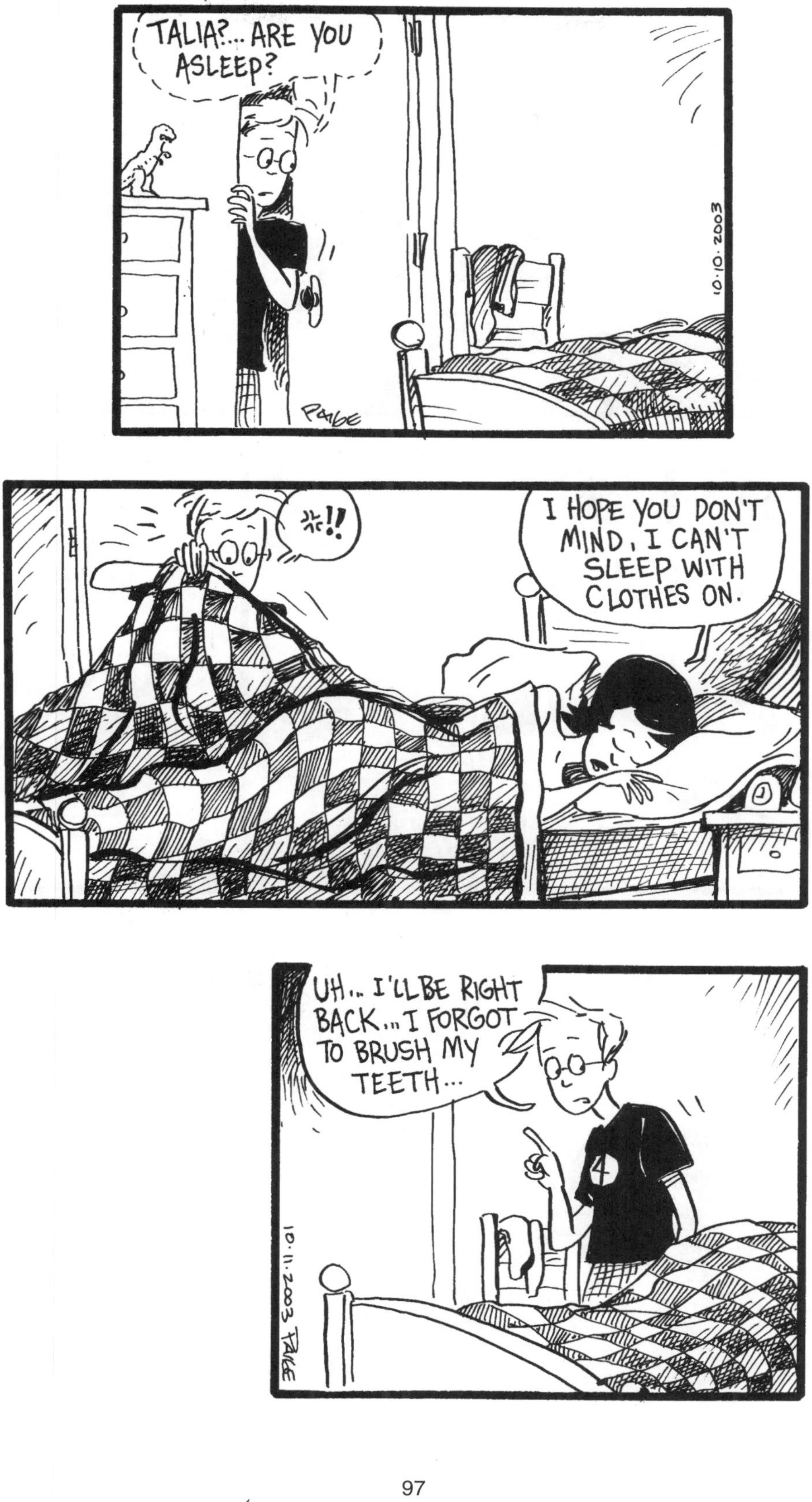
TALIA?... ARE YOU ASLEEP?
10.10.2003
PAIGE
I HOPE YOU DON'T MIND, I CAN'T SLEEP WITH CLOTHES ON.
UH... I'LL BE RIGHT BACK... I FORGOT TO BRUSH MY TEETH...
10.11.2003
PAIGE

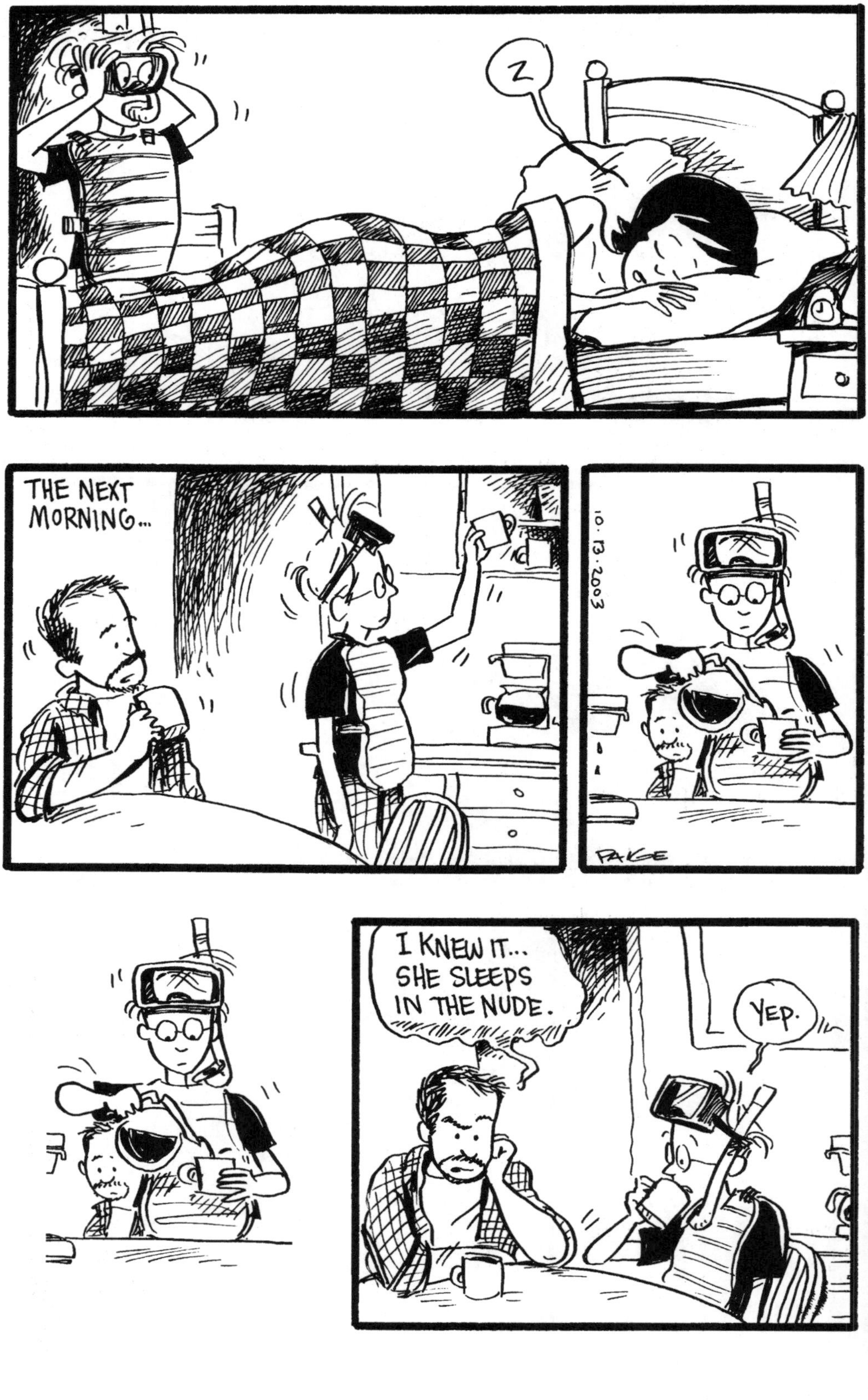
Z
THE NEXT MORNING...
10·13·2003
PAIGE
I KNEW IT... SHE SLEEPS IN THE NUDE.
YEP.

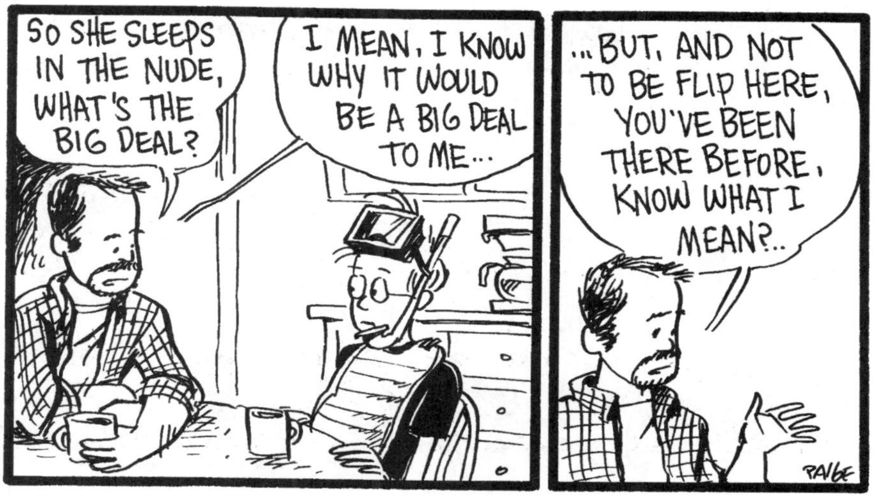
SO SHE SLEEPS IN THE NUDE, WHAT'S THE BIG DEAL?
I MEAN, I KNOW WHY IT WOULD BE A BIG DEAL TO ME...
...BUT, AND NOT TO BE FLIP HERE, YOU'VE BEEN THERE BEFORE, KNOW WHAT I MEAN?..
PAIGE

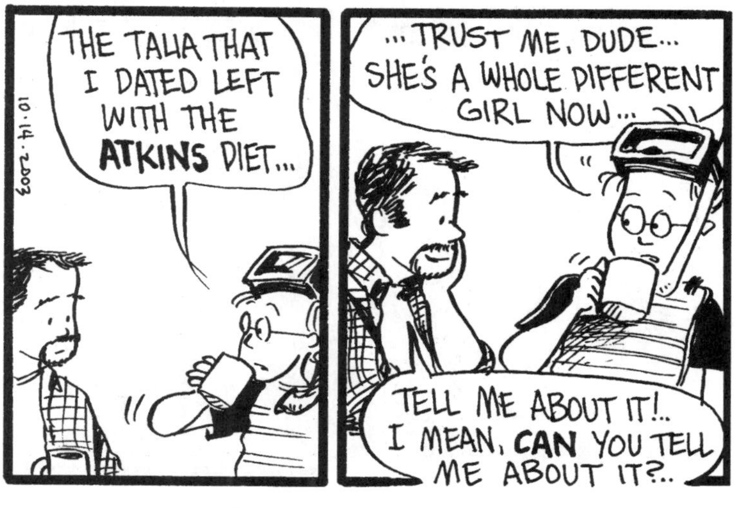
10.14.2003
THE TALIA THAT I DATED LEFT WITH THE **ATKINS** DIET...
...TRUST ME, DUDE... SHE'S A WHOLE DIFFERENT GIRL NOW...
TELL ME ABOUT IT!.. I MEAN, **CAN** YOU TELL ME ABOUT IT?..

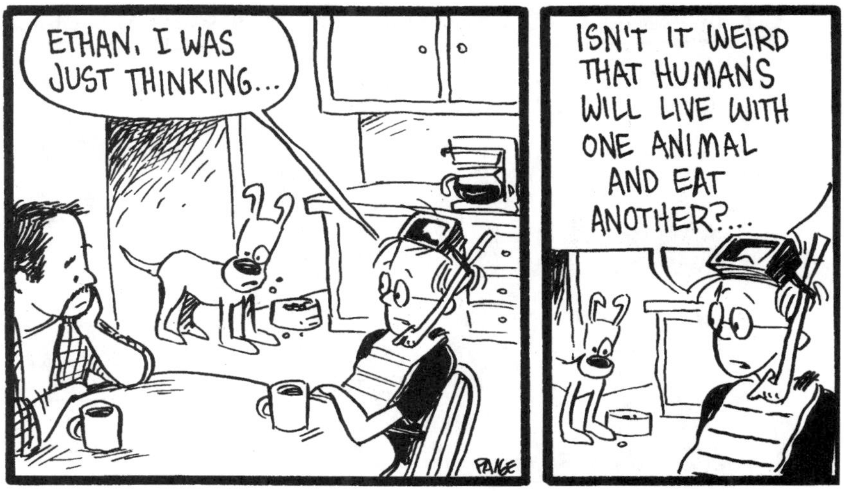
ETHAN, I WAS JUST THINKING...
PAIGE
ISN'T IT WEIRD THAT HUMANS WILL LIVE WITH ONE ANIMAL AND EAT ANOTHER?...

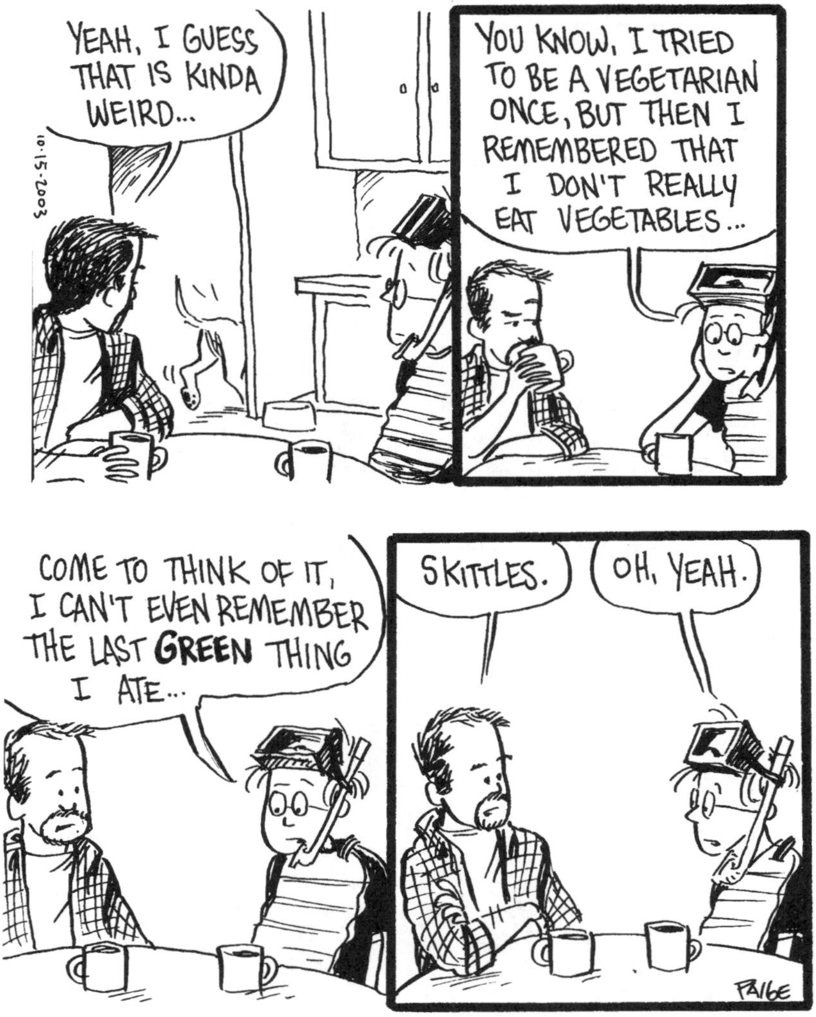
10·15·2003
YEAH, I GUESS THAT IS KINDA WEIRD...
YOU KNOW, I TRIED TO BE A VEGETARIAN ONCE, BUT THEN I REMEMBERED THAT I DON'T REALLY EAT VEGETABLES...
COME TO THINK OF IT, I CAN'T EVEN REMEMBER THE LAST **GREEN** THING I ATE...
SKITTLES.
OH, YEAH.
PAIGE

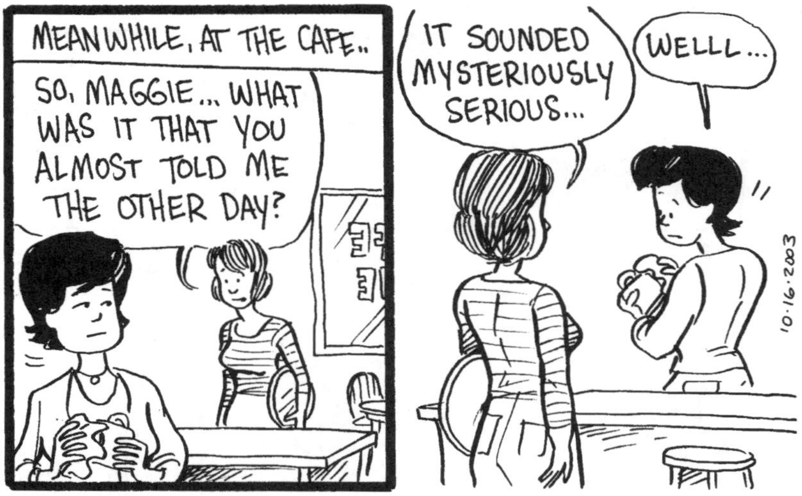
MEANWHILE, AT THE CAFE..
SO, MAGGIE... WHAT WAS IT THAT YOU ALMOST TOLD ME THE OTHER DAY?
IT SOUNDED MYSTERIOUSLY SERIOUS...
WELLL...
10·16·2003

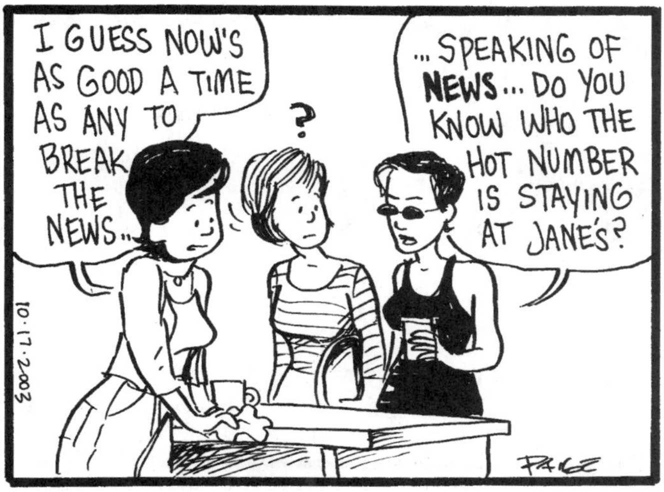
I GUESS NOW'S AS GOOD A TIME AS ANY TO BREAK THE NEWS...
?
... SPEAKING OF NEWS... DO YOU KNOW WHO THE HOT NUMBER IS STAYING AT JANE'S?
10.17.2003
PAIGE

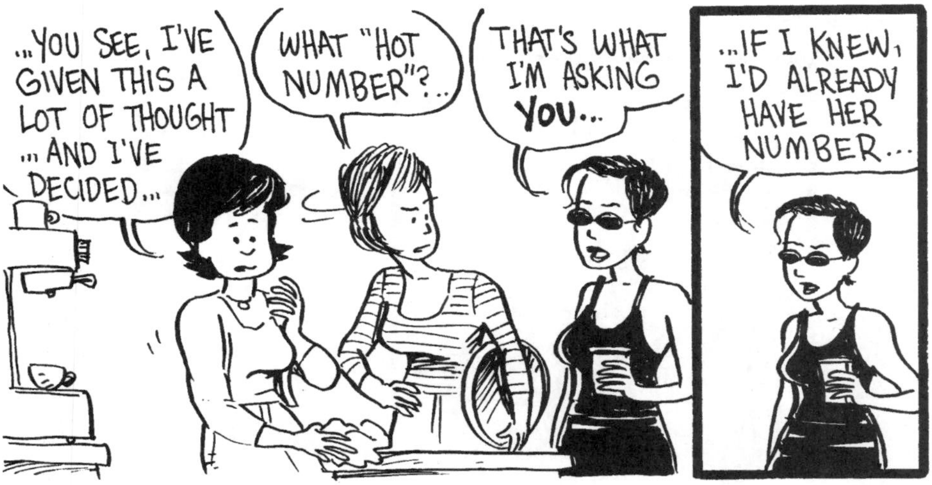
... YOU SEE, I'VE GIVEN THIS A LOT OF THOUGHT ... AND I'VE DECIDED...
WHAT "HOT NUMBER"?...
THAT'S WHAT I'M ASKING YOU...
...IF I KNEW, I'D ALREADY HAVE HER NUMBER...

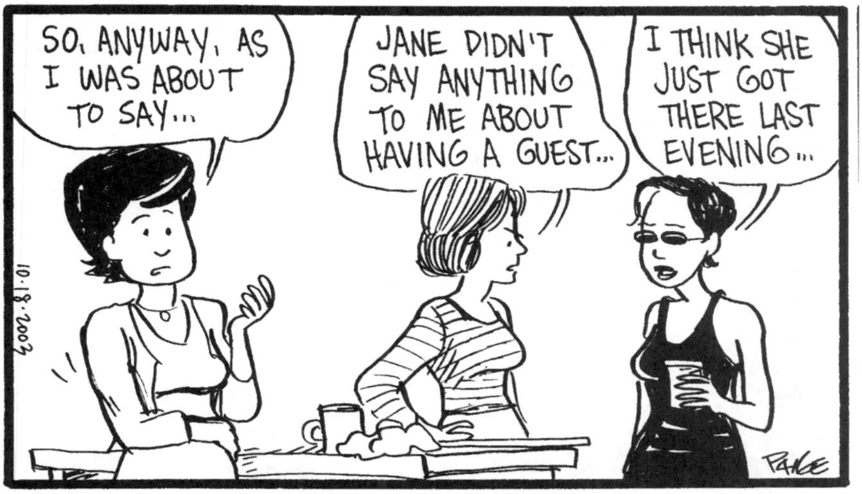
SO, ANYWAY, AS I WAS ABOUT TO SAY...
JANE DIDN'T SAY ANYTHING TO ME ABOUT HAVING A GUEST...
I THINK SHE JUST GOT THERE LAST EVENING...
10.18.2003
PAIGE

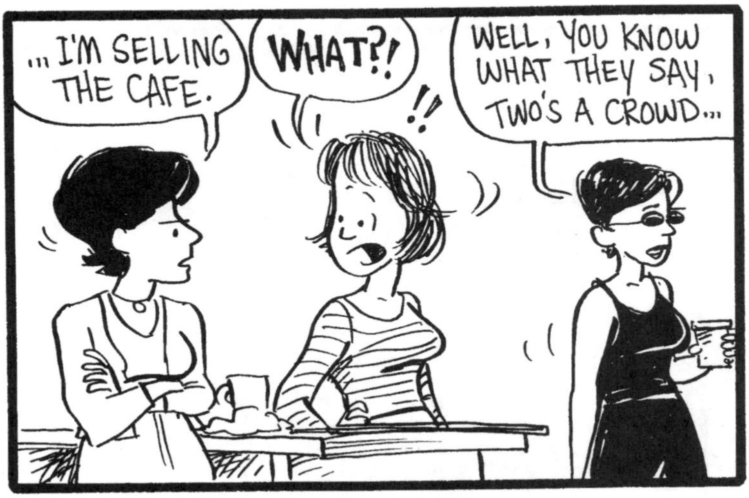
...I'M SELLING THE CAFE.
WHAT?!
!!
WELL, YOU KNOW WHAT THEY SAY, TWO'S A CROWD...

Meanwhile, at Jane and Ethan's...

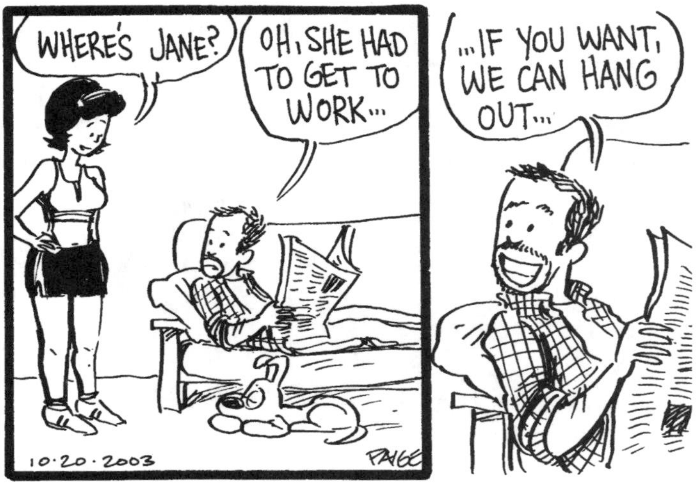
WHERE'S JANE?
OH, SHE HAD TO GET TO WORK...
...IF YOU WANT, WE CAN HANG OUT...
10·20·2003
PAIGE

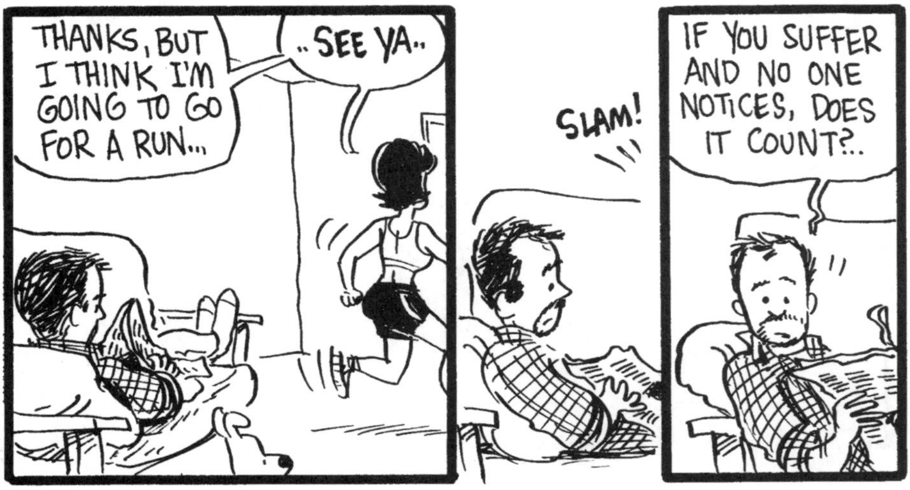
THANKS, BUT I THINK I'M GOING TO GO FOR A RUN...
..SEE YA..
SLAM!
IF YOU SUFFER AND NO ONE NOTICES, DOES IT COUNT?..

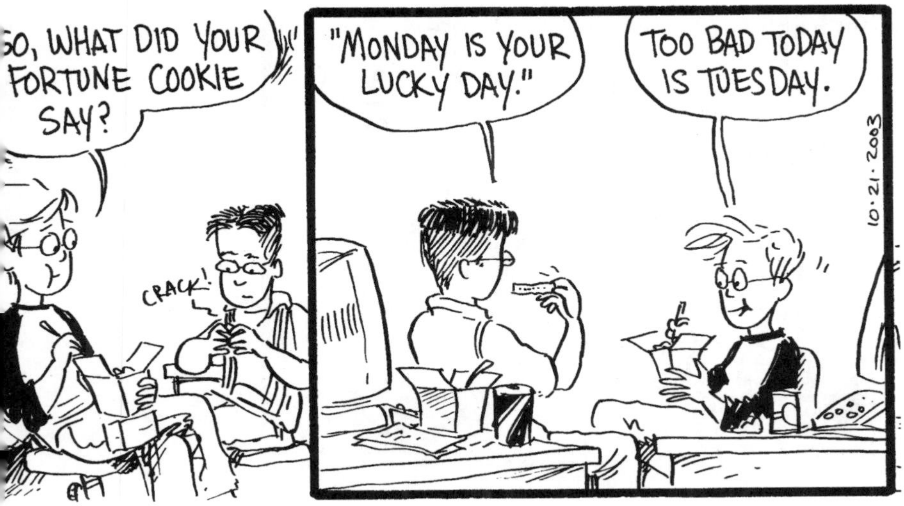
SO, WHAT DID YOUR FORTUNE COOKIE SAY?
CRACK!
"MONDAY IS YOUR LUCKY DAY."
TOO BAD TODAY IS TUESDAY.
10·21·2003

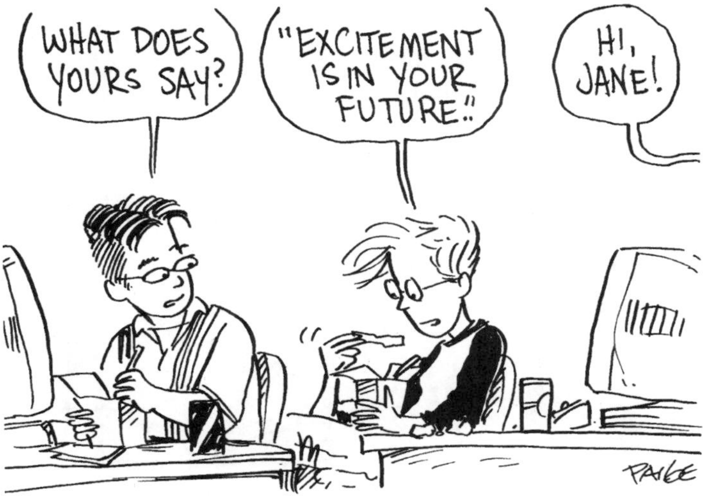
WHAT DOES YOURS SAY?
"EXCITEMENT IS IN YOUR FUTURE."
HI, JANE!
PAIGE

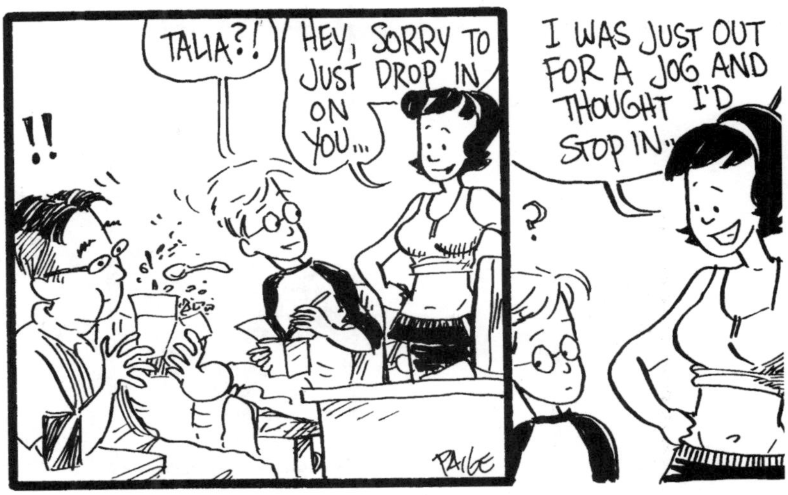
!!
TALIA?!
HEY, SORRY TO JUST DROP IN ON YOU...
I WAS JUST OUT FOR A JOG AND THOUGHT I'D STOP IN...
?
PAIGE

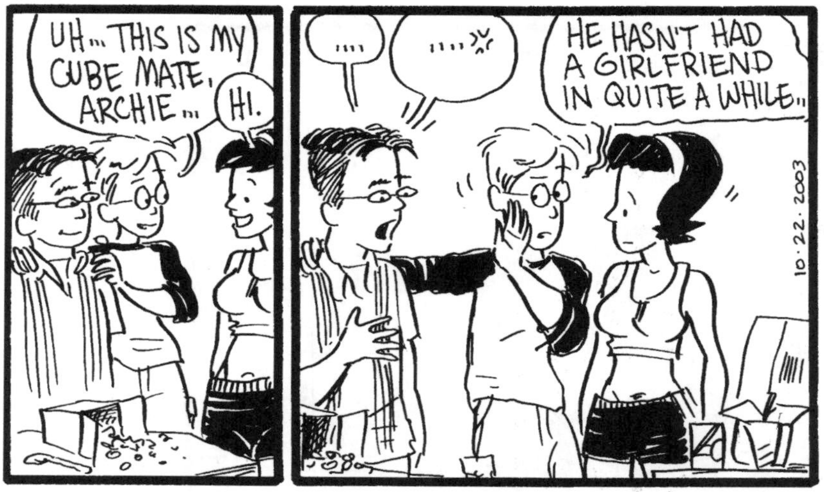
UH... THIS IS MY CUBE MATE, ARCHIE...
HI.
....
HE HASN'T HAD A GIRLFRIEND IN QUITE A WHILE..
10·22·2003

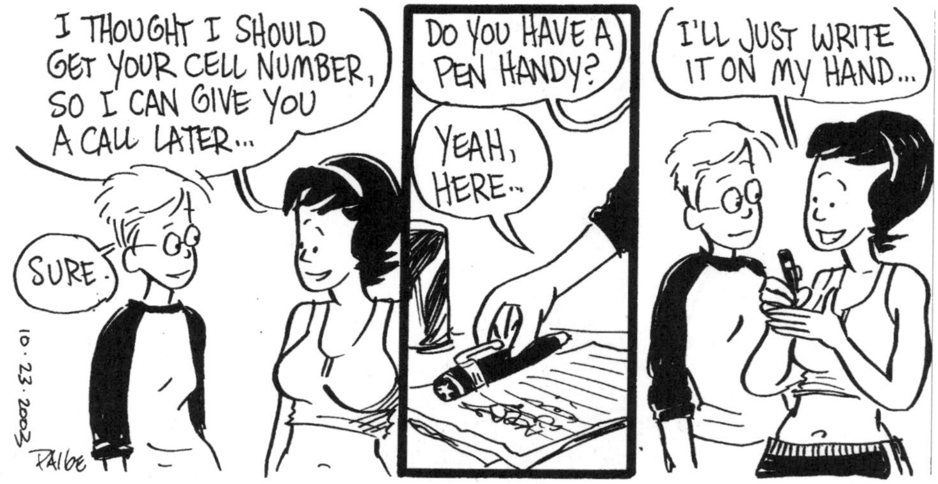
I THOUGHT I SHOULD GET YOUR CELL NUMBER, SO I CAN GIVE YOU A CALL LATER...
SURE.
10·23·2003
PAIGE
DO YOU HAVE A PEN HANDY?
YEAH, HERE..
I'LL JUST WRITE IT ON MY HAND...

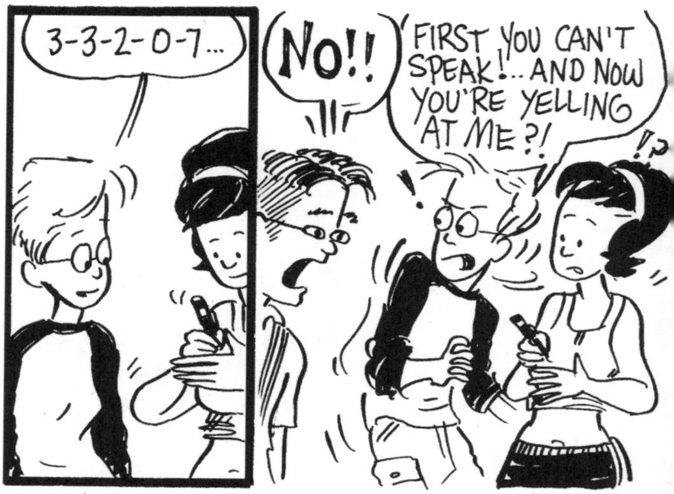
3-3-2-0-7...
NO!!
FIRST YOU CAN'T SPEAK!.. AND NOW YOU'RE YELLING AT ME?!

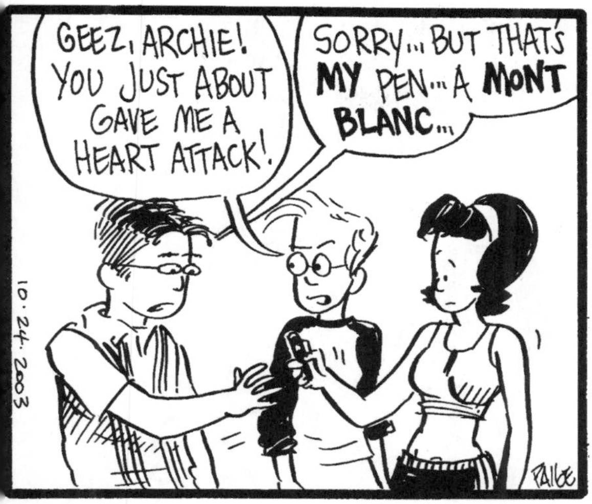
GEEZ, ARCHIE! YOU JUST ABOUT GAVE ME A HEART ATTACK!
SORRY... BUT THAT'S **MY** PEN... A **MONT BLANC**...
10 · 24 · 2003
PAIGE

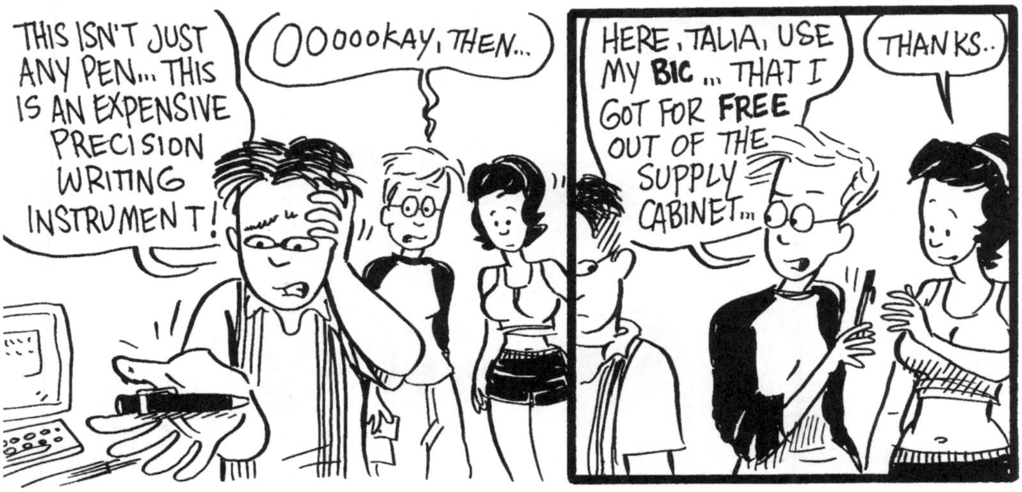
THIS ISN'T JUST ANY PEN... THIS IS AN EXPENSIVE PRECISION WRITING INSTRUMENT!
OOoooKAY, THEN...
HERE, TALIA, USE MY **BIC**... THAT I GOT FOR **FREE** OUT OF THE SUPPLY CABINET...
THANKS..

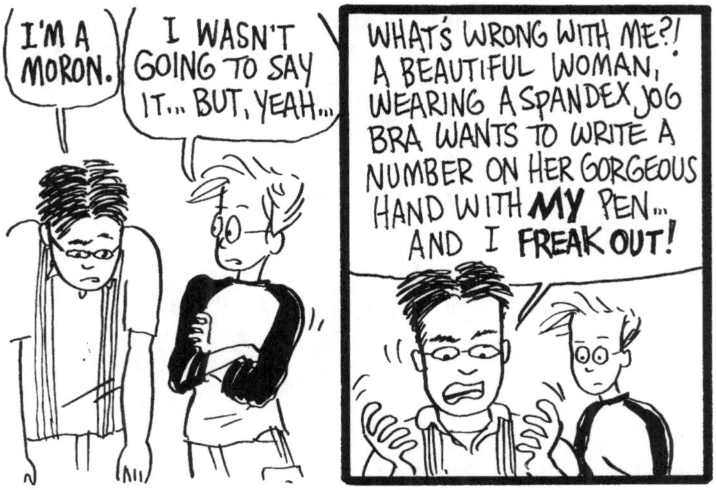
I'M A MORON.
I WASN'T GOING TO SAY IT... BUT, YEAH...
WHAT'S WRONG WITH ME?! A BEAUTIFUL WOMAN, WEARING A SPANDEX JOG BRA WANTS TO WRITE A NUMBER ON HER GORGEOUS HAND WITH **MY** PEN... AND I **FREAK OUT**!

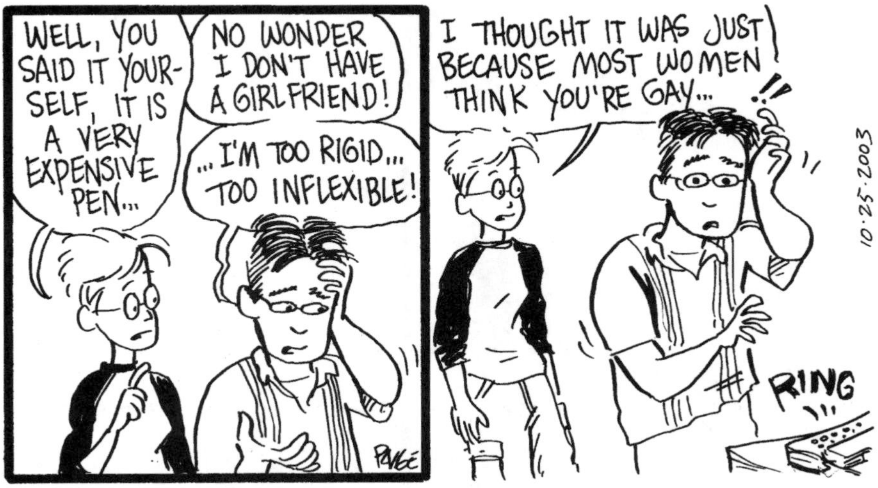
WELL, YOU SAID IT YOURSELF, IT IS A VERY EXPENSIVE PEN...
NO WONDER I DON'T HAVE A GIRLFRIEND!
...I'M TOO RIGID... TOO INFLEXIBLE!
PAIGE
I THOUGHT IT WAS JUST BECAUSE MOST WOMEN THINK YOU'RE GAY...
!!
RING
10·25·2003

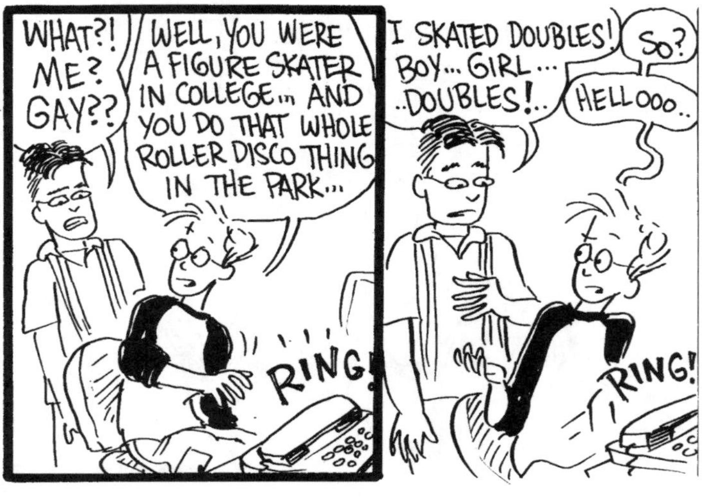
WHAT?! ME? GAY??
WELL, YOU WERE A FIGURE SKATER IN COLLEGE... AND YOU DO THAT WHOLE ROLLER DISCO THING IN THE PARK...
RING!
I SKATED DOUBLES! BOY... GIRL... ..DOUBLES!..
SO?
HELLOOO..
RING!

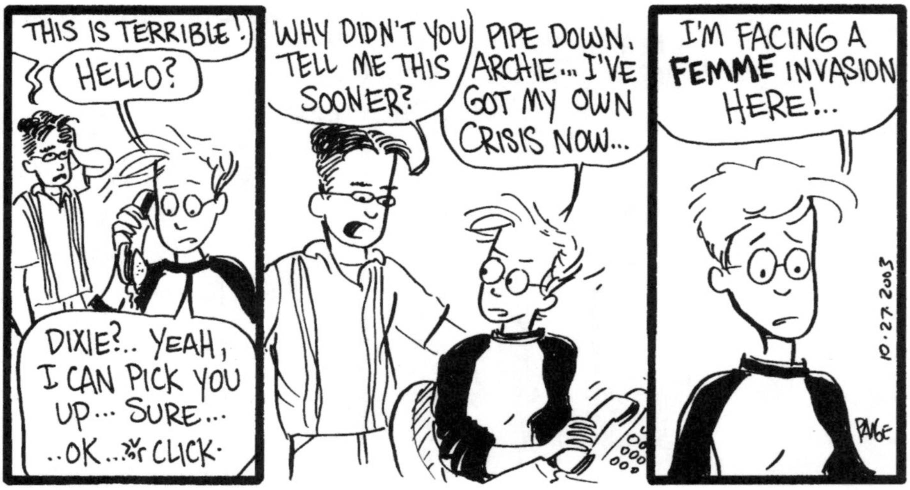
THIS IS TERRIBLE!
HELLO?
DIXIE?.. YEAH, I CAN PICK YOU UP... SURE... ..OK... CLICK
WHY DIDN'T YOU TELL ME THIS SOONER?
PIPE DOWN, ARCHIE... I'VE GOT MY OWN CRISIS NOW...
I'M FACING A FEMME INVASION HERE!..
10·27·2003
PAIGE

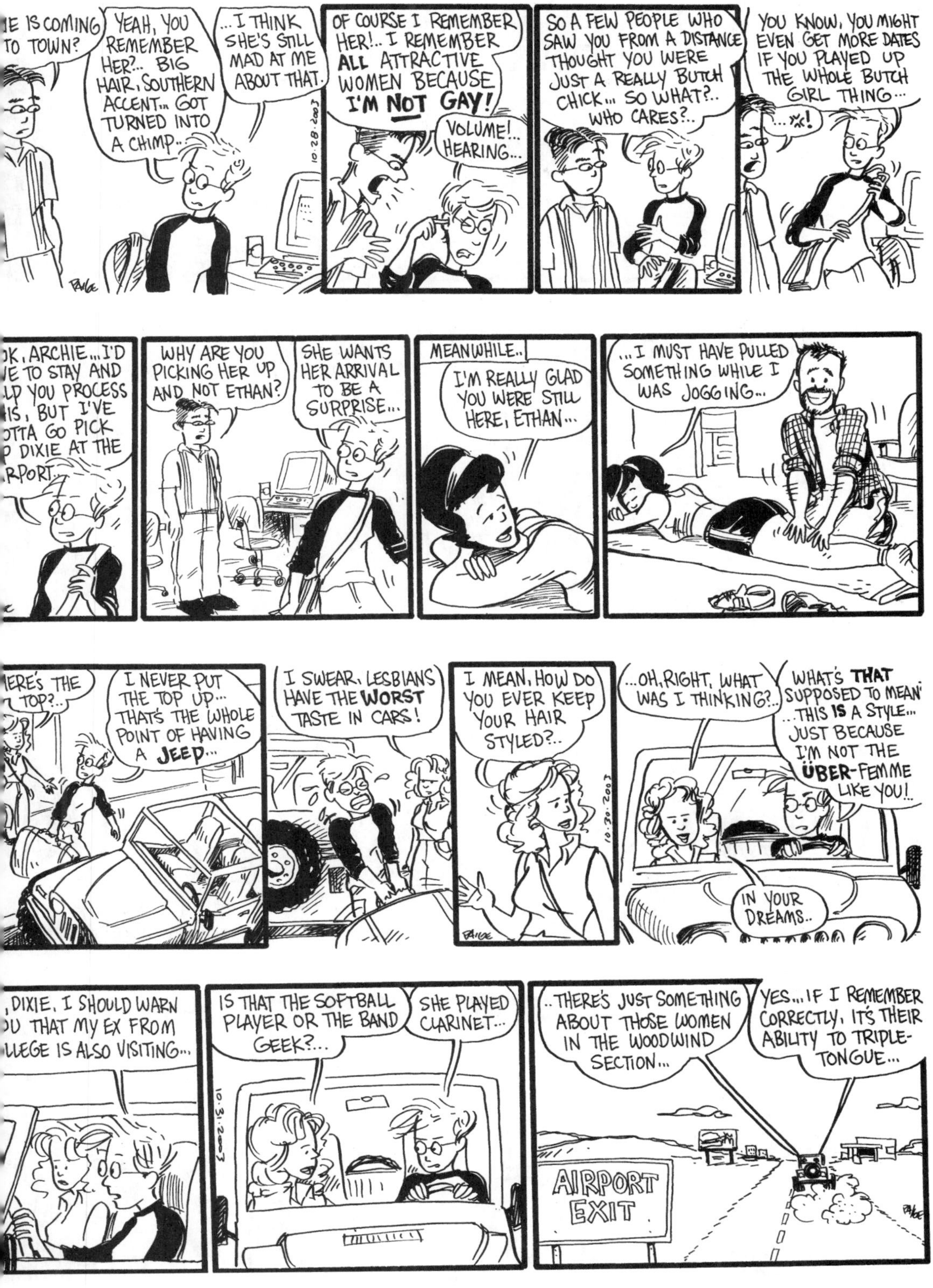

...E IS COMING TO TOWN?
YEAH, YOU REMEMBER HER?.. BIG HAIR, SOUTHERN ACCENT... GOT TURNED INTO A CHIMP...
...I THINK SHE'S STILL MAD AT ME ABOUT THAT.
10.28.2003
OF COURSE I REMEMBER HER!.. I REMEMBER ALL ATTRACTIVE WOMEN BECAUSE I'M NOT GAY!
VOLUME!... HEARING...
SO A FEW PEOPLE WHO SAW YOU FROM A DISTANCE THOUGHT YOU WERE JUST A REALLY BUTCH CHICK... SO WHAT?.. WHO CARES?..
YOU KNOW, YOU MIGHT EVEN GET MORE DATES IF YOU PLAYED UP THE WHOLE BUTCH GIRL THING...
...%!
...OK, ARCHIE... I'D ...E TO STAY AND ...LP YOU PROCESS ...IS, BUT I'VE ...OTTA GO PICK ...P DIXIE AT THE ...RPORT...
WHY ARE YOU PICKING HER UP AND NOT ETHAN?
SHE WANTS HER ARRIVAL TO BE A SURPRISE...
MEANWHILE..
I'M REALLY GLAD YOU WERE STILL HERE, ETHAN...
...I MUST HAVE PULLED SOMETHING WHILE I WAS JOGGING...
...ERE'S THE ... TOP?..
I NEVER PUT THE TOP UP... THAT'S THE WHOLE POINT OF HAVING A JEEP...
I SWEAR, LESBIANS HAVE THE WORST TASTE IN CARS!
I MEAN, HOW DO YOU EVER KEEP YOUR HAIR STYLED?..
10.30.2003
...OH, RIGHT, WHAT WAS I THINKING?..
WHAT'S THAT SUPPOSED TO MEAN ...THIS IS A STYLE... JUST BECAUSE I'M NOT THE ÜBER-FEMME LIKE YOU!..
IN YOUR DREAMS..
..., DIXIE, I SHOULD WARN ...OU THAT MY EX FROM ...LLEGE IS ALSO VISITING...
10.31.2003
IS THAT THE SOFTBALL PLAYER OR THE BAND GEEK?..
SHE PLAYED CLARINET...
..THERE'S JUST SOMETHING ABOUT THOSE WOMEN IN THE WOODWIND SECTION...
YES... IF I REMEMBER CORRECTLY, IT'S THEIR ABILITY TO TRIPLE-TONGUE...
AIRPORT EXIT

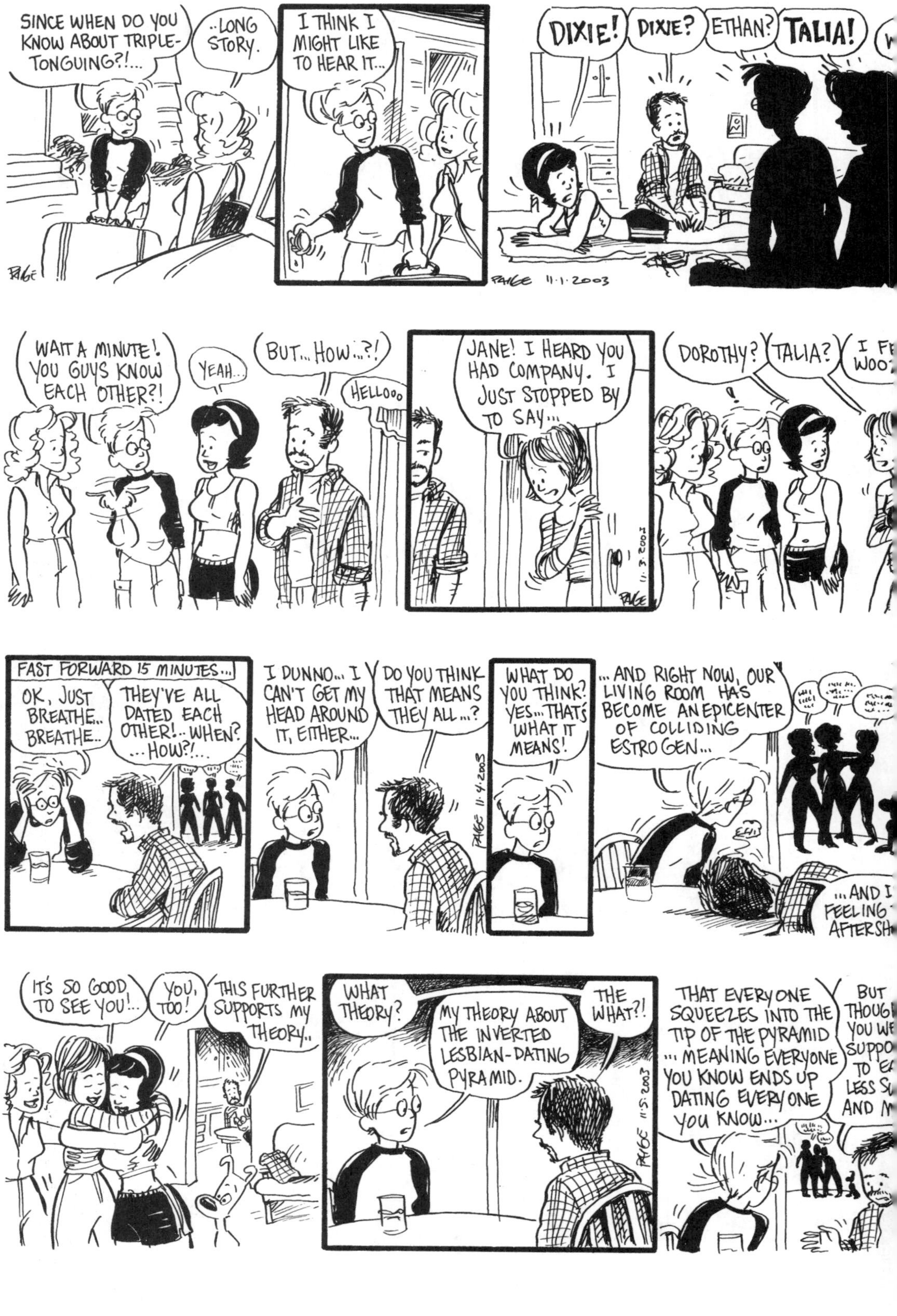
SINCE WHEN DO YOU KNOW ABOUT TRIPLE-TONGUING?!...
..LONG STORY.
I THINK I MIGHT LIKE TO HEAR IT...
DIXIE!
DIXIE?
ETHAN?
TALIA!
PAIGE 11·1·2003
WAIT A MINUTE! YOU GUYS KNOW EACH OTHER?!
YEAH..
BUT... HOW...?!
HELLOooo
JANE! I HEARD YOU HAD COMPANY. I JUST STOPPED BY TO SAY...
11·3·2003
DOROTHY?
TALIA?
FAST FORWARD 15 MINUTES...
OK, JUST BREATHE.. BREATHE..
THEY'VE ALL DATED EACH OTHER!.. WHEN? ...HOW?!...
I DUNNO... I CAN'T GET MY HEAD AROUND IT, EITHER...
DO YOU THINK THAT MEANS THEY ALL...?
PAIGE 11·4·2003
WHAT DO YOU THINK? YES... THAT'S WHAT IT MEANS!
...AND RIGHT NOW, OUR LIVING ROOM HAS BECOME AN EPICENTER OF COLLIDING ESTROGEN...
IT'S SO GOOD TO SEE YOU!..
YOU, TOO!
THIS FURTHER SUPPORTS MY THEORY..
WHAT THEORY?
MY THEORY ABOUT THE INVERTED LESBIAN-DATING PYRAMID.
THE WHAT?!
PAIGE 11·5·2003
THAT EVERYONE SQUEEZES INTO THE TIP OF THE PYRAMID ...MEANING EVERYONE YOU KNOW ENDS UP DATING EVERYONE YOU KNOW...

Chapter 3

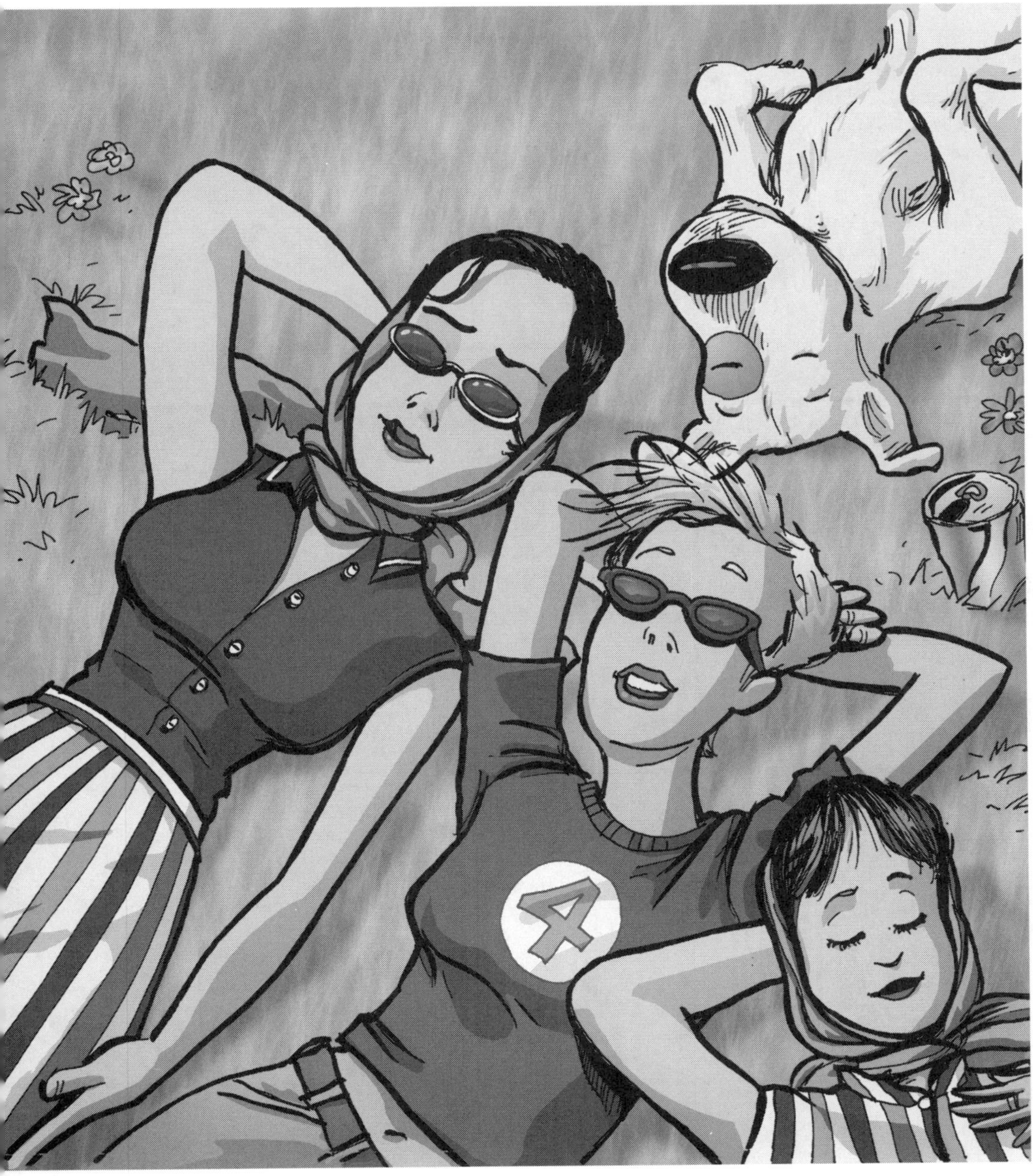

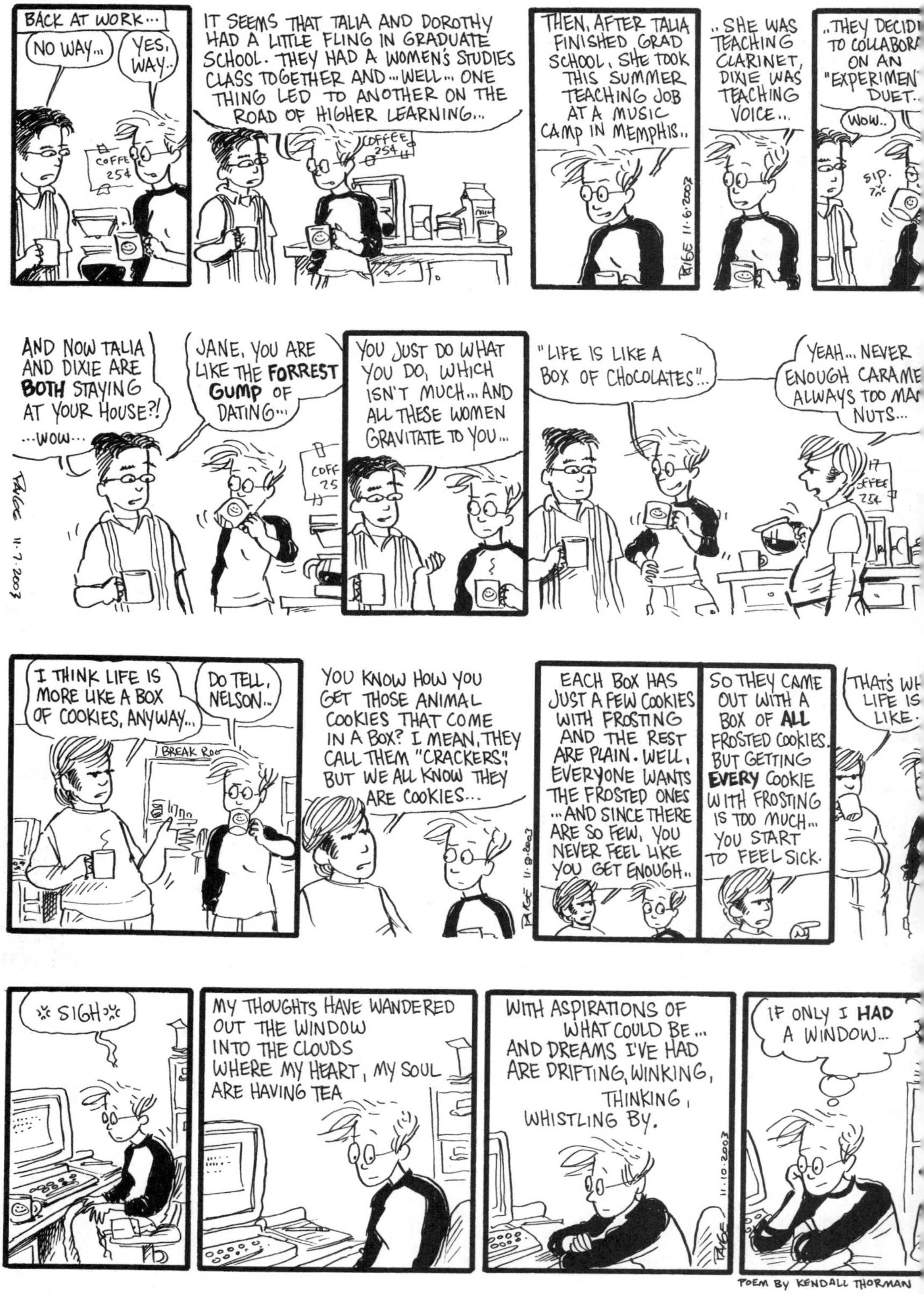
BACK AT WORK...
NO WAY...
YES, WAY..
COFFEE 25¢
IT SEEMS THAT TALIA AND DOROTHY HAD A LITTLE FLING IN GRADUATE SCHOOL. THEY HAD A WOMEN'S STUDIES CLASS TOGETHER AND... WELL... ONE THING LED TO ANOTHER ON THE ROAD OF HIGHER LEARNING...
THEN, AFTER TALIA FINISHED GRAD SCHOOL, SHE TOOK THIS SUMMER TEACHING JOB AT A MUSIC CAMP IN MEMPHIS..
PAIGE 11·6·2003
..SHE WAS TEACHING CLARINET, DIXIE WAS TEACHING VOICE...
..THEY DECID
TO COLLABORA
ON AN
"EXPERIMEN
DUET..
WOW..
SIP.
AND NOW TALIA AND DIXIE ARE **BOTH** STAYING AT YOUR HOUSE?!
...WOW...
PAIGE 11·7·2003
JANE, YOU ARE LIKE THE **FORREST GUMP** OF DATING...
YOU JUST DO WHAT YOU DO, WHICH ISN'T MUCH... AND ALL THESE WOMEN GRAVITATE TO YOU...
"LIFE IS LIKE A BOX OF CHOCOLATES"...
YEAH... NEVER
ENOUGH CARAME
ALWAYS TOO MA
NUTS...
I THINK LIFE IS MORE LIKE A BOX OF COOKIES, ANYWAY...
DO TELL, NELSON...
BREAK ROO
YOU KNOW HOW YOU GET THOSE ANIMAL COOKIES THAT COME IN A BOX? I MEAN, THEY CALL THEM "CRACKERS," BUT WE ALL KNOW THEY ARE COOKIES...
PAIGE 11·8·2003
EACH BOX HAS JUST A FEW COOKIES WITH FROSTING AND THE REST ARE PLAIN. WELL, EVERYONE WANTS THE FROSTED ONES ...AND SINCE THERE ARE SO FEW, YOU NEVER FEEL LIKE YOU GET ENOUGH..
SO THEY CAME OUT WITH A BOX OF **ALL** FROSTED COOKIES. BUT GETTING **EVERY** COOKIE WITH FROSTING IS TOO MUCH... YOU START TO FEEL SICK.
THAT'S WH
LIFE IS
LIKE.
SIGH
MY THOUGHTS HAVE WANDERED OUT THE WINDOW INTO THE CLOUDS WHERE MY HEART, MY SOUL ARE HAVING TEA
WITH ASPIRATIONS OF WHAT COULD BE... AND DREAMS I'VE HAD ARE DRIFTING, WINKING, THINKING, WHISTLING BY.
PAIGE 11·10·2003
IF ONLY I **HAD** A WINDOW...
POEM BY KENDALL THORMAN

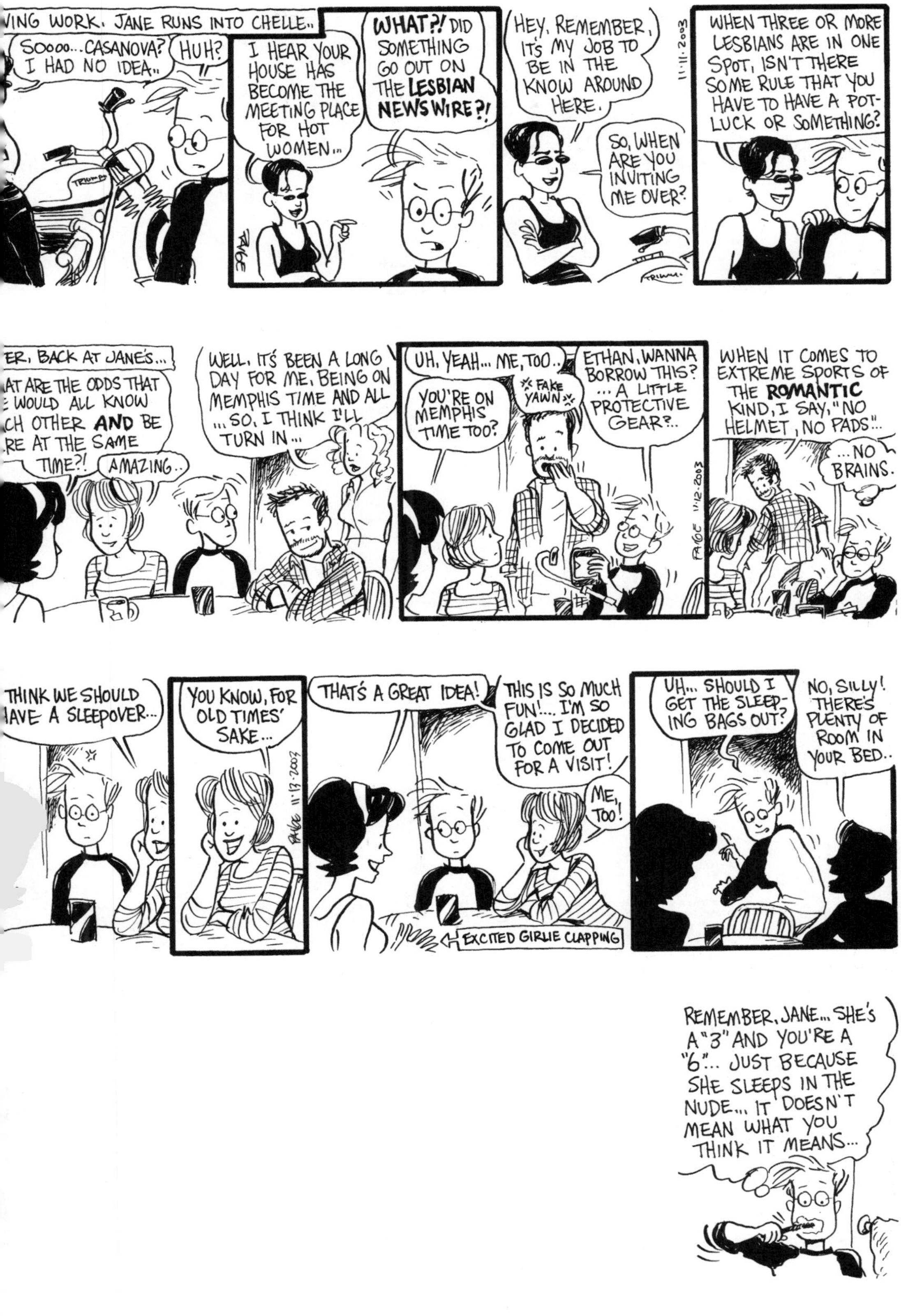

VING WORK, JANE RUNS INTO CHELLE..
SOOOO...CASANOVA? I HAD NO IDEA..
HUH?
I HEAR YOUR HOUSE HAS BECOME THE MEETING PLACE FOR HOT WOMEN..
WHAT?! DID SOMETHING GO OUT ON THE LESBIAN NEWS WIRE?!
HEY, REMEMBER, IT'S MY JOB TO BE IN THE KNOW AROUND HERE.
SO, WHEN ARE YOU INVITING ME OVER?
11·11·2003
WHEN THREE OR MORE LESBIANS ARE IN ONE SPOT, ISN'T THERE SOME RULE THAT YOU HAVE TO HAVE A POT-LUCK OR SOMETHING?
ER, BACK AT JANE'S...
AT ARE THE ODDS THAT WOULD ALL KNOW CH OTHER AND BE RE AT THE SAME TIME?!
AMAZING..
WELL, IT'S BEEN A LONG DAY FOR ME, BEING ON MEMPHIS TIME AND ALL ...SO, I THINK I'LL TURN IN...
UH, YEAH... ME, TOO..
YOU'RE ON MEMPHIS TIME TOO?
FAKE YAWN
ETHAN, WANNA BORROW THIS? ...A LITTLE PROTECTIVE GEAR?..
11·12·2003
WHEN IT COMES TO EXTREME SPORTS OF THE ROMANTIC KIND, I SAY, "NO HELMET, NO PADS"...
...NO BRAINS.
THINK WE SHOULD AVE A SLEEPOVER...
YOU KNOW, FOR OLD TIMES' SAKE...
11·13·2003
THAT'S A GREAT IDEA!
THIS IS SO MUCH FUN!... I'M SO GLAD I DECIDED TO COME OUT FOR A VISIT!
ME, TOO!
EXCITED GIRLIE CLAPPING
UH... SHOULD I GET THE SLEEP-ING BAGS OUT?
NO, SILLY! THERE'S PLENTY OF ROOM IN YOUR BED..
REMEMBER, JANE... SHE'S A "3" AND YOU'RE A "6"... JUST BECAUSE SHE SLEEPS IN THE NUDE... IT DOESN'T MEAN WHAT YOU THINK IT MEANS...

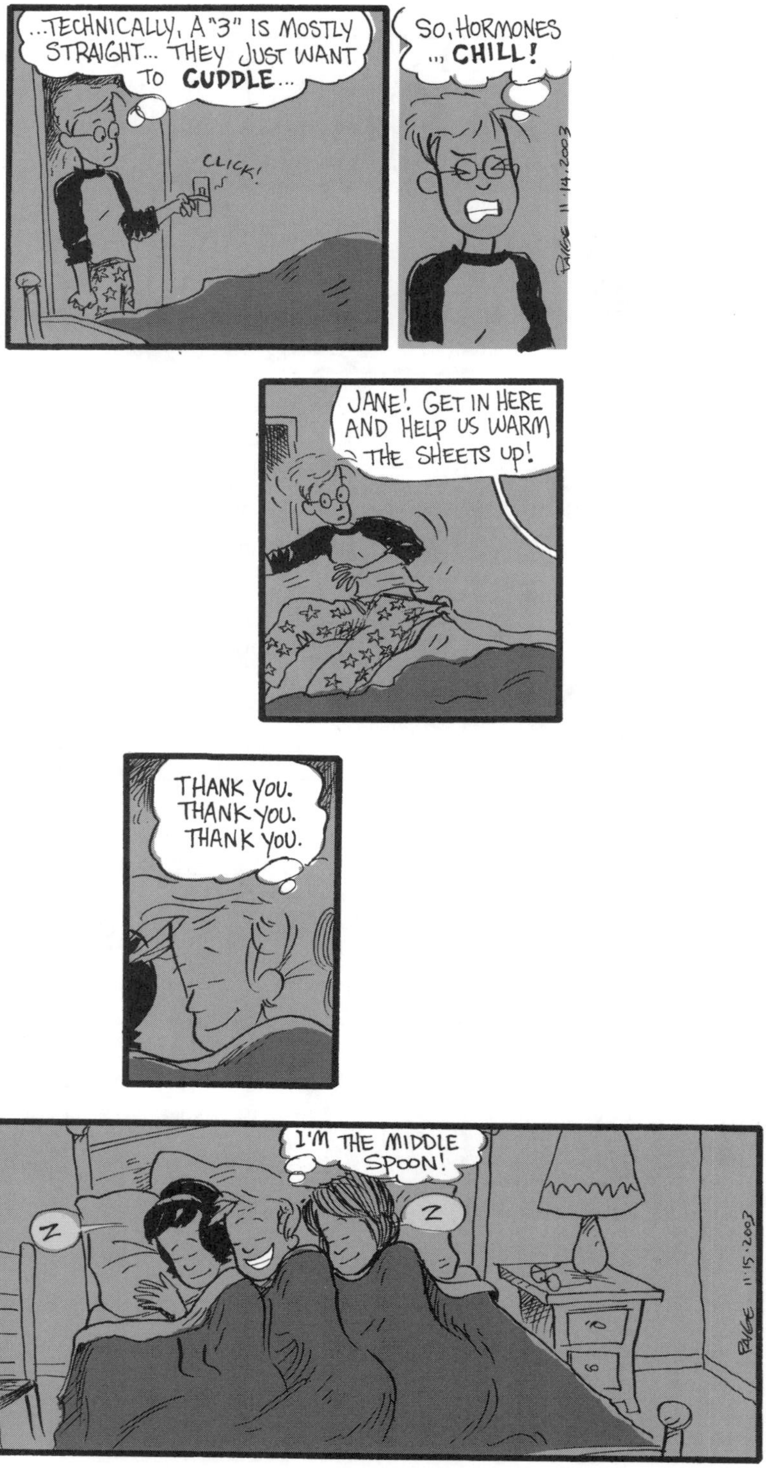
...TECHNICALLY, A "3" IS MOSTLY STRAIGHT... THEY JUST WANT TO CUDDLE...
CLICK!
SO, HORMONES ..., CHILL!
PAIGE 11.14.2003
JANE! GET IN HERE AND HELP US WARM THE SHEETS UP!
THANK YOU. THANK YOU. THANK YOU.
I'M THE MIDDLE SPOON!
Z
Z
PAIGE 11.15.2003

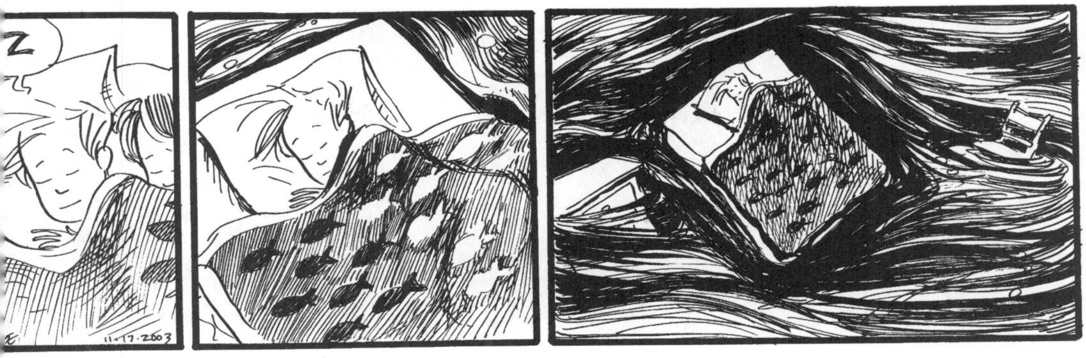
Z
11·17·2003

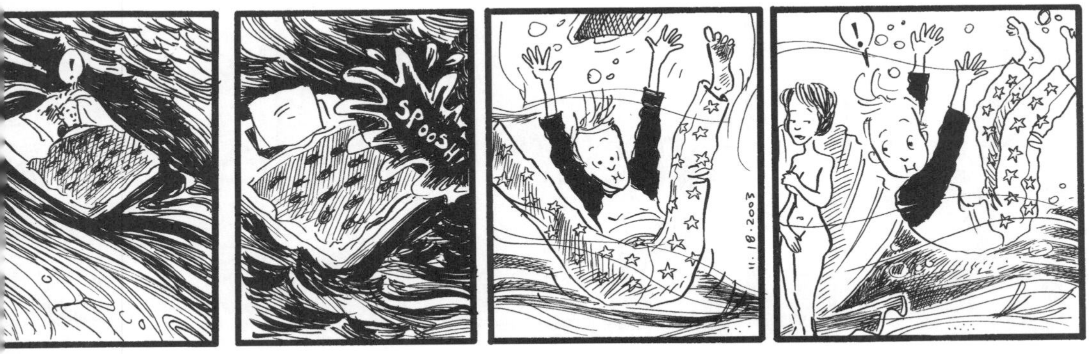
!
SPOOSH!
11·18·2003
!

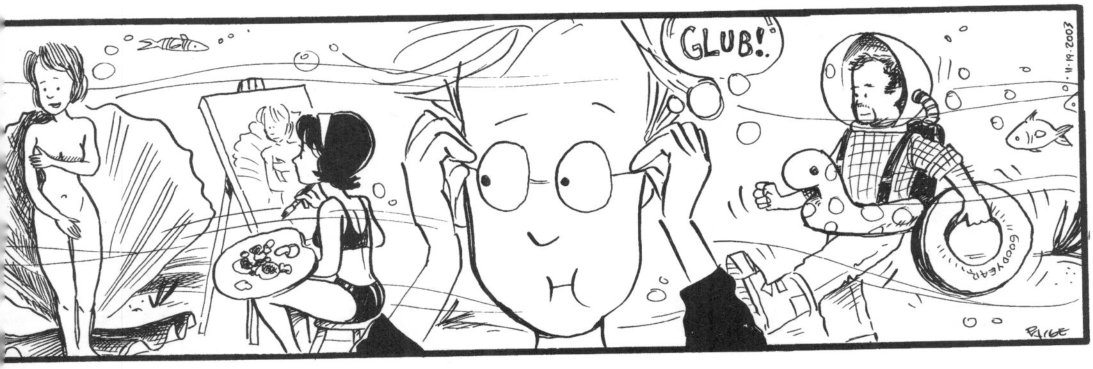
GLUB!
11·19·2003
GOODYEAR

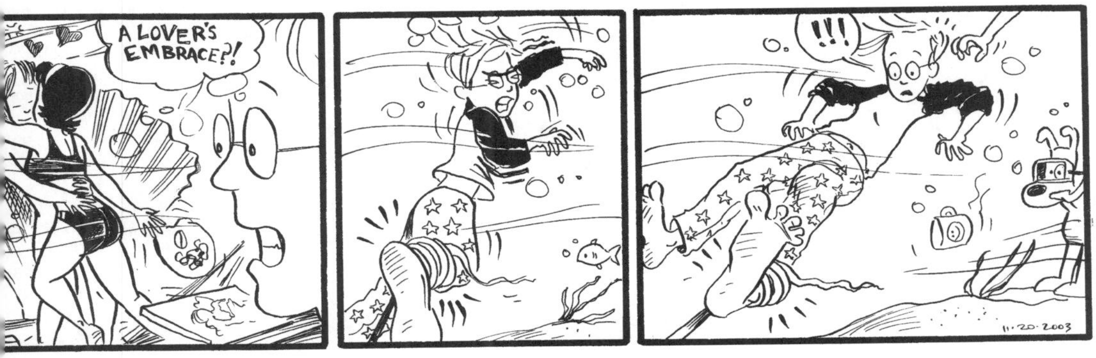
A LOVER'S EMBRACE?!
!!!
11·20·2003

11-21-2003
11-22-2003
COUGH COUGH!
AAAAAH
JANE, TALIA AND I WENT FOR A WALK. WE DIDN'T WANT TO DISTURB YOUR SOUND SLEEP. ~XO DOROTHY
11.24.2003
PAIGE
WHAT WAS THAT?...THE DOOR?...
I THINK IT WAS JANE LEAVING FOR WORK...
STRANGE... USUALLY SHE AT LEAST HAS ONE CUP OF COFFEE BEFORE SHE LEAVES...
11-25-2003
SO... YOU'RE FRIENDS DIDN'T GIVE YOU A HARD TIME ABOUT COMING BACK TO CALIFORNIA?..."THE LAND OF FRUITS AND NUTS"!!
THERE ONLY ON NUT I'M INTEREST IN...
PAIGE

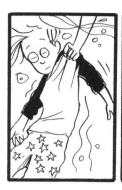

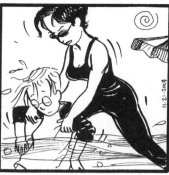

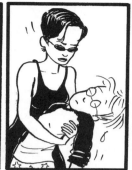

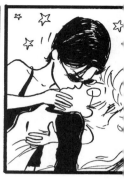

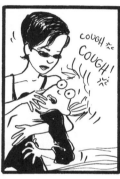

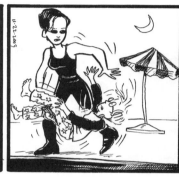

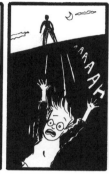

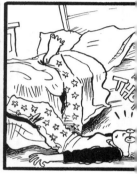

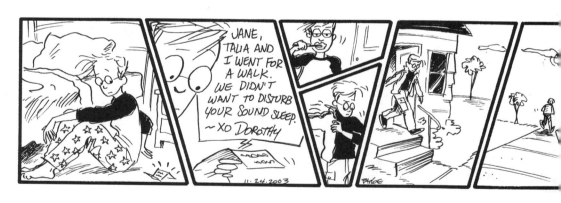

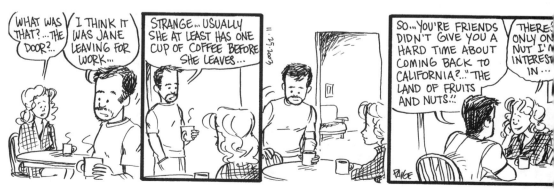

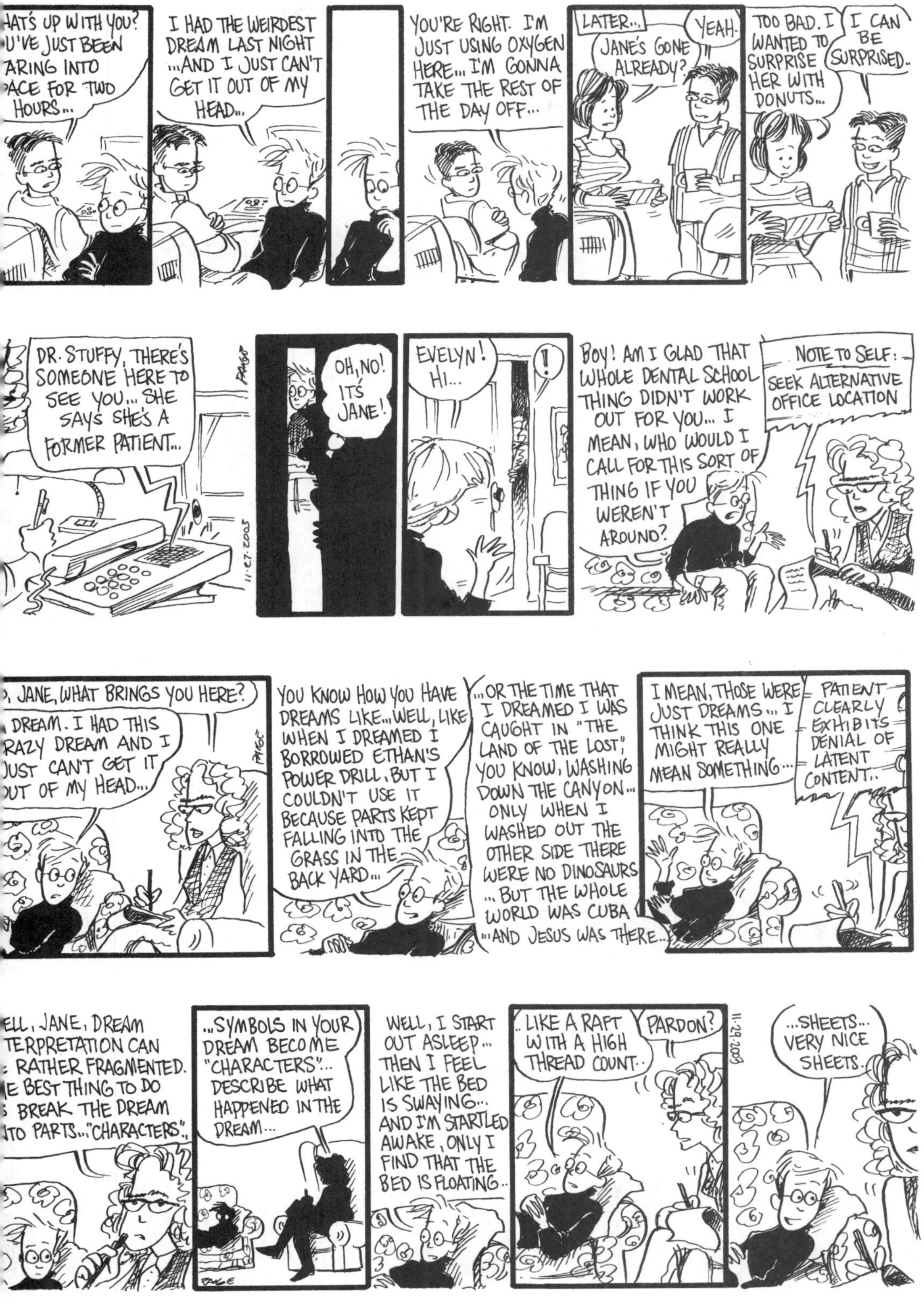
HAT'S UP WITH YOU? U'VE JUST BEEN ARING INTO ACE FOR TWO HOURS...
I HAD THE WEIRDEST DREAM LAST NIGHT ...AND I JUST CAN'T GET IT OUT OF MY HEAD...
YOU'RE RIGHT. I'M JUST USING OXYGEN HERE... I'M GONNA TAKE THE REST OF THE DAY OFF...
LATER...
JANE'S GONE ALREADY?
YEAH.
TOO BAD. I WANTED TO SURPRISE HER WITH DONUTS...
I CAN BE SURPRISED..
DR. STUFFY, THERE'S SOMEONE HERE TO SEE YOU... SHE SAYS SHE'S A FORMER PATIENT...
PAIGE
11-27-2003
OH, NO! IT'S JANE!
EVELYN! HI...
!
BOY! AM I GLAD THAT WHOLE DENTAL SCHOOL THING DIDN'T WORK OUT FOR YOU... I MEAN, WHO WOULD I CALL FOR THIS SORT OF THING IF YOU WEREN'T AROUND?
NOTE TO SELF: SEEK ALTERNATIVE OFFICE LOCATION
, JANE, WHAT BRINGS YOU HERE?
DREAM. I HAD THIS RAZY DREAM AND I UST CAN'T GET IT UT OF MY HEAD...
PAIGE
YOU KNOW HOW YOU HAVE DREAMS LIKE... WELL, LIKE WHEN I DREAMED I BORROWED ETHAN'S POWER DRILL, BUT I COULDN'T USE IT BECAUSE PARTS KEPT FALLING INTO THE GRASS IN THE BACK YARD...
...OR THE TIME THAT I DREAMED I WAS CAUGHT IN "THE LAND OF THE LOST," YOU KNOW, WASHING DOWN THE CANYON... ONLY WHEN I WASHED OUT THE OTHER SIDE THERE WERE NO DINOSAURS ... BUT THE WHOLE WORLD WAS CUBA ...AND JESUS WAS THERE...
I MEAN, THOSE WERE JUST DREAMS... I THINK THIS ONE MIGHT REALLY MEAN SOMETHING...
PATIENT CLEARLY EXHIBITS DENIAL OF LATENT CONTENT..
ELL, JANE, DREAM TERPRETATION CAN RATHER FRAGMENTED. E BEST THING TO DO BREAK THE DREAM TO PARTS..."CHARACTERS"...
...SYMBOLS IN YOUR DREAM BECOME "CHARACTERS"... DESCRIBE WHAT HAPPENED IN THE DREAM...
PAIGE
WELL, I START OUT ASLEEP... THEN I FEEL LIKE THE BED IS SWAYING... AND I'M STARTLED AWAKE, ONLY I FIND THAT THE BED IS FLOATING...
.. LIKE A RAFT WITH A HIGH THREAD COUNT..
PARDON?
11-29-2003
...SHEETS... VERY NICE SHEETS..

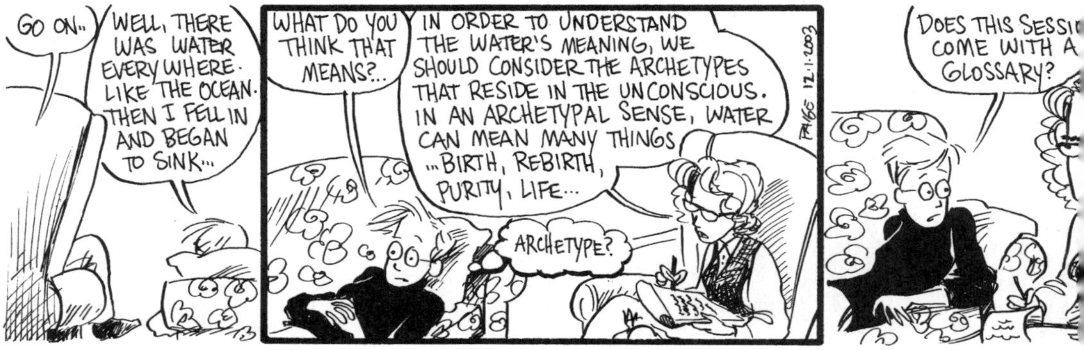
GO ON..
WELL, THERE WAS WATER EVERYWHERE. LIKE THE OCEAN. THEN I FELL IN AND BEGAN TO SINK...
WHAT DO YOU THINK THAT MEANS?..
IN ORDER TO UNDERSTAND THE WATER'S MEANING, WE SHOULD CONSIDER THE ARCHETYPES THAT RESIDE IN THE UNCONSCIOUS. IN AN ARCHETYPAL SENSE, WATER CAN MEAN MANY THINGS ...BIRTH, REBIRTH, PURITY, LIFE...
ARCHETYPE?
PAIGE 12.1.2003
DOES THIS SESSI
COME WITH A
GLOSSARY?

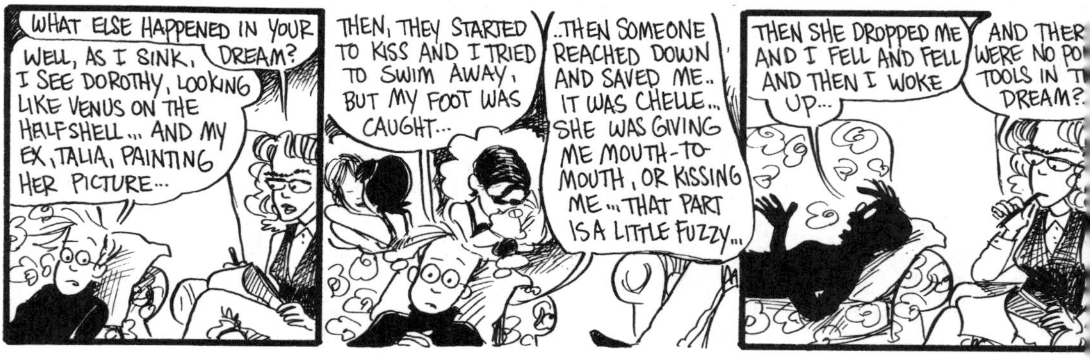
WHAT ELSE HAPPENED IN YOUR DREAM?
WELL, AS I SINK, I SEE DOROTHY, LOOKING LIKE VENUS ON THE HALFSHELL... AND MY EX, TALIA, PAINTING HER PICTURE...
THEN, THEY STARTED TO KISS AND I TRIED TO SWIM AWAY, BUT MY FOOT WAS CAUGHT...
..THEN SOMEONE REACHED DOWN AND SAVED ME.. IT WAS CHELLE... SHE WAS GIVING ME MOUTH-TO-MOUTH, OR KISSING ME... THAT PART IS A LITTLE FUZZY...
THEN SHE DROPPED ME AND I FELL AND FELL AND THEN I WOKE UP...
AND THER
WERE NO PO
TOOLS IN T
DREAM?..

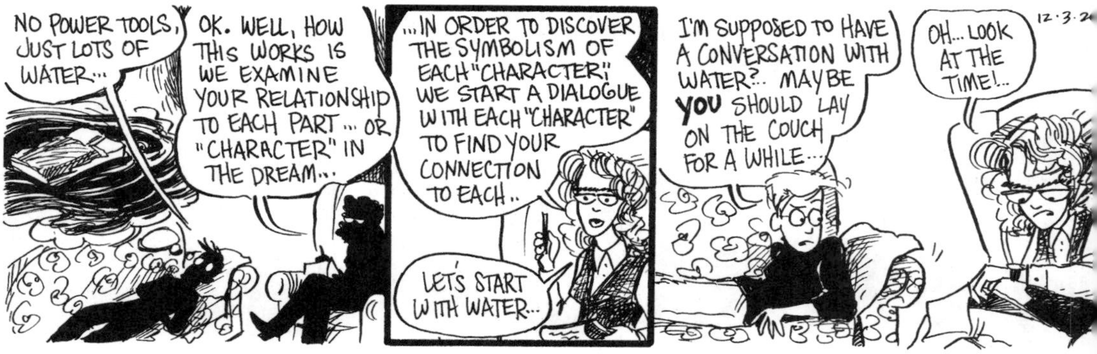
NO POWER TOOLS, JUST LOTS OF WATER...
OK. WELL, HOW THIS WORKS IS WE EXAMINE YOUR RELATIONSHIP TO EACH PART... OR "CHARACTER" IN THE DREAM...
...IN ORDER TO DISCOVER THE SYMBOLISM OF EACH "CHARACTER," WE START A DIALOGUE WITH EACH "CHARACTER" TO FIND YOUR CONNECTION TO EACH..
LET'S START WITH WATER..
I'M SUPPOSED TO HAVE A CONVERSATION WITH WATER?.. MAYBE YOU SHOULD LAY ON THE COUCH FOR A WHILE...
OH... LOOK AT THE TIME!..
12.3.2

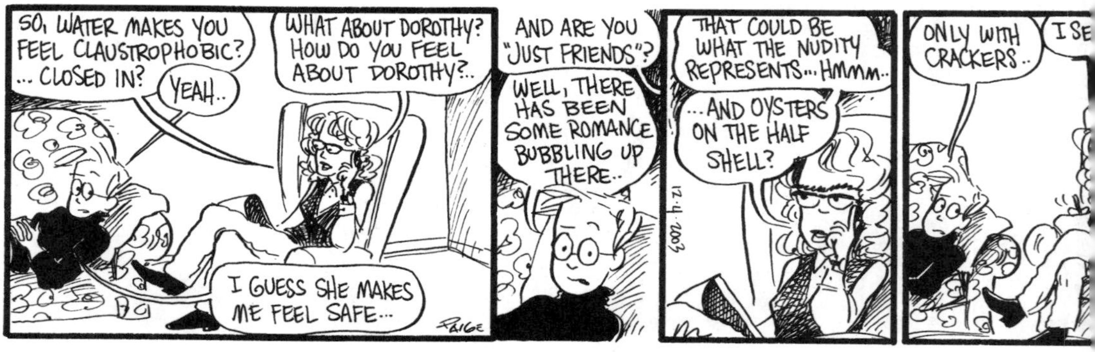
SO, WATER MAKES YOU FEEL CLAUSTROPHOBIC? ... CLOSED IN?
YEAH..
WHAT ABOUT DOROTHY? HOW DO YOU FEEL ABOUT DOROTHY?..
I GUESS SHE MAKES ME FEEL SAFE...
PAIGE
AND ARE YOU "JUST FRIENDS"?
WELL, THERE HAS BEEN SOME ROMANCE BUBBLING UP THERE..
12.4.2003
THAT COULD BE WHAT THE NUDITY REPRESENTS... HMMM..
...AND OYSTERS ON THE HALF SHELL?
ONLY WITH CRACKERS..
I SE

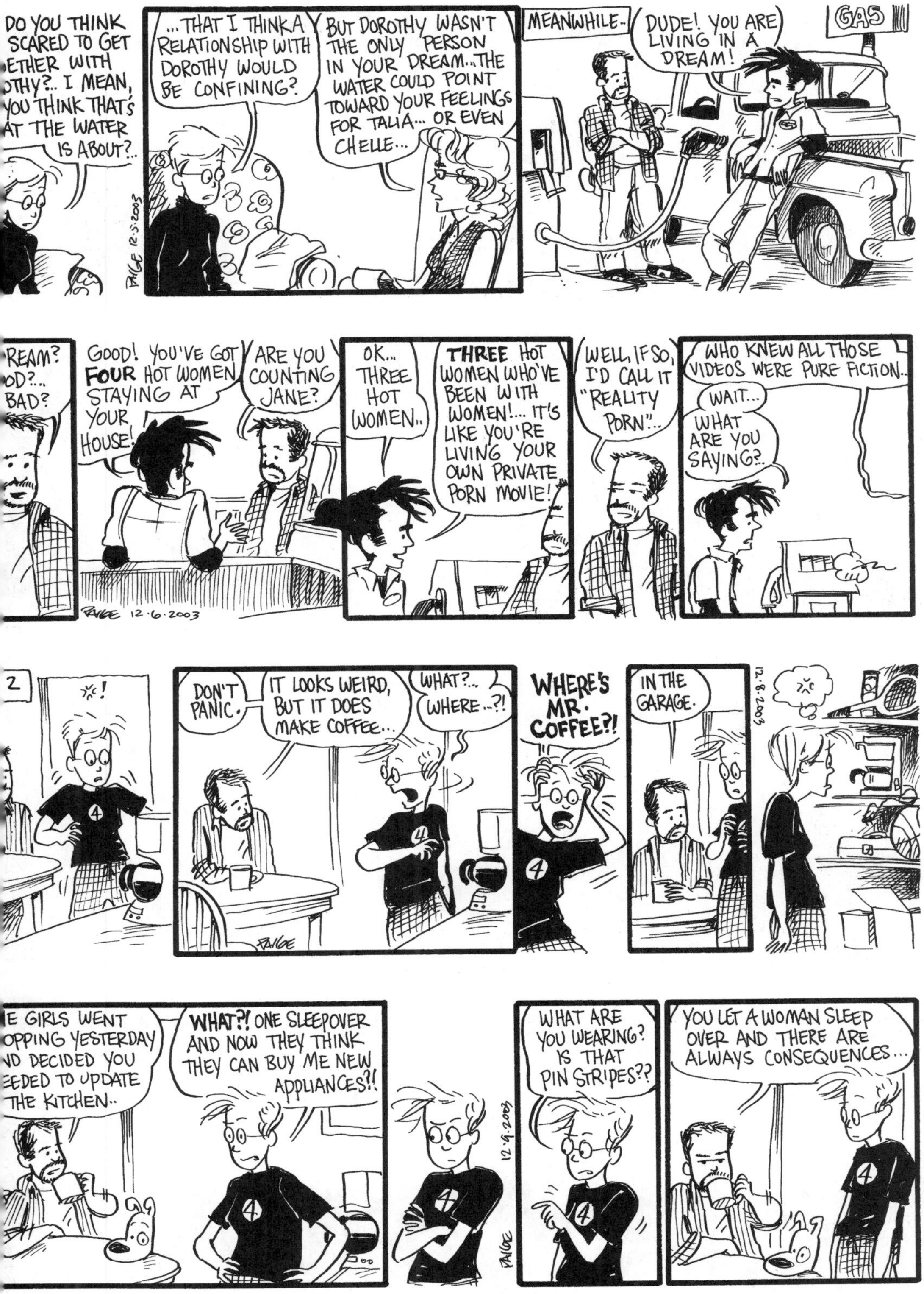

DO YOU THINK SCARED TO GET ETHER WITH OTHY?.. I MEAN, YOU THINK THAT'S AT THE WATER IS ABOUT?..
...THAT I THINK A RELATIONSHIP WITH DOROTHY WOULD BE CONFINING?
BUT DOROTHY WASN'T THE ONLY PERSON IN YOUR DREAM... THE WATER COULD POINT TOWARD YOUR FEELINGS FOR TALIA... OR EVEN CHELLE...
PAIGE 12·5·2003
MEANWHILE..
DUDE! YOU ARE LIVING IN A DREAM!
GAS
REAM? OD?.. BAD?
GOOD! YOU'VE GOT FOUR HOT WOMEN STAYING AT YOUR HOUSE!
ARE YOU COUNTING JANE?
OK... THREE HOT WOMEN..
THREE HOT WOMEN WHO'VE BEEN WITH WOMEN!... IT'S LIKE YOU'RE LIVING YOUR OWN PRIVATE PORN MOVIE!
WELL, IF SO, I'D CALL IT "REALITY PORN"...
WHO KNEW ALL THOSE VIDEOS WERE PURE FICTION..
WAIT...
WHAT ARE YOU SAYING?..
PAIGE 12·6·2003
2
DON'T PANIC.
IT LOOKS WEIRD, BUT IT DOES MAKE COFFEE...
WHAT?... WHERE..?!
WHERE'S MR. COFFEE?!
IN THE GARAGE.
PAIGE
12·8·2003
E GIRLS WENT OPPING YESTERDAY ND DECIDED YOU EEDED TO UPDATE THE KITCHEN..
WHAT?! ONE SLEEPOVER AND NOW THEY THINK THEY CAN BUY ME NEW APPLIANCES?!
12·9·2003
WHAT ARE YOU WEARING? IS THAT PIN STRIPES??
YOU LET A WOMAN SLEEP OVER AND THERE ARE ALWAYS CONSEQUENCES...
PAIGE

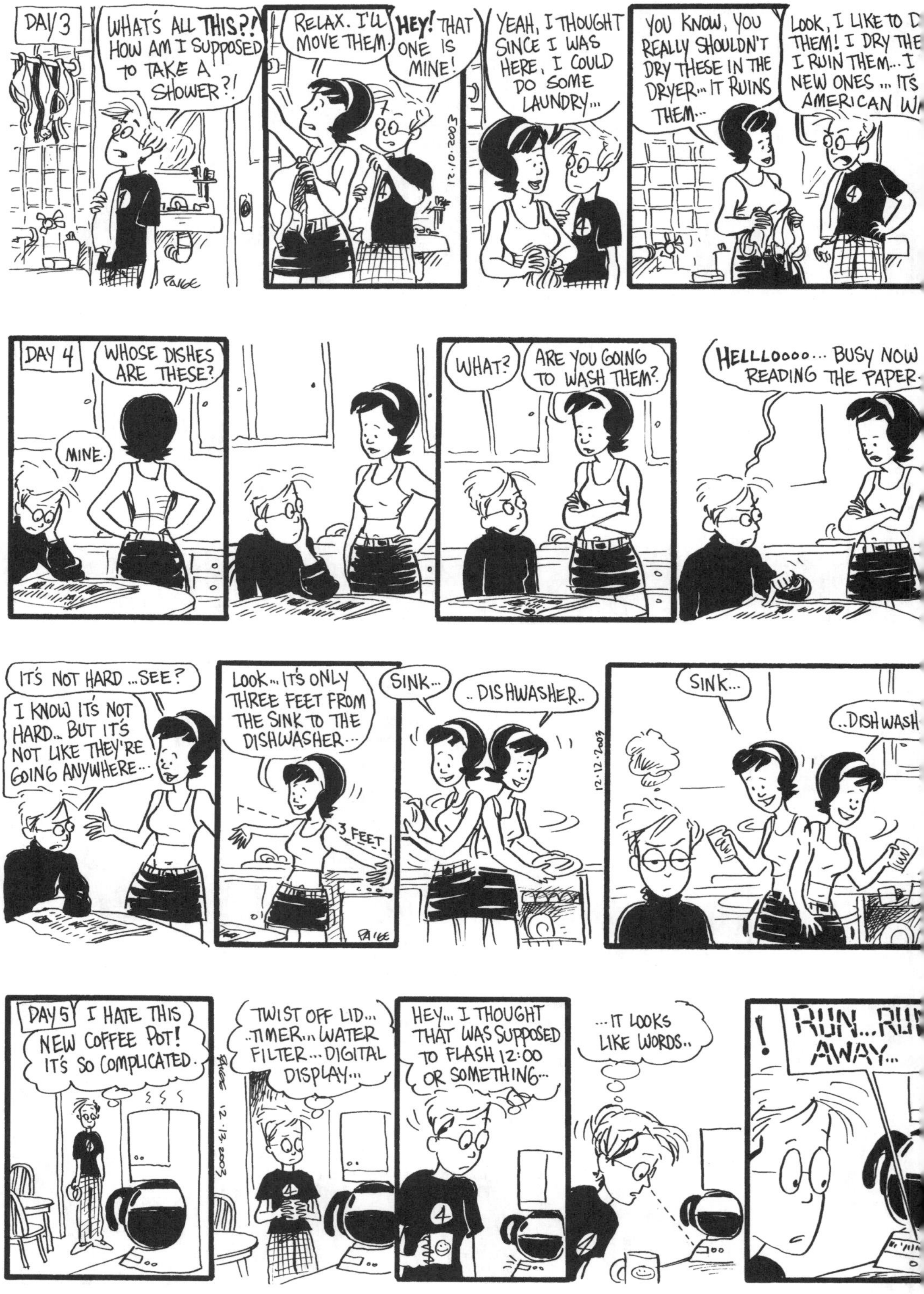

DAY 3
WHAT'S ALL THIS?! HOW AM I SUPPOSED TO TAKE A SHOWER?!
PAIGE
RELAX. I'LL MOVE THEM.
HEY! THAT ONE IS MINE!
12.10.2003
YEAH, I THOUGHT SINCE I WAS HERE, I COULD DO SOME LAUNDRY...
YOU KNOW, YOU REALLY SHOULDN'T DRY THESE IN THE DRYER... IT RUINS THEM...
LOOK, I LIKE TO
THEM! I DRY
I RUIN THEM... I
NEW ONES ... IT'S
AMERICAN
DAY 4
WHOSE DISHES ARE THESE?
MINE.
WHAT?
ARE YOU GOING TO WASH THEM?
HELLLoooo... BUSY NOW
READING THE PAPER
IT'S NOT HARD ...SEE?
I KNOW IT'S NOT HARD... BUT IT'S NOT LIKE THEY'RE GOING ANYWHERE...
LOOK... IT'S ONLY THREE FEET FROM THE SINK TO THE DISHWASHER...
3 FEET
PAIGE
SINK...
.. DISHWASHER..
12.12.2003
SINK...
..DISHWASH
DAY 5
I HATE THIS NEW COFFEE POT! IT'S SO COMPLICATED.
PAIGE
12.13.2003
TWIST OFF LID... ..TIMER... WATER FILTER... DIGITAL DISPLAY...
HEY... I THOUGHT THAT WAS SUPPOSED TO FLASH 12:00 OR SOMETHING...
...IT LOOKS LIKE WORDS..
!
AWAY...

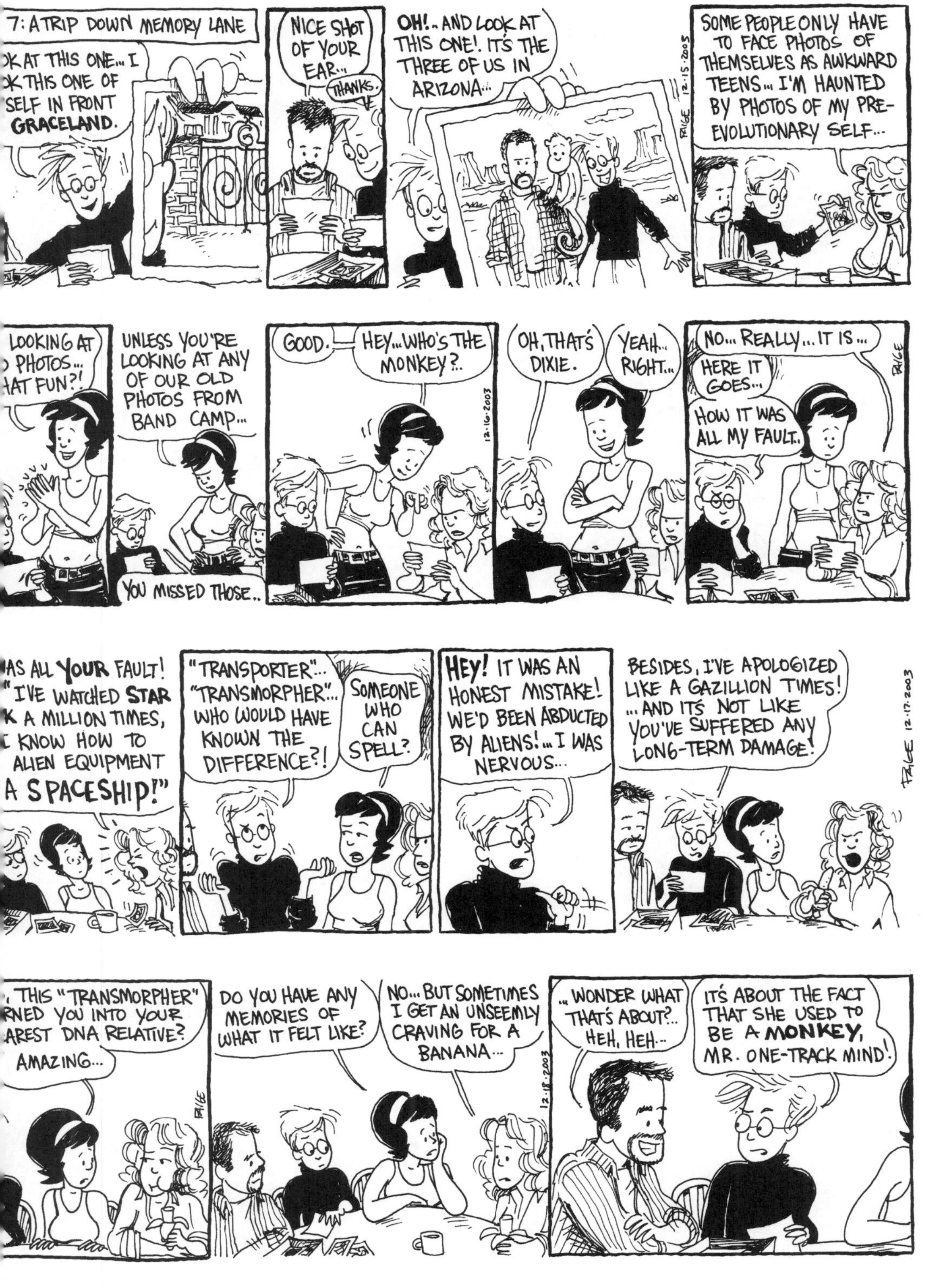
7: A TRIP DOWN MEMORY LANE
OK AT THIS ONE... I OK THIS ONE OF SELF IN FRONT GRACELAND.
NICE SHOT OF YOUR EAR...
THANKS.
OH!.. AND LOOK AT THIS ONE! IT'S THE THREE OF US IN ARIZONA...
12·15·2003
PAIGE
SOME PEOPLE ONLY HAVE TO FACE PHOTOS OF THEMSELVES AS AWKWARD TEENS... I'M HAUNTED BY PHOTOS OF MY PRE-EVOLUTIONARY SELF...
LOOKING AT PHOTOS... HAT FUN?!
UNLESS YOU'RE LOOKING AT ANY OF OUR OLD PHOTOS FROM BAND CAMP...
YOU MISSED THOSE..
GOOD.
HEY... WHO'S THE MONKEY?..
12·16·2003
OH, THAT'S DIXIE.
YEAH... RIGHT...
NO... REALLY... IT IS...
HERE IT GOES...
HOW IT WAS ALL MY FAULT.
PAIGE
AS ALL YOUR FAULT! "I'VE WATCHED STAR K A MILLION TIMES, KNOW HOW TO ALIEN EQUIPMENT A SPACESHIP!"
"TRANSPORTER"... "TRANSMORPHER"... WHO WOULD HAVE KNOWN THE DIFFERENCE?!
SOMEONE WHO CAN SPELL?
HEY! IT WAS AN HONEST MISTAKE! WE'D BEEN ABDUCTED BY ALIENS! ... I WAS NERVOUS...
BESIDES, I'VE APOLOGIZED LIKE A GAZILLION TIMES! ... AND IT'S NOT LIKE YOU'VE SUFFERED ANY LONG-TERM DAMAGE!
PAIGE 12·17·2003
, THIS "TRANSMORPHER" RNED YOU INTO YOUR AREST DNA RELATIVE? AMAZING...
PAIGE
DO YOU HAVE ANY MEMORIES OF WHAT IT FELT LIKE?
NO... BUT SOMETIMES I GET AN UNSEEMLY CRAVING FOR A BANANA...
12·18·2003
... WONDER WHAT THAT'S ABOUT?.. HEH, HEH..
IT'S ABOUT THE FACT THAT SHE USED TO BE A MONKEY, MR. ONE-TRACK MIND!

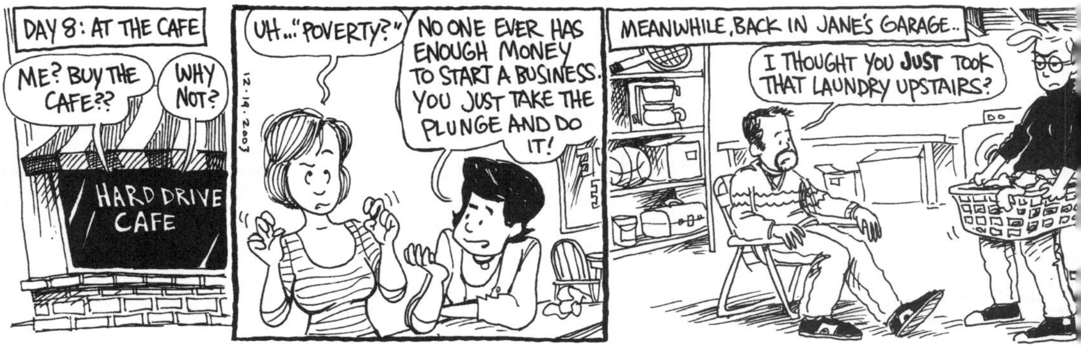

DAY 8: AT THE CAFE
ME? BUY THE CAFE??
WHY NOT?
HARD DRIVE CAFE
12·19·2003
UH... "POVERTY?"
NO ONE EVER HAS ENOUGH MONEY TO START A BUSINESS. YOU JUST TAKE THE PLUNGE AND DO IT!
MEANWHILE, BACK IN JANE'S GARAGE..
I THOUGHT YOU **JUST** TOOK THAT LAUNDRY UPSTAIRS?

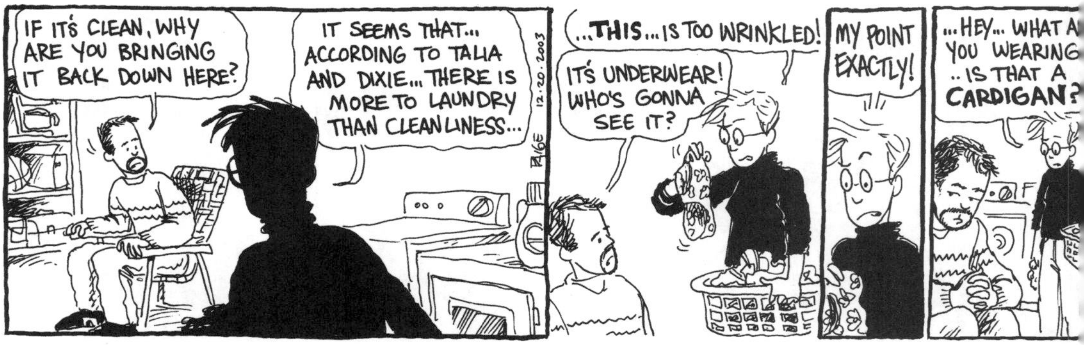

IF IT'S CLEAN, WHY ARE YOU BRINGING IT BACK DOWN HERE?
IT SEEMS THAT... ACCORDING TO TALIA AND DIXIE... THERE IS MORE TO LAUNDRY THAN CLEANLINESS...
12·20·2003
PAIGE
...**THIS**... IS TOO WRINKLED!
IT'S UNDERWEAR! WHO'S GONNA SEE IT?
MY POINT EXACTLY!
...HEY... WHAT A
YOU WEARING
..IS THAT A **CARDIGAN?**

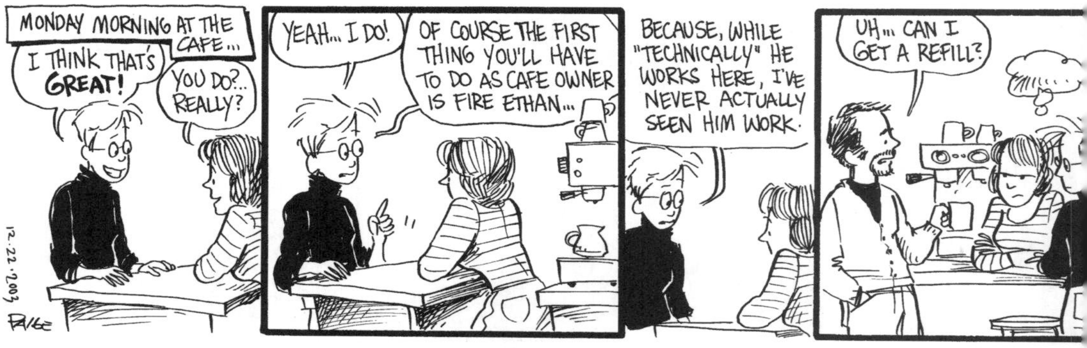

MONDAY MORNING AT THE CAFE...
I THINK THAT'S **GREAT!**
YOU DO?.. REALLY?
12·22·2003
PAIGE
YEAH... I DO!
OF COURSE THE FIRST THING YOU'LL HAVE TO DO AS CAFE OWNER IS FIRE ETHAN...
BECAUSE, WHILE "TECHNICALLY" HE WORKS HERE, I'VE NEVER ACTUALLY SEEN HIM WORK.
UH... CAN I GET A REFILL?

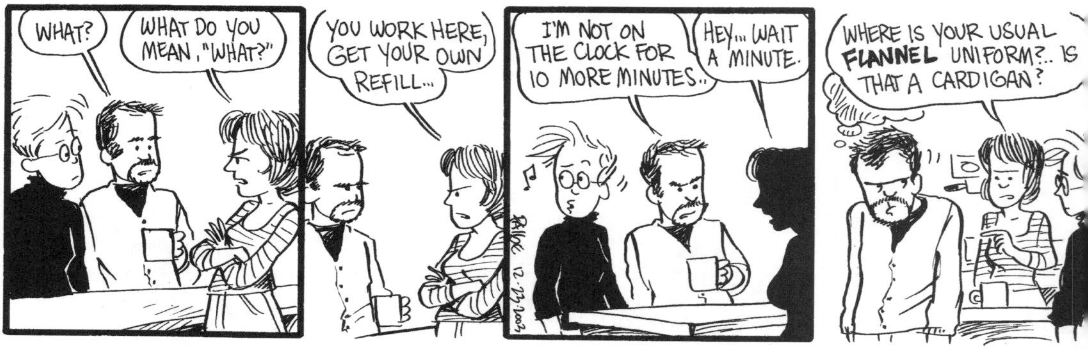

WHAT?
WHAT DO YOU MEAN, "WHAT?"
YOU WORK HERE, GET YOUR OWN REFILL...
PAIGE
12·23·2003
I'M NOT ON THE CLOCK FOR 10 MORE MINUTES..
HEY... WAIT A MINUTE.
WHERE IS YOUR USUAL **FLANNEL** UNIFORM?.. IS THAT A CARDIGAN?

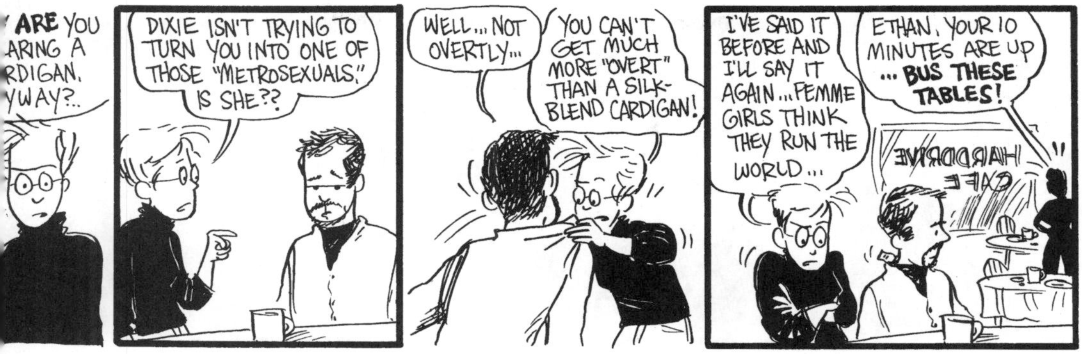
ARE YOU
ARING A
RDIGAN,
YWAY?..
DIXIE ISN'T TRYING TO TURN YOU INTO ONE OF THOSE "METROSEXUALS," IS SHE??
WELL... NOT OVERTLY...
YOU CAN'T GET MUCH MORE "OVERT" THAN A SILK-BLEND CARDIGAN!
I'VE SAID IT BEFORE AND I'LL SAY IT AGAIN... FEMME GIRLS THINK THEY RUN THE WORLD...
ETHAN, YOUR 10 MINUTES ARE UP ... BUS THESE TABLES!

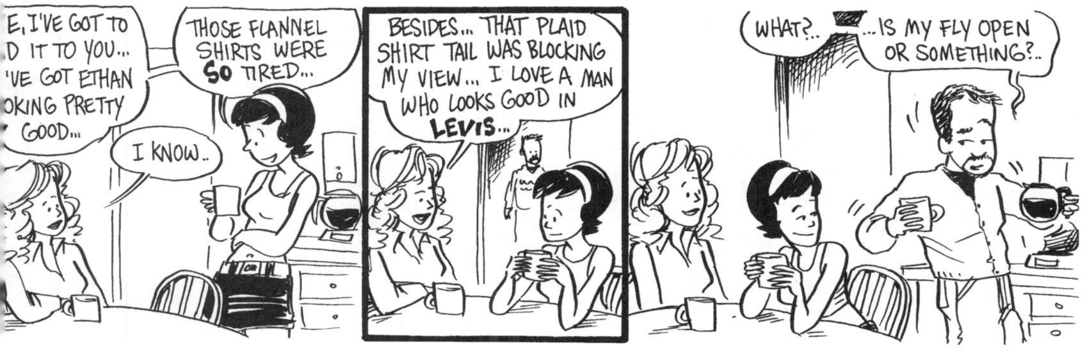
E, I'VE GOT TO
D IT TO YOU...
'VE GOT ETHAN
OKING PRETTY
GOOD...
THOSE FLANNEL SHIRTS WERE SO TIRED...
I KNOW..
BESIDES... THAT PLAID SHIRT TAIL WAS BLOCKING MY VIEW... I LOVE A MAN WHO LOOKS GOOD IN LEVIS...
WHAT?..
...IS MY FLY OPEN OR SOMETHING?..

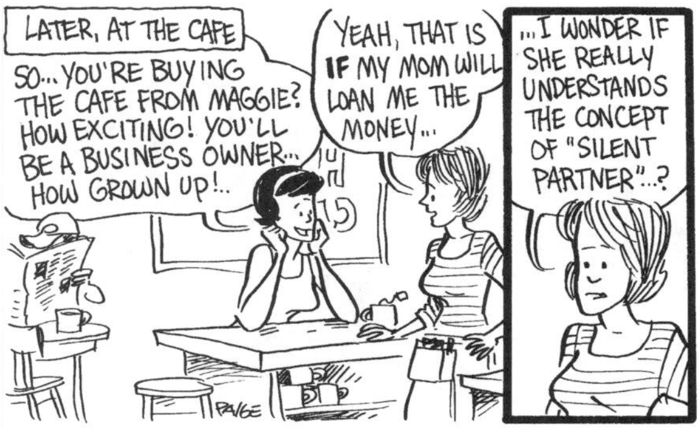
LATER, AT THE CAFE
SO... YOU'RE BUYING THE CAFE FROM MAGGIE? HOW EXCITING! YOU'LL BE A BUSINESS OWNER... HOW GROWN UP!..
YEAH, THAT IS IF MY MOM WILL LOAN ME THE MONEY...
...I WONDER IF SHE REALLY UNDERSTANDS THE CONCEPT OF "SILENT PARTNER"..?
PAIGE

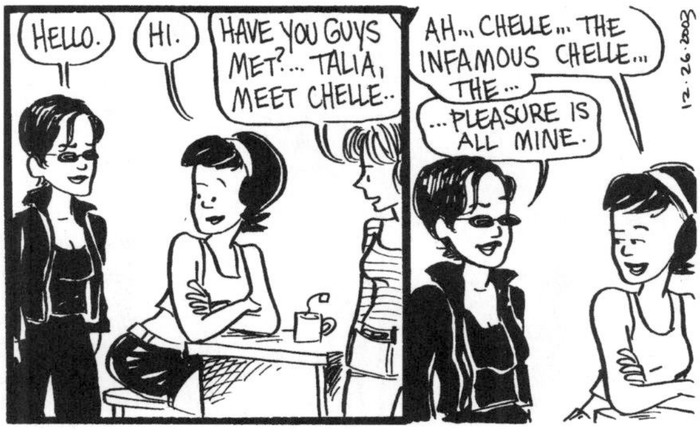
HELLO.
HI.
HAVE YOU GUYS MET?... TALIA, MEET CHELLE..
AH... CHELLE... THE INFAMOUS CHELLE... THE...
...PLEASURE IS ALL MINE.
12.26.2003

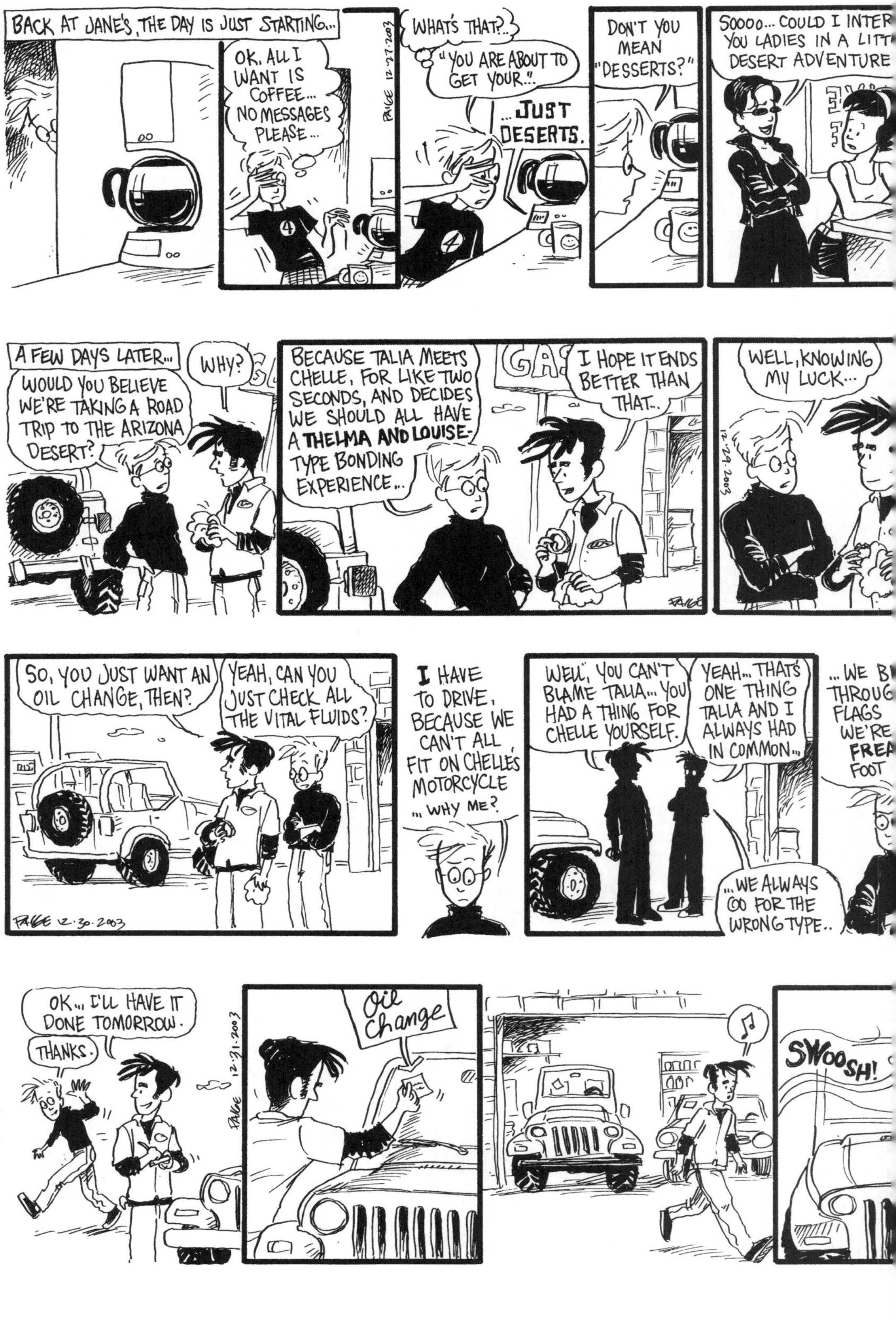

BACK AT JANE'S, THE DAY IS JUST STARTING...
OK, ALL I WANT IS COFFEE... NO MESSAGES PLEASE...
PAIGE 12·27·2003
WHAT'S THAT?..
"YOU ARE ABOUT TO GET YOUR.."
...JUST DESERTS.
DON'T YOU MEAN "DESSERTS?"
SOOOO... COULD I INTER
YOU LADIES IN A LITT
DESERT ADVENTURE
A FEW DAYS LATER...
WOULD YOU BELIEVE WE'RE TAKING A ROAD TRIP TO THE ARIZONA DESERT?
WHY?
BECAUSE TALIA MEETS CHELLE, FOR LIKE TWO SECONDS, AND DECIDES WE SHOULD ALL HAVE A THELMA AND LOUISE-TYPE BONDING EXPERIENCE...
I HOPE IT ENDS BETTER THAN THAT...
PAIGE
12·29·2003
WELL, KNOWING MY LUCK...
SO, YOU JUST WANT AN OIL CHANGE, THEN?
YEAH, CAN YOU JUST CHECK ALL THE VITAL FLUIDS?
PAIGE 12·30·2003
I HAVE TO DRIVE, BECAUSE WE CAN'T ALL FIT ON CHELLE'S MOTORCYCLE ... WHY ME?
WELL, YOU CAN'T BLAME TALIA... YOU HAD A THING FOR CHELLE YOURSELF.
YEAH... THAT'S ONE THING TALIA AND I ALWAYS HAD IN COMMON...
...WE ALWAYS GO FOR THE WRONG TYPE..
...WE B
THROUG
FLAGS
WE'RE
FREA
FOOT
OK... I'LL HAVE IT DONE TOMORROW.
THANKS.
PAIGE 12·31·2003
Oil Change
SWOOSH!

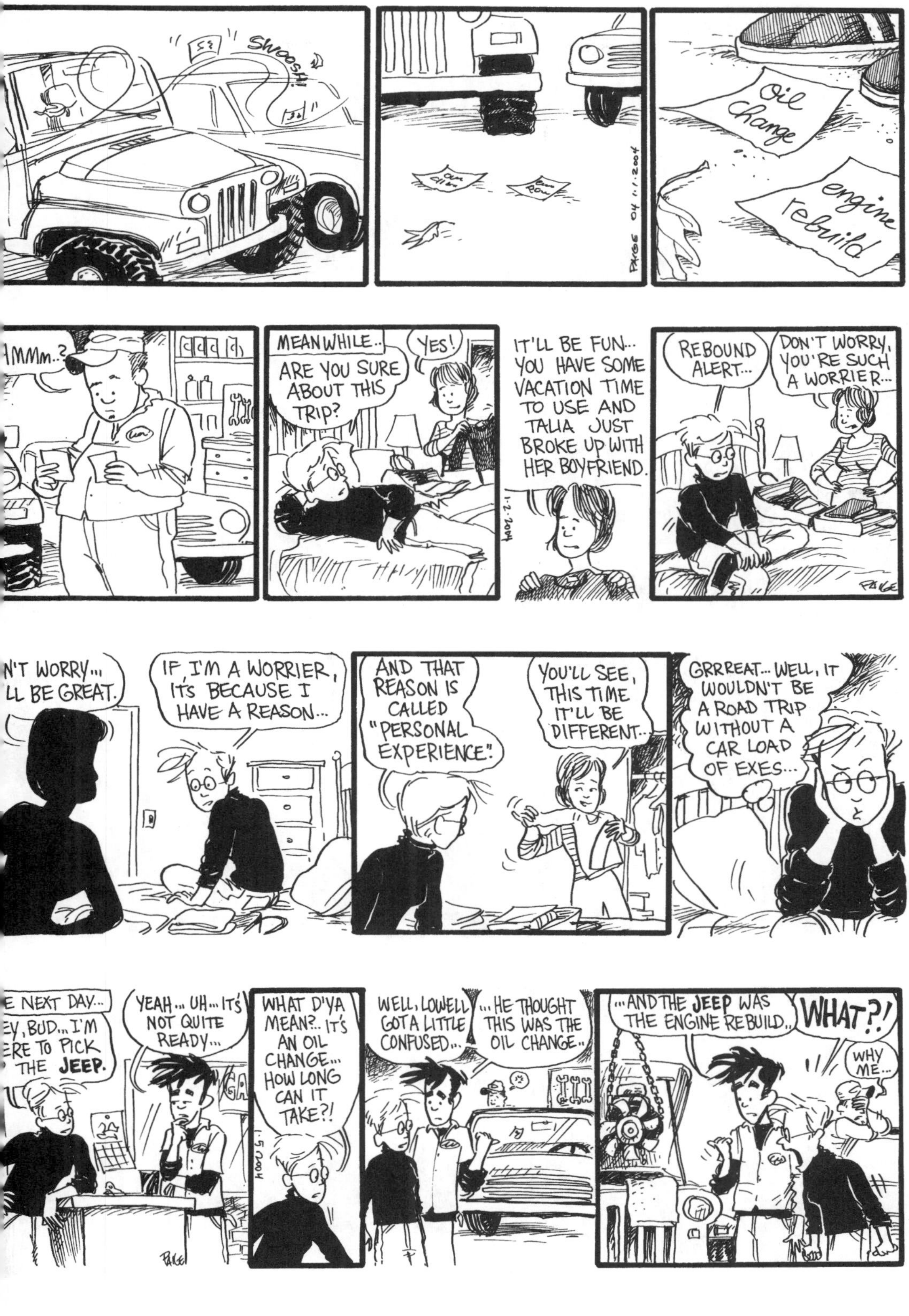

SWOOSH!
Oil Change
engine rebuild
HMMm..?
MEANWHILE..
ARE YOU SURE ABOUT THIS TRIP?
YES!
IT'LL BE FUN... YOU HAVE SOME VACATION TIME TO USE AND TALIA JUST BROKE UP WITH HER BOYFRIEND.
REBOUND ALERT...
DON'T WORRY, YOU'RE SUCH A WORRIER...
N'T WORRY... LL BE GREAT.
IF I'M A WORRIER, IT'S BECAUSE I HAVE A REASON...
AND THAT REASON IS CALLED "PERSONAL EXPERIENCE".
YOU'LL SEE, THIS TIME IT'LL BE DIFFERENT...
GRRREAT... WELL, IT WOULDN'T BE A ROAD TRIP WITHOUT A CAR LOAD OF EXES...
E NEXT DAY...
EY, BUD... I'M ERE TO PICK THE JEEP.
YEAH... UH... IT'S NOT QUITE READY...
WHAT D'YA MEAN?.. IT'S AN OIL CHANGE... HOW LONG CAN IT TAKE?!
WELL, LOWELL GOT A LITTLE CONFUSED...
...HE THOUGHT THIS WAS THE OIL CHANGE...
...AND THE JEEP WAS THE ENGINE REBUILD...
WHAT?!
WHY ME...

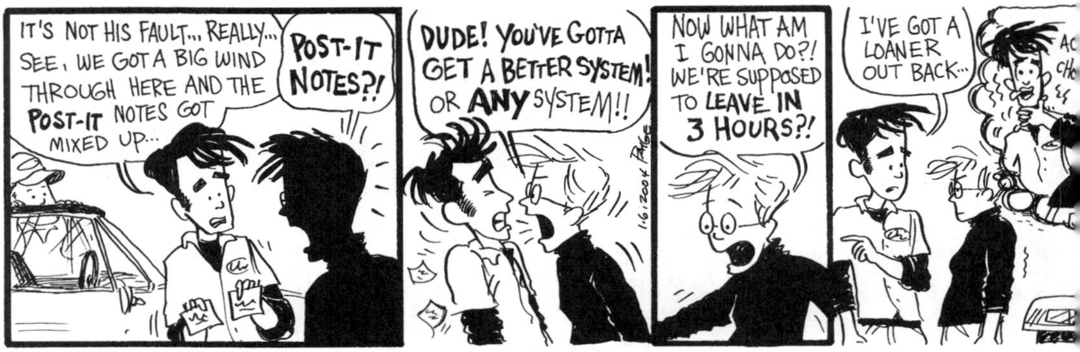
IT'S NOT HIS FAULT... REALLY... SEE, WE GOT A BIG WIND THROUGH HERE AND THE POST-IT NOTES GOT MIXED UP...
POST-IT NOTES?!
DUDE! YOU'VE GOTTA GET A BETTER SYSTEM! OR ANY SYSTEM!!
PAIGE 1.6.2004
NOW WHAT AM I GONNA DO?! WE'RE SUPPOSED TO LEAVE IN 3 HOURS?!
I'VE GOT A LOANER OUT BACK...

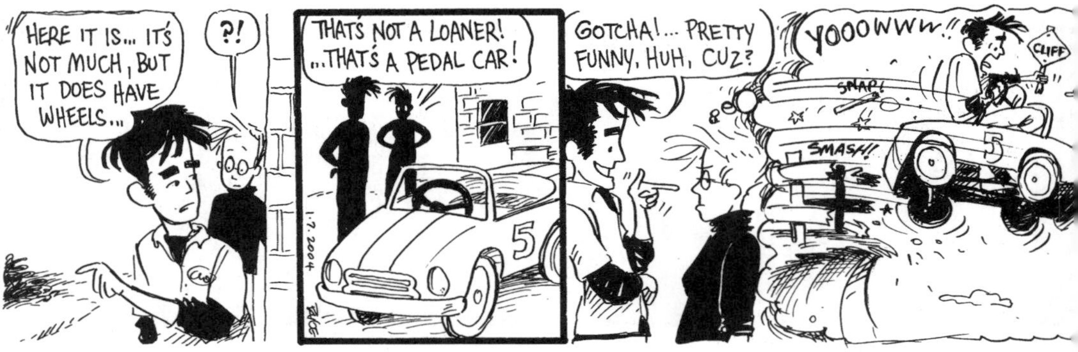
HERE IT IS... IT'S NOT MUCH, BUT IT DOES HAVE WHEELS...
?!
THAT'S NOT A LOANER! ...THAT'S A PEDAL CAR!
1.7.2004 PAIGE
GOTCHA!... PRETTY FUNNY, HUH, CUZ?
YOOOWWW!!
CLIFF
SNAP!
SMASH!!
5

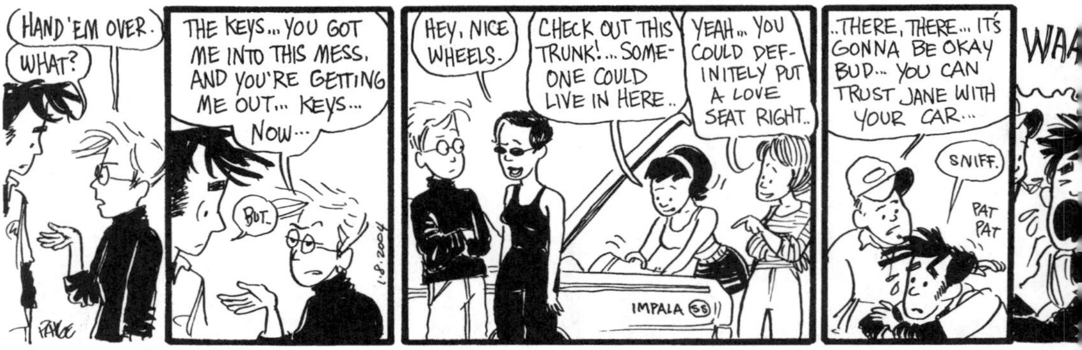
HAND 'EM OVER.
WHAT?
PAIGE
THE KEYS... YOU GOT ME INTO THIS MESS, AND YOU'RE GETTING ME OUT... KEYS... NOW...
BUT...
1.8.2004
HEY, NICE WHEELS.
CHECK OUT THIS TRUNK!... SOME-ONE COULD LIVE IN HERE...
YEAH... YOU COULD DEF-INITELY PUT A LOVE SEAT RIGHT...
IMPALA 58
..THERE, THERE... IT'S GONNA BE OKAY BUD... YOU CAN TRUST JANE WITH YOUR CAR...
SNIFF.
PAT PAT
WAA

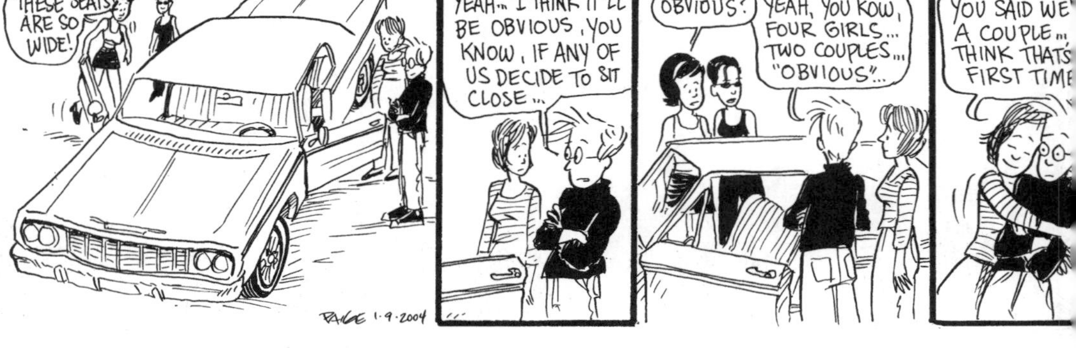
THESE SEATS ARE SO WIDE!
PAIGE 1.9.2004
YEAH... I THINK IT'LL BE OBVIOUS, YOU KNOW, IF ANY OF US DECIDE TO SIT CLOSE...
OBVIOUS?
YEAH, YOU KOW, FOUR GIRLS... TWO COUPLES... "OBVIOUS"...
YOU SAID WE' A COUPLE... THINK THAT'S FIRST TIME

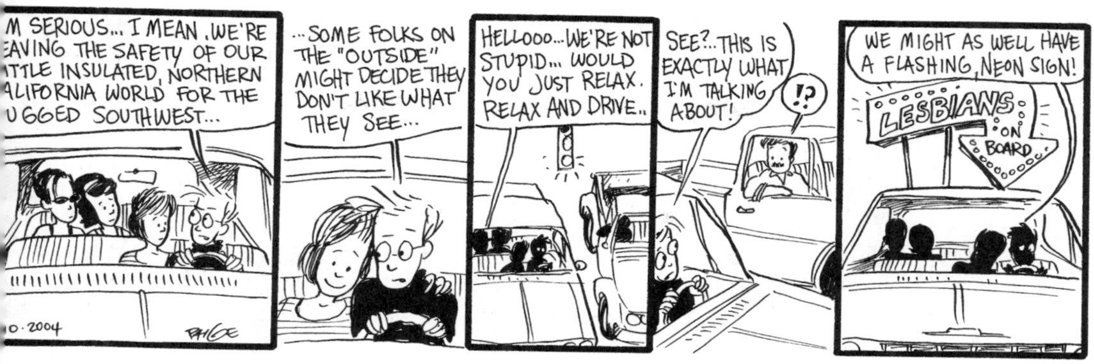
M SERIOUS... I MEAN, WE'RE
EAVING THE SAFETY OF OUR
TTLE INSULATED, NORTHERN
ALIFORNIA WORLD FOR THE
UGGED SOUTHWEST...
0·2004
PAIGE
...SOME FOLKS ON THE "OUTSIDE" MIGHT DECIDE THEY DON'T LIKE WHAT THEY SEE...
HELLOOO... WE'RE NOT STUPID... WOULD YOU JUST RELAX. RELAX AND DRIVE..
SEE?...THIS IS EXACTLY WHAT I'M TALKING ABOUT!
!?
WE MIGHT AS WELL HAVE A FLASHING, NEON SIGN!
LESBIANS ON BOARD

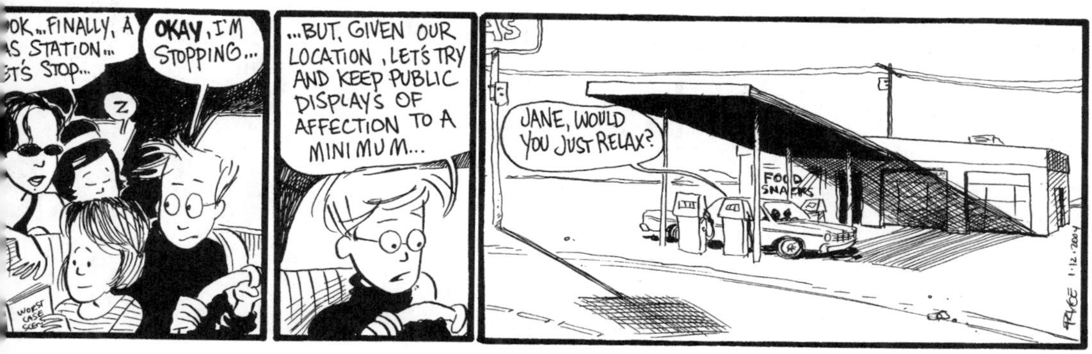
OK... FINALLY, A
AS STATION...
T'S STOP...
OKAY, I'M STOPPING...
Z
...BUT, GIVEN OUR LOCATION, LET'S TRY AND KEEP PUBLIC DISPLAYS OF AFFECTION TO A MINIMUM...
JANE, WOULD YOU JUST RELAX?
1·12·2004
PAIGE

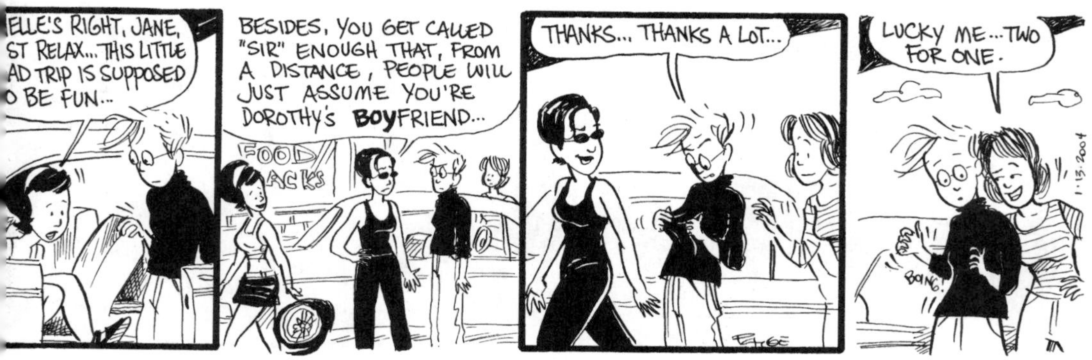
ELLE'S RIGHT, JANE,
ST RELAX... THIS LITTLE
AD TRIP IS SUPPOSED
O BE FUN...
BESIDES, YOU GET CALLED "SIR" ENOUGH THAT, FROM A DISTANCE, PEOPLE WILL JUST ASSUME YOU'RE DOROTHY'S **BOY**FRIEND...
THANKS... THANKS A LOT...
PAIGE
LUCKY ME...TWO FOR ONE.
BOING!
1·13·2004

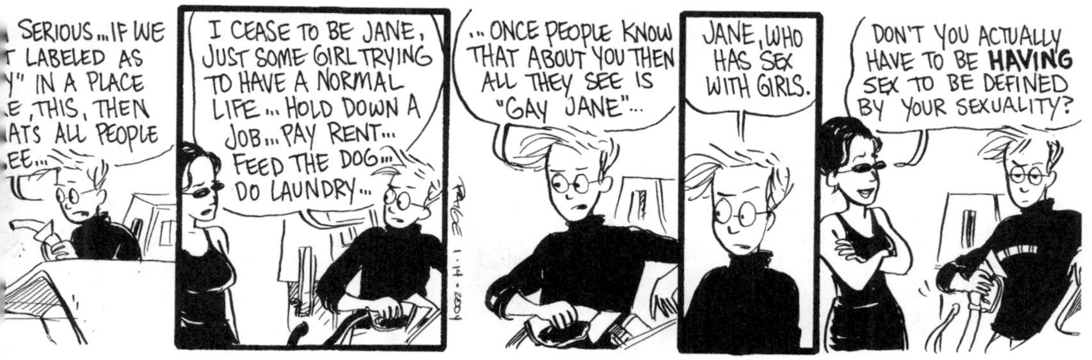
SERIOUS...IF WE
T LABELED AS
Y" IN A PLACE
E, THIS, THEN
ATS ALL PEOPLE
EE...
I CEASE TO BE JANE, JUST SOME GIRL TRYING TO HAVE A NORMAL LIFE... HOLD DOWN A JOB... PAY RENT... FEED THE DOG... DO LAUNDRY...
PAIGE 1·14·2004
...ONCE PEOPLE KNOW THAT ABOUT YOU THEN ALL THEY SEE IS "GAY JANE"...
JANE, WHO HAS SEX WITH GIRLS.
DON'T YOU ACTUALLY HAVE TO BE **HAVING** SEX TO BE DEFINED BY YOUR SEXUALITY?

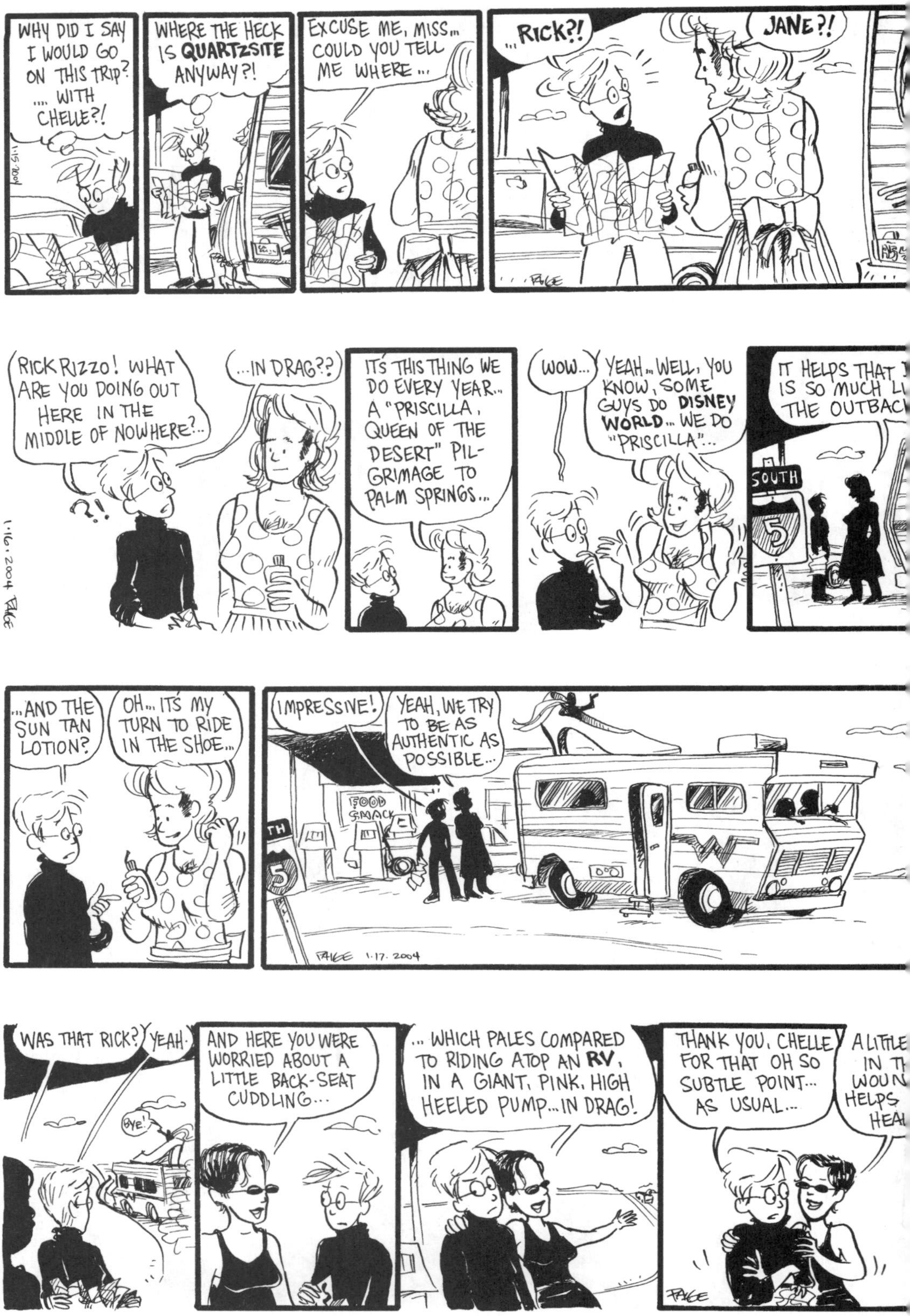
WHY DID I SAY I WOULD GO ON THIS TRIP? .... WITH CHELLE?!
1.15.2004
WHERE THE HECK IS **QUARTZSITE** ANYWAY?!
EXCUSE ME, MISS... COULD YOU TELL ME WHERE...
... **RICK?!**
JANE?!
PAIGE
RICK RIZZO! WHAT ARE YOU DOING OUT HERE IN THE MIDDLE OF NOWHERE?...
?!
...IN DRAG??
IT'S THIS THING WE DO EVERY YEAR... A "PRISCILLA, QUEEN OF THE DESERT" PILGRIMAGE TO PALM SPRINGS...
WOW...
YEAH... WELL, YOU KNOW, SOME GUYS DO **DISNEY WORLD**... WE DO "PRISCILLA"...
IT HELPS THAT
IS SO MUCH
THE
SOUTH
5
1.16.2004 PAIGE
...AND THE SUN TAN LOTION?
OH... IT'S MY TURN TO RIDE IN THE SHOE...
IMPRESSIVE!
YEAH, WE TRY TO BE AS AUTHENTIC AS POSSIBLE...
FOOD SHACK
TH
5
PAIGE 1.17.2004
WAS THAT RICK?
YEAH.
BYE!
AND HERE YOU WERE WORRIED ABOUT A LITTLE BACK-SEAT CUDDLING...
... WHICH PALES COMPARED TO RIDING ATOP AN **RV**, IN A GIANT, PINK, HIGH HEELED PUMP... IN DRAG!
THANK YOU, CHELLE FOR THAT OH SO SUBTLE POINT... AS USUAL...
A LITTLE
IN
HELPS
PAIGE

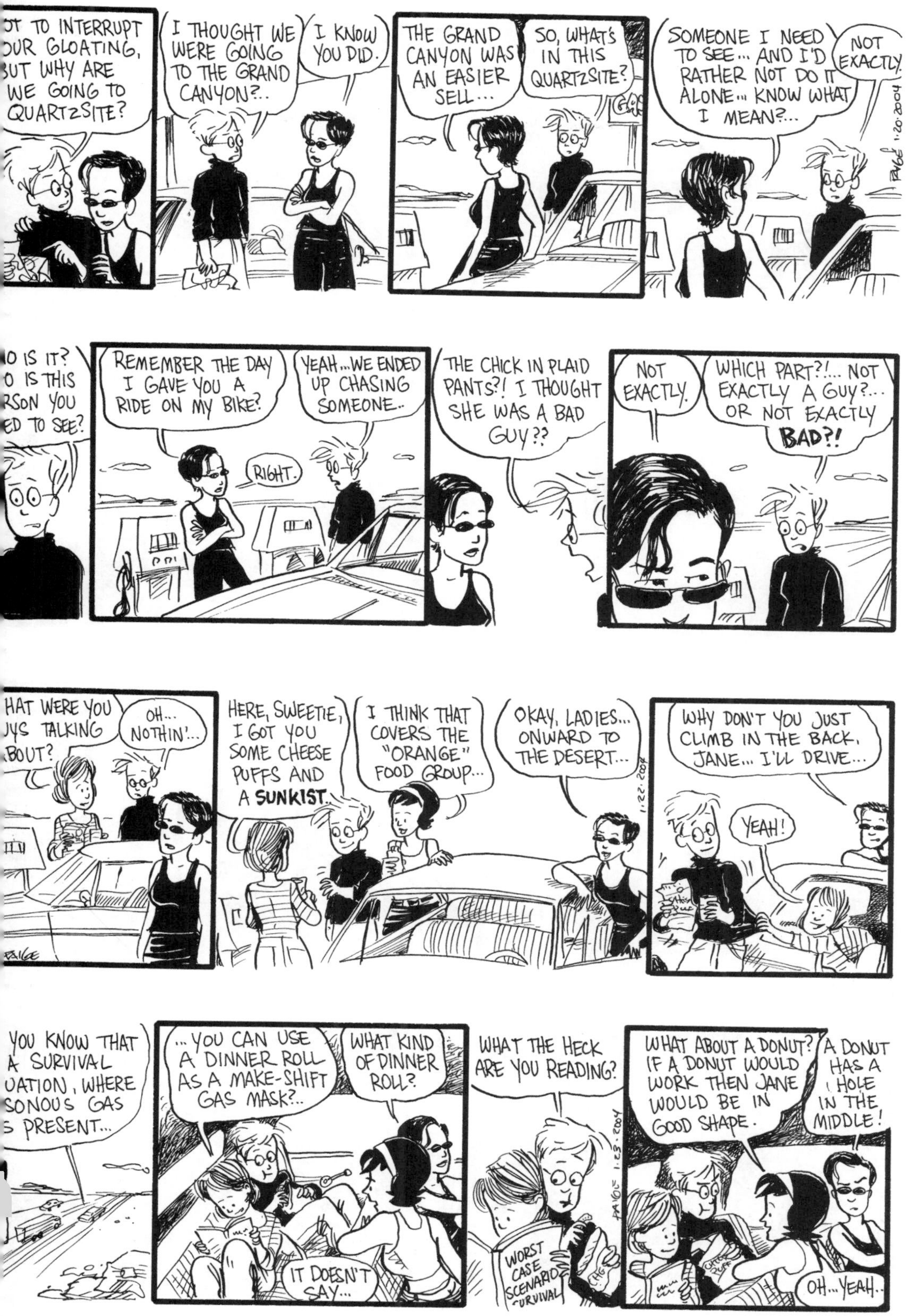
OT TO INTERRUPT OUR GLOATING, BUT WHY ARE WE GOING TO QUARTZSITE?
I THOUGHT WE WERE GOING TO THE GRAND CANYON?...
I KNOW YOU DID.
THE GRAND CANYON WAS AN EASIER SELL...
SO, WHAT'S IN THIS QUARTZSITE?
SOMEONE I NEED TO SEE... AND I'D RATHER NOT DO IT ALONE... KNOW WHAT I MEAN?...
NOT EXACTLY.
1-20-2004
PAIGE
O IS IT? O IS THIS RSON YOU ED TO SEE?
REMEMBER THE DAY I GAVE YOU A RIDE ON MY BIKE?
YEAH... WE ENDED UP CHASING SOMEONE..
RIGHT.
THE CHICK IN PLAID PANTS?! I THOUGHT SHE WAS A BAD GUY??
NOT EXACTLY.
WHICH PART?!... NOT EXACTLY A GUY?... OR NOT EXACTLY BAD?!
HAT WERE YOU UYS TALKING BOUT?
OH... NOTHIN'...
PAIGE
HERE, SWEETIE, I GOT YOU SOME CHEESE PUFFS AND A SUNKIST.
I THINK THAT COVERS THE "ORANGE" FOOD GROUP...
OKAY, LADIES... ONWARD TO THE DESERT...
1-22-2004
WHY DON'T YOU JUST CLIMB IN THE BACK, JANE... I'LL DRIVE...
YEAH!
YOU KNOW THAT A SURVIVAL UATION, WHERE SONOUS GAS S PRESENT...
...YOU CAN USE A DINNER ROLL AS A MAKE-SHIFT GAS MASK?...
WHAT KIND OF DINNER ROLL?
IT DOESN'T SAY...
WHAT THE HECK ARE YOU READING?
WORST CASE SCENARIO SURVIVAL
1-23-2004
PAIGE
WHAT ABOUT A DONUT? IF A DONUT WOULD WORK THEN JANE WOULD BE IN GOOD SHAPE.
A DONUT HAS A HOLE IN THE MIDDLE!
OH... YEAH..

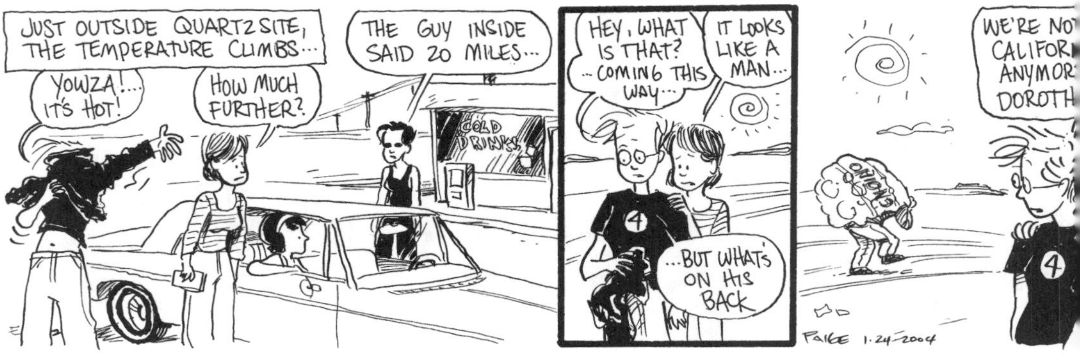
JUST OUTSIDE QUARTZSITE, THE TEMPERATURE CLIMBS...
YOWZA!... IT'S HOT!
HOW MUCH FURTHER?
THE GUY INSIDE SAID 20 MILES...
COLD DRINKS
HEY, WHAT IS THAT? ...COMING THIS WAY...
IT LOOKS LIKE A MAN...
...BUT WHAT'S ON HIS BACK
ONIONS
WE'RE NO
CALIFOR
ANYMOR
DOROTH
PAIGE 1·24·2004

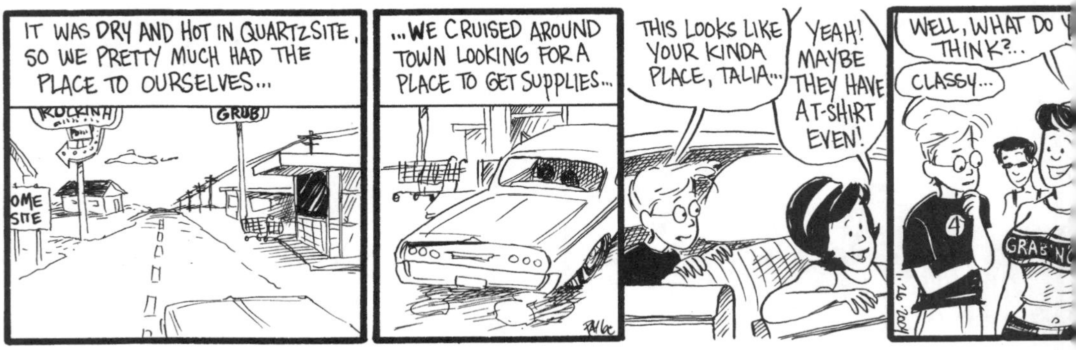
IT WAS DRY AND HOT IN QUARTZSITE, SO WE PRETTY MUCH HAD THE PLACE TO OURSELVES...
ROCKIN H
POOL
GRUB
OME SITE
...WE CRUISED AROUND TOWN LOOKING FOR A PLACE TO GET SUPPLIES...
PAIGE
THIS LOOKS LIKE YOUR KINDA PLACE, TALIA...
YEAH! MAYBE THEY HAVE A T-SHIRT EVEN!
WELL, WHAT DO
THINK?...
CLASSY...
GRAB'N
1·26·2004

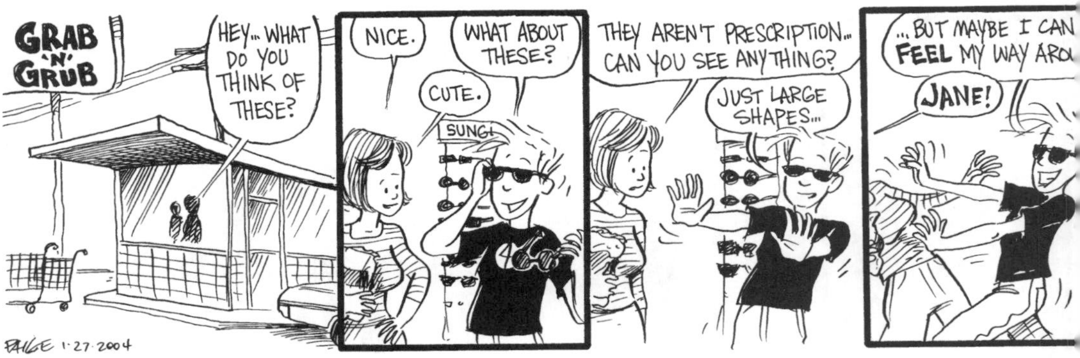
GRAB 'N' GRUB
HEY... WHAT DO YOU THINK OF THESE?
PAIGE 1·27·2004
NICE.
WHAT ABOUT THESE?
CUTE.
SUNGL
THEY AREN'T PRESCRIPTION... CAN YOU SEE ANYTHING?
JUST LARGE SHAPES...
...BUT MAYBE I CAN FEEL MY WAY ARO
JANE!

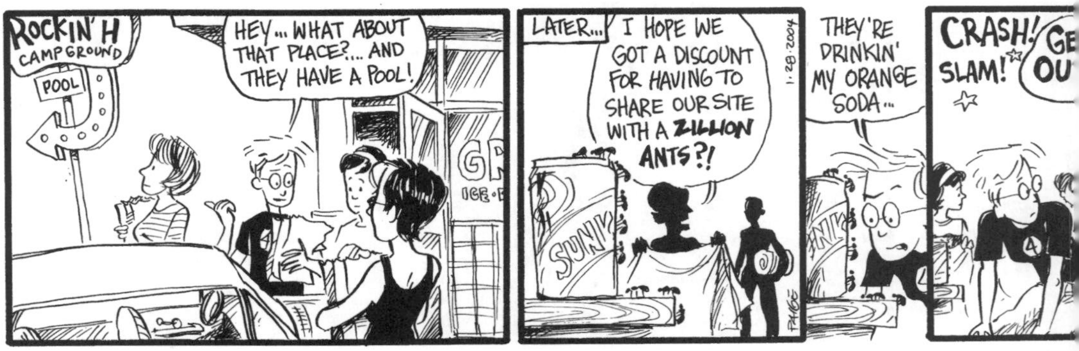
ROCKIN' H CAMPGROUND
POOL
HEY... WHAT ABOUT THAT PLACE?... AND THEY HAVE A POOL!
ICE
LATER...
I HOPE WE GOT A DISCOUNT FOR HAVING TO SHARE OUR SITE WITH A ZILLION ANTS?!
1·28·2004
SUNNY
PAIGE
THEY'RE DRINKIN' MY ORANGE SODA...
CRASH! SLAM!
GE OU

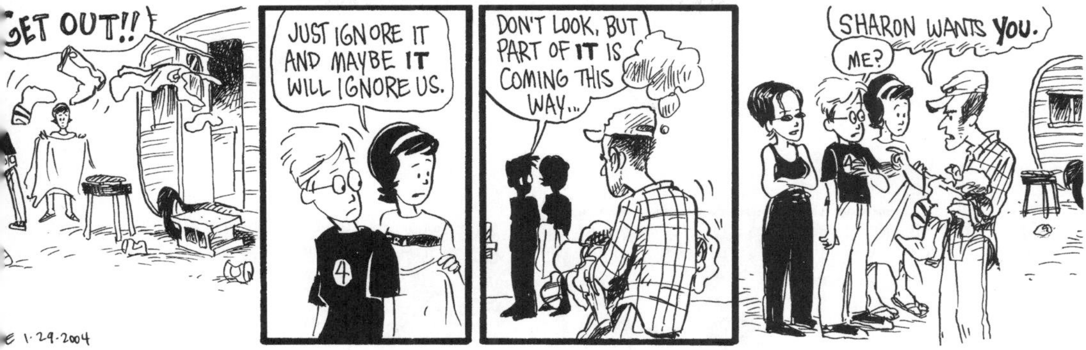
GET OUT!!
JUST IGNORE IT AND MAYBE IT WILL IGNORE US.
DON'T LOOK, BUT PART OF IT IS COMING THIS WAY...
SHARON WANTS YOU.
ME?
1·29·2004

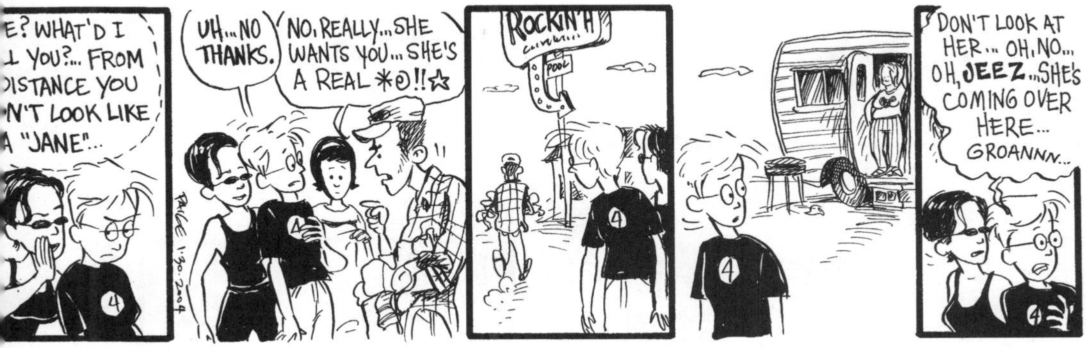
E? WHAT'D I L YOU?... FROM DISTANCE YOU N'T LOOK LIKE A "JANE"...
UH...NO THANKS.
NO, REALLY...SHE WANTS YOU... SHE'S A REAL *@!!☆
1·30·2004
ROCKIN'H
POOL
DON'T LOOK AT HER... OH, NO... OH, JEEZ...SHE'S COMING OVER HERE... GROANNN...

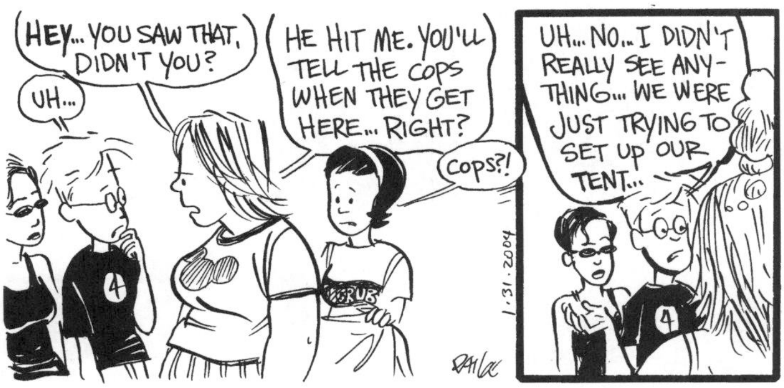
HEY... YOU SAW THAT, DIDN'T YOU?
UH...
HE HIT ME. YOU'LL TELL THE COPS WHEN THEY GET HERE... RIGHT?
COPS?!
1·31·2004
UH... NO.. I DIDN'T REALLY SEE ANYTHING... WE WERE JUST TRYING TO SET UP OUR TENT...

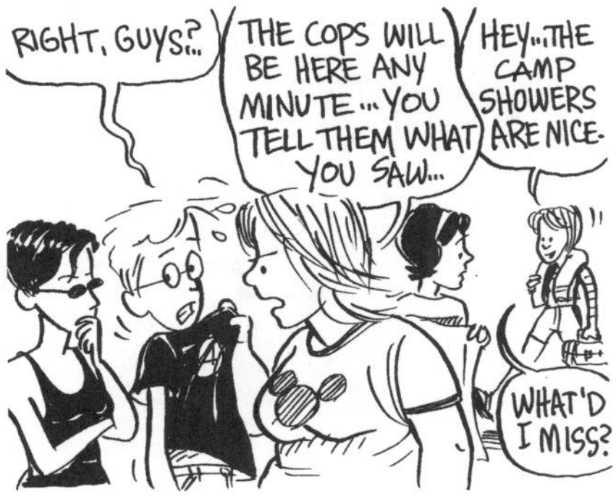
RIGHT, GUYS?...
THE COPS WILL BE HERE ANY MINUTE ... YOU TELL THEM WHAT YOU SAW...
HEY...THE CAMP SHOWERS ARE NICE.
WHAT'D I MISS?

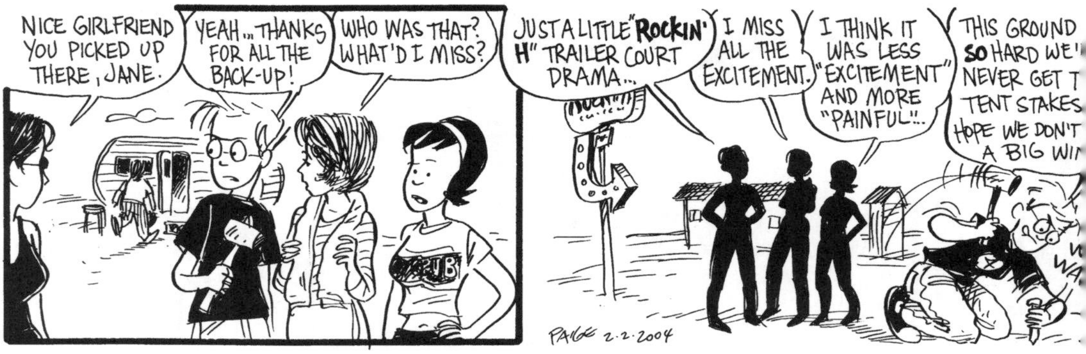
NICE GIRLFRIEND YOU PICKED UP THERE, JANE.
YEAH... THANKS FOR ALL THE BACK-UP!
WHO WAS THAT? WHAT'D I MISS?
JUST A LITTLE "ROCKIN' H" TRAILER COURT DRAMA...
I MISS ALL THE EXCITEMENT.
I THINK IT WAS LESS "EXCITEMENT" AND MORE "PAINFUL"!..
THIS GROUND SO HARD NEVER GET TENT STAKES HOPE WE DON'T A BIG
PAIGE 2.2.2004

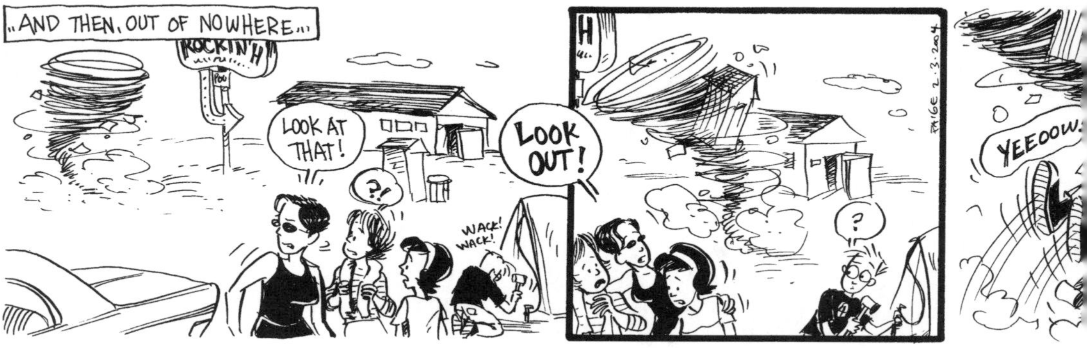
...AND THEN, OUT OF NOWHERE...
ROCKIN' H
LOOK AT THAT!
?!
WACK! WACK!
LOOK OUT!
?
PAIGE 2.3.2004

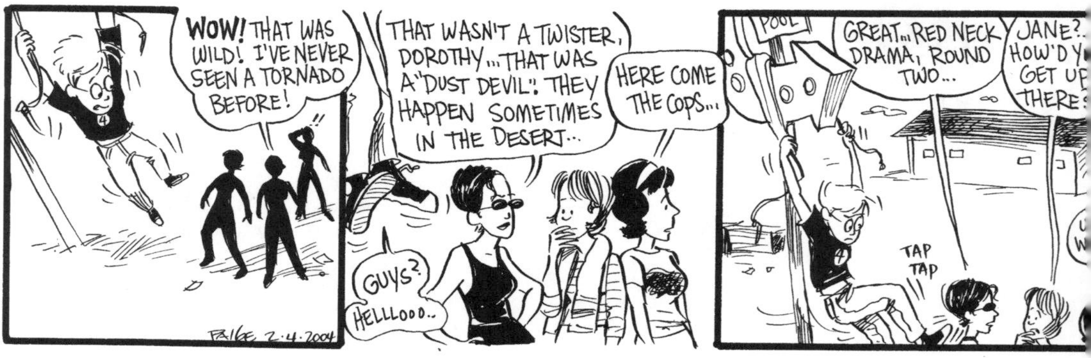
WOW! THAT WAS WILD! I'VE NEVER SEEN A TORNADO BEFORE!
PAIGE 2.4.2004
THAT WASN'T A TWISTER, DOROTHY... THAT WAS A "DUST DEVIL". THEY HAPPEN SOMETIMES IN THE DESERT...
HERE COME THE COPS...
GUYS? HELLLOOO..
POOL
GREAT... RED NECK DRAMA, ROUND TWO...
JANE?..
TAP TAP

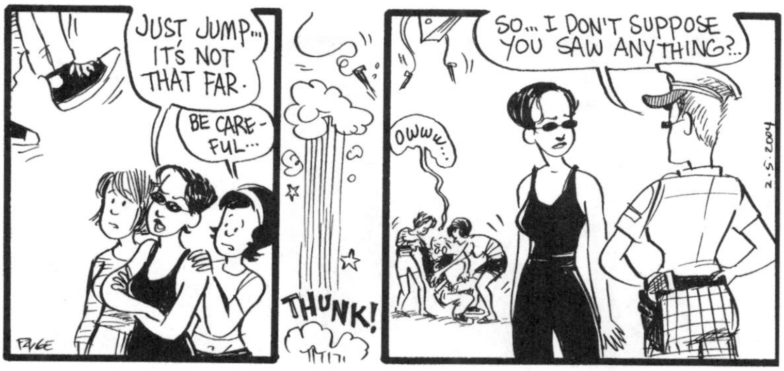
JUST JUMP... IT'S NOT THAT FAR.
BE CAREFUL...
THUNK!
PAIGE
OWWW...
SO... I DON'T SUPPOSE YOU SAW ANYTHING?..
2.5.2004

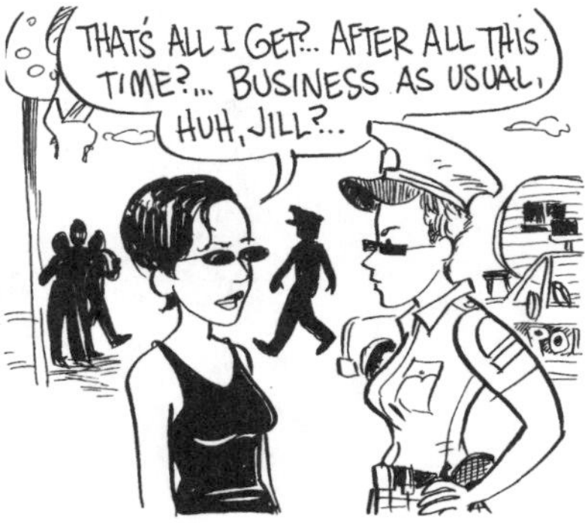
THAT'S ALL I GET?.. AFTER ALL THIS TIME?... BUSINESS AS USUAL, HUH, JILL?..

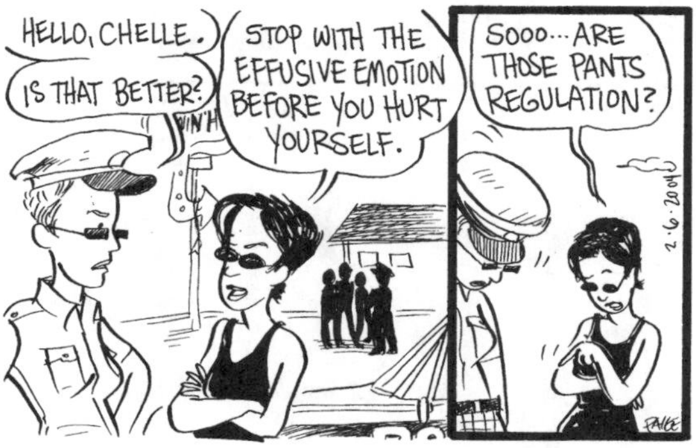
HELLO, CHELLE.
IS THAT BETTER?
STOP WITH THE EFFUSIVE EMOTION BEFORE YOU HURT YOURSELF.
SOOO... ARE THOSE PANTS REGULATION?
2.6.2004
PAIGE

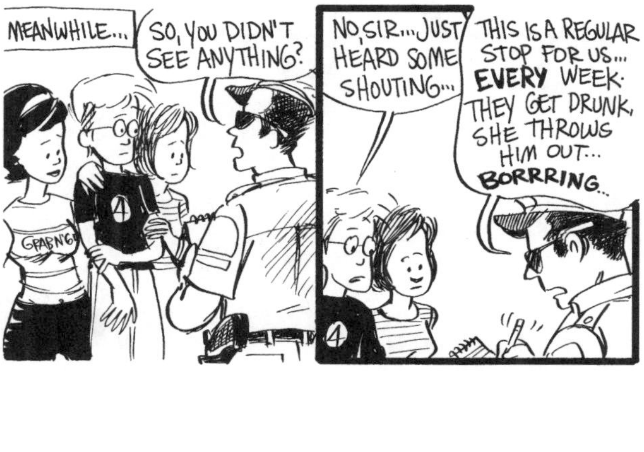
MEANWHILE...
SO, YOU DIDN'T SEE ANYTHING?
NO, SIR... JUST HEARD SOME SHOUTING...
THIS IS A REGULAR STOP FOR US... EVERY WEEK. THEY GET DRUNK, SHE THROWS HIM OUT... BORRRING...

THERE WAS NOTHING NEW TO REPORT... SO AFTER A HALF HOUR, THE COPS LET JOHN GO AND WERE ON THEIR WAY...

I CAME ALL THE WAY OUT HERE TO BE WITH HER. HITCH HIKED FROM SAN DIEGO... AND THIS IS THE THANKS I GET?!

I WAS REALLY DOING SOMETHING WITH MY LIFE 'TIL I MET THAT WENCH!

I'M FINISHED WITH HER... REALLY.

HOW SAD. YOU KNOW, EVEN THOUGH HE SAID IT, HE'LL PROBABLY GO BACK FOR MORE.

WHAT A CYCLE OF MISERY...

WELL, IT'S NOT LIKE HE'S ALONE IN THAT BEHAVIOR...

SPEAK FOR YOURSELF.

YES, WE ALL REPEAT PATTERNS IN RELATIONSHIPS THAT ARE UNHEALTHY.

ALRIGHT, MS. PERFECT. WHO WAS THAT COP IN THE PLAID PANTS?

THAT LOOKED LIKE A REPEAT PATTERN TO ME... NEXT SUBJECT.

NIGHT HAS FALLEN ON OUR LITTLE CAMPSCENE AND ONLY TWO REMAIN BY THE CRACKLING FIRE...
PAIGE 2·10·2004
DIDN'T CHELLE TURN IN? I'M SURPRISED YOU'RE STILL SITTING HERE...
I THOUGHT YOU WERE INTO HER?
I AM.
BUT I THINK SHE'S THE SORT OF GAL WHO COULD DO WITH A LITTLE "WAITING"...
Life is Good

IMPRESSIVE SELF-CONTROL, TALIA.
THANKS...
... BESIDES. I THINK YOU'RE MUCH HARDER TO GET QUALITY TIME WITH...

ARE WE TALKING QUALITY TIME HERE?
OR, YOU KNOW, QUALITY TIME?
Life is good
2·11·2004
I'M JUST CURIOUS ABOUT WHAT'S GOING ON WITH YOU AND DOROTHY
OH.

I DIDN'T KNOW YOU GUYS WERE... WELL... A COUPLE...
BUT YOU'RE SEEMING VERY ATTENTIVE TO EACH OTHER ON THIS TRIP..
UH...

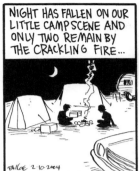

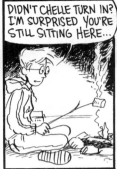

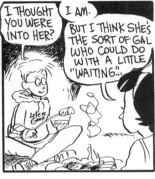

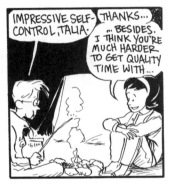

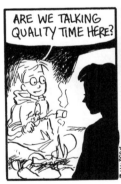

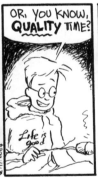

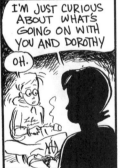

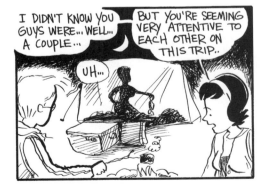

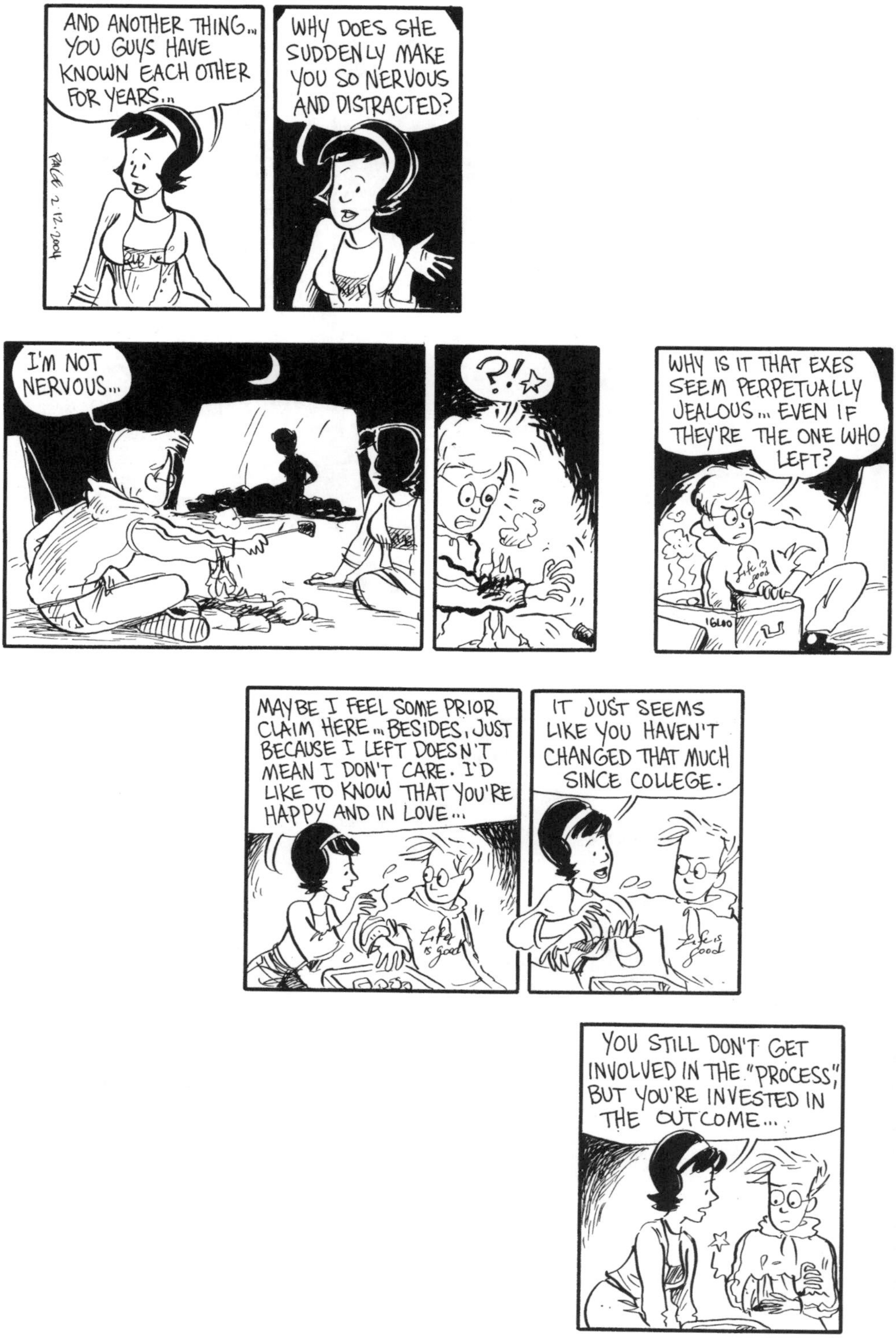
AND ANOTHER THING... YOU GUYS HAVE KNOWN EACH OTHER FOR YEARS...
WHY DOES SHE SUDDENLY MAKE YOU SO NERVOUS AND DISTRACTED?
I'M NOT NERVOUS...
?!☆
WHY IS IT THAT EXES SEEM PERPETUALLY JEALOUS... EVEN IF THEY'RE THE ONE WHO LEFT?
MAYBE I FEEL SOME PRIOR CLAIM HERE... BESIDES, JUST BECAUSE I LEFT DOESN'T MEAN I DON'T CARE. I'D LIKE TO KNOW THAT YOU'RE HAPPY AND IN LOVE...
IT JUST SEEMS LIKE YOU HAVEN'T CHANGED THAT MUCH SINCE COLLEGE.
YOU STILL DON'T GET INVOLVED IN THE "PROCESS," BUT YOU'RE INVESTED IN THE OUTCOME...

WHAT'S THAT SUPPOSED TO MEAN?!
I GET INVOLVED IN PROCESSES ALL THE TIME!
PULEEZE!
PAIGE 2.14.2004

YOU ARE SO COMPLETELY PASSIVE...
THINGS JUST SORT OF HAPPEN TO YOU...
IT'S LIKE YOU CAN SEE THINGS COMING, BUT YOU DON'T MOVE AWAY FROM THE SITE OF IMPACT...

SITE OF IMPACT, HUH?...GIVE ME ONE GOOD EXAMPLE...
YOU AND CHELLE.

YOU GUYS COULDN'T BE ANY MORE WRONG FOR EACH OTHER AND YET, YOU CAN'T STAY AWAY FROM HER.
I'M AWAY FROM HER... AT LEAST TEN FEET...
2.16.2004
BUT YOU'RE ON THIS TRIP...
BUT...

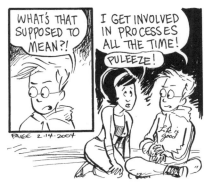

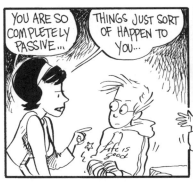

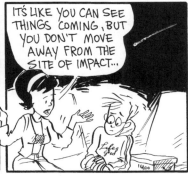

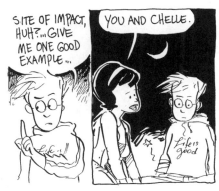

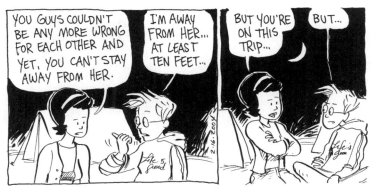

THIS ISN'T ABOUT YOU AND CHELLE ANYWAY...
BUT...
PAIGE 2·17·2004
LOOK, I LIKE DOROTHY. OBVIOUSLY... I MEAN, WE HAD THAT FLING IN COLLEGE...
SO, I'M NOT DOWN ON DOROTHY... ALL I'M SAYING IS PAY ATTENTION.
LIVE DELIBERATELY. DON'T JUST BE ATTRACTED TO THE ATTRACTION... MAKE A CHOICE AND INVEST YOURSELF IN IT.
WHO ARE YOU? AND WHAT HAVE YOU DONE WITH TALIA?..

I'M SERIOUS, JANE. THINK ABOUT IT.
SWEET DREAMS.
2·18·2004

PAIGE

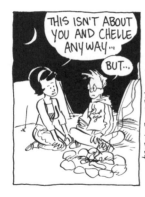

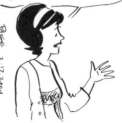

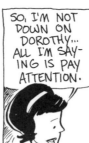

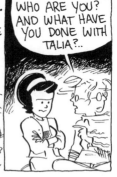

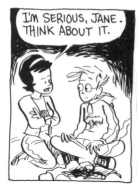

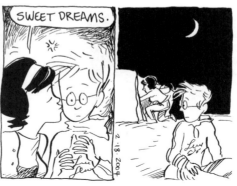

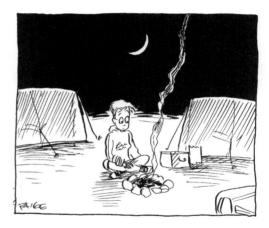

I DON'T KNOW WHAT SHE'S TALKING ABOUT. I'M NOT PASSIVE!...

I MEAN, THERE WAS ANNE, IN HIGH SCHOOL...

SHE WAS MY BEST FRIEND AND WE USED TO HAVE LOTS OF SLEEP OVERS...

AND IT DID SEEM LIKE SHE WANTED TO BE MORE THAN FRIENDS.

...BUT, WHO KNEW SHE'D TURN OUT TO BE GAY?

WE COULD SHOWER TOGETHER... TO CONSERVE WATER, OF COURSE...

LET'S SEE... THEN THERE WAS TALIA, THIRTY POUNDS HEAVIER...

WE WERE ROOMMATES AT BAND CAMP...

I DEFINITELY MADE THE FIRST MOVE...

TALIA, DO YOU HAVE SOME CONDITIONER I COULD BORROW? ...I'M OUT...

JANE!... I THOUGHT YOU'D NEVER ASK!

UMPH!

137

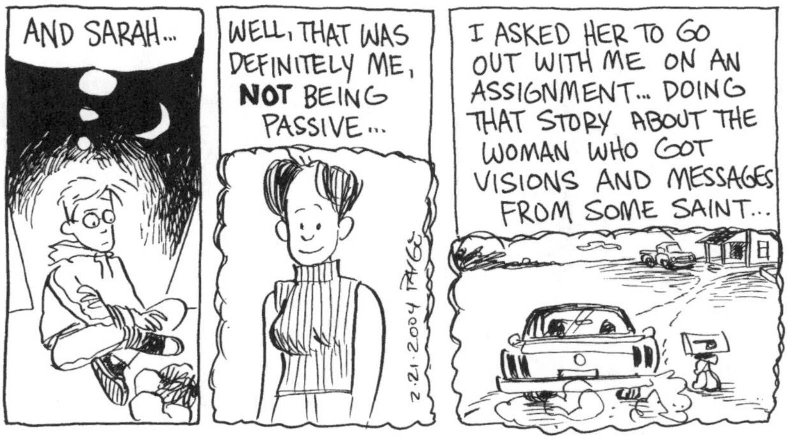
AND SARAH...
WELL, THAT WAS DEFINITELY ME, NOT BEING PASSIVE...
2.21.2004 PAIGE
I ASKED HER TO GO OUT WITH ME ON AN ASSIGNMENT... DOING THAT STORY ABOUT THE WOMAN WHO GOT VISIONS AND MESSAGES FROM SOME SAINT...

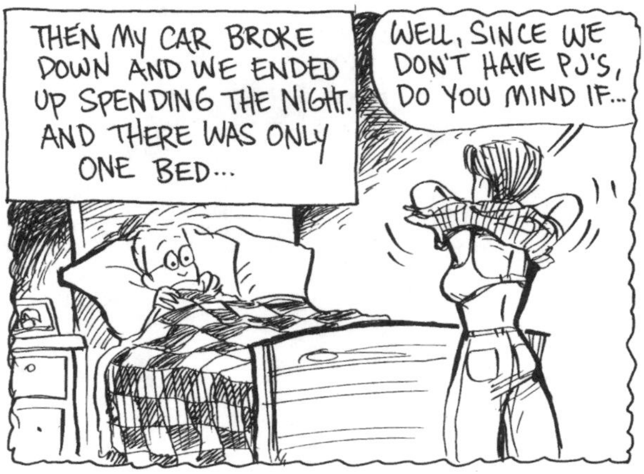
THEN MY CAR BROKE DOWN AND WE ENDED UP SPENDING THE NIGHT. AND THERE WAS ONLY ONE BED...
WELL, SINCE WE DON'T HAVE PJ'S, DO YOU MIND IF...

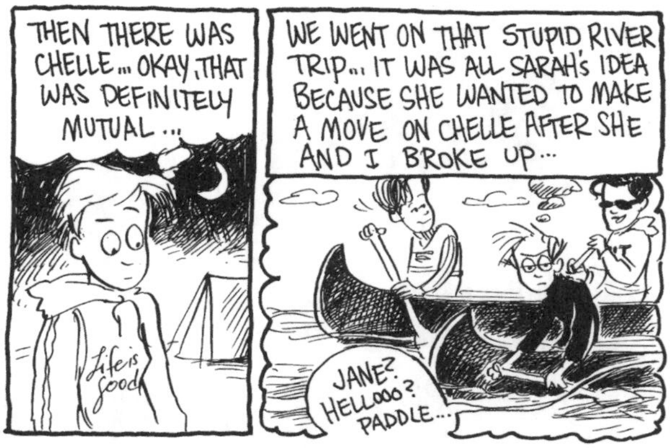
THEN THERE WAS CHELLE... OKAY, THAT WAS DEFINITELY MUTUAL...
Life is good
WE WENT ON THAT STUPID RIVER TRIP... IT WAS ALL SARAH'S IDEA BECAUSE SHE WANTED TO MAKE A MOVE ON CHELLE AFTER SHE AND I BROKE UP...
JANE? HELLOOO? PADDLE...

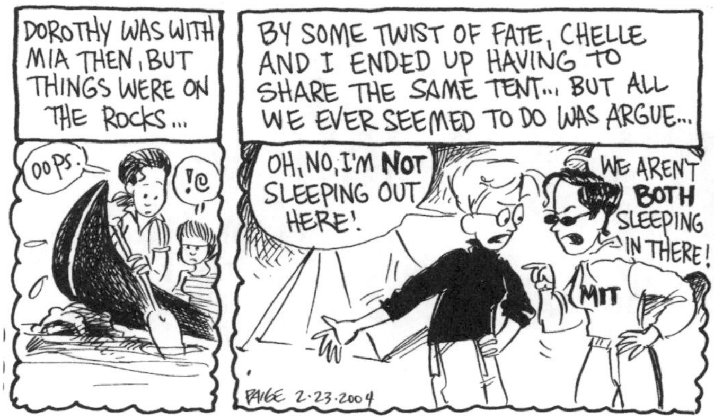
DOROTHY WAS WITH MIA THEN, BUT THINGS WERE ON THE ROCKS...
OOPS!
!@
BY SOME TWIST OF FATE, CHELLE AND I ENDED UP HAVING TO SHARE THE SAME TENT... BUT ALL WE EVER SEEMED TO DO WAS ARGUE...
OH, NO, I'M NOT SLEEPING OUT HERE!
WE AREN'T BOTH SLEEPING IN THERE!
MIT
PAIGE 2.23.2004

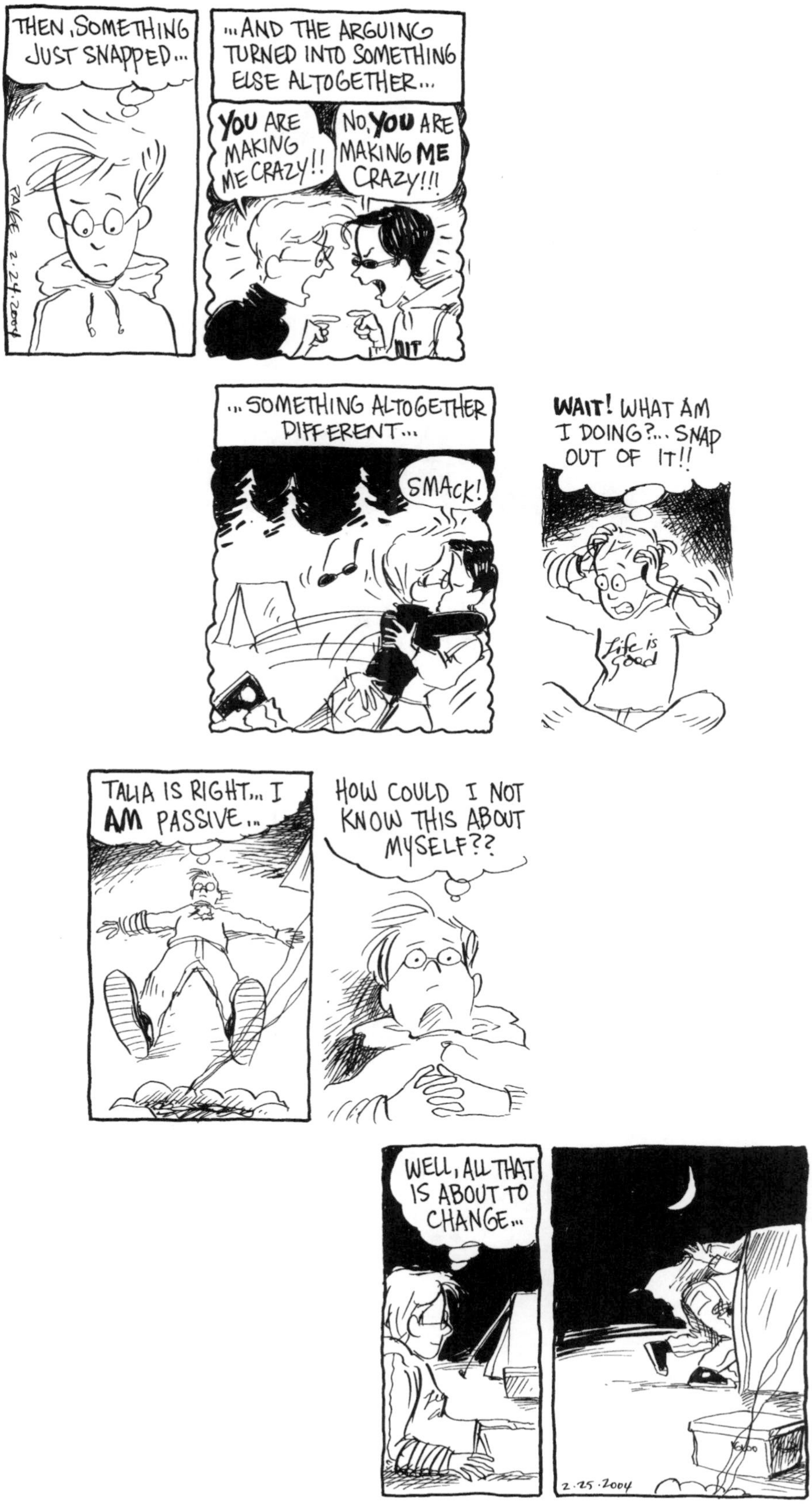
THEN, SOMETHING JUST SNAPPED...
PAIGE 2.24.2004
...AND THE ARGUING TURNED INTO SOMETHING ELSE ALTOGETHER...
YOU ARE MAKING ME CRAZY!!
NO, YOU ARE MAKING ME CRAZY!!!
...SOMETHING ALTOGETHER DIFFERENT...
SMACK!
WAIT! WHAT AM I DOING?... SNAP OUT OF IT!!
Life is Good
TALIA IS RIGHT... I AM PASSIVE...
HOW COULD I NOT KNOW THIS ABOUT MYSELF??
WELL, ALL THAT IS ABOUT TO CHANGE...
2.25.2004

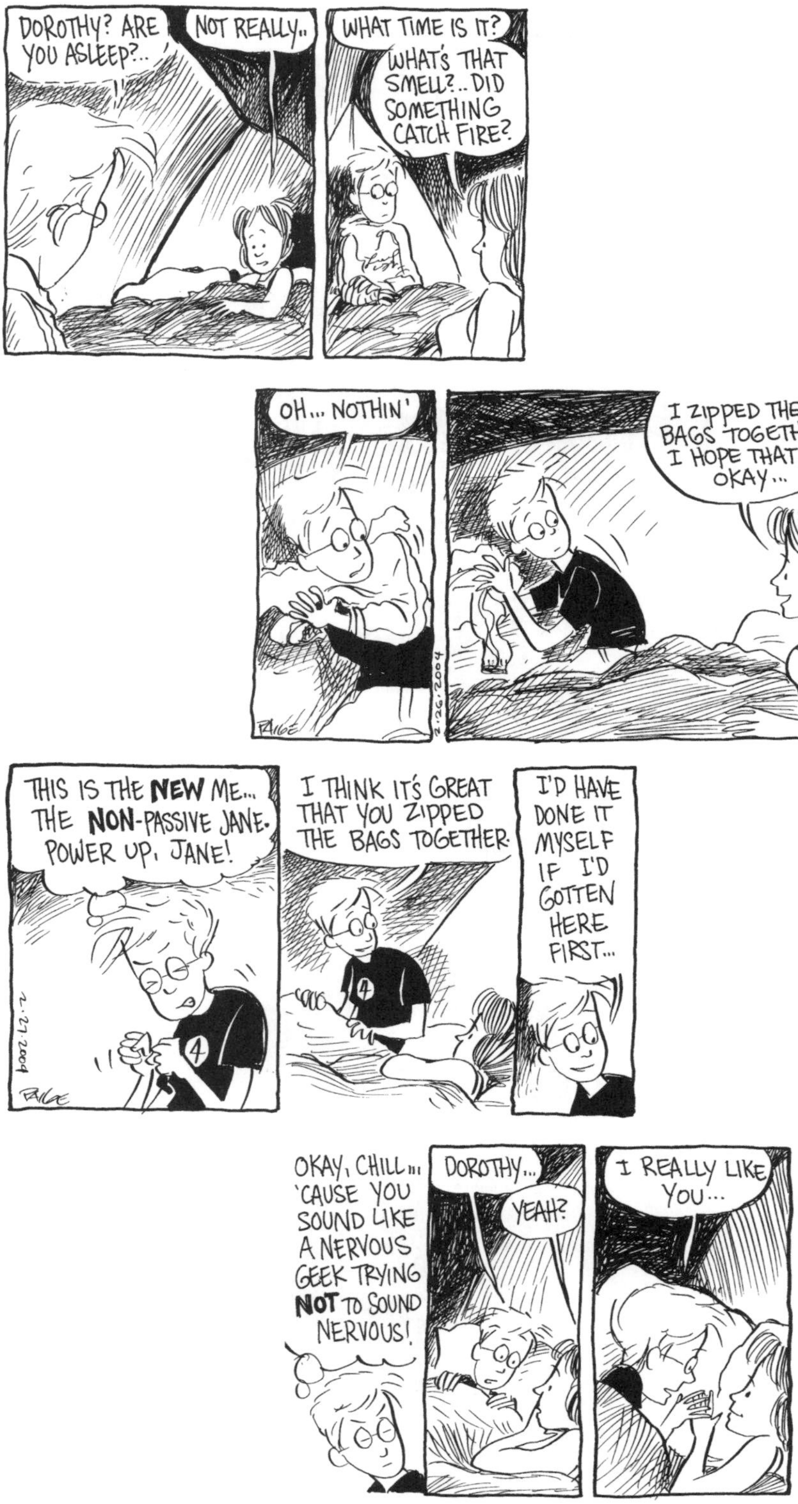
DOROTHY? ARE YOU ASLEEP?...
NOT REALLY..
WHAT TIME IS IT?
WHAT'S THAT SMELL?.. DID SOMETHING CATCH FIRE?
OH... NOTHIN'
I ZIPPED THE BAGS TOGETHER, I HOPE THAT'S OKAY...
2.26.2004
PAIGE
THIS IS THE NEW ME... THE NON-PASSIVE JANE. POWER UP, JANE!
I THINK IT'S GREAT THAT YOU ZIPPED THE BAGS TOGETHER.
I'D HAVE DONE IT MYSELF IF I'D GOTTEN HERE FIRST...
2.27.2004
PAIGE
OKAY, CHILL... 'CAUSE YOU SOUND LIKE A NERVOUS GEEK TRYING NOT TO SOUND NERVOUS!
DOROTHY...
YEAH?
I REALLY LIKE YOU...

I REALLY LIKE YOU TOO JANE... THIS TRIP HAS MADE ME REALIZE SOMETHING...
2·28·2004

...ISN'T IT AMAZING? HERE WE WERE, ALL THIS TIME, RIGHT UNDER EACH OTHER'S NOSES...
SOMETIMES IT'S THOSE CLOSEST TO US... THOSE THAT WE SHOULD KNOW, THAT ELLUDE US...
THAT'S BEAUTIFUL. DID YOU WRITE THAT?
UH... NO.
UM... I READ IT IN A BOOK...
...ABOUT FISHING...
PAIGE

CUT!
JANE'S WORLD
WE INTERRUPT OUR DAILY COMIC TO READ A BIT OF FAN MAIL...
3·1·2004
Dear Jane, Is this really a lesbian comic if no one ever gets laid? Your friend, Steven
UH... LET'S LOOK AT ANOTHER LETTER FOLKS..
Dear Jane, When is there going to be some real action in "Jane's World?" ~Anxiously waiting, Steven
HEH, HEH..
COUGH
ONE MORE?
Dear Jane, Can Someone in your comic please have sex? And when you draw the pictures can you please show some
CENSORED
Voyeuristically yours, Steven
!?
OK, FOLKS! ROLL TAPE!

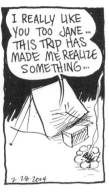

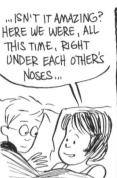

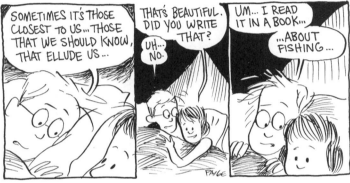

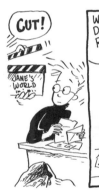

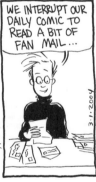

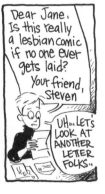

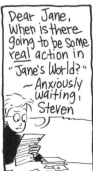

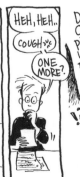

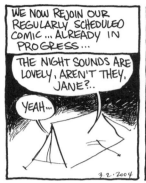

WE NOW REJOIN OUR REGULARLY SCHEDULED COMIC ... ALREADY IN PROGRESS...
THE NIGHT SOUNDS ARE LOVELY, AREN'T THEY, JANE?..
YEAH...
SO, DOROTHY, WHAT DID YOU MEAN WHEN YOU SAID THIS TRIP MADE YOU REALIZE SOMETHING?
3.2.2004

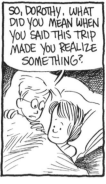

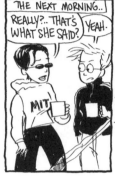

THE NEXT MORNING..
REALLY?.. THAT'S WHAT SHE SAID?
YEAH.
MIT
SHE SAID THAT SPENDING THIS TIME WITH TALIA MADE HER REMEMBER WHY SHE FELL FOR HER IN THE FIRST PLACE.
PAIGE
WELL, THAT EXPLAINS A LOT...
I'M SO CONFUSED!
MIT

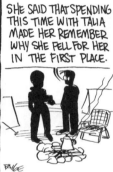

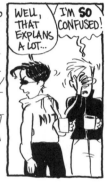

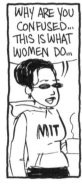

WHY ARE YOU CONFUSED... THIS IS WHAT WOMEN DO...
MIT
THEY ALWAYS USE THE INDIRECT METHOD... EVEN AS KIDS... THEY NEVER WENT RIGHT UP TO THE PERSON THEY LIKED ON THE PLAYGROUND...
...THEY GOT THEIR BEST FRIEND TO DO IT.
MIT
PAIGE
3.3.2004

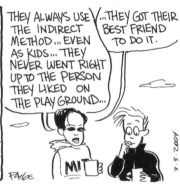

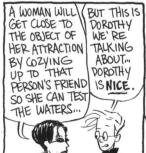

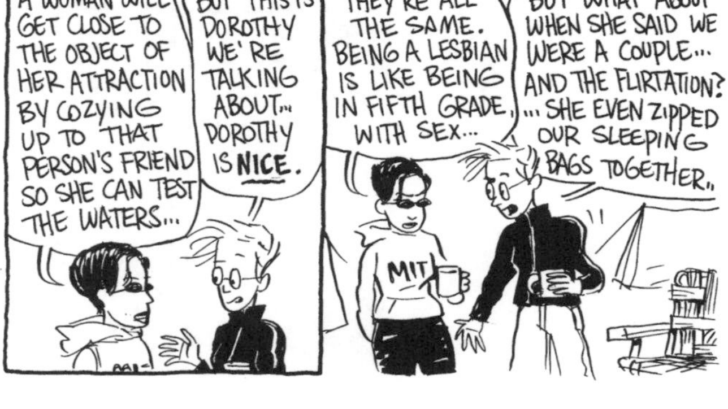

A WOMAN WILL GET CLOSE TO THE OBJECT OF HER ATTRACTION BY COZYING UP TO THAT PERSON'S FRIEND SO SHE CAN TEST THE WATERS...
BUT THIS IS DOROTHY WE'RE TALKING ABOUT... DOROTHY IS NICE.
THEY'RE ALL THE SAME. BEING A LESBIAN IS LIKE BEING IN FIFTH GRADE, WITH SEX...
BUT WHAT ABOUT WHEN SHE SAID WE WERE A COUPLE... AND THE FLIRTATION? ... SHE EVEN ZIPPED OUR SLEEPING BAGS TOGETHER..
MIT

IT WAS A CLASSIC JEALOUSY PLAY.
IT WAS?
SHE WAS FLIRTING WITH YOU TO SEE IF SHE WOULD GET A REACTION FROM TALIA.
3.4.2004

HEY... THAT'S WHY TALIA STAYED AND TALKED TO ME BY THE FIRE... SHE WAS WAY TOO INTERESTED IN WHAT WAS GOING ON WITH DOROTHY AND ME...
IT WASN'T ABOUT ME BEING PASSIVE AT ALL!...
WELL, YOU **ARE** PASSIVE...
...CAN YOU WARM THIS UP?
SHE WAS JUST TRYING TO FIND OUT IF I'D MADE A MOVE!
PAIGE

THIS IS ALL JUST SO TYPICALLY DYSFUNCTIONAL.
I GOT NO WHERE WITH TALIA LAST NIGHT. NOW I SEE WHY.... SHE DID ALLUDE TO SOME REKINDLED ATTRACTION...
3.5.2004
PAIGE

...BUT THE WAY SHE SAID IT I THOUGHT SHE WAS TALKING ABOUT YOU...
ME?
...BUT OBVIOUSLY SHE MEANT DOROTHY.
HEY! THAT'S NOT OBVIOUS TO ME!
SSHH... THEY'RE WALKING BACK FROM THE SHOWERS...

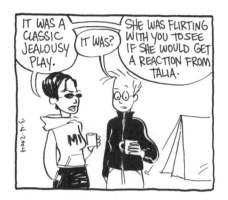

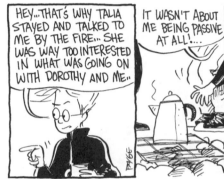

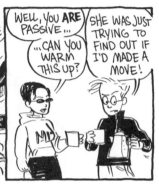

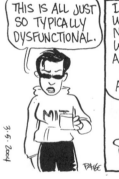

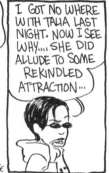

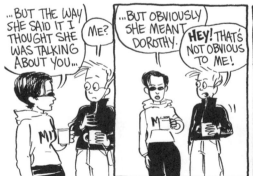

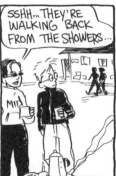

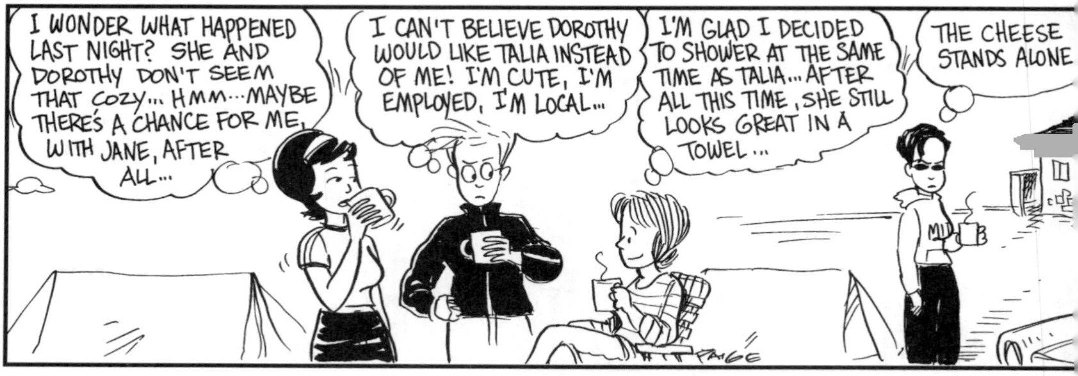
I WONDER WHAT HAPPENED LAST NIGHT? SHE AND DOROTHY DON'T SEEM THAT COZY... HMM...MAYBE THERE'S A CHANCE FOR ME, WITH JANE, AFTER ALL...
I CAN'T BELIEVE DOROTHY WOULD LIKE TALIA INSTEAD OF ME! I'M CUTE, I'M EMPLOYED, I'M LOCAL...
I'M GLAD I DECIDED TO SHOWER AT THE SAME TIME AS TALIA... AFTER ALL THIS TIME, SHE STILL LOOKS GREAT IN A TOWEL...
THE CHEESE STANDS ALONE
PAIGE

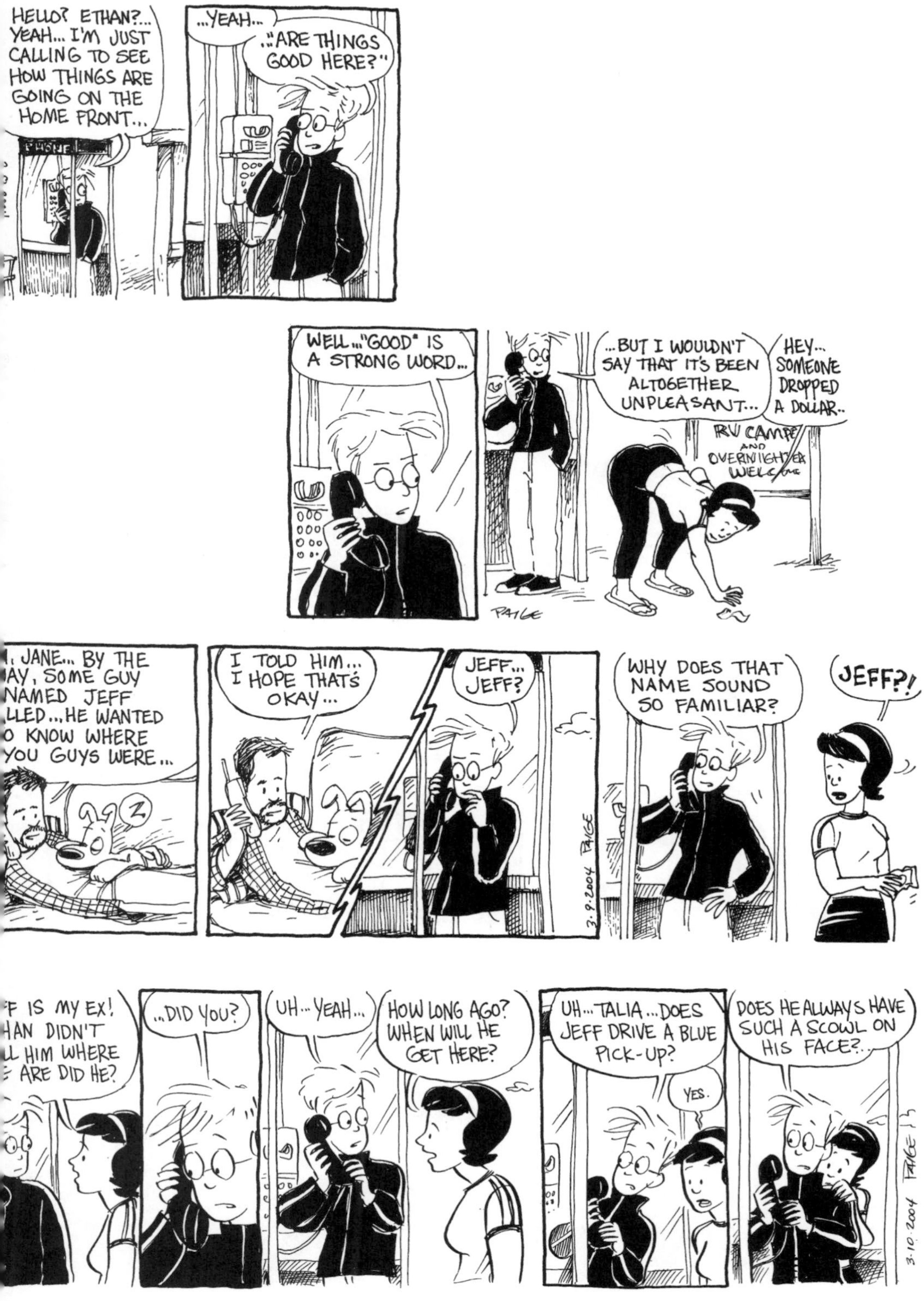
HELLO? ETHAN?... YEAH... I'M JUST CALLING TO SEE HOW THINGS ARE GOING ON THE HOME FRONT...
PHONE
...YEAH...
..."ARE THINGS GOOD HERE?"
WELL..."GOOD" IS A STRONG WORD...
...BUT I WOULDN'T SAY THAT IT'S BEEN ALTOGETHER UNPLEASANT...
HEY... SOMEONE DROPPED A DOLLAR..
RV CAMPE AND OVERNIGHTER WELC
PAIGE
, JANE... BY THE AY, SOME GUY NAMED JEFF LLED... HE WANTED O KNOW WHERE YOU GUYS WERE...
I TOLD HIM... I HOPE THAT'S OKAY...
JEFF... JEFF?
WHY DOES THAT NAME SOUND SO FAMILIAR?
JEFF?!
3.9.2004 PAIGE
F IS MY EX! HAN DIDN'T L HIM WHERE ARE DID HE?
...DID YOU?
UH... YEAH...
HOW LONG AGO? WHEN WILL HE GET HERE?
UH... TALIA... DOES JEFF DRIVE A BLUE PICK-UP?
YES.
DOES HE ALWAYS HAVE SUCH A SCOWL ON HIS FACE?...
3.10.2004 PAIGE

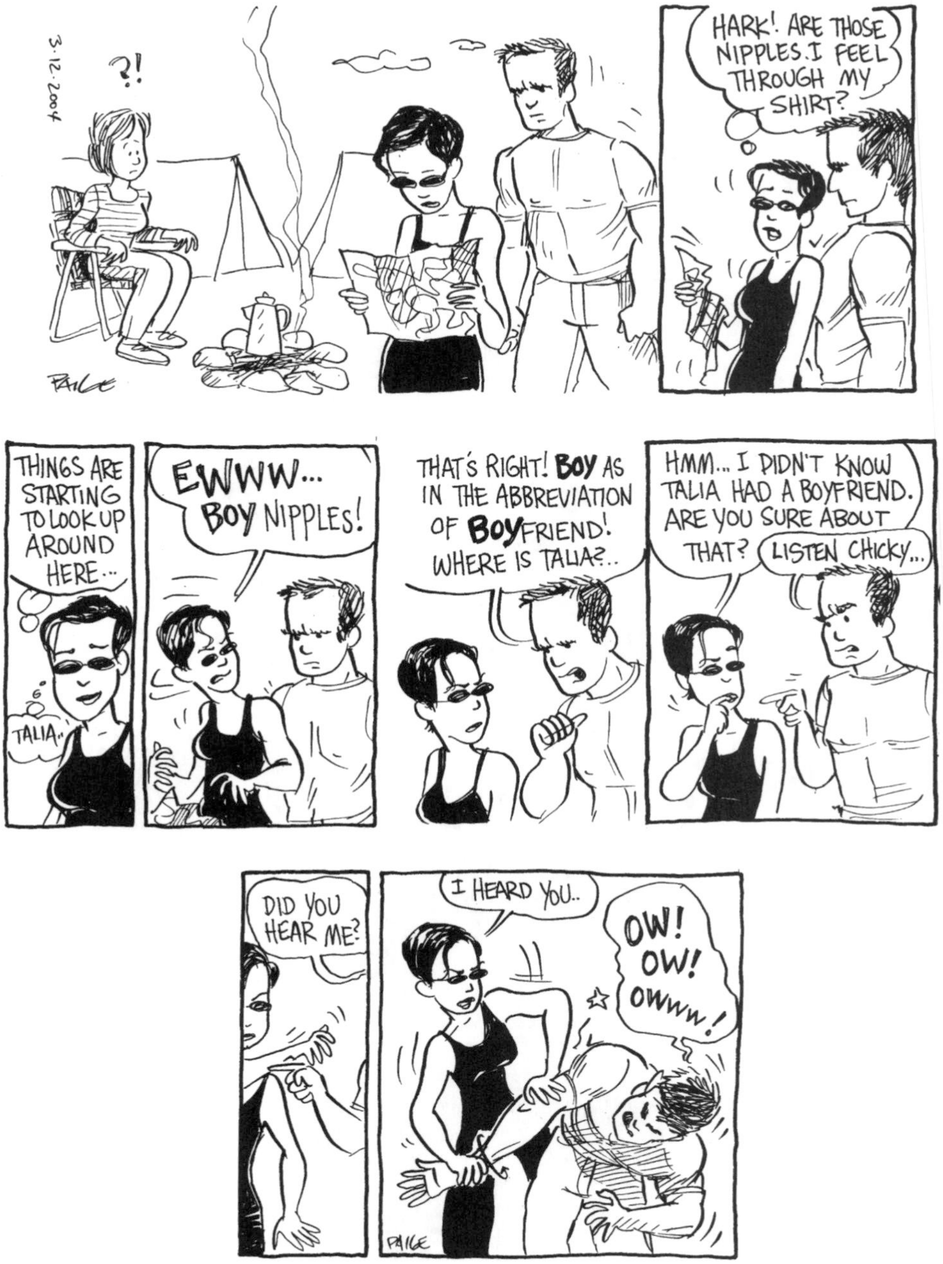
3.12.2004
?!
PAIGE
HARK! ARE THOSE NIPPLES I FEEL THROUGH MY SHIRT?
THINGS ARE STARTING TO LOOK UP AROUND HERE...
TALIA..
EWWW... BOY NIPPLES!
THAT'S RIGHT! BOY AS IN THE ABBREVIATION OF BOYFRIEND! WHERE IS TALIA?..
HMM... I DIDN'T KNOW TALIA HAD A BOYFRIEND. ARE YOU SURE ABOUT THAT?
LISTEN CHICKY...
DID YOU HEAR ME?
I HEARD YOU..
OW! OW! OWww!
PAIGE

3.15.2004
WHAT'S JEFF DOING HERE? I THOUGHT YOU GUYS BROKE UP...
WE DID, SORT OF...
COME ON... I THINK WE SHOULD GET OVER THERE BEFORE CHELLE HURTS HIM...
....

HOW DO YOU "SORT OF" BREAK UP WITH SOMEONE?
PAIGE
3.16.2004
I LEFT HIM A MESSAGE ON HIS ANSWERING MACHINE.
THAT'S SO LAME!

AND HERE I THOUGHT YOU'D EVOLVED.
I CAN BE EVOLVED AND STILL TRY AND AVOID CON-FRONTATION...
WELL, I MAY BE PASSIVE, BUT AT LEAST I'M NOT A BIG CHICKEN!
...OH, WAIT...
..YES, I AM..
PAIGE

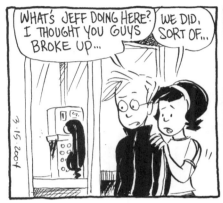

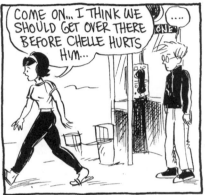

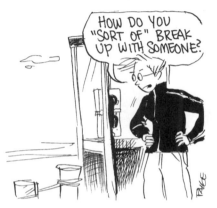

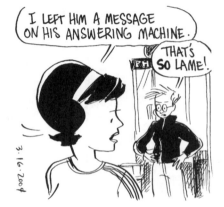

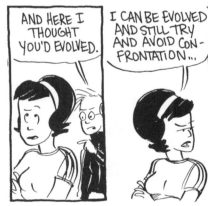

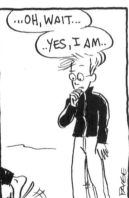

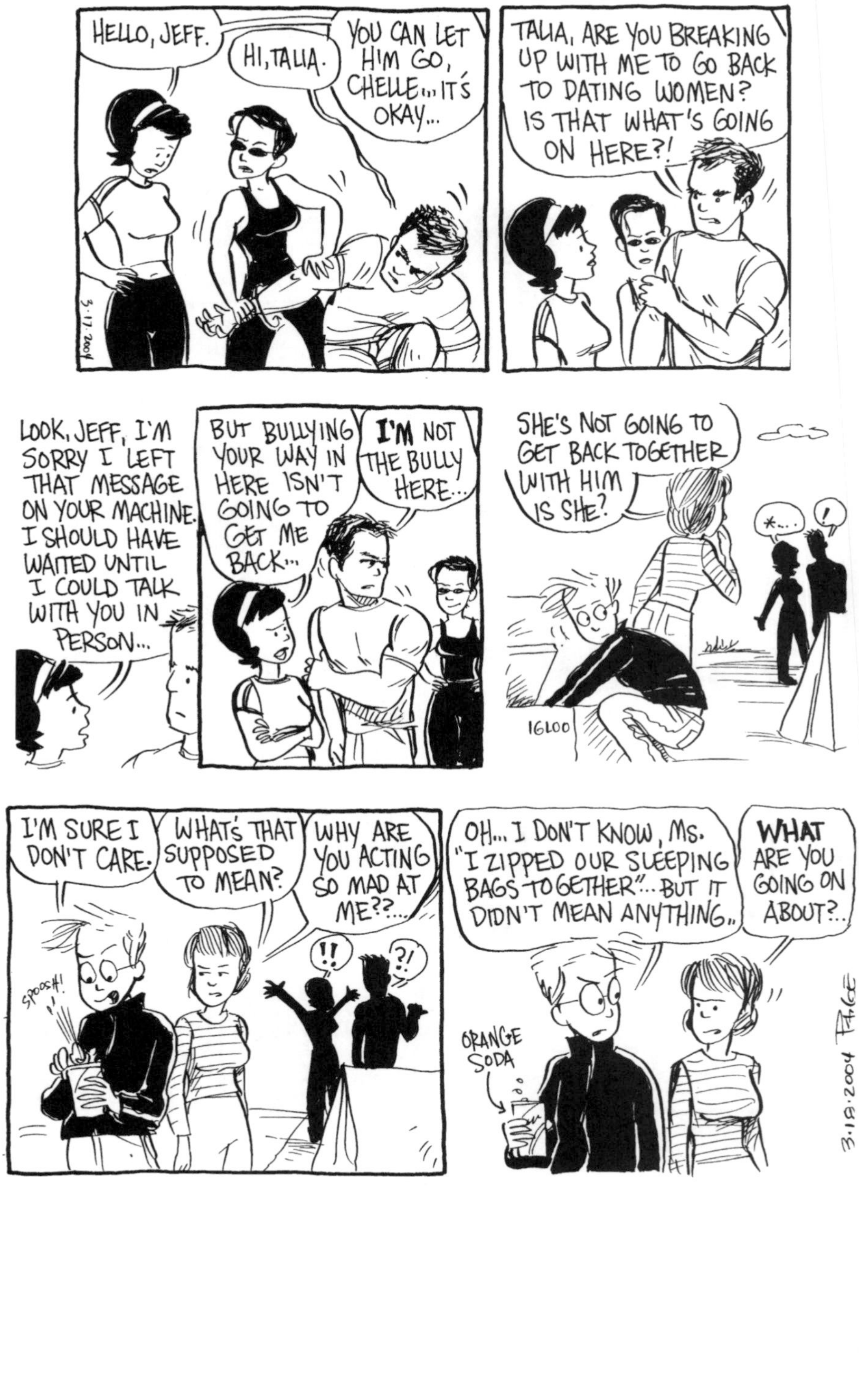
HELLO, JEFF.
HI, TALIA.
YOU CAN LET HIM GO, CHELLE... IT'S OKAY...
3.17.2004
TALIA, ARE YOU BREAKING UP WITH ME TO GO BACK TO DATING WOMEN? IS THAT WHAT'S GOING ON HERE?!
LOOK, JEFF, I'M SORRY I LEFT THAT MESSAGE ON YOUR MACHINE. I SHOULD HAVE WAITED UNTIL I COULD TALK WITH YOU IN PERSON...
BUT BULLYING YOUR WAY IN HERE ISN'T GOING TO GET ME BACK...
I'M NOT THE BULLY HERE...
SHE'S NOT GOING TO GET BACK TOGETHER WITH HIM IS SHE?
*...
!
IGLOO
I'M SURE I DON'T CARE.
WHAT'S THAT SUPPOSED TO MEAN?
WHY ARE YOU ACTING SO MAD AT ME??...
SPOOSH!
!!
?!
OH... I DON'T KNOW, MS. "I ZIPPED OUR SLEEPING BAGS TOGETHER"... BUT IT DIDN'T MEAN ANYTHING..
WHAT ARE YOU GOING ON ABOUT?..
ORANGE SODA
3.18.2004
PAIGE

MIXED SIGNALS... THAT'S WHAT I'M TALKING ABOUT!
YOU AND YOUR MIXED SIGNALS!
YOU WERE DEFINITELY FLIRTING WITH ME THIS WHOLE TRIP!
SO?
PAIGE
3.19.2004
SO?!..SO, YOU WERE FLIRTING WITH ME, BUT YOU'RE INTERESTED IN TALIA!
AGAIN, I SAY...SO?
IT'S NOT LIKE YOU WERE INTERESTED IN HER...YOU'VE PRACTICALLY BEEN AFRAID OF HER SINCE SHE GOT HERE!
ARRGH... NEVER MIND!
NO, WAIT. YOU'RE OBVIOUSLY UPSET...WE SHOULD TALK THIS OUT..
I DON'T WANT TO TALK ABOUT IT...
WELL, SULKING ISN'T GOING TO SOLVE ANYTHING!
OH... I DUNNO... IT FEELS PRETTY DARN GOOD...
PAIGE
LOOK! ME... SULKING...
WHATE
HMMM...FEELS SOOO GOOD!
SUIT YOURSELF, JANE..

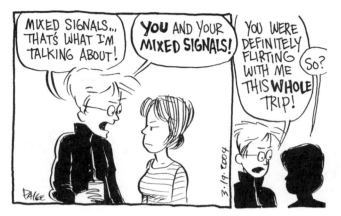

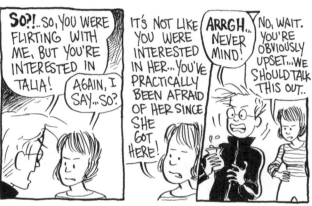

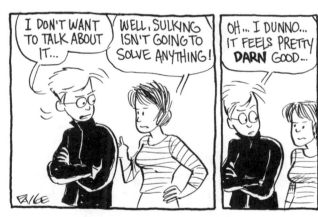

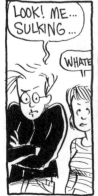

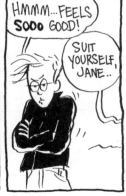

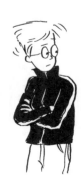

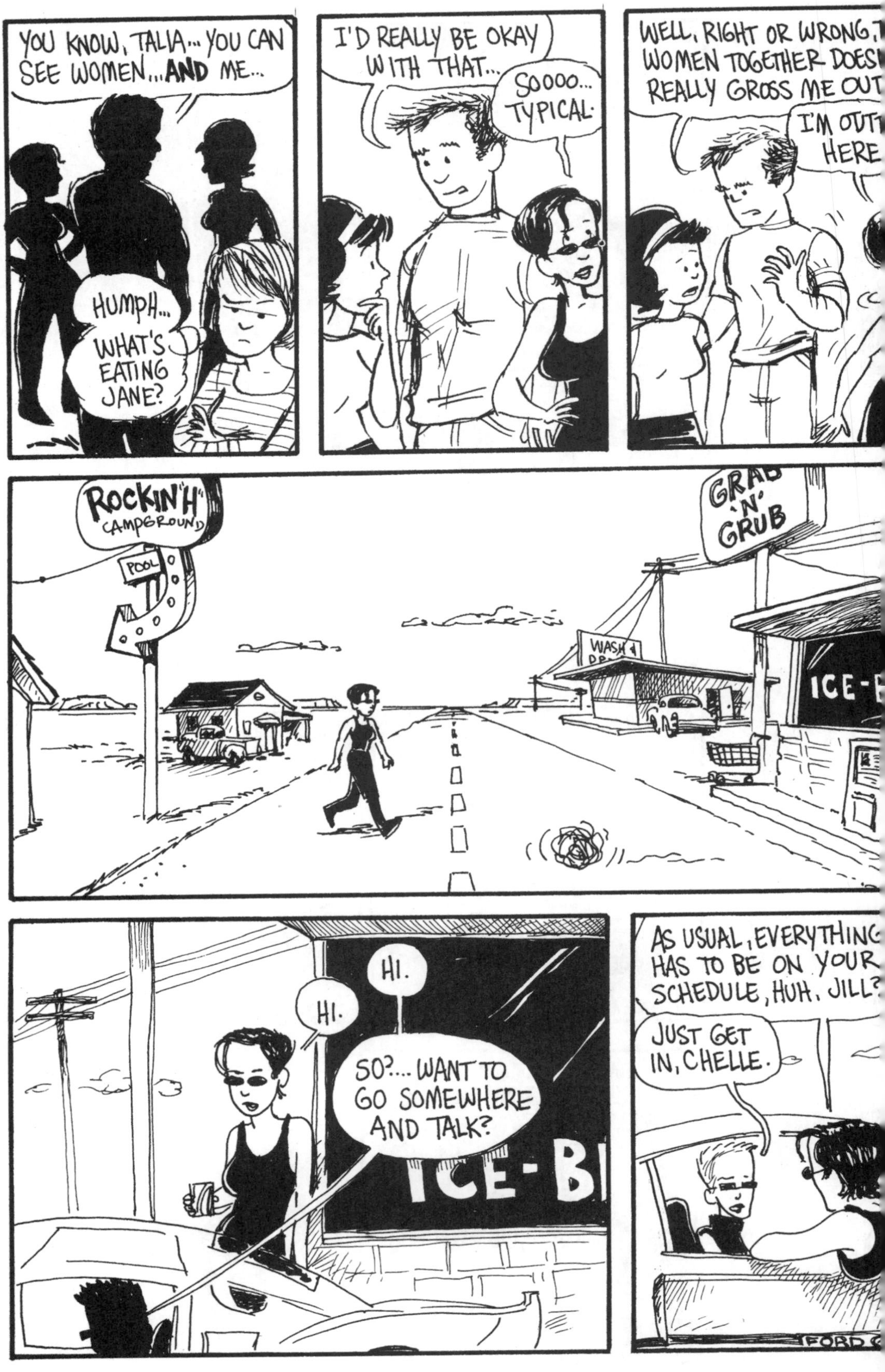
YOU KNOW, TALIA... YOU CAN SEE WOMEN... AND ME...
HUMPH...
WHAT'S EATING JANE?
I'D REALLY BE OKAY WITH THAT...
SOOOO... TYPICAL.
WELL, RIGHT OR WRONG, T
WOMEN TOGETHER DOES
REALLY GROSS ME OUT
I'M OUTT HERE
ROCKIN' "H" CAMPGROUND
POOL
GRAB 'N' GRUB
WASH &
ICE-
HI.
HI.
SO?... WANT TO GO SOMEWHERE AND TALK?
ICE-B
AS USUAL, EVERYTHING HAS TO BE ON YOUR SCHEDULE, HUH, JILL?
JUST GET IN, CHELLE.
FORD

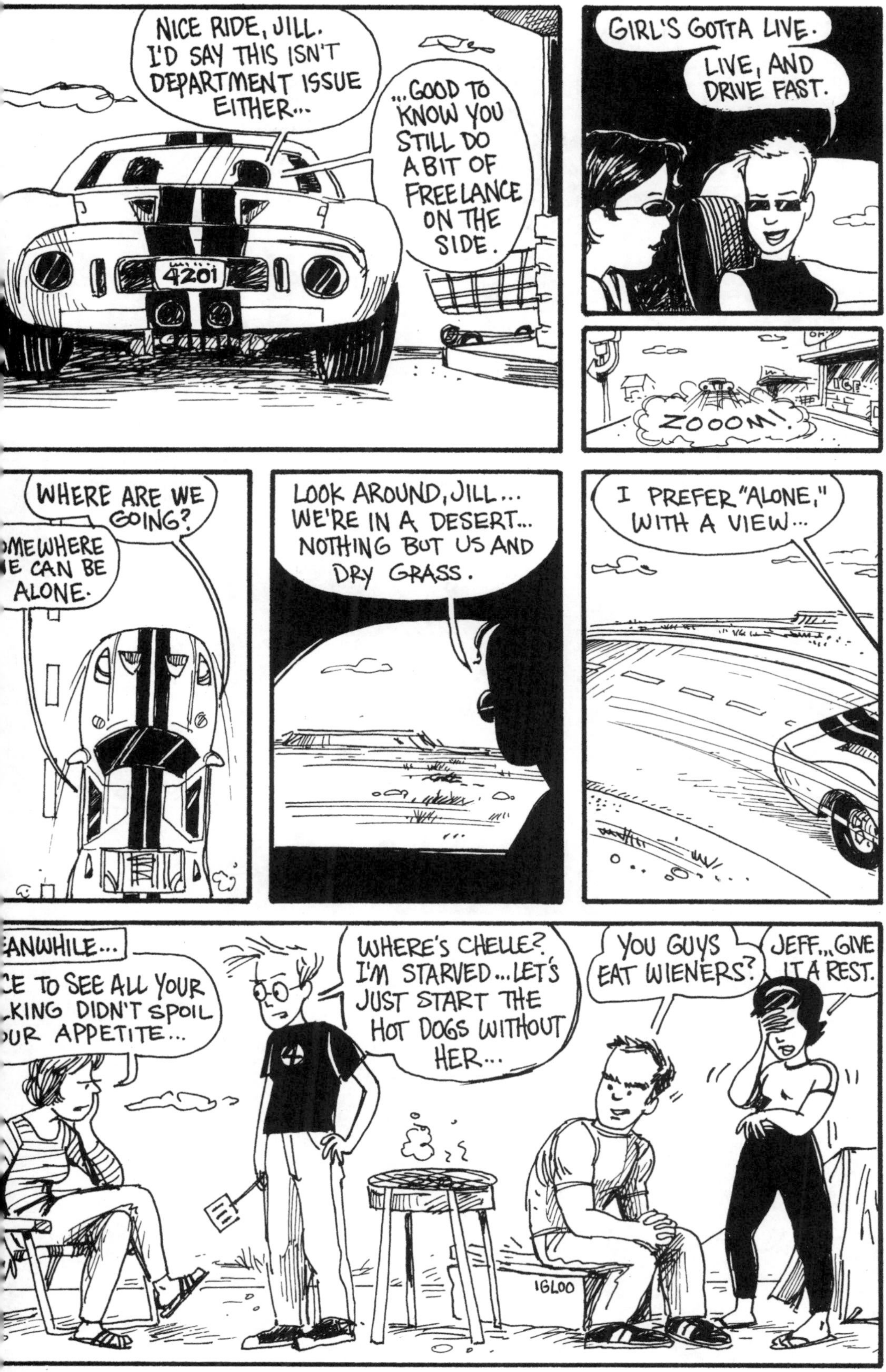
NICE RIDE, JILL. I'D SAY THIS ISN'T DEPARTMENT ISSUE EITHER...
...GOOD TO KNOW YOU STILL DO A BIT OF FREELANCE ON THE SIDE.
4201
GIRL'S GOTTA LIVE.
LIVE, AND DRIVE FAST.
ZOOOM!
WHERE ARE WE GOING?
LOOK AROUND, JILL... WE'RE IN A DESERT... NOTHING BUT US AND DRY GRASS.
I PREFER "ALONE," WITH A VIEW...
WHERE'S CHELLE? I'M STARVED...LET'S JUST START THE HOT DOGS WITHOUT HER...
YOU GUYS EAT WIENERS?
JEFF...GIVE IT A REST.
IGLOO

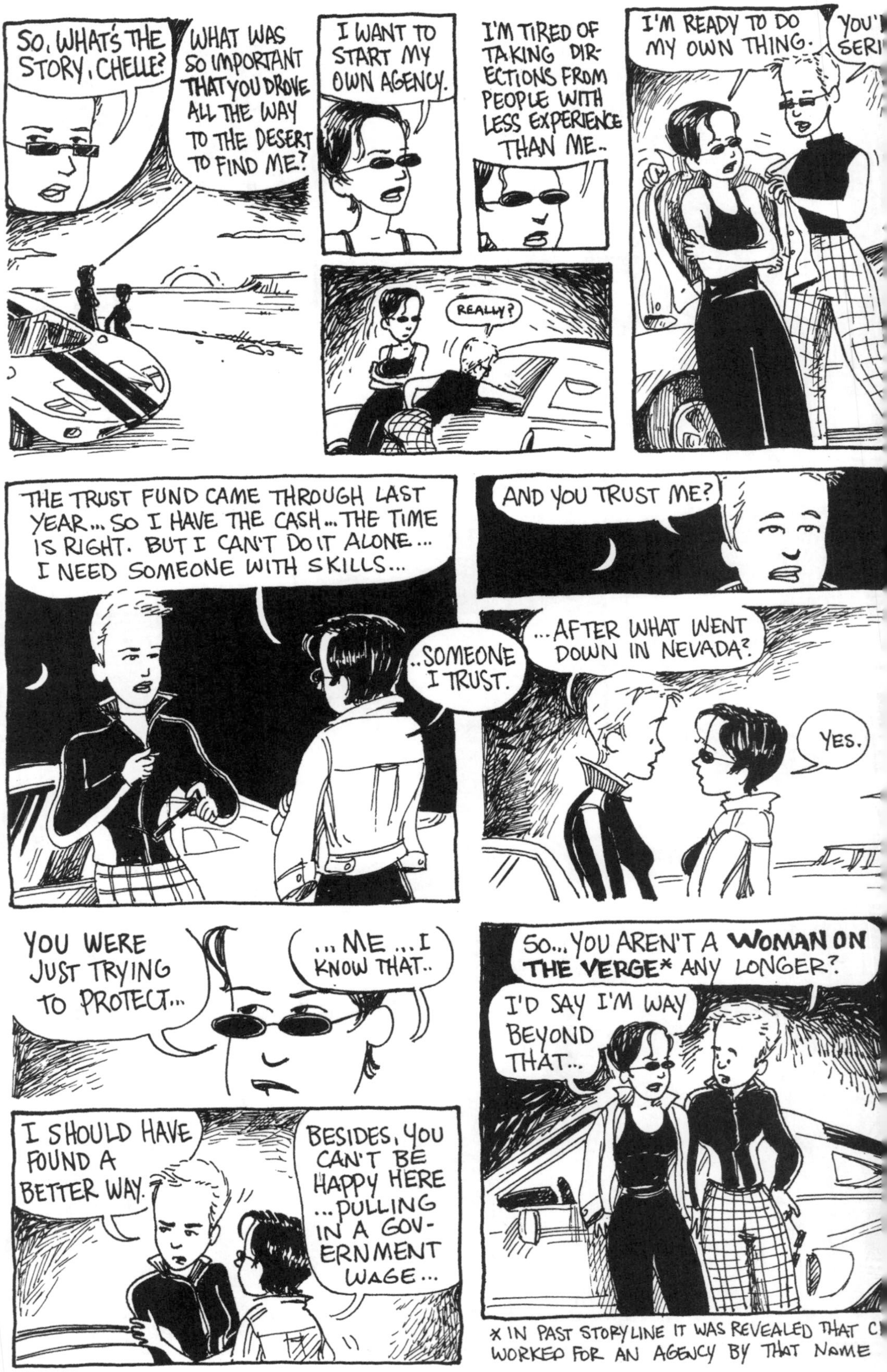
SO, WHAT'S THE STORY, CHELLE?
WHAT WAS SO IMPORTANT THAT YOU DROVE ALL THE WAY TO THE DESERT TO FIND ME?
I WANT TO START MY OWN AGENCY.
I'M TIRED OF TAKING DIRECTIONS FROM PEOPLE WITH LESS EXPERIENCE THAN ME..
REALLY?
I'M READY TO DO MY OWN THING.
THE TRUST FUND CAME THROUGH LAST YEAR... SO I HAVE THE CASH... THE TIME IS RIGHT. BUT I CAN'T DO IT ALONE... I NEED SOMEONE WITH SKILLS...
...SOMEONE I TRUST.
AND YOU TRUST ME?
...AFTER WHAT WENT DOWN IN NEVADA?
YES.
YOU WERE JUST TRYING TO PROTECT...
...ME ...I KNOW THAT..
I SHOULD HAVE FOUND A BETTER WAY.
BESIDES, YOU CAN'T BE HAPPY HERE ...PULLING IN A GOVERNMENT WAGE...
SO... YOU AREN'T A WOMAN ON THE VERGE* ANY LONGER?
I'D SAY I'M WAY BEYOND THAT...
* IN PAST STORYLINE IT WAS REVEALED THAT C
WORKED FOR AN AGENCY BY THAT NAME

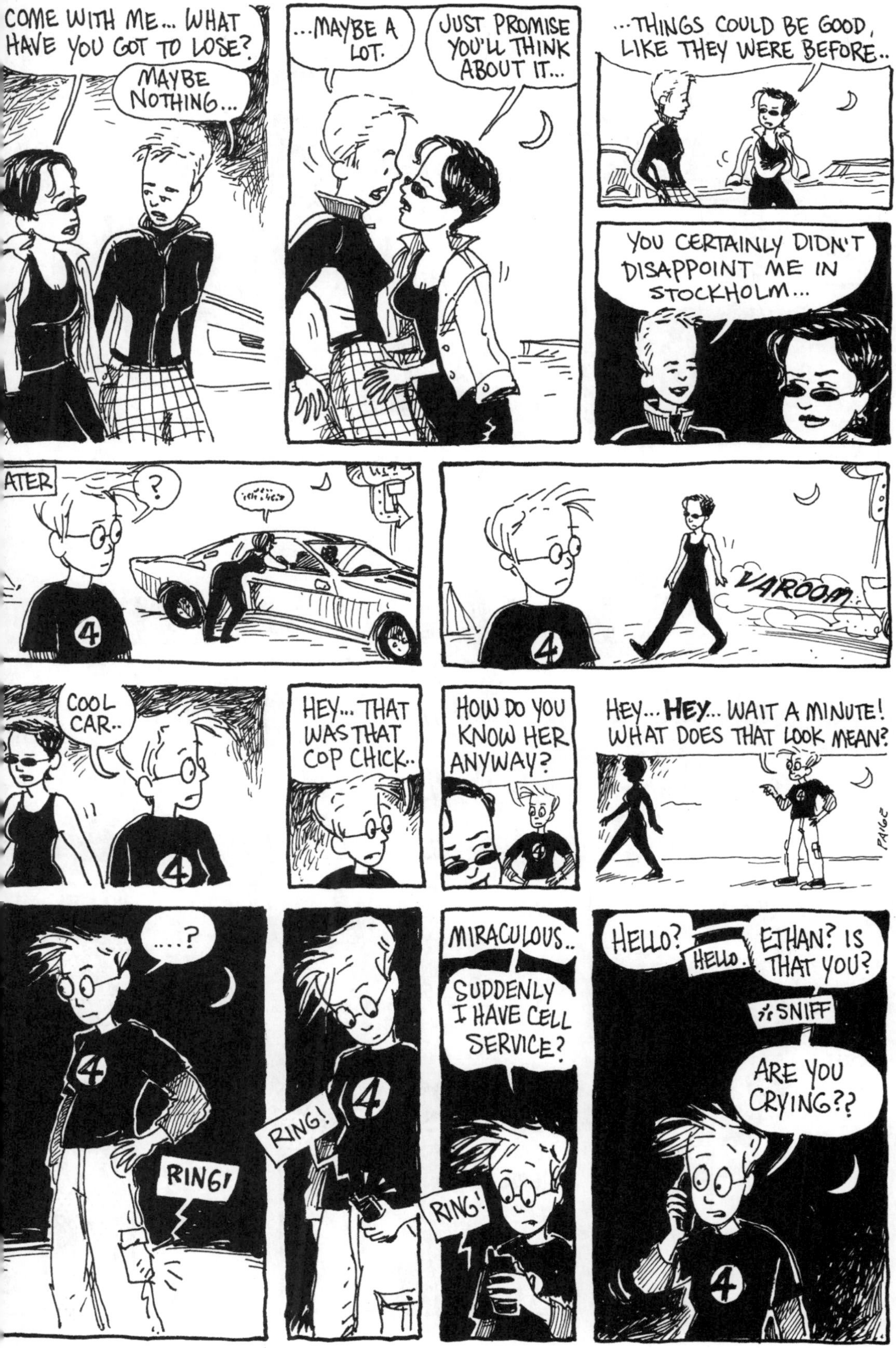
COME WITH ME... WHAT HAVE YOU GOT TO LOSE?
MAYBE NOTHING...
...MAYBE A LOT.
JUST PROMISE YOU'LL THINK ABOUT IT...
...THINGS COULD BE GOOD, LIKE THEY WERE BEFORE..
YOU CERTAINLY DIDN'T DISAPPOINT ME IN STOCKHOLM...
ATER
?
VAROOM
COOL CAR..
HEY... THAT WAS THAT COP CHICK..
HOW DO YOU KNOW HER ANYWAY?
HEY... HEY... WAIT A MINUTE! WHAT DOES THAT LOOK MEAN?
PAIGE
....?
RING!
RING!
MIRACULOUS..
SUDDENLY I HAVE CELL SERVICE?
RING!
HELLO?
HELLO.
ETHAN? IS THAT YOU?
SNIFF
ARE YOU CRYING??

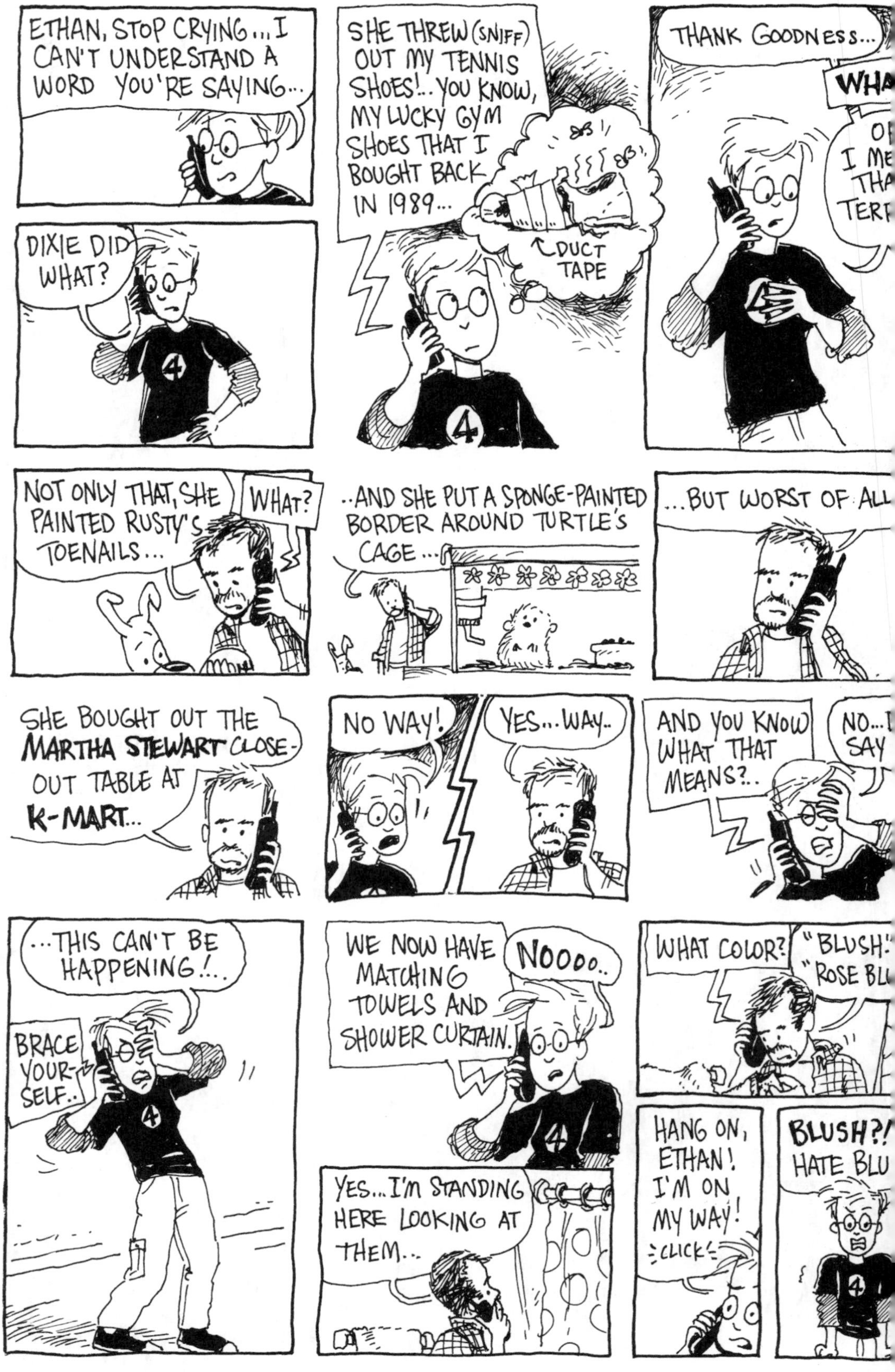
ETHAN, STOP CRYING... I CAN'T UNDERSTAND A WORD YOU'RE SAYING...
DIXIE DID WHAT?
SHE THREW (SNIFF) OUT MY TENNIS SHOES!.. YOU KNOW, MY LUCKY GYM SHOES THAT I BOUGHT BACK IN 1989...
DUCT TAPE
THANK GOODNESS...
WHA
O
I ME
THA
TERR
NOT ONLY THAT, SHE PAINTED RUSTY'S TOENAILS...
WHAT?
..AND SHE PUT A SPONGE-PAINTED BORDER AROUND TURTLE'S CAGE...
...BUT WORST OF ALL
SHE BOUGHT OUT THE MARTHA STEWART CLOSE-OUT TABLE AT K-MART...
NO WAY!
YES...WAY..
AND YOU KNOW WHAT THAT MEANS?..
NO...
SAY
...THIS CAN'T BE HAPPENING!...
BRACE YOURSELF..
WE NOW HAVE MATCHING TOWELS AND SHOWER CURTAIN.
NOOOO..
YES... I'M STANDING HERE LOOKING AT THEM...
WHAT COLOR?
"BLUSH"
"ROSE BL
HANG ON, ETHAN! I'M ON MY WAY!
CLICK
BLUSH?!
HATE BLU

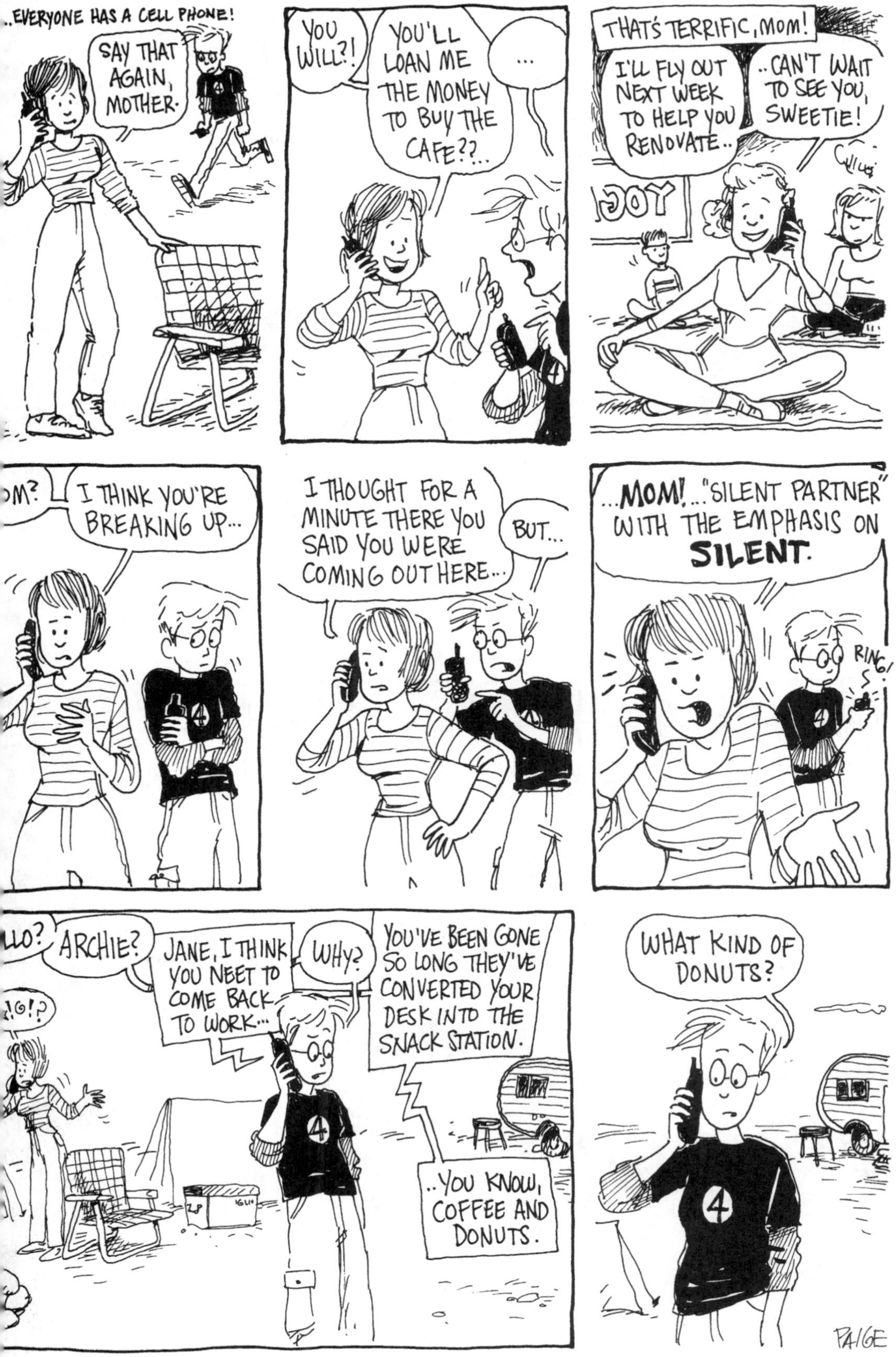
..EVERYONE HAS A CELL PHONE!
SAY THAT AGAIN, MOTHER.
YOU WILL?!
YOU'LL LOAN ME THE MONEY TO BUY THE CAFE??...
...
THAT'S TERRIFIC, MOM!
I'LL FLY OUT NEXT WEEK TO HELP YOU RENOVATE..
..CAN'T WAIT TO SEE YOU, SWEETIE!
OM?
I THINK YOU'RE BREAKING UP...
I THOUGHT FOR A MINUTE THERE YOU SAID YOU WERE COMING OUT HERE...
BUT...
...MOM!..."SILENT PARTNER" WITH THE EMPHASIS ON SILENT.
RING!
LLO?
ARCHIE?
JANE, I THINK YOU NEET TO COME BACK TO WORK...
WHY?
YOU'VE BEEN GONE SO LONG THEY'VE CONVERTED YOUR DESK INTO THE SNACK STATION.
..YOU KNOW, COFFEE AND DONUTS.
WHAT KIND OF DONUTS?
PAIGE

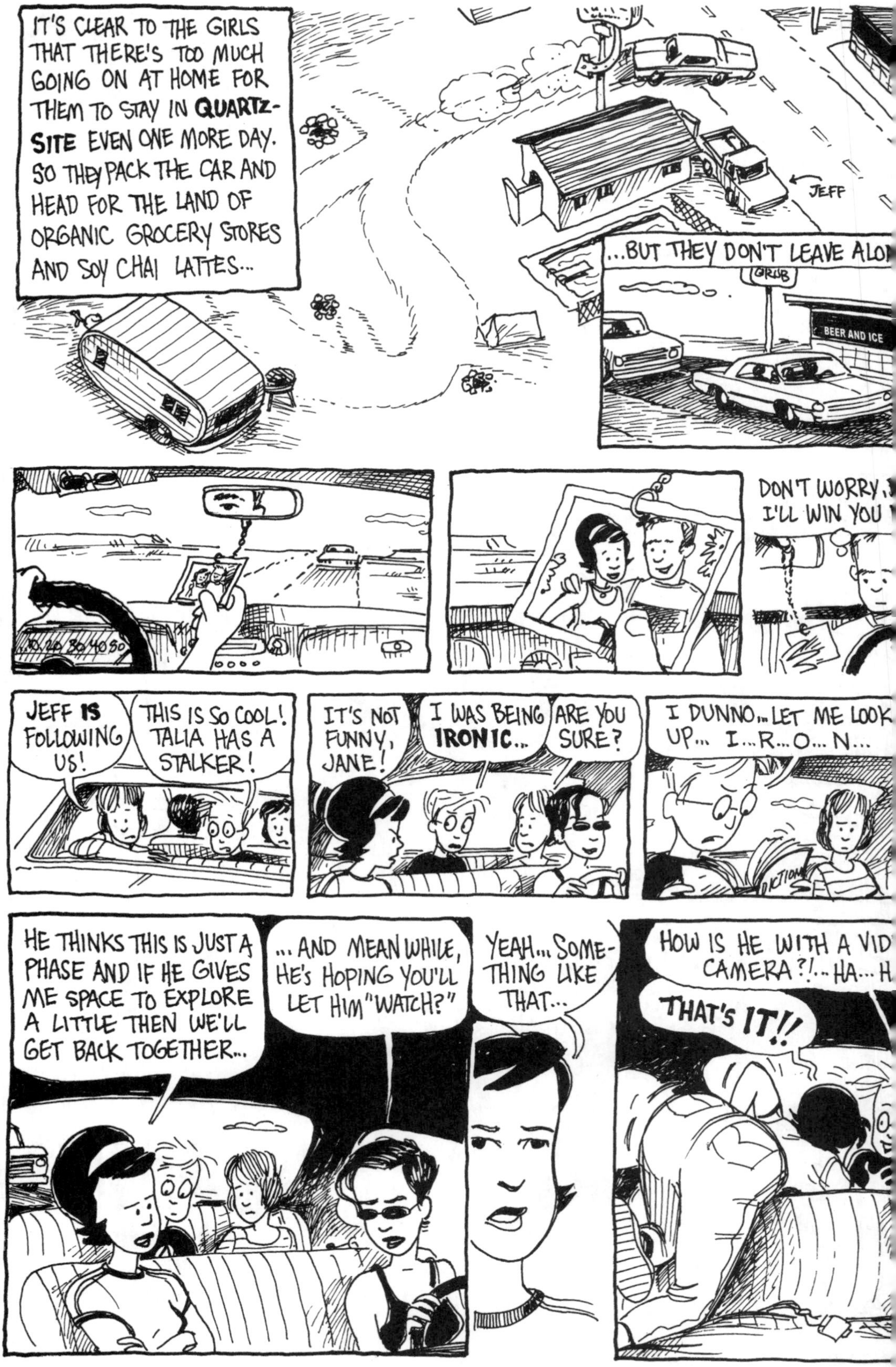
IT'S CLEAR TO THE GIRLS THAT THERE'S TOO MUCH GOING ON AT HOME FOR THEM TO STAY IN QUARTZSITE EVEN ONE MORE DAY. SO THEY PACK THE CAR AND HEAD FOR THE LAND OF ORGANIC GROCERY STORES AND SOY CHAI LATTES...
JEFF
...BUT THEY DON'T LEAVE ALO
GRUB
BEER AND ICE
DON'T WORRY,
I'LL WIN YOU
JEFF IS FOLLOWING US!
THIS IS SO COOL! TALIA HAS A STALKER!
IT'S NOT FUNNY, JANE!
I WAS BEING IRONIC...
ARE YOU SURE?
I DUNNO... LET ME LOOK UP... I...R...O...N...
HE THINKS THIS IS JUST A PHASE AND IF HE GIVES ME SPACE TO EXPLORE A LITTLE THEN WE'LL GET BACK TOGETHER...
...AND MEAN WHILE, HE'S HOPING YOU'LL LET HIM "WATCH?"
YEAH... SOMETHING LIKE THAT...
HOW IS HE WITH A VID CAMERA?!... HA... H
THAT'S IT!!

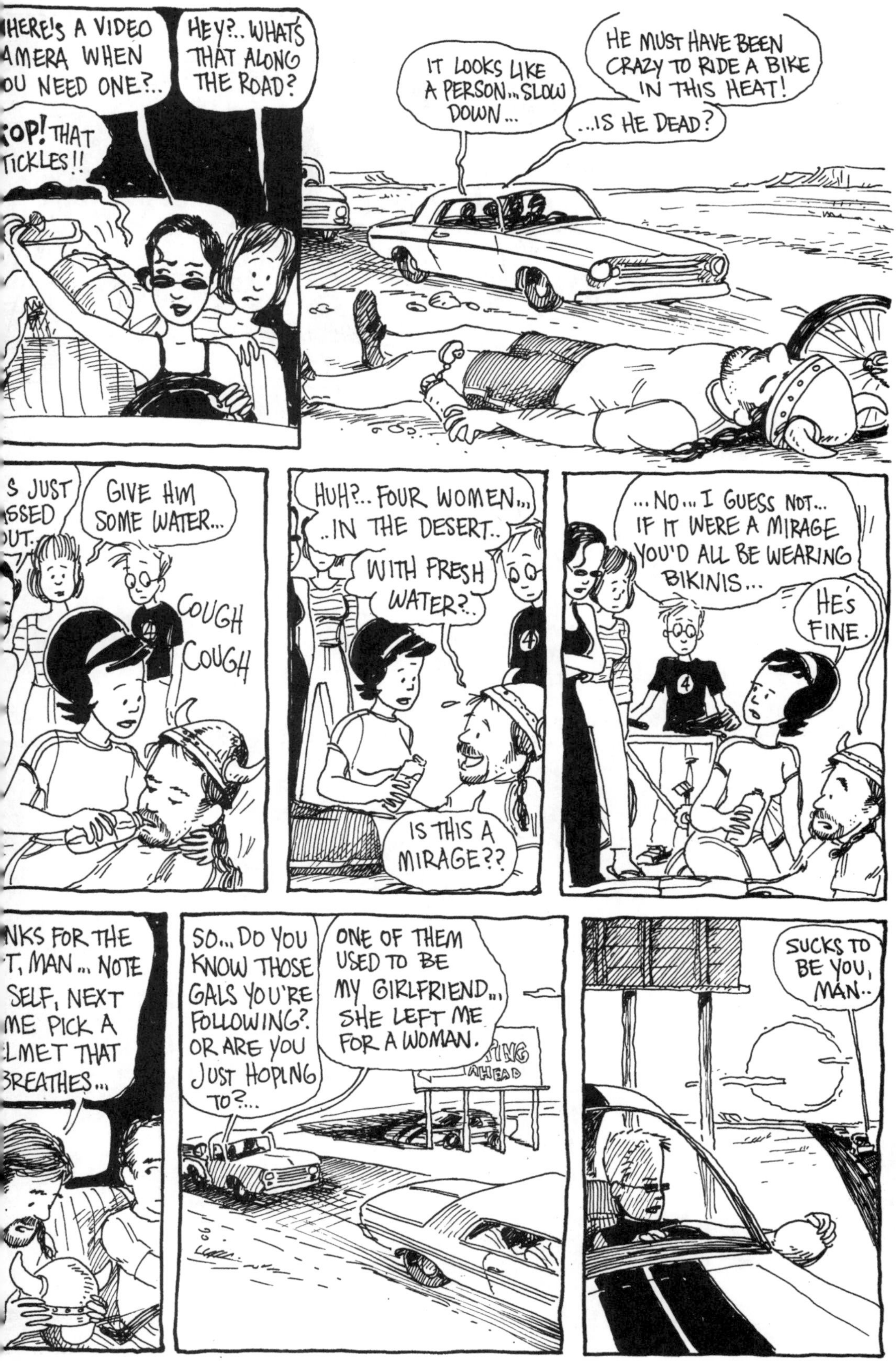
HERE'S A VIDEO
AMERA WHEN
OU NEED ONE?..
HEY?.. WHAT'S THAT ALONG THE ROAD?
OP! THAT TICKLES!!
IT LOOKS LIKE A PERSON... SLOW DOWN...
HE MUST HAVE BEEN CRAZY TO RIDE A BIKE IN THIS HEAT!
...IS HE DEAD?
S JUST
SSED
UT.
GIVE HIM SOME WATER...
COUGH COUGH
HUH?.. FOUR WOMEN... ..IN THE DESERT..
WITH FRESH WATER?..
IS THIS A MIRAGE??
...NO... I GUESS NOT... IF IT WERE A MIRAGE YOU'D ALL BE WEARING BIKINIS...
HE'S FINE.
NKS FOR THE
T, MAN... NOTE
SELF, NEXT
ME PICK A
LMET THAT
BREATHES...
SO... DO YOU KNOW THOSE GALS YOU'RE FOLLOWING? OR ARE YOU JUST HOPING TO?...
ONE OF THEM USED TO BE MY GIRLFRIEND... SHE LEFT ME FOR A WOMAN.
AHEAD
SUCKS TO BE YOU, MAN..

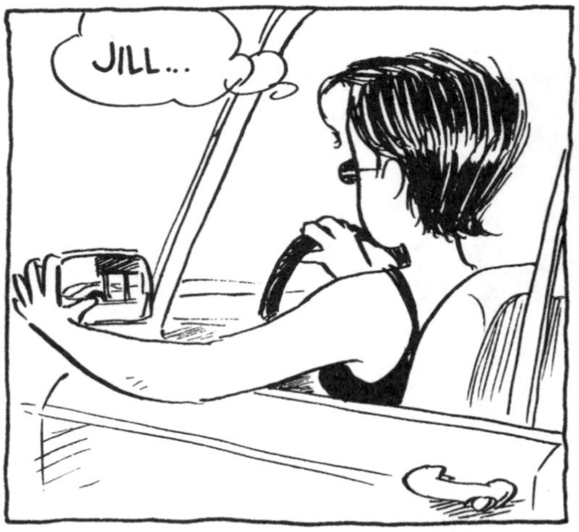
JILL...

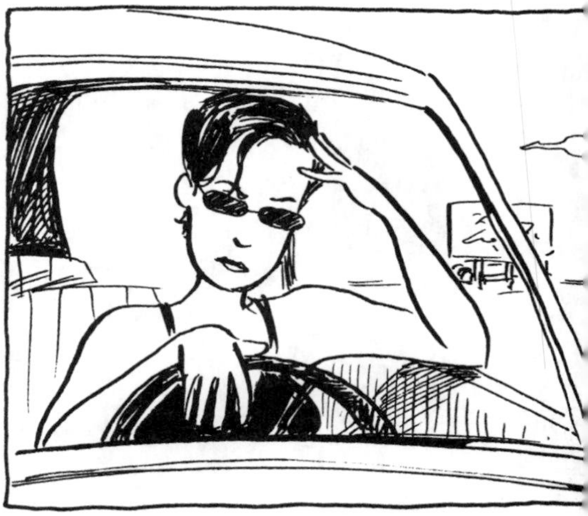

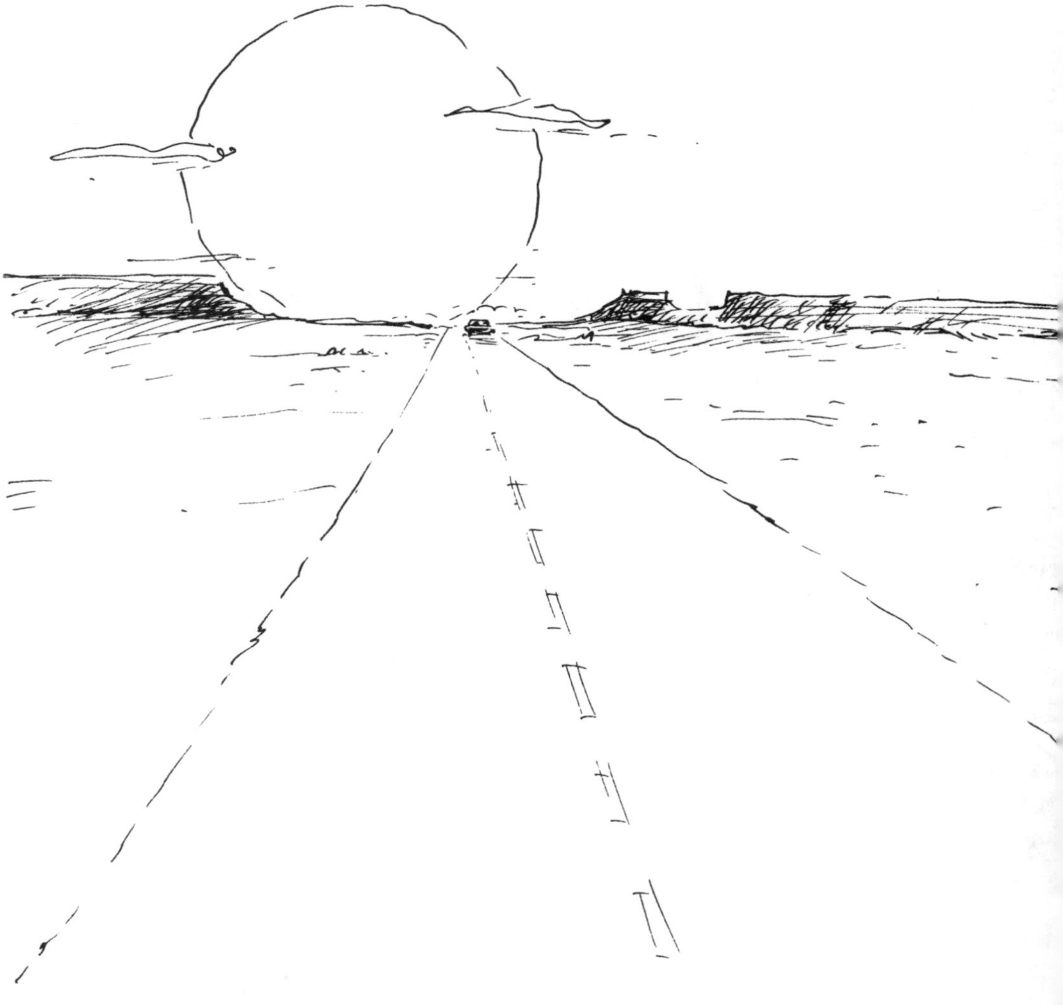

To be continued.

jane's world rewind

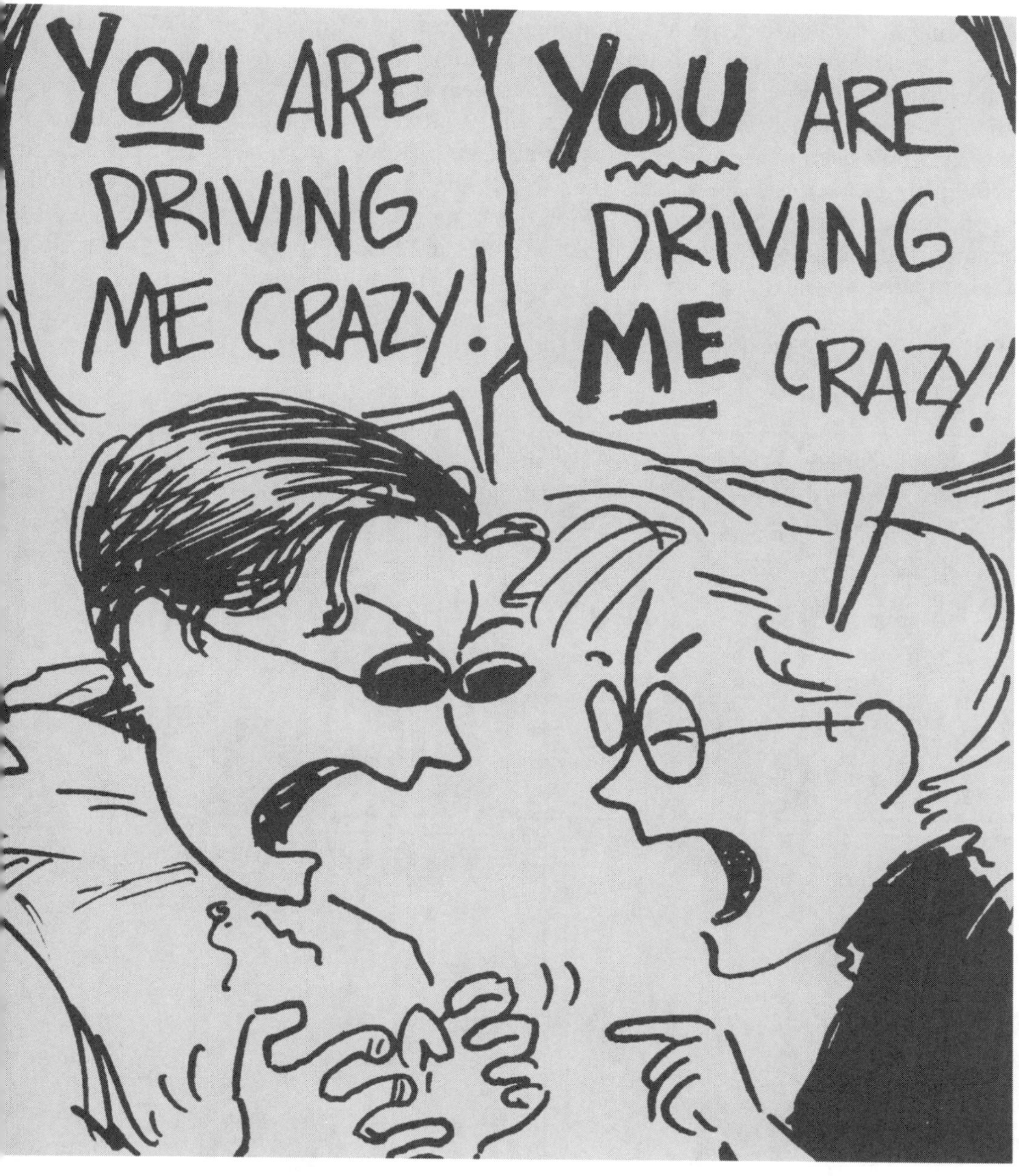
YOU ARE DRIVING ME CRAZY!
YOU ARE DRIVING ME CRAZY!

Author's note: *This is the first in a series of "rewind" sequences from previous issues of Jane's World. These missing chapters are events that couldn't be aired on Comics.com because of the required "G" rating, but are important to the ongoing story of Jane and her pals.*

Jane's World Rewind: Jane and Chelle, first conta

In Issue 4, alien abduction precipitates a bit of fallout for Jane. Sarah breaks up with Jane loses her job at the paper and is forced to take a job at the local Quicki-Mart. To add insul injury, Sarah rides with Chelle in the Pride parade. Jane decides to try and win Sarah back suggesting the two of them go on a little canoe and camping trip. Not hip to Jane's plan, S invites Chelle, Dorothy and Mia along. In desperation, Jane talks Ethan into coming so sh won't have to paddle her canoe alone. There's a near collision on the river in which Jane a Ethan get tossed out of their canoes... Ethan with a broken arm. Cindy, Jane's old trainer fi the gym who's been going to night school to become a forest ranger, sees the river calamit unfold just in time to save Jane and Ethan from a soggy end. Dorothy, overcome with old ings for Ethan, rides with him to the hospital, leaving Mia to wonder if this is the end of th romance. Sarah comforts Mia, which forces Chelle and Jane to share a tent. This is a glimp of what really happened between the ending of Issue 4 and the beginning of Issue 5.

Further proof that opposites attract... Jane and Chelle... first contact...

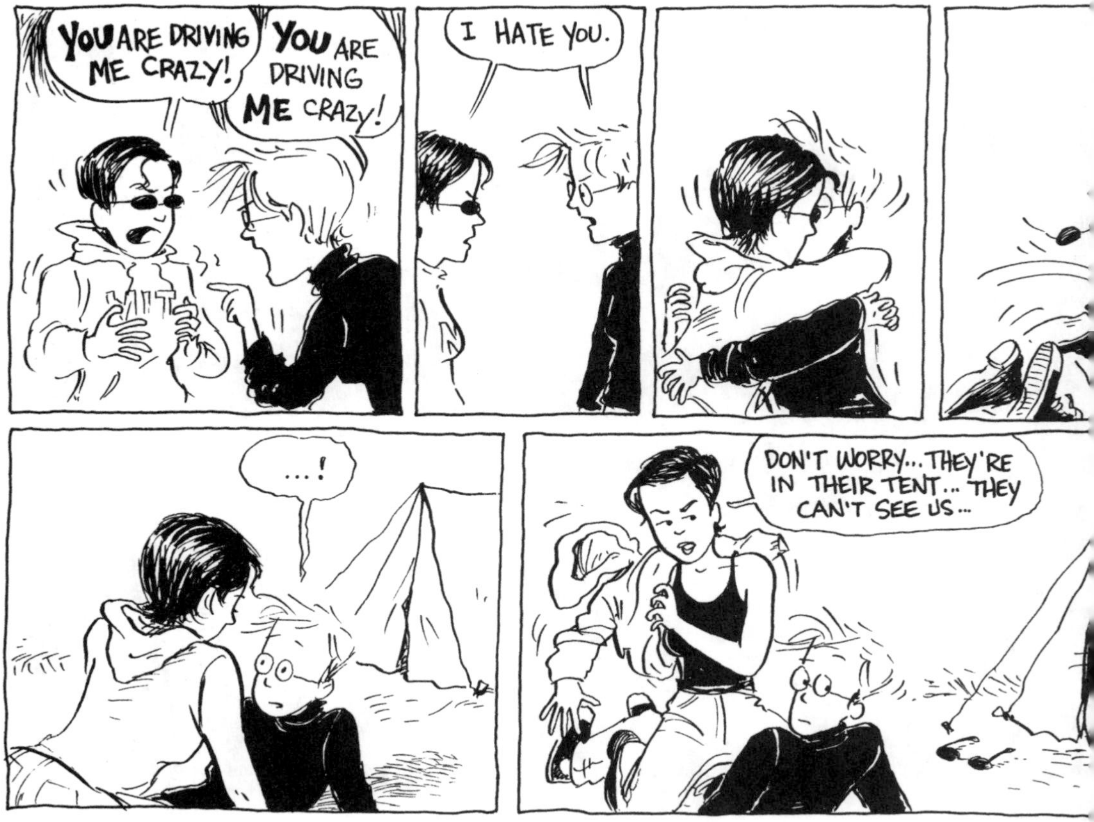

YOU ARE DRIVING ME CRAZY!
YOU ARE DRIVING ME CRAZY!
I HATE YOU.
...!
DON'T WORRY... THEY'RE IN THEIR TENT... THEY CAN'T SEE US...

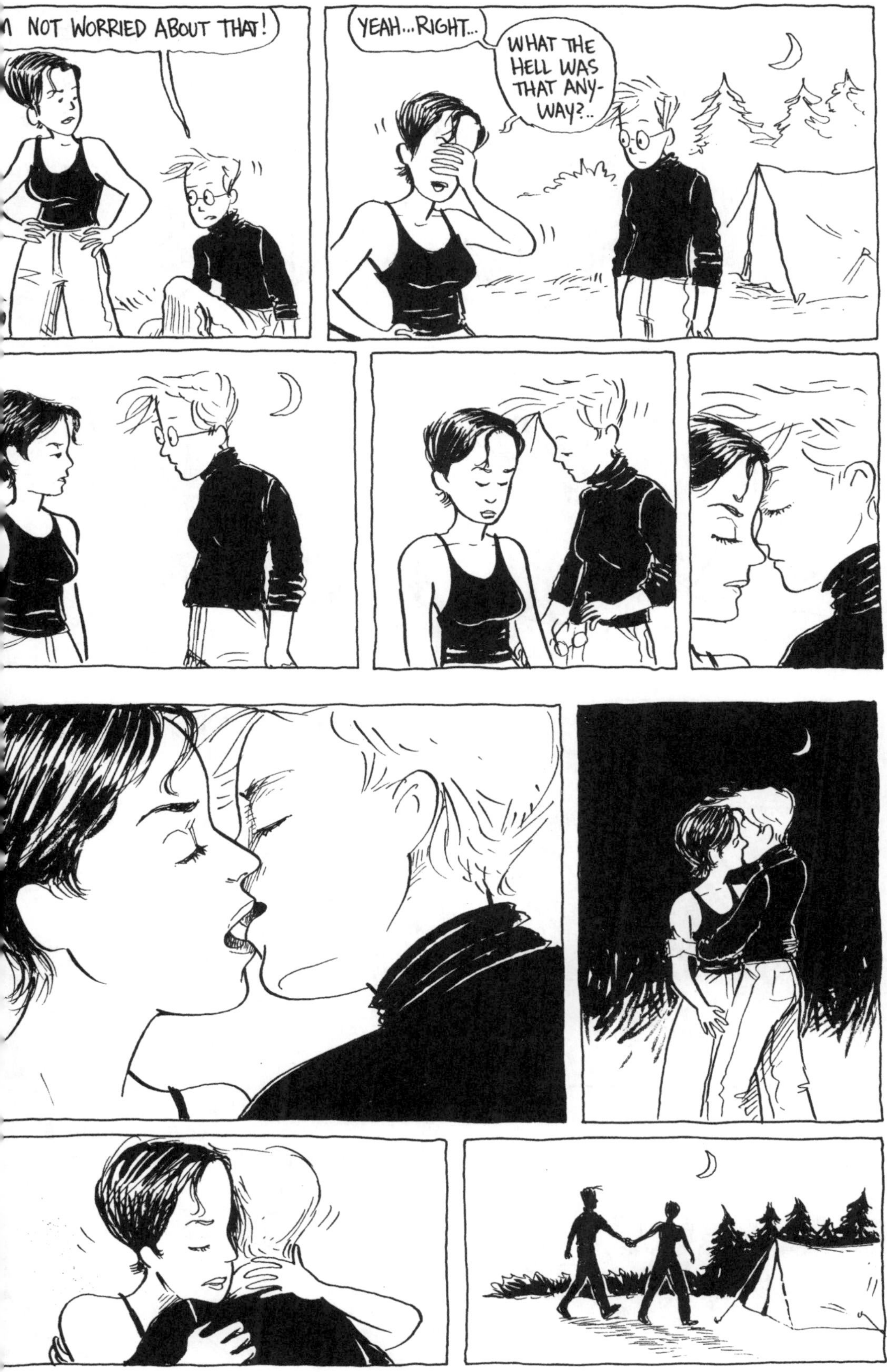
M NOT WORRIED ABOUT THAT!
YEAH... RIGHT...
WHAT THE HELL WAS THAT ANY-WAY?...

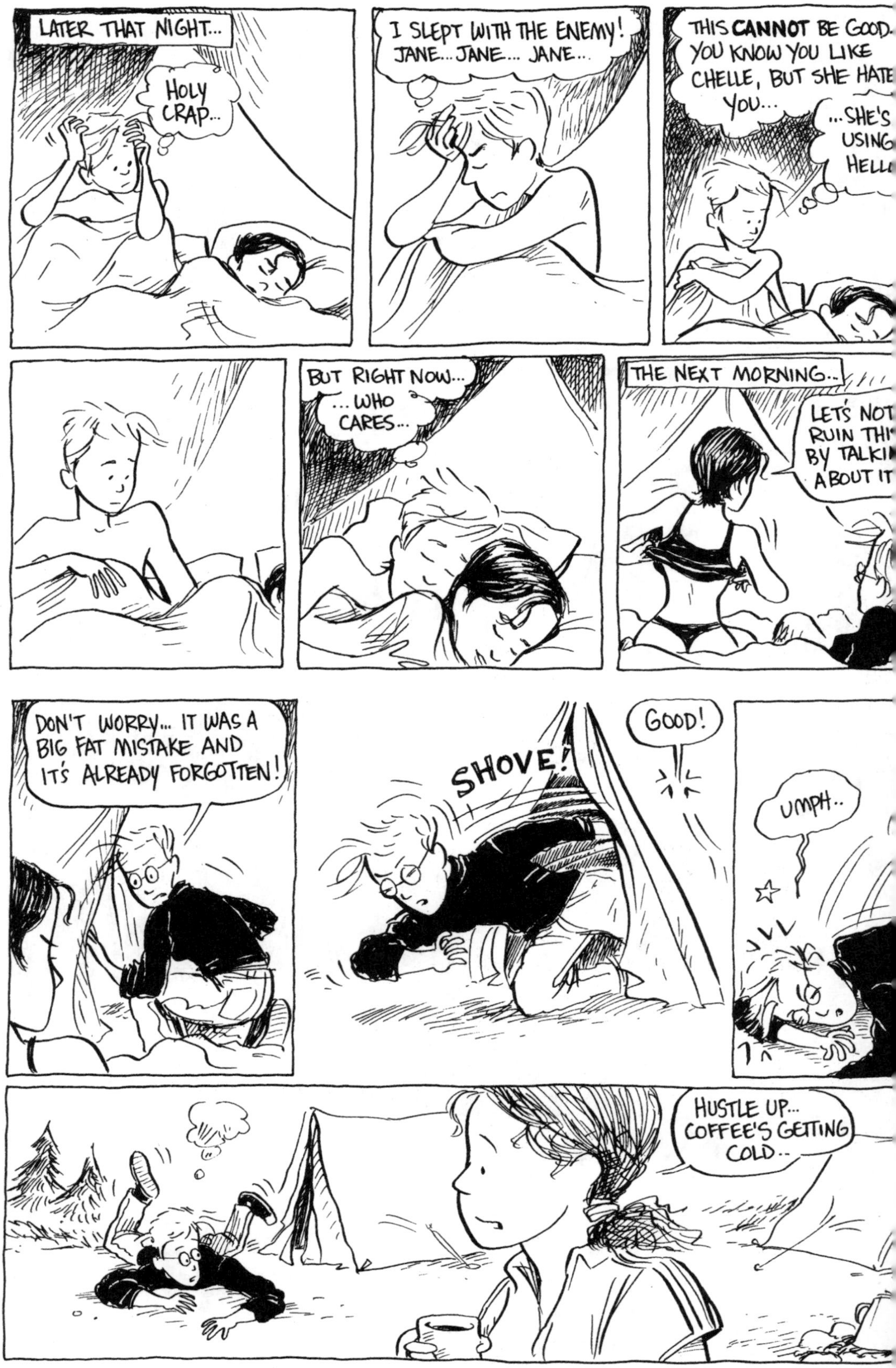
LATER THAT NIGHT...
HOLY CRAP...
I SLEPT WITH THE ENEMY! JANE... JANE... JANE...
THIS CANNOT BE GOOD. YOU KNOW YOU LIKE CHELLE, BUT SHE HATE YOU...
...SHE'S USING HELL
BUT RIGHT NOW... ...WHO CARES...
THE NEXT MORNING..
LET'S NOT RUIN THI BY TALKI ABOUT IT
DON'T WORRY... IT WAS A BIG FAT MISTAKE AND IT'S ALREADY FORGOTTEN!
SHOVE!
GOOD!
UMPH..
HUSTLE UP... COFFEE'S GETTING COLD..

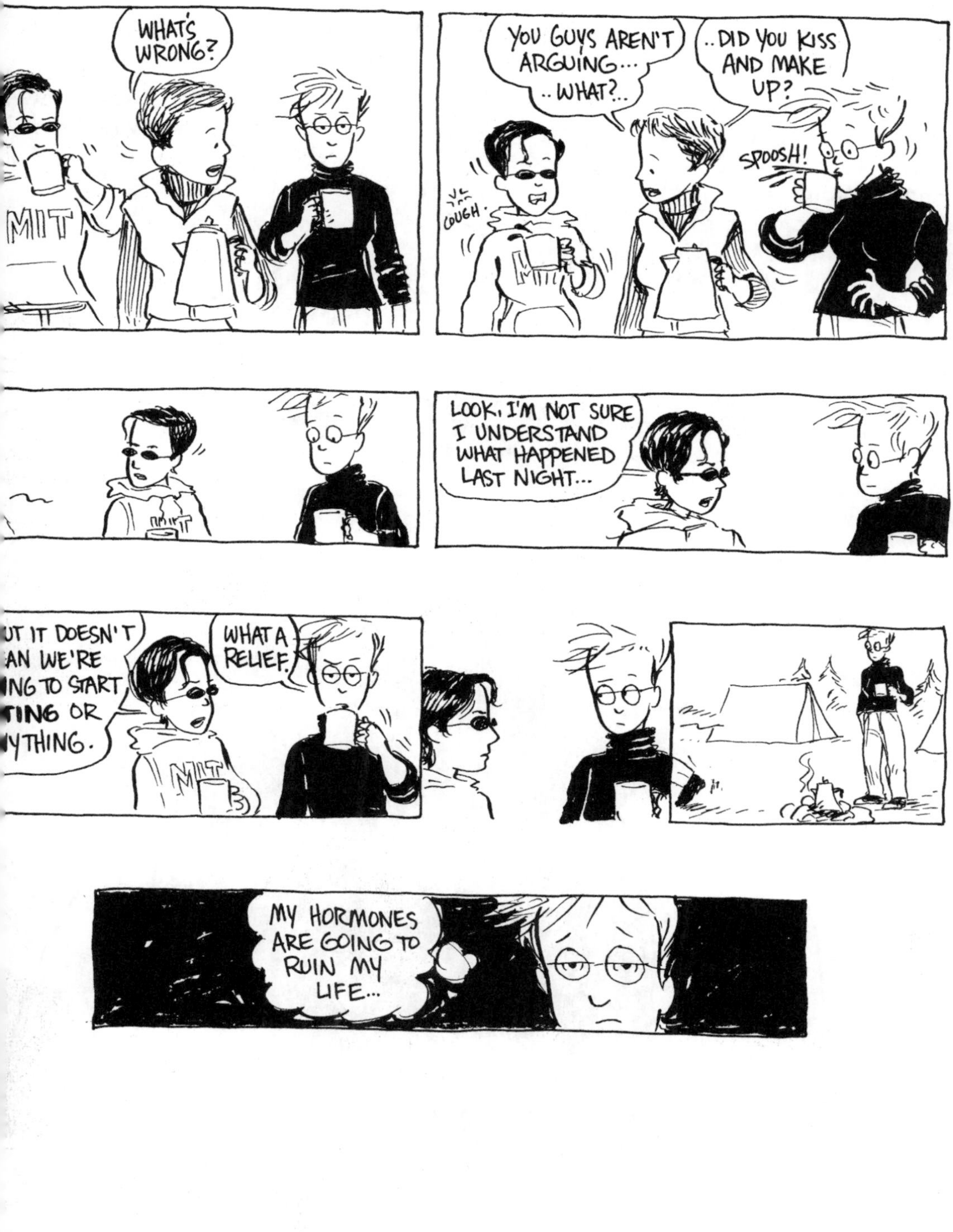
WHAT'S WRONG?
YOU GUYS AREN'T ARGUING... ..WHAT?..
..DID YOU KISS AND MAKE UP?
COUGH.
SPOOSH!
LOOK, I'M NOT SURE I UNDERSTAND WHAT HAPPENED LAST NIGHT...
UT IT DOESN'T AN WE'RE NG TO START TING OR YTHING.
WHAT A RELIEF.
MY HORMONES ARE GOING TO RUIN MY LIFE...

Jane's World Gallery

The next couple of pages were inspired by a thread on the Jane forum. Several f were discussing who would play the different cast members of Jane's World if a movie were in production. Eavesdropping on this web discussion inspired me to tr and envision the characters as real people, rather than comic characters. Here's a sampling of what I came up with. Unfortunately, Dorothy and Bud are missing, so I'll work on those for a later issue.

Since it is Jane's comic I guess it's only fair that she's first up in the gallery.

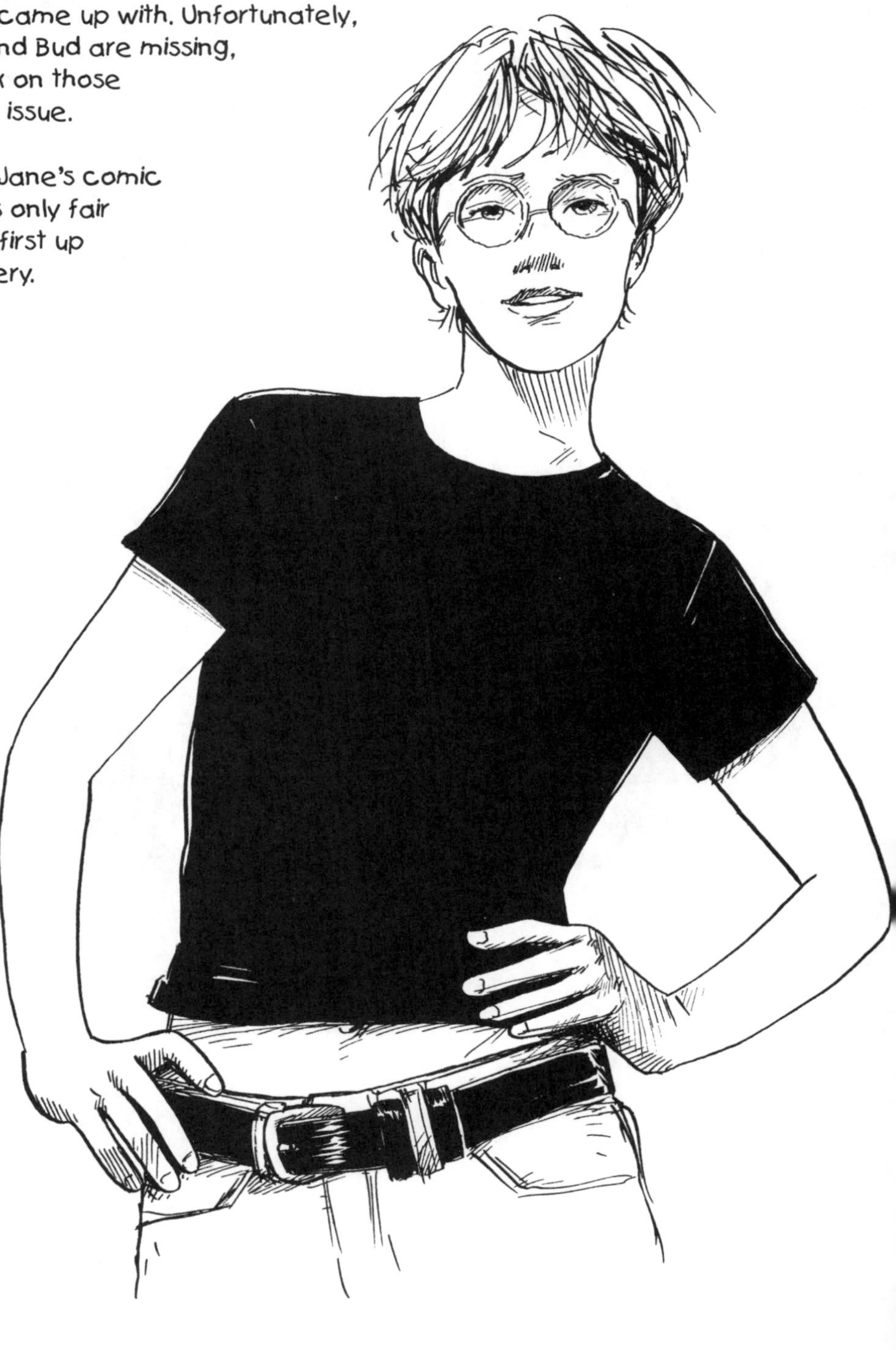

Ethan is up next as Jane's long-time costar.

Chelle, without the shades.

And to finish up this first round,
new-comer, bad girl, Jill.

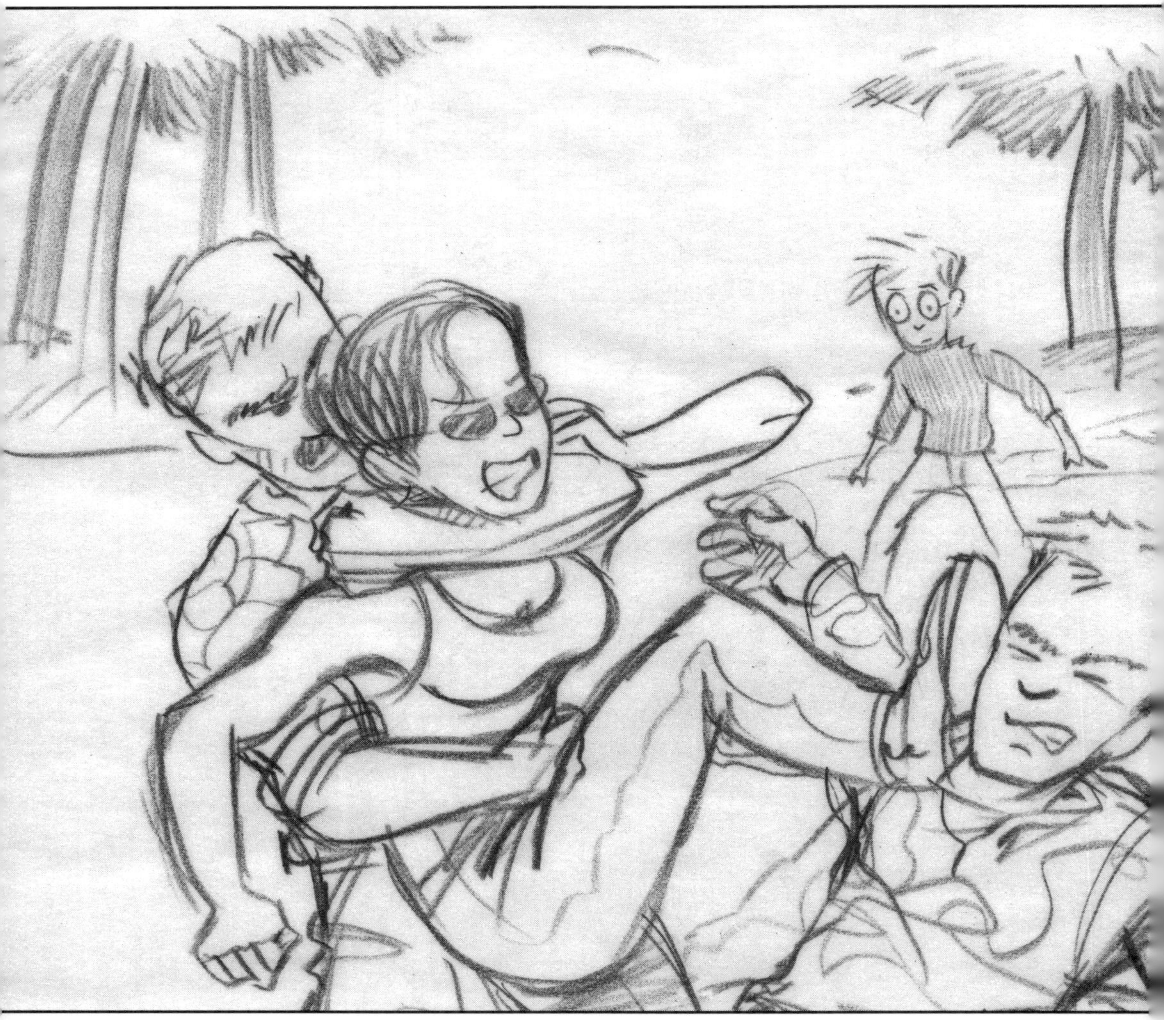